Managing Sport Facilities and Major Events

From corporate boxes to sprinklers, food outlets to toilets, first aid to media, facility and event managers are accountable for the success of sporting ventures and events.

Managing Sport Facilities and Major Events explains how to get the job done. With detailed international case studies in each chapter, the book offers a systematic guide to the management issues and practical problems that sports managers must address to ensure financial, sporting and ethical success.

Chapters cover feasibility assessment, market research, event bidding and branding, risk analysis, contract and project management, corporate structure, quality assurance, budgeting, facility management, staffing, occupational health and safety, and contractual considerations—as well as economic, social, community and environmental issues.

Written by an international team of expert scholars, *Managing Sport Facilities and Major Events* is an invaluable student text and professional reference.

Hans Westerbeek is Head of School, **Aaron Smith** is Associate Professor and Director of Research and **Paul Emery** is Lecturer in the School of Sport, Tourism and Hospitality Management at La Trobe University, Melbourne. **Paul Turner** and **Linda van Leeuwen** are Senior Lecturers in the Bowater School of Management and Marketing at Deakin University, Melbourne. **Christine Green** is Assistant Professor in the Department of Kinesiology and Health Education at the University of Texas at Austin.

Managing Sport Facilities and Major Events

Hans Westerbeek, Aaron Smith,
Paul Turner, Paul Emery, Christine Green
and Linda van Leeuwen

Routledge
Taylor & Francis Group

LONDON AND NEW YORK

First published in Australia in 2005
by Allen & Unwin, PO Box 8500, St Leonards, NSW 1590, Australia

This edition published 2006
by Routledge
2 Park Square, Milton Park, Abingdon, Oxon OX14 4RN

Simultaneously published in the USA
by Routledge
270 Madison Ave, New York, NY 10016

Routledge is an imprint of the Taylor & Francis Group, an informa business

© 2005 Hans Westerbeek, Aaron Smith, Paul Turner,
Paul Emery, Christine Green, Linda van Leeuwen

Typeset in Sabon by Keystroke, 28 High Street, Tettenhall, Wolverhampton
Printed and bound in Great Britain by TJ International Ltd, Padstow, Cornwall

This edition not for sale outside the UK, Europe, the USA, China,
South Korea, Japan or Taiwan.

British Library Cataloguing in Publication Data
A catalogue record for this book is available from the British Library

Library of Congress Cataloging in Publication Data
Managing sport facilities and major events/Hans Westerbeek . . . [et al.].
   p. cm.
  Includes bibliographical references and index.
  ISBN 0–415–40108–9 (hardback) – ISBN 0–415–40109–7 (pbk.)
1. Sports facilities – Management. I. Westerbeek, Hans. II. Title.
GV401.W47 2006
796. 06'9—dc22   2006007555

ISBN10: 0–415–40108–9 (hbk)
ISBN10: 0–415–40109–7 (pbk)

ISBN13: 978–0–415–40108–1 (hbk)
ISBN13: 978–0–415–40109–8 (pbk)

Contents

Figures and tables

Preface

The foot races came first. The course was set out for them from the starting post, and they raised a dust upon the plain as they all flew forward at the same moment. Clytoneus came in first by a long way; he left everyone else behind him by the length of the furrow that a couple of mules can plough in a fallow field. They then turned to the painful art of wrestling, and here Euryalus proved to be the best man. Amphialus excelled all the others in jumping, while at throwing the disc there was no one who could approach Elatreus. Alcinous's son Laodamas was the best boxer, and he it was who presently said, when they had all been diverted with the games, 'Let us ask the stranger whether he excels in any of these sports; he seems very powerfully built; his thighs, calves, hands, and neck are of prodigious strength, nor is he at all old, but he has suffered much lately, and there is nothing like the sea for making havoc with a man, no matter how strong he is'. (Homer 800 BC, *The odyssey*, excerpt from Book VIII)

Coming together to compete in sporting events, or to sit on the sidelines admiring the achievements of others, hosting festivals to celebrate the beauty of the arts, or dining on the best food available and drinking the best wines in order to celebrate the turning of another year, historians and archaeologists have uncovered ample evidence of people coming together to mark special occasions. Homer kindly provides us with the opportunity to look back some 3000 years in order to make us realise that major events, and in particular sporting events, have been around for a long time. With the Athens Olympic Games of 2004 well and truly behind us now, and all the challenges that the local organising committee were confronted with in regard to the (on time!) construction of facilities that were purposely built to host the games, we are left to wonder what has changed in those 3000 years. Not much, some will say; we still fight wars and the Olympic Games still strive to bring the youth of the world together in a truce. Others may want to argue that we have much advanced since the ancient times, and that 'civilisation' is now world-wide rather than limited to Greeks of Homer, Plato or Hercules' times. We do not attempt to answer this question in this book. What the authors do want to stress is that since the beginning of human history, the reasons for people coming together have not changed greatly. We argue that major (sporting) events, and the facilities that host them, are all about creating togetherness, enjoyment and a fantastic leisure experience; a good time away from the pressures and realities of everyday life.

The purpose of this book therefore is to overview and discuss the issues that underpin the success of, first of all, the construction and operation of the facilities that host major events, and second, the conception and operation of the event itself. Our logic to deal with the management of facilities and major events in one book is simple: one does not exist without the other; they are in a symbiotic relationship.

Bringing together two fields of study and application that have traditionally been dealt with separately was a stimulating challenge. Providing the reader with an overview of what sport facility and event management is all about was relatively easy but in order to ensure that this book also provides the necessary depth of discussion we decided to work with six different content experts rather than a few generalists. At the time of writing, these content experts were residing in three different continents. The Asia-Pacific perspective was provided by Westerbeek, Smith, Turner and van Leeuwen who all live in Australia. Paul Emery provided the European, and in particular, the UK perspective from Newcastle in England, and Christine Green, residing in Texas, ensured that the contents of the book are relevant from the perspective of the facility and event industries in the United States. This has led to an exciting variety of insights and case studies, as well as in-depth discussion of a range of important issues such as facility design and construction, event operations, bidding for major events, facility and event performance management and what the key success factors are for running sport facilities and events.

Although this book has been written as an overall collaborative and integrative effort, authors have each taken responsibility for different chapters. Hans Westerbeek wrote Chapters 1 and 4; Aaron Smith was in charge of Chapters 3 and 5; Paul Turner wrote Chapters 6 and 7; Paul Emery headed up Chapters 2 and 9; Christine Green put together Chapters 10 and 11; and Linda van Leeuwen not only wrote Chapter 8 but also meticulously reviewed and edited a number of drafts of the book, including the final. Linda also compiled the case studies for Chapters 1, 2, 3 and 9. We kindly thank Emma Sherry for preparing the case study in Chapter 10, and David Shilbury for preparing the case study in Chapter 11. As the editor of the Sport Management series (Allen & Unwin), we would also like to acknowledge David Shilbury's support throughout the process of writing the book, and his hard work on the final proof checking. Last but not least we would like to thank Jeanmarie Morosin, our editor at Allen & Unwin, who combined understanding for yet another delay with sheer determination and efficiency to hit the very ambitious production deadlines.

Hans Westerbeek, Aaron Smith, Paul Turner, Paul Emery,
Christine Green and Linda van Leeuwen

1

Introduction to sport facility and event management

Chapter focus

Structure, size and trends in the sport facility and sport event sectors

Key success factors of operating sport facilities and running sport events

Developing new sport facilities: feasibility analysis

Developing new sport facilities: design and construction issues

Developing new sport facilities: preparing facility management infrastructure

Operating the new sport facility: attracting events

Operating the new sport facility: preparing event management infrastructure

Attracting customers: marketing the sport facility and the sport events

Running the sport event: event operations

Measuring facility and event performance: a scorecard approach to success

Measuring facility and event performance: impact on and for stakeholders

CHAPTER OBJECTIVES

In this chapter, we will:
- Provide an outline of the changing nature of the sport facility and event sectors.
- Provide an overview of the structure of this book.
- Supply a broad survey of the structure, size and trends that typify the facility and events sectors.
- Identify a number of new markets for sporting events and discuss the implications for the construction of new facilities.
- Outline the added value of new facilities and events to user and non-user groups.
- Demonstrate the need for and application of managerial skills to facility and event operations.

If you build it, they will come . . .

Throughout the last two decades of the twentieth century, many managers of newly established sport and entertainment facilities were confronted with the inaccuracy of the well-known industry credo: if you build it, they will come. Times have changed quite rapidly. Modern-day sport and entertainment venues are vastly different in their appearance and functionality compared with the previous generation of facilities. As we will discuss shortly, not only is the market for sport and entertainment events expanding and becoming more diversified but the needs of old and new customers have changed as well, leading to the changing functionality of new venues.

The changing nature of facility and event management

The current generation of stadia incorporate multipurpose facilities and have a sharper focus on catering for corporate hospitality, which in turn affects attendance (patterns) at events. With the corporate dollar an increasingly important source of revenue for facility and event operators, more space in facilities is being devoted to corporate clients, necessitating a reassessment of facility and event positioning strategies. This leads logically to a reassessment of the facility's (and its tenants') target markets. Based on this shift from what were largely 'community' customers to a wider range of clients (including the much more cashed-up corporate clients), Roberts (1999) notes a change in approach to funding the construction of contemporary sport facilities.

As a result of the reluctance of sport fans and local community to fund developments with tax dollars (as opposed to the previous generation of stadia developed two or three decades ago, where funding often consisted of near 100 per cent tax money), facility and event organisations have turned their attention to identifying alternative funding strategies. Not only are sport and entertainment venues more likely to be privately funded and owned, but this situation has resulted in the 'unbundling' of commercial activities (concessions, pouring rights, merchandising rights, media rights) that can operate through the facility. Corporations are prepared to pay top dollars for luxury boxes and club seating. The value of stadium naming rights has risen dramatically and stadium precincts are 'increasingly becoming the beating heart of a total entertainment destination which means in-stadium rights has been extended by the development of the surrounding zones with cinemas, other sports facilities, and restaurants. The common denominator is that each is forward contracted to deliver revenue at set times' (Roberts 1999, p. 18).

Britcher (2000, p. 26) notes that the new Staples Center in Los Angeles is

> a 1 million-square foot building [and] contains 20,000 seats, 160 luxury suites on three levels at the mid-level, 3000 premier club seats, [a] premier club, [a] grand reserve club, Fox Network Television studio, Fox Network Sports Bar and a large team store selling team apparel for all four professional sports franchises. The naming rights to the venue sold for more than US$120 million.

With high-quality facilities such as the Staples Center, which are fitted and resourced to service a demanding on-site (corporate) audience and a remote (television) audience, comes the need to continuously improve the levels of service quality. Not only do customers demand higher-quality events on the field, and more of them—they also wish to be served in a way that matches the event and its facility surroundings. Well-trained, friendly, immaculately dressed and highly knowledgeable staff are required to serve better food to sophisticated, information- and spectacle-hungry audiences in more convenient, ergonomically outfitted physical surroundings. In summary, changing customer needs have driven a change in the type (and number) of events that are organised, in turn leading to facilities that are purpose-built to cater to a wider variety of audiences and events. The higher quality of the new venues has led to higher customer expectations, which in turn has sparked a sharper focus on delivering high-quality service by facility and event owners.

Overview of book contents

What does all of this mean in the context of this book? First of all, you will have noticed in the title of the book that we have combined the management of facilities and events. As is suggested in the introduction above, the sport or entertainment event is inextricably linked to the place and location in which it is being organised and hosted. High-profile events require high-profile facilities; high-quality events require high-quality facilities; big events require big facilities; community events require facilities that cater for the needs of community groups, and so on. The type of event brings with it an endless list of requirements, the fulfilment of which determines the eventual success or failure of the event. Transport to and from the event, overnight visitors' accommodation, a sizable target market that is willing and able to attend the event, climatic conditions at the event location, specific athlete or entertainers' requirements such as playing surface or acoustics—all are just a start to the list of matters that need consideration when matching the facility (location) with the event. In other words, a book on facility management is incomplete when the events that are to be hosted at the facility are not discussed. The same principle would apply to a book that dealt with event management without considering the event location. Although many of the examples used in the book will be related to professional sport, it needs to be understood that our facility and event definitions extend beyond the professional sport arena. That is, it is our intention to provide a context for the establishment and organisation of participative and spectator events, for community and elite events, and for profit and non-profit events. These events can be and are hosted in facilities ranging from state-of-the-art sporting 'temples' to local community halls. However, in the interests of providing a clear focus, we will look for our examples largely in the sport and recreation industry. An industry is a collection of suppliers to a marketplace that principally provide products that are substitutable. In this book we will position 'sport facilities' and 'sport events' as sub-industries or sectors of the wider sport and recreation industry.

This book is also intended to provide you with an extensive insight into the different markets that are served by the events sector—to better understand how, when and why to build new facilities, and to take a long-term perspective when managing either facilities or events. The latter is important in order to stay ahead of the developments in a sector that is long-term capital-intensive. In other words, if you incorrectly assess the needs of the target markets, leading to financing and building the wrong facilities, the (financial) consequences will also have a long-term impact. Rather than providing a purely 'technical' approach to how to plan and operate facilities and how to organise events, we have taken the perspective of the facility and event manager as our guide to writing this book. We will take you through the process of building a new facility, considering the research and preparation that goes into assessing the feasibility of setting up a new facility and event business. Having done this, we will guide you through the processes of building the facility and operating it by organising events in it, ultimately leading to intermediate performance monitoring and to determining the levels of success achieved.

In this first chapter, we provide a broad insight into the structure, size and trends that typify the facility and events sectors. This 'big picture' information is used in Chapter 2 to briefly elaborate on the key drivers of success when planning, designing, building and operating sport and entertainment venues, and when planning and organising events. Although there is a wide range of performance indicators that can—and need to—be considered when monitoring and measuring the successful management of facilities and events, we will limit our discussion in Chapter 2 to three key drivers of success. These are time, quality, and money. In Chapters 10 and 11 we will elaborate on measuring facility and event success by applying a scorecard approach to performance measurement (Chapter 10), and by looking at the impact of facilities and events from an economic, social, community and environmental point of view (Chapter 11).

Having considered the drivers of success, in Chapter 3 you are shown the steps through a process described as the feasibility analysis. Before committing to the major investment that comes with building large venues, a significant amount of research needs to be conducted in order to ensure its viability. In this chapter we will analyse the stakeholders of both the newly planned facility and the events that might be hosted there. We will conduct a geographic analysis, an analysis of all potential customers and, finally, a financial analysis in order to determine overall feasibility of the new venue. Based on the outcome of research, in Chapter 4 we will consider design and building issues, ultimately leading to a comprehensive insight into facility and event logistics. This information can then be used in a building brief. Assuming that the facility has now been built, in Chapter 5 the facility management organisation is established—in other words, what needs to be done in order to operate successfully within the physical structures of the venue, which types of qualified personnel and how many of them we need, and what type of infrastructure is required. Having established a facility management organisation, we can start the process of organising our own events or, indeed, attracting events to our venue.

In Chapter 6 we will discuss the process of bidding for major events, how to structure the event management network, and how to start the process of event planning in the case of a successful bid. This process is continued in Chapter 7, where we start integrating our facility and event information. In other words, the venue now needs to be transformed to event mode, and an event project management structure needs to be merged with the existing facility management organisation. From both a facility and event perspective, this is also the time when risk management issues are considered.

In Chapter 8 we turn our attention to attracting the all-important customers (often better known as participants and spectators) to our venue and to our events. This can be done in a variety of ways, including the marketing of the venue itself, marketing the events, or positioning either the facility or the event based on specific strengths of the organisation (e.g. its ability to deliver exceptional service). In Chapter 9 we focus on the actual event, and on event operations from the perspectives of staffing, scheduling, crisis management, service delivery, risk management, financial management and, of course, actual event management. As noted, an in-depth discussion of performance measurement will be conducted in Chapters 10 and 11, before we conclude the book in the epilogue. In the next section we overview briefly how events have always been an important part of human societies, leading to what we now call the facility and event management sector.

The emergence of the facility and event management sector

As already noted, we refer to one sector (facilities and events) rather than two separate sectors, which we justify by the fact that events cannot exist without the facilities that host them. We also argue that excellent sport facility managers require substantial knowledge of how to organise world-class events. Event managers, in turn, require a wide range of facility management skills in order to make their events top-class. It goes without saying that 'facilities' in our sector discussion refers only to those facilities that are suited to host events. It makes little sense to also consider, for example, offices of a major bank or the retail facilities of a supermarket chain as part of our industry discussion.

Special events have always been part of human history. Anthropologists have traced human civilisation for tens of thousands of years, and at the heart of their observations are the 'special events' that typify and explain tribal behaviour of that time and place. The supposed longest continuous human civilisation on the planet, that of the Aboriginal people of Australia, can be traced back 40 000 years, and many of their ancient rites and rituals survive into modern times. Rites and rituals represent 'special and important occasions' for members of the tribe or community, which either mark significant changes in position and responsibility or are more general celebrations or commemorations of significant moments in time, such as the arrival of spring, or the passing of an elder tribesperson. Many of the sites of these rituals were secret and sacred, and remain so today. In other words, the special 'event' is closely tied to a special 'place'. One without the other loses its significance.

From more modern times, records have shown that special events did not diminish in importance in the context of different societies. The Scandinavian Vikings celebrated successful explorations and hosted large festivities to honour their gods, as did the American Indians. The ancient Greeks conducted large athletic festivals to celebrate human excellence as a direct expression of honouring their gods, and the Romans organised gladiatorial events at massive colosseums to entertain the crowds and also to facilitate a culture of preparation for combat. Hundreds of years before the discovery of gunpowder in Europe, the Chinese would celebrate the arrival of the new year with elaborate displays of fireworks, and throughout the European Middle Ages more localised events would lead to the development of many country-specific events that still exist today. Examples are the 'Oktoberfest' in Germany and the 'Elfstedentocht' (eleven-city tour speed skating event) in the Netherlands. Largely through European imperialism (leading to the 'export' of domestic events) and the industrial revolution, events became more international.

Better information flow and transport infrastructure allowed people to travel more widely and created opportunities for joint celebrations. Events such as the first modern Olympic Games in 1896 are precursors to a movement that saw the 1900s become the first century of truly international events. After an initial facility 'boom' during the ancient Greek and Roman civilisations, when hugely impressive venues (you can still go and have a look!) were purpose-built to host major events, a second building frenzy took place during the latter stages of the nineteenth century. The development of internationally standardised football codes in particular led to the building of many stadia in the USA, the UK and mainland Europe, as well as Australia, that could host up to 100 000 spectators. Many of those facilities have now been recycled three or four times in order to cater to the quality standards of the third millennium. If in the 1890s the second facility building boom was initiated, then societal changes in the 1990s led to the third global development period. Directly related to the 'continuous improvement' of facilities and events is the ongoing professionalisation of facility and event managers. In order to remain well prepared to deliver on ever-increasing quality standards, managers need a continuous flow of cutting-edge information and management systems, which is one of the main reasons for the publication of this book. We now discuss the global trends that have been and are still transforming the facility and events industry, leading to the construction boom of the 1990s and to the growing number and variety of events that are being organised today.

Trends driving the growth of the facility and event management sector

Editor of the *Sports Facility Reports* Paul Anderson (2000) observed that 57 teams in the four major US professional sports leagues (MLB, NBA, NFL, NHL) are playing in facilities that were constructed between 1990 and 2000. Moreover, 10 teams constructed new facilities in the 1980s and 15 teams were involved in major upgrades or renovations of the facilities they were playing in during the 1990s. On top of that, 13 teams will move into newly constructed facilities in the third millennium and another 15 teams are in the process of planning to renovate or build a new facility. This means that by 2005 approximately 84 per cent of all major league teams will be playing in facilities that have been either renovated or newly constructed since 1980.

In the English Premier League, total attendance has recently been restricted by stadium capacity. The competition provides an interesting example of the importance of the variable 'stadium capacity' when interpreting overall attendance figures per club and per league. Boon (1999) compared average league attendance for the 1997/98 season with ground capacity and found that, although all clubs in the Premier League averaged an occupancy rate of 90 per cent, the top five clubs had occupancy rates of 98 per cent or higher. This was sufficient evidence for more than half of the clubs in the League to become involved in stadium renovation or new construction. However, the reverse turned out to be the case for less successful teams (often first, second and third division teams). Boosting stadium capacity in order to improve gate receipts may well have a negative effect on attendance, leading to the conclusion (Boon 1999, p. 15) that there is

> a clear need for some lower division clubs to temper their dream stadium plans with a degree of realism. It may be great to have a 20,000 capacity stadium, but an average attendance of only 4,000 creates a negative atmosphere. A 10,000 or 12,000 capacity stadium can provide a better atmosphere and—paradoxically—increased support.

It is a fact that the average occupancy rate of 90 per cent for Premier League teams drops to 69 per cent for division one, 47 per cent for division two and 33 per cent for division three (Boon 1999). Westerbeek and Smith (2003) noted two recent examples of Dutch soccer clubs moving to new facilities. Building new facilities with greater capacity shows the potential of these venues when the clubs operate in unsaturated spectator markets. Ajax Amsterdam moved from the 29 500 capacity de Meer Stadium to the Amsterdam Arena (48 000 seats), which raised Ajax's average attendance from 29 000 to 41 275. Vitesse Arnhem's move from 'Monnikehuize' (capacity 11 000) to the 'Gelredome' (capacity 26 500) raised average attendance from 8000 to 23 080. Boon's observation is particularly significant, in that having 'excess capacity' in stadia is not necessarily desirable for football clubs. Match-day attendance can be positively stimulated by a limited supply of seats in the stadium. It might therefore be better to talk about optimum capacity, rather than maximum capacity.

The situation in Australia may serve as another example. Historically, the most popular domestic football competition, the Australian Football League (national governing body for the sport of Australian Rules football), was organised along the lines of most European soccer competitions. AFL clubs owned or leased their own football stadia and most home matches were played there. The Australian Rules football competition was predominantly based in the heartland of the code, the city of Melbourne, and in 'the old days' was a competition between different suburbs. About 15 years ago a sea change occurred in Australian football. For the code to remain financially healthy and competitive against 'new' booming sports such as basketball and soccer, the competition's operating systems needed dramatic rationalisation. League administrators, the AFL Commission, turned the League into a national competition, in the process setting up teams in different states, some of which were new teams and some teams relocated from Melbourne. A facility rationalisation strategy was adopted by the League as one of the drivers of success for the national competition. Clubs had to move from their small, outdated and often unsafe suburban stadia to the few AFL-designated playing facilities throughout the country. In Melbourne in particular this led to multiple teams adopting either the Melbourne Cricket Ground (MCG) or Waverley Park, recently replaced by the state-of-the-art Telstra Dome, as their home ground. Both the MCG (currently being redeveloped) and the Telstra Dome offer a range of facilities, from 'purchase at the gate' access to long-term corporate box leases. The moral of the story? The market in a domestic football competition such as the AFL is not able to sustain a wide range of low-capacity yet high-quality outfitted (corporate hospitality) stadia. Rather, costs need to be shared by a number of professional clubs playing at the same venue, in the process cross-subsidising the maintenance of high-quality entertainment opportunities at a limited number of venues. (Here it also needs to be stated that the playing surface required for Australian rules football is about twice as big as a soccer pitch, leading to bigger and wider venues. Larger crowds are therefore needed to create a good game atmosphere; hence, consumption of football needs to be artificially concentrated by limiting the number of consumption outlets.)

Other reasons to build new facilities

Apart from these 'capacity-specific' reasons to become involved in the construction of new facilities, Anderson (2000) provided five features that may explain the global 'facility boom'. First, he argues that it is more efficient to build new facilities than to renovate existing facilities in an effort to upgrade them to current standards and expectations. Second, new facilities are likely to become more than just an entertainment venue. Modern facilities are integrated into comprehensive community localities that include residential, office and retail space. Third, new facilities are more likely, through the novelty factor and expanded services, to boost attendance. Fourth, when certain sporting teams or competitions as a whole come to play in new facilities, competitors will have to follow or suffer the consequences of becoming a less attractive entertainment option for the fans. Finally, the 'increasing cost theory' posits that only new facilities can generate the necessary revenue streams to return a profit to the operators of the facility. We have already explained that corporate customers have become more important to the facility and event bottom line than the revenues generated from the 'average spectator'. A more recent move in the USA to revert to building 'single-purpose' facilities—that is, baseball- or football-only grounds—is directly linked to wanting to control all revenue streams generated through the sport facility rather than share them with co-tenants. It can also be seen from Table 1.1 that, when looking at the five major professional sporting leagues in the USA, the trend is away from paying for the construction of new sports arenas with public money; hence the need to create a 'return on private investment'.

As can be seen in Table 1.1, Major League Baseball is the only sport that has slightly increased the amount of public funding spent on building new stadia in the 1990s. This in itself does not come as a big surprise, given the fact that baseball, like no other sport in the USA, is the sport of the people. 'Funding' baseball from the public purse is least likely to meet with public backlash; hence it attracts the highest proportion of public funding of all major sports, and is the only sport that has increased its level of public funding throughout the 1990s. Ice hockey and soccer, in particular, seem to be perceived as sports that need to generate their own, private support. They are indeed niche market operators, compared with their all-American counterparts of football, baseball and basketball. The averages across leagues show a clear trend towards privately funding the establishment of new sporting facilities.

In Australia, the Telstra Dome in Melbourne is 100 per cent privately funded. The stadium incorporates a retractable roof covering an oval-sized pitch capable of hosting cricket and Australian Rules matches, seats just over 50 000 spectators, and has been tagged the 'corporate dome', given its strong focus on catering to the corporate dollar. The stadium was proposed to the market as an investment project and was completed with a range of major equity partners as venue shareholders. The growing requirement to 'return on invest-

Table 1.1 Proportion of sport facilities built in the USA with public funding pre-1990 compared with those built in 1990 or later

League	Constructed before 1990 % Public funding (no. of facilities)	Constructed 1990 or later % Public funding (no. of facilities)
National Hockey League	100 (5)	42 (23)
Major League Baseball	69 (11)	73 (17)
National Football League	87 (13)	67 (18)
National Basketball Association	50 (6)	42 (20)
Major League Soccer	100 (8)	55 (5)
Average across leagues	*81 (43)*	*54 (83)*

Source: Adapted from *Sports Facility Reports* (2002).

ment' further explains the focus on catering for the more lucrative corporate customers. Although the stadium did not turn a profit during its first few years of operation, leading to shareholder buyouts, the facility continues to be privately owned.

Australia's premier sporting stadium, the Melbourne Cricket Ground, is currently undergoing a major redevelopment. In summary, the facility is being redeveloped into 'a major entertainment destination', rather than just a place to host some sporting contests. A range of daytime cafés, bars and restaurants combined with conferencing facilities will encourage seven-day traffic at the venue. This is further boosted by a number of sporting museums that will be hosted in the facility, including the Gallery of Sport, the Olympic Museum and the Sport Australia Hall of Fame. Approximately 70 per cent of the existing stadium will have been redeveloped when capacity of the venue is brought back to its original 100 000 seats, in readiness for the 2006 Commonwealth Games. Funding for this near $A600 million project largely comes from private sources. On the back of preparing for the 2006 Commonwealth Games, the federal government has committed $A90 million, but a large proportion of the loan repayments—$A29 million per annum, to be precise—is generated by the 83 000 members of the Melbourne Cricket Club (MCC). The MCC has had the long-term management of the MCG, on behalf of the state government and the MCG Trust, and has recently secured the rights to manage the facility until 2042, also extending the club's lease of the members' reserve until 2067. The loan is to be repaid in 20 years. Other funding comes from the Australian Football League, the most important tenant of the facility, at $A5 million per annum, and from renegotiated service supplier contracts such as catering, security, advertising and ground sponsorships (Melbourne Cricket Club 2002). It needs no further explanation that with such levels of capital commitment, facilities such as the MCG need to host a continual supply of new events.

Growth in the number and type of events

When we take a closer and separate look at the events sector, we can also observe an extended period of significant growth. The president of the US-based International Festivals and Events Association, Steve Schmader, used the example of the small city of Boise in Idaho, with an estimated population of 400 000 (Zoltak 2002). The city hosts 150 festivals and events yearly that are large enough to require police support. With the country's more than 15 000 cities, and using a conservative estimate of 10 events or festivals per city, this leads to 150 000 events being organised in the USA alone per year. According to the Travel Industry Association of America, this translates to 111.2 million person trips per year, leading to a higher room-night demand than in, for example, the conventions industry. Overall, the industry is estimated to be worth $US15 billion per annum (Zoltak 2002).

According to Goldblatt (2000), there are four reasons that largely explain the growth in the number of events organised worldwide. The first reason relates to the demographic shift that is currently changing the makeup of most of the developed first world. The population of most Western nations is ageing rapidly, leading to more older people—lots more. Not only do older people have more time, they also have more money to spend during that time; and because they are growing older there are also more reasons to celebrate. The second reason relates to the exponential development of new technology, which in turn leads to a high-tech environment in which human contact (both face-to-face communication and physical contact) becomes increasingly rare. To balance their high-tech lives, people are looking for 'high-touch' opportunities to preserve their humanness. Events are excellent providers of 'high-touch' experiences. Booming economies around the world (at this time 'September 11' has put only a temporary stop to this growth) constitute the third reason for growth in the event sector. In particular, tourism and leisure industries have benefited from the extra disposable income earned in many countries around the world. Moreover, the events we are referring to here are obviously not limited to sport. As a matter of fact, sport represents only a small part of the global events industry, which includes cultural festivals, food festivals, art fairs and religious gatherings. However, sport is one area of events that is experiencing significant growth. The final reason leading to growth in the number of events relates to time. Time, particularly in Western nations, has become a precious commodity to be traded against other valuables. Work and leisure have merged to become almost a continuum in the West. People are opting for more, shorter breaks, which in turn should offer different experiences every time. Gone are the days of families travelling to the same holiday destination for 20 years in succession. More varied events, throughout the whole year, are needed to satisfy the requirements of increasingly diversified and demanding customers— customers who are prepared to pay for those events that allow them to 'economise' on the time they have available.

New markets for sporting events and implications for facilities

Westerbeek and Smith (2003) used the work of futurist Rolf Jensen (1999) to identify a number of marketplaces for sport products of the future. Rolf Jensen argued that wealthy, developed nations are about to enter what he called the 'Dream Society'. Humankind has moved from hunting and gathering to farming in an agricultural society. With the industrial revolution, the UK and other Western European nations, as well as the USA, entered the industrial society. Growing wealth as a result of dramatic technological advances resulted in people moving from the country to urban centres; cities were constructed, which in turn facilitated the establishment of transport infrastructure. People and organisations also became involved in what we now define as 'planning'. Increasingly, people allowed themselves the luxury of forgoing short-term results for longer-term prosperity. About three decades ago, the leading industrial nations moved into the so-called information society. Because production jobs were largely automated, knowledge became more important than capital. Intellectual capital is now valued more highly than physical capital. In the information society, however, success is still predominantly measured in tangible, materialistic wealth. According to Jensen (1999), the Dream Society will drive people towards achieving the emotional wealth that typified the very early human societies. The Dream Society is the ultimate societal type, because it combines material wealth (we no longer struggle to survive) with emotional wealth and fulfilment. The Dream Society perspective neatly fits in with the trends explaining the growth of the events industry, as observed by Goldblatt (2000). New events and more of them need new facilities (and also more of them). This is why it is prudent for sport facility and event managers to take stock and imagine what types of products are likely to be delivered through their facilities and with their event management structures. Westerbeek and Smith (2003) have proposed six new markets for sport products in the 'DreamSport Society'. These markets are sport entertainment, sport fantasy, sport quality, sport identity, sport tradition and sport conscience.

New markets for sport products

Sport entertainment[1]

People have an increasing emotional need for adventure, as evidenced by the escalation of such activities as bungee jumping and extreme sports. The sport theatregoer, who attends sporting contests with the express desire for entertainment and spectacle, exemplifies this need for adventure. Theatregoers of the future, however, are more about being entertained by satisfying their need for adventure than merely sitting on the sidelines and passively watching a sporting contest. This is not to say that theatregoers necessarily want to be *in* the game, but in order to realise their emotional peak they must have some influence *on* the game. As this is impossible in a practical sense, they instead require an interactive *presence* to best fill their emotional needs. What does this mean for facility and event managers? Well, if interactivity is the key, then technology that facilitates spectators' emotional connection to the sport product by engaging them in ways they have never experienced before will triumph, and will ultimately revolutionise sport delivery. This will have vast consequences for facility design and construction. It also needs to be noted that, although we are looking forward to future consumption behaviour, those facility and event managers that want to remain ahead of the game will need to incorporate the opportunities to deliver those products in their design and construction plans today!

Sport fantasy

Achieving the emotional need that can be described as togetherness revolves around products that can bring consumers together. Naturally, most sport teams and some events capitalise on this emotional bond that sport can provide better than any other products including beer, fast cars and film. At the heart of this emotional requirement is the desire for comradeship and direction. In other words, the interest in sport—whether conscious or not—is more about the other fans that sport attracts than about the game itself. This can be seen in participation-based events like University Games, the Gay Games and the Masters Games. However, only a comparative minority of people seeking to fulfil this need for togetherness do so directly through involvement in sport. Most attempt to meet this need through 'champ-following', particularly of team sports. The champ follower of the future is different in that he or she selects winning teams to support because these provide a convenient opportunity to experience the pleasure of togetherness that only success can deliver.

Champ followers are principally motivated to watch sport because they have an interest in a specific team or club that is winning. They are reluctant to watch sport by themselves. The new champ followers will increasingly look for opportunities to share the emotional experience of sport consumption with other like-minded individuals and groups, to share around their winning affiliation and reinforce to themselves that the world is viewing them as a winner. For facility and event managers this has some implications. First of all, champ followers do not necessarily meet in the traditional stadium. Increasingly they are using the

---

[1]   Parts of this section have been published earlier in Westerbeek, H. & Smith, A. (2003). *Sport Business in the Global Marketplace*. Palgrave, London. Permission to reuse this material was kindly granted by the authors.

Internet to chat with kindred spirits all around the world. Merely sitting in a stadium with other sports fans is not enough. Champ followers must derive a sense of importance from belonging to the group; the others in the group must care about their presence and recognise them as winners, just like the team they are supporting. Channelling sport exclusively through pay television is therefore a certain way to ensure that the new champ followers will find it more difficult to access the groups they need in order to reach satisfaction. Facility and event managers need to offer a range of opportunities to share that 'winning feeling' with other 'winners'.

It is important to note that Westerbeek and Smith (2003) see the boundaries between the different markets as not necessarily concrete. The need for togetherness can be found in other fan types, and the new champ follower is not exclusively interested in meeting an emotional need for togetherness.

Sport quality

The sport quality segment of the DreamSport Society is a combination of the expression of care and the intrinsic enjoyment of the sport product being consumed. Sport organisations are full of opportunities for members and fans to demonstrate that they care. Volunteers are the backbone of club-based sport systems like those in Europe and Australasia. The composition of the sport quality segment reflects a slightly new role for the sporting aficionado who has traditionally been interested in sport because it possesses the intrinsic aesthetics that they find alluring, or even addictive. In the DreamSport Society, the new aficionado is no longer satisfied with the position of semi-detached sports lover. The visual pleasure of watching a good game is not enough as other competing products offer more than quality skills on show, seeking to reach consumers on an emotional level. New aficionados want the quality sport experience to reach a deeper level—one that allows them to fulfil their need to show they care intensely about their sport and the level at which it is played. For athletes to appeal to this segment, they need to care as well—care about the people and communities that allow them to reap the benefits of their superior athletic performances. The move towards athletes being viewed and positioned as 'good corporate citizens' is of particular interest to the celebrity marketers. Sport performers will continue to earn their sometimes outrageous salaries only if they show their fans they care about them. Sometimes this comes naturally to athletes, for example to Australian tennis ace Patrick Rafter, who has set up his own charity, the Cherish the Children Foundation, and is also the patron of several others. Other athletes may need the assistance of their agents to select appropriate charities to support and donate parts of their earnings to, in order to convince the public that they do care about the communities that they benefit so much from. From the event management point of view in particular, those events that offer a 'care' factor are most likely to attract the sport quality niche of the events marketplace.

From the sport quality perspective, the influence of the almighty dollar or pound can be significant. Trends and pressures that affect the intrinsic quality of the sport itself will determine the commitment of the sport quality aficionado. For example, where economic imperatives drive the amount of money associated with sport and force the evolution of new 'elite of elite' leagues, and foster the development of super-athletes to perform in these competitions, the sport quality segment will happily consume sport. However, where these pressures erode the quality of the game, or manipulate it to an extent that the 'pure' element of the game is lost, then the segment will react unfavourably. This segment will make assessments about the value of the sport's quality, and this value assessment will be mediated by the actual ability of segment members to show that they care about quality.

Sport identity

Sport fans have a history of eliciting a sense of identity and meaning from their association with sport teams and clubs. The sport identity segment of the DreamSport Society combines the emotional need for identity. Jensen (1999) refers to this as the 'who-am-I' need, with the strength of conviction held by the passionate partisan. The sport identity segment will seek the emotional satisfaction of a strong sense of belonging and identity, married with the unwavering loyalty of the passionate fan. At the superficial level the sport identity segment comprises focused sport watchers, keenly observant about the state of the game and their team, and compelled by the most trivial team-related information. However, at the deeper level, this segment is looking for self-definition. At this deeper level, that search is realised by a close affiliation with a team or club, where a personal identity can be moulded indistinguishably with a club or a supporter group. As a result, the sport identity group define themselves in a way that is consistent with their association with a team of choice. For facility designers, this means that the 'space' allocated to these passionate fans needs to reflect their passion for the team they follow, and to offer opportunities to claim that space as if it were theirs. From the event point of view, it is important to note that these passionate fans are willing to spend significant sums of money in pursuit of ongoing self-identification through the purchase of sport-spectating services like tickets and pay television subscriptions, memorabilia, merchandise, endorsed products like club credit cards or home loans, and product extensions like junk food and beer. But they can also be easily alienated. As with any of the segments, forces that interfere with the identification process are harmful to this consumer. For example, when fans are locked out of venues in favour of corporate ticket holders and hospitality services, there will be a distancing of the fans from their beloved club and a consequent weakening of their identity.

Sport tradition

The sport tradition segment is a particularly interesting one from a facility management point of view. The emotional need to be met relates to the 'peace of mind' that comes through reminiscing about better times in the past. Of course, history is important to sports fans, but none so much as the sport tradition segment. Sport traditionalists are born of a combination of the 'peace of mind' element, which focuses on the good feelings and 'old-time' values that the consumption of some products can elicit, and the reclusive partisan sport fans, who will come back to fandom from the bench when the right set of circumstances seizes their interests. The sport tradition fans are therefore sophisticated in the way they assess the value of sport watching. Their emotional interest is engaged when sport can offer them a chance to reignite past values, to bask in a new winning streak that reminds them of the glory days, or to inspire them with confidence and trust. This is why corporatisation can disenfranchise the fan and take sport away from that special traditional base that is so important. On the other hand, corporatisation in the form of corporate hospitality, for example, can offer some of the special treatment that the sport tradition segment needs to satisfy its sense of personal service and value. Technology and innovation can also deprive this segment of the personal touches that sport can provide, such as the suburban stadium that is replaced by a heartless but architecturally stunning multi-purpose venue, or the old memorabilia-filled pub or bar that was sold to make way for yuppie apartments. Major League Baseball in the USA has continually managed to attract reclusive partisans to the game, in the normal cycles in which they take intermittent interest. Many of the MLB clubs are, or have been, involved in stadium renovation or rebuilding in the style that was prominent at the height of baseball's community success during the early 1900s.

Sport conscience

The final segment we are using to help sport facility and event managers focus on the future has been named sport conscience. The name is a reflection of the emotional requirements of consumers more interested in the broader picture than they are necessarily with sports or clubs themselves. The important element is a sincere desire that something worthwhile is accomplished that affects people at a greater level than the mere enjoyment of sport participation or spectatorship. There is a moral conviction at work. Allied to this is a sense of community. The main consumers in this segment are the community partisans, who are concerned with the needs of others in their association with sport. In particular, this fan type attends sport to please others and to contribute to the community interest. These are the mothers and fathers who bring the half-time tea or oranges, provide the taxis and coach the team. These are also the individuals who turn up to the local game because the team 'needs the support', or because they view it as a manifestation of their community pride.

A combination of the community partisan and the need for some conviction to be realised can be seen in the sport conscience segment. Their principal emotional necessities revolve around feelings of moral righteousness, usually achieved through benefits to the community or at least to people other than themselves. These people use sport, like some people use charity, to alleviate guilt and to sustain a sense of personal rectitude. They will buy only the shoes that were manufactured in 'appropriate' circumstances, consume healthy, organically grown foods, and attend sporting contests and events that show them to be worthy community contributors. These are the consumers that need to be targeted by the organisers of community festivals or mass participation events such as the Gay Games and the Masters Games, and of sports (events) with definitive moral philosophies about such issues as racism and gender inequality.

Table 1.2 provides an overview of sport product examples in all DreamSport Society marketplaces. It can be seen that the days are gone of the simple football match as the only 'sport product' hosted in a sport arena or community sport facility. For (recreational) *sport entertainment* people visit theme parks or jump off cliffs, for *sport fantasy* they interact with other fans online or at events, for *sport quality* they volunteer at events in a meaningful manner, for *sport identity* they publicly support teams that offer them opportunities to be 'part of the family', for *sport tradition* facilities and service providers replicate the 'good old days', and for *sport conscience* people will support those events and athletes that contribute to society as a whole.

In this table's overview of the type of products that will be delivered to the DreamSport Society marketplaces, also outlined are the implications for facility and event managers when

Table 1.2 DreamSport products and implications for facility and event managers

DreamSport Society marketplaces	Example products	Implications for facility and event managers
Sport entertainment	Sport-themed consumption (theme park, museum, facility tours) Sport tourism products (sport adventure packages to Queenstown, New Zealand including rafting, bungee jumping etc.)	Customer in the game Customer part of the action Active manipulation or influence on outcome Facility features to allow for integration of the 'spectating' and 'participating' roles
Sport fantasy	Team-based spectatorship (Newcastle United, Los Angeles Lakers, Collingwood Football Club) International, event-based (based on nationality or alma mater) spectatorship (at the Olympic Games or at the World University Games)	Integration of online and onsite togetherness Vastly expanding marketplaces through online supporter communities In-stadium interactive and 'between fans' communication features
Sport quality	Team-based volunteerism (domestic teams, ethnically based teams, local clubs) International event-based volunteerism (e.g. the Athens 2004 Olympic Games)	Culturally sensitive event communication (understand us and care about us) Events that give back or contribute to the community Events that incorporate opportunities to help others Athletes who care about fans 'Pure' (drug-free, traditional rules) sport
Sport identity	Sport participation products (Auskick, as a national participation program marketed by the Australian Football League) Sport spectatorship products (FIFA World Cup and fanatic country/team support) Packaged athlete and team products (Tiger Woods, Manchester United, the Brazilian soccer team)	Separate 'space' allocated within the facility to passionate partisans Opportunities during events to publicly express the passion people feel for a team or athlete Fit between the object of passionate following and tangible products offered for sales to commodify that relationship
Sport tradition	Sport-themed consumption (theme park, museum, facility tours Hallmark sporting events (Wimbledon) Broadcast- and film-produced sporting entertainment (the FA Cup final) Sport tourism (the British Lions Rugby Union tour)	Traditional architecture Traditional or recycled building materials Re-creation of 'old' experiences Marketing programs that have a high 'hero and ritual' content
Sport conscience	Culturally specific sport sponsorship based on convictions (e.g. sun protection products and surf lifesaving in Australia) Culturally global sport sponsorship based on convictions (Coca-Cola and the Olympic Games)	'Green' buildings 'Green' events Corporate sport citizenship Sport, facilities and events as tools to 'make things better'

they consider the delivery of these products. It has now also become clear that few facilities can cater to the needs of all sport consumers. In the remainder of this book we will therefore consider the following types of sport event facilities:

- natural facilities (e.g. speed skating contests on natural ice such as lakes or canals);
- spectator facilities (e.g. football stadia);
- participative facilities (e.g. gymnasia or community swimming pools);
- multi-use facilities (e.g. facilities that include retractable or removable seating systems, allowing them to be used for community and elite purposes).

The added value of facilities and events to user and non-user groups

As noted earlier, we will comment on the drivers of facility and event success more elaborately in Chapter 2, and will consider performance management issues in Chapters 10 and 11. This chapter concludes with a closer look at how the construction of facilities and the hosting of events are justified by the organisers and governments that determine how (community) resources are invested. There are four areas that are most often used to show to investors or to the local community why a new facility or major event will add value to all stakeholders involved. These areas are:

- community development
- economic development
- destination development
- social and cultural development.

Community development

As has been shown, communities of local, regional or national citizens have significantly contributed to the establishment of new facilities and to the attraction of hallmark sporting events to their cities and regions. However, only recently have governments realised that they are to be publicly accountable for the community resources they invest in venues and sporting events. Not only are they accountable economically—that is, to show professional financial management skills—but they also need to outline how community resources are used to provide a return for the community. This is when the establishment of facilities and the attraction and organisation of events are considered in light of added value. For example, will the new facility offer more opportunities for local community members to come together, to get to know each other better, to organise or become involved in community events, to allow minority communities to congregate and integrate with other community members? A multi-purpose facility such as the Melbourne Sport and Aquatic Centre (MSAC) in Melbourne, Australia, is an example of this. The venue offers facilities for elite and community sport in swimming, basketball, netball, volleyball, table tennis, squash, badminton, and general health and fitness; it further accommodates a number of state sporting organisations' offices. In short, the facility brings people from different (sporting) backgrounds together. With regard to events, do they provide community members with the opportunity to experience new cultures? Do the events, indeed, bring people together? Events can be used to showcase the uniqueness of local communities to the rest of the world, or at a more local level to invite people from various communities to come along and meet their neighbours. However, where community development remains a quite 'intangible' way of justifying the new facilities and events, calculating the economic effect of facilities and events on communities clearly focuses on measurable (quantifiable) contributions to the host society.

Economic development

Economic impact studies are attempts to demonstrate how expenditure related to the sporting event circulates through the economy. A positive economic impact (leading to economic benefits) can result from spending by visitors (locals, non-business and business 'tourists') on food, accommodation and transport. Added to this is the expenditure of government authorities and private investors when new event-related infrastructure is developed. In addition to this direct impact, there is the contribution of indirect spending when businesses produce goods and services (e.g. building materials) for organisations that spend money directly related to the event. Finally, there is a component called induced impact, when extra income gained by employees of firms that create direct and indirect impact is spent in the economy. The most common economic benefits that are the result of positive economic impact are the generation of new jobs, an increase in tourism in the region, the attraction of new business to the region, the growth of existing businesses, and a legacy of new or upgraded capital works (including sport facilities) for the region. A report by AT Kearny (2002) notes that the net economic impact for hosts of the Olympic Games can be quite significant, as is outlined in Table 1.3.

Destination development

The information age has resulted in an increased conceptual proximity of nations, cities and people. Lightning-fast long-distance exchange of information is leading to the redevelopment of urban regions from monocentric to polycentric cities. New economy cities are typified by the concentration of knowledge-based services and activities, not by building around a church or city hall. In other words, commercial activities are becoming the new centres of agglomeration and these centres both compete and cooperate with each other. Berg, Braun and Otgaar (2000), at the European Institute for Comparative Urban Research (EURICUR) in Rotterdam (the Netherlands), argue that the potentially successful polycentric city will be formed around knowledge-generating institutions like multinationals, universities and research organisations.

Table 1.3 Impact of hosting the Olympic Games on national economies

Host city	Net economic impact ($US billion)	Impact as % of GDP of the host country
Seoul (1988)	2.6	1.40
Barcelona (1992)	16.6	2.90
Atlanta (1996)	5.1	0.07
Sydney (2000)	4.3	1.00

Source: Adapted from AT Kearny (2002).

From that perspective it is no longer sufficient to be (or become) a city that is built in an attractive location. Potential (and current) citizens, business organisations, investors and visitors determine whether a city is attractive enough to be considered as a destination. Access to information, new knowledge, cultural services and a healthy environment are becoming the competitive drivers of success for cities to attract 'clients'. In other words, how can cities be marketed as an attractive alternative for all identified client groups? Increasingly, sport is being used as one of the drivers of city marketing strategies. This is because sport events allow targeting of all (domestic and international) client groups through one powerful medium. As Spain's second city, Barcelona struggled to be recognised and accepted as an attractive alternative to Madrid. With the successful hosting of the 1992 Olympic Games at the core of Barcelona's regeneration strategy, it is now one of the most attractive cities in Europe, boosting modern transport systems, a clean and revitalised coastal environment, a massively (re)developed living environment, and a revived cultural and social awareness among its citizens. The number of annual overnight stays grew from 3.8 million in 1990 to 4.3 million in the year of the Olympics, to a massive 7.4 million in 1998. In other words, sport is being used as a powerful destination development tool (Berg, Braun & Otgaar 2000).

Social and cultural development

There are a multitude of social benefits that can be identified, and it is common for governments and event organisers to highlight those benefits that are most likely to fit current policy and generate positive attitudes towards the event. From a sport-specific development point of view the event will contribute to the exposure of the sport, the development and preparation of officials and volunteers, and the generation of event-specific knowledge. The net benefits to the sport include new knowledge, experienced people and marketing benefits. Nor should the contribution of the event to national identity and citizenship be underestimated—in other words, the development of 'esprit de corps' of a nation or city. Furthermore, the event can contribute to programs that focus on youth development, gender equity, multiculturalism, and health and fitness. One category of social benefits that is increasingly identified as a priority is the area of environmental legacy. Benefits that the event needs to deliver to its host society include the development of new environmental policies, the contribution to human health, the active pursuit of resource conservation, and pollution prevention and environmental protection. Stated differently, it is not sufficient for the event to merely ensure that the natural environment is not damaged: rather, the event will be used as the instigator for enriching the living environment and, hence, will leave an environmental legacy. The Sydney 2000 Olympic Games may serve as an example. They were tagged 'the green games', largely because the principal site of competition at Homebush had been a toxic waste dump for years before it was singled out as the future venue of the Games. The whole site was cleaned before the new venues were constructed, and the nearby Olympic athlete village was developed to become a thriving suburb after the Olympics. All houses in the Olympic village have been sold and are currently occupied by a new Sydney community of predominantly young families.

Cultural benefits may relate to the level of inclusiveness of linguistic and cultural aspects of the event. How accessible is the event to cultural minorities? And is the event actively used and promoted to offer minority groups opportunities to participate? The alternative is obviously that governments need to spend taxes on developing cultural inclusiveness programs of their own (hence the need to conduct a cost–benefit analysis). The IOC has enforced the inclusion of a cultural program directly linked to the hosting of the Olympic Games, to offer the host city opportunities to produce cultural benefits. Not only does it allow the host nation to expose its particular culture and its values to the rest of the world (media benefits), but the inclusion of arts and heritage groups and activities in the event's program will deliver 'inclusiveness' benefits to a large cross-section of the host society.

Summary

In this chapter we have provided an outline of the changing nature of the sport facility and event sector. Because of its changing nature, the sector more than ever needs managers who are skilled in the areas of managing facilities *and* events. Throughout the rest of this book, you will be taken through the processes that range from establishing the facility and event infrastructure, to the actual running and performance evaluation of facilities and events. These processes will be outlined on the back of knowledge about the structure, size and trends that typify the facility and events sectors. The latter information is of critical importance, because it largely determines which markets the facility and its events need to cater for. This is why we have identified a number of new markets for sporting events and discussed the implications for the construction of new facilities. In this age of economic rationalisation and increasing social awareness, the business plan for constructing new facilities and attracting expensive events needs to be broader than a mere outline of the economic benefits. Our brief overview of the added value of new facilities and events to user *and* non-user groups presages a more detailed discussion of these issues in chapters to come.

Case study

Melbourne Sports and Aquatic Centre: customer needs and relationship management

This chapter's discussion of six different DreamSport Society marketplaces centred on the future needs of facility and event customers. Meeting customer needs is essential to the success of any facility or event, but customer needs are many and varied and continue to evolve.

One facility that meets the needs of many different customer groups and continues to adapt to changing customer needs is the Melbourne Sports and Aquatic Centre (MSAC). Located at the edge of attractive parkland and within close proximity to the central business district, this impressive multi-purpose centre caters to a diversity of sport and leisure participants, spectators and organisations. The facility comprises a 2000 seat show court, eight-court basketball hall, 12-court badminton hall, 27-court table tennis/volleyball hall, 10-court squash centre, 75-metre 10-lane swimming pool with spectator seating for 2000, 14-board diving facility, multi-purpose pool, 25-metre lap pool, water slide, wave pool, fully equipped fitness centre, and a wellness centre. The MSAC also houses a number of retail outlets, crèches, a café, bar, function and meeting rooms, as well as office space for various sport associations.

However, it's not only its multi-purpose nature that enables the MSAC to meet so many customer needs. The centre prides itself on creative programming and the identification and exploitation of market opportunities. For example, it was the first facility of its type in Australia to capitalise on using licensed Nemo-themed pool equipment, attracting a great number of junior and family customers to its wave pool. The MSAC has also moved into the lucrative corporate training and development market, attracting the business of many Melbourne firms seeking to fulfil a range of staff development objectives, such as improved teamwork and problem solving. Furthermore, in 2004 the MSAC launched the Melbourne School of Sport and Recreation Management. The School caters to the unmet professional development needs of Melbourne's sport management professionals. Its services range from career management to breakfast seminar series and from conferences to short courses in such areas as marketing and customer service.

As impressive as the MSAC is, redevelopments are currently under way including a 50-metre outdoor swimming pool, additional office space for sport associations, a second hydrotherapy pool, a multistorey car park, and a permanent 3000 seat grandstand for state, national and international competitions. The redevelopments were largely driven by Melbourne's securing the 2006 Commonwealth Games (M2006). The MSAC will be one of the key Commonwealth Games facilities, hosting aquatics events as well as squash and table tennis. Thus, by the end of 2005, when the redevelopments are complete, the MSAC will be able to meet the needs of even more customers.

One of the biggest challenges the MSAC confronts in meeting customer needs is when it has to close its doors to many, and sometimes all, of its customers due to the staging of a major event. When the Formula One Grand Prix comes to town each year in early March, the MSAC closes its doors for nearly a week to all customers except those using the aquatics area and the fitness and wellness centres. The MSAC and the Formula One race track are both located in the one area, and it is operationally impossible for the MSAC to stay open to everyone while the event is being run literally right outside its front door. In 2006, the Formula One Grand Prix will be rescheduled to late February or April to accommodate the Commonwealth Games scheduled for 15–26 March. Given the 'bump-in' and 'bump-out' requirements for each event, and the fact that the entire centre will be closed to everyone except M2006 customers during the actual games, the MSAC will not be meeting the needs of its normal customers for potentially one month!

Q. Select two of the MSAC's customer groups (i.e. individuals such as basketballers rather than organisations such as one of the sport associations) and develop some creative strategies that the MSAC could implement to ensure that their needs are met during the period of Formula One–Commonwealth Games closure. (Think outside the square—for example, can other 'partner' organisations help here?)

Many of the challenges the MSAC confronts (e.g. forced closure due to the Grand Prix) are best dealt with via effective relationship management. The importance of developing and maintaining relationships is a theme central to many other chapters in this book. For example, Chapter 4 emphasises the importance of developing strategic relationships and working collaboratively when it comes to designing and constructing sport facilities, and Chapter 8 discusses the importance of facility and event managers engaging in relationship marketing with many of their more important customer groups.

In a business context, relationships go beyond networking and a round of golf. They are built on an organisation's capacity to assist another to achieve its objectives. The MSAC has many business customers that are just as dependent on the centre as MSAC is on them. When the MSAC closes for the 2006 Grand Prix and Commonwealth Games, these business customers will be more inconvenienced than the individuals (e.g. the basketballers) who use the centre.

This book is a resource for facility and event managers as well as students aspiring to work in the field. While not necessarily taught in sport management education programs, central to anyone's success in this field is the ability to seek out, nurture and maintain relationships with key stakeholders. In addition to the key success factors discussed in Chapter 2, successful relationship management is essential to the effective operation of any facility or event.

Q. Identify at least 10 of the MSAC's business customers.

Q. Select two of these business customers and describe the interdependent nature of their relationship with the MSAC.

Q. Using the same two business customers, develop some creative strategies that the MSAC could implement to ensure that at least some of these customers' needs are met during the period of closure. (Again, think outside the square—can other 'partner' organisations help here?)

Q. Once again, using the same two business customers, develop some creative strategies that the MSAC could implement (before, during and after the closure) to maintain positive relationships with them.

2

Key success factors of operating sport facilities and running sport events

Chapter focus
Structure, size and trends in the sport facility and sport event sectors
Key success factors of operating sport facilities and running sport events
Developing new sport facilities: feasibility analysis
Developing new sport facilities: design and construction issues
Developing new sport facilities: preparing facility management infrastructure
Operating the new sport facility: attracting events
Operating the new sport facility: preparing event management infrastructure
Attracting customers: marketing the sport facility and the sport events
Running the sport event: event operations
Measuring facility and event performance: a scorecard approach to success
Measuring facility and event performance: impact on and for stakeholders

CHAPTER OBJECTIVES

In this chapter, we will:
*   Demonstrate the complexities of real-life sport management through the introduction and analysis of an international sports event.
*   Provide an applied overview of the management lifecycle phases of a sports event and facility, from the perspective of the local organising committee.
*   Identify the distinguishing features of a major sport event.
*   Introduce the basics of performance management by adopting a systems approach to organisational analysis.
*   Discuss the key success factors and project drivers of managing sport facilities and events.

The foundations to success

Whereas Chapter 1 sets the scene and provides an essential overview of the current and future sport facility and event industry, this chapter will primarily establish the framework for the successful planning, design, building, operation and evaluation of sport facilities and events. As in any business setting, continuously exceeding performance expectations presupposes a comprehensive understanding of the relevant concepts, principles and processes of management. For this reason, we introduce the boundaries and constraints of effective facility and event management, providing a holistic context for applying the analytical processes and tools that will be introduced in subsequent chapters.

To ensure practical relevance and meaning, we begin with a case study of a specific major sport event—namely, the 2002 Commonwealth Games hosted in the city of Manchester, England. Through analysis of this international sports event, which includes facility building and development, a conceptual framework is presented from which most event and facility managers can operate. In particular, the project management principles of the lifecycle concept, systems theory and the micro-management drivers of quality, time and cost are discussed from both theoretical and practical perspectives. Adopting this approach will demonstrate the complexity of real-life sport management, as well as highlighting the importance of clarifying organisational and individual relationships that determine performance measurement. Understanding the often diverse and sometimes conflicting inter- and intra-organisational requirements of contemporary sport will help more informed managers to reliably analyse and predict human behaviour, and thereby meet the ultimate goal of optimising sustainable organisational performance.

The XVII Commonwealth Games, Manchester 2002

So what is the nature and scope of this event? The Commonwealth Games (the Games) involves participants from 47 Commonwealth nations and their dependants (independent communities that have been historically derived from the republican government of England). Spanning every continent of the globe and constituting 1.7 billion people (30 per cent of the world's population), this elite-athlete, multi-sport competition is owned by an international governing body (the Commonwealth Games Federation, or CGF) and is hosted by a different Commonwealth country every four years. Further similarities to the Olympic Games include the fact that the CGF operates through a constitution, as well as protocols, regulations and codes of conduct in awarding the hosting of the event to a country (a Commonwealth Games Association, or CGA) seven years in advance of the implementation of the event. (See http://www.thecgf.com.)

From the perspective of Manchester (the 2002 host city and local organiser of the CGA), Table 2.1 summarises the general nature of this particular case study as well as many of the practical logistics involved in managing the XVII Commonwealth Games.

The XVII Commonwealth Games of Manchester 2002 has been selected as our sport event case study because it conforms to Torkildsen's (1999) general characteristics of an event (e.g. a clearcut starting and finishing point; fixed, absolute deadlines; one-off organisation, normally superimposed on other work; and typically involving large risks as well as many opportunities). Furthermore, the event includes many of the distinctive and complex sport

Table 2.1 Summary details of the XVII Commonwealth Games, Manchester 2002

Event aspect	The XVII Commonwealth Games, Manchester 2002
What	10-day world-class competitive event, involving 17 sports (14 individual; 3 team) and 72 Commonwealth nations
When	England's candidate city chosen—February 1994 Host candidate country chosen—November 1995 XVII Commonwealth Games Event held at Manchester, England, 25 July–4 August 2002
Who	5250 athletes/team officials; 1000 technical officials; 4500 accredited media; 9000 volunteers; 1 million spectators; 1 billion television audience (110 broadcast territories with a total of more than 1500 broadcast hours)

How

Event Organisational Basic Structure

```
              CGF
               │
               ▼
             CGCE
               │
               ▼
  ISF ◄──►   LOC   ◄──► Media
   
  SE                    S & P
           Volunt.
  SubCo                 Others
```

Key

CGF—Commonwealth Games Federation (*event owner*)

CGCE—Commonwealth Games Council for England (*National Commonwealth Games Association—CGA*)

LOC—Manchester 2002 Ltd (*local organising/operating company established through Manchester City Council*)

ISF—International Sport Federations (e.g. IAAF; FINA)

SE—Sport England (major funder of the Games through the national Lottery)

SubCo—subcontractors (e.g. IDEO, which designed the baton that included sensors to detect, monitor and convert the holder's pulse to a light beam)

Volunt.—Volunteers

Media—e.g. BBC was the host broadcaster and UK rights holder (15 hours of live television per day; 1000 hours of interactive television of up to 5 events at any one time)

S & P—official sponsors (e.g. ASDA, clothing; Adecco, staffing) and partners (e.g. United Utilities, water and electricity partner)

Others—e.g. tourism agencies, regeneration bodies, local charities, health action zones

Budget—The local organising committee operational budget was £130.6 million (twice that of the initial breakeven bid projections), of which sponsorship, ticket sales, merchandising and television rights constituted £51 million and £79.6 million came from taxpayers and Sport England.

Facilities—19 venues (all except one within 5 miles of the Manchester Games centre). Two facilities (aquatics and athletics/opening and closing stadium) minimally needed to be built at an additional cost of £150 million.

Other	• Alongside the Games was the 'Spirit of Friendship Festival' (11 March–10 August 2002). This acted as a promotional catalyst 'for a vibrant and engaging celebration of the modern Commonwealth', enabling a wider target audience reach than just sport, the north-west of England, or the duration of the Games. This included a comprehensive support program of sport, education, art, culture, community, and the Queen's Golden Jubilee celebratory activities linked by the common yet distinctive themes of 'diversity and inclusion'.

	• The 'Inclusive Commonwealth Games' became the enduring quality of the Games with equality of opportunity for all: elite athletes with a disability were included within the Games program and medal table for the first time ever; spectator ticket prices were affordable to all, with more than 10 000 free tickets being given to young people, community and disadvantaged groups.
	• The event became the centrepiece for the Queen's Golden Jubilee celebrations: in the Baton Relay (the equivalent of the Olympic Torch Relay), the baton, containing the Queen's message, departed London's Buckingham Palace on 11 March (Commonwealth Day) and travelled 63 000 miles across five continents, before being read by the Queen at the Games Opening Ceremony (25 July).
Example of the event outputs/ outcomes	• Regarded as the 'biggest and most successful yet' (Commonwealth Games 2002) and 'the affordable games that will leave a legacy of sport rather than a legacy of debt' (Ives 2002, p. 1).
	• Economic impact estimates: secured Manchester more than £600 million in public and private investment; created the equivalent of more than 6100 full-time jobs; short-term doubling/trebling of local trade, long-term boosting the number of visitors to the area by an estimated 300 000 each year (Yates 2002, pp. 12–13).
	• 'Team England's most successive sport medal tally ever' – 165 medals (54 gold) (West 2002).
	• The post-hoc evaluation by Sport England website voters revealed that 87% of the English public thought that the games were a good use of money, 56% would play more sport because of the Games, and 88% believed that the Games improved the image of English sport (Sport England 2002).

N.B. Further information related to the Manchester Commonwealth Games case study can be obtained from the event home page (http://www.commonwealthgames.com).

Sources: Sports Council (1994); Commonwealth Games (2002); Guardian Media Group (2002); Ives (2002); Sport England (2002); West (2002); and Yates (2002).

event management features of major sports events as suggested by Emery (2003) and summarised by the acronym STUDIES (see Table 2.2).

Due to the unique temporal and multi-organisational requirements of this major sport event, it is clearly one of the more complex projects to manage. But in addition, and as previously mentioned in Table 2.1, the event in 2002 included the building of new facilities (such as the athletics/opening and closing stadium as well as the aquatics centre), as well as the use of 17 other established sport venues used to host the event. In this sense it provides an excellent contemporary case study, because it potentially incorporates a broad array of practical issues and perspectives from which to focus on sport event and facility management.

To better appreciate the depth of management encountered in this project, however, our main stakeholder focus here will be on the local organising event committee (the operating company of Manchester 2002 Ltd, or M2002), both as event host and venue manager. Whereas the former will involve the very difficult task of effectively managing vertical and horizontal stakeholders as a low-level contractor, the latter will more specifically address Manchester City Council's venue management of the athletics and opening/closing ceremony stadia. In both cases a high-pressure project management environment was encountered due to the immovable Opening Ceremony deadline. This demanded effective and efficient management by Manchester City Council, along with the development of a sound rationale for its involvement.

Table 2.2 Distinguishing features of many major sport events

Distinctive features	Manchester 2002 Commonwealth Games example
Scale/scope of logistics	• Manchester secured more than £600 million in investment: Sport England alone invested £165 million in the event. • More than 23 000 staff were involved in administering the event, of which 9000 were volunteers.
Temporary nature	• Manchester 2002 Ltd was a temporary dynamic organisation established to manage the event (e.g. 700 staff were involved one month before the event; 23 000 staff during the event; and the organisation was dissolved 6 months after the event) (Done 2002).
Unique	• This event was founded on historical rather than geographical grounds, and in sharing a common language and family background it is reported to create a unique atmosphere and hence is commonly referred to as the 'Friendly Games' (Phillips 2002). • The City of Manchester had never previously hosted the event or anything remotely similar.
Demand	• Nearly 600 000 tickets (80%) were sold at least 10 days before the event start date. Such was the late demand that the event was predicted to break the 94% of sales established by the hugely popular Sydney Olympic Games (Yates 2002).
International involvement	• This family of 72 independent sovereign states spreads across five continents, constitutes 1.7 billion people (30% of the world's population), and involves participants representing a broad cross-section of the world's faiths, races, languages and cultures (Commonwealth Games Federation 2001).
Event history & culture	• The idea was born in the 1890s although the first Commonwealth Games were not held until 1930, where they involved 400 athletes from 11 countries and were hosted in Hamilton, Canada. • Possessing the overriding Commonwealth Games Federation vision 'to promote a unique, friendly world class Games and to develop sport for the benefit of the Commonwealth' (Commonwealth Games Federation 2001), all decisions are reported to be based on the core values of 'humanity, equality and destiny' (Commonwealth Games 2002).
Stakeholders	• Organisational complexity includes at least three levels of multi-organisation management from public, private and voluntary sectors. It is not unusual for an event of this size to operate agreements with more than 700 different organisations to successfully deliver the event.

Source: Adapted from Emery (2003).

The 'why' of Manchester City Council involvement

Despite receiving social, community and financial objections, the local government organisation of Manchester City Council (MCC) decided to bid to host the potentially elite, international and capital-intensive project of the 2002 Commonwealth Games. The reason for its decision lies within both the historical and cultural background of the city, as well as the perceived power of sport to act as a marketing vehicle to breathe new life into the city and region.

At the turn of the millennium, Manchester City, with a population of around 430 000, was typically regarded as a depressed former industrial area. As Sport England (2002, p. 14) elaborates:

> Over the last three decades or so, East Manchester has declined from being a nation-ally important area of mature industry and settled population to become one of the most intense concentrations of deprivation in the country, unable to retain either busi-nesses or residents.

Having already witnessed the global appeal and local community 'feel-good factor' of sport through the renowned success of Manchester United Football Club, MCC decided to adopt a strategy of hosting world-class sport events to revitalise the region and simultaneously achieve its corporate objectives. As the leader of the Council explained (Leese 2002, p. 20):

> We bid for the games as a catalyst to regenerate our city and to boost our profile worldwide ... The Commonwealth Games are the catalyst, the focus and the founda-tion for a comprehensive and co-ordinated range of multi-million pound investment ... that will drive up the quality of life for Manchester people.

The choice of strategy was therefore justified on the basis that, if successful, it would trans-form the image of the area into an attractive one in which to invest and live, against a time frame that would be unprecedented by any other means. This specifically meant Manchester (2002) establishing the following unique mission:

- to deliver an outstanding sporting spectacle of world significance, celebrating athletic excellence, cultural diversity and the unique atmosphere of the 'Friendly Games';
- to deliver a successful Games on behalf of all competitors, spectators and stakeholders;
- to leave a lasting legacy of new sporting facilities and social, physical and economic regeneration; and
- to set a new benchmark for hosting international sporting events in the UK and the lasting benefit they can generate for all those involved.

Such a mission was then converted into more specific objectives, such as the following pub-licly shared regeneration targets (Sport England 2002, pp. 14–15):

- doubling the population of the North Manchester area to 60 000 in the next decade;
- building 12 500 new homes and improving 7000 existing ones;
- developing North Manchester Business Park, offering up to 10 000 new jobs;
- constructing a new district centre, next to the main stadium, offering new homes, shops and employment;
- improving educational standards; and
- producing an integrated transport system.

Having now hosted the event, the city and region appear to be well on target to exceed such performance measures and, as reported by McKinnon (2002, p. 1), chief executive of City Centre Management:

You don't get the true value [of the investment] until well after the Games have finished
... We've had thirty years of regeneration concentrated into six years but investment
in the city is not going to stop now.

In essence, the rationale behind MCC's involvement with the event was based on creating added
value through community, economic, destination as well as social and cultural development
means. In hindsight, to achieve the dream of hosting the most significant multidisciplinary
sporting event held in England since the 1948 Olympics was a complex and high-risk endeav-
our for any city to undertake. On the one hand, appraising the strategic fit between internal
resources (facilities, people and money) and the required external demands of the event revealed
that many 'fit-for-purpose' facilities already existed in the northwest region. These included:

- *The Manchester Evening News Arena* (the largest indoor arena in Europe, which opened
  in 1995; seats up to 21 000 spectators; is currently used for major sport events and concerts as well as being the home of the local professional ice hockey and basketball teams)
  would act as the Games venue for the netball and boxing finals.
- *The Greater Manchester Exhibition Centre* (G-MEX), which opened in 1986, was able to
  host the Games Press Centre, gymnastics, judo, weightlifting and wrestling events.
- Similarly, local leisure centres such as the *Forum Centre* (used for the Games preliminary
  boxing rounds and as training centre) and the *Belle Vue Leisure Centre* (the Games
  hockey centre) were both within easy reach of the city centre and required low levels of
  investment to adapt them to meet the needs of the CGF.

On the other hand, to compete with the other international bids as well as meet the long-term
operational facility performance needs of the future (increased revenue streams, efficiency
gains and seven-day traffic; see Chapter 1), additional new world-class facilities were
required. Given the norm that local government budgets are unlikely to include the sort of
capital development funds required to build such major sport stadia, at least one or more
business partners were demanded to realise the MCC strategy and fund the project.

As this was a world-class sports event of national significance to future mega-event
bidding, the obvious first point of contact was Sport England (the national quango and
leading sports development agency and distributor of lottery funds). Possessing the remit to
enhance world-class sport and community opportunities, Sport England fortunately decided
to wholeheartedly support the bid, and soon became the major funder of M2002. It committed £165 million to the project, of which £135 million was dedicated to facility building
and £30 million went towards running costs (Sport England 2002).

Without Sport England or an alternative partner to source the project, the Games simply
would not have taken place in Manchester. However, partnership, which is commonly
regarded as a necessity in contemporary sport provision, brings with it both benefits and
(often unforeseen) shortfalls. The general advantages of partnerships (which are particularly
complicated in the hosting of major sport events) are perhaps most obviously developed for
the synergies that they create. For example, they are likely to be built on organisational
specialism(s), and provide the opportunity to reduce resource commitment and organisational risk when compared with sole ownership. The disadvantages relate to a distinct lack
of power and control over the management processes, which in turn makes the achievement
of performance targets that much more difficult. Moreover, they typically involve very

complex decision making and time-consuming communications that demand a full understanding of each partner's expectations. Fortunately, in the case of Sport England, this agenda was very clear and closely aligned with that of MCC, as illustrated in Table 2.3.

New state-of-the-art sport facilities were therefore designed and built for the 2002 Games, and Table 2.4 provides just two examples of these—further evidence of how M2002 managed to incorporate Sport England's sporting legacy investment needs in its strategic sport facility plan.

Managing the project

Having determined to host the event in established and new specialist sport facilities, Manchester City Council was required to effectively manage the project. In practice this meant identifying what needed to be done, by whom and when, and then implementing the plan of action to achieve the short- and long-term performance targets of all stakeholders. Clearly, this was a daunting management task, of considerable magnitude and complexity. Theoretical and practical experience over the years suggested to MCC that there was only one solution—namely, to adopt a general to specific focus, understanding the project as a whole before breaking it down into subprojects or more manageable phases. Starting at the general level and progressing to the specific, MCC realised that all sports events and facilities can be

Table 2.3 Sport England objectives

Objective	Example of proposed activity to achieve objective
Present a world-class sport environment	• Building of new state-of-the-art sport facilities and establishing an appropriate elite support network
Achieve a lasting legacy for sport	• Sport facility usage—regional home for the English Institute of Sport and guaranteed community use after the event • Commonwealth Curriculum pack—web-based active learning package linked to the national curriculum • Passport 2002—a scheme focusing on the young to participate in a range of health, citizenship and sport activities • Active Sports Talent Camps in nine sports—10 000 young able and disabled participants and 4500 coaches, officials and volunteers
Provide a catalyst for regeneration	• Create a sustainable development of homes, shops, workspaces and community facilities through the New Islington Estate • Establish North Manchester Business Park (160-hectare site) and Openshaw Business Centre (500 jobs) • Develop East Manchester Sport Action Zone—a community sport activity project in an area of high social and economic deprivation
Support Team England	• £3.5 million additional support to increase the chances of Games medal success focusing on sports outside of the national World Class programs (e.g. bowls and wrestling) • £750 000 dedicated to team manager, education and development of athlete familiarisation programs in Manchester prior to the Games

Sources: Guardian Media Group (2002) and Sport England (2002).

Table 2.4 Examples of world-class sporting facilities built for the Manchester Commonwealth Games

Facility	Facility features, funding and use after the Commonwealth Games

Sportcity	*Facility features*
	 • Focal point for the Manchester Commonwealth Games, providing the venue for the track cycling, table tennis and squash competitions
	 • Site area of 146 acres (largest integrated sports development in Britain), including:
	   – 3500 seat National Cycling Centre
	   – 1500 seat, seven-court national squash centre
	   – **Manchester Athletics Centre**, featuring a 200-metre indoor track and 400 metre outdoor track
	   – Indoor tennis centre, with six indoor and six outdoor courts
	   – 38 000 seat **City of Manchester Stadium**—to host the opening and closing ceremonies, as well as the athletics and rugby sevens competitions
	   – Sports science and medicine facilities
	 Funding
	 Total project costs—£116.2 million (Sport England Lottery Fund of £92 million)
	 Use after the games
	 • **Sportcity** will become the regional headquarters of the English Institute of Sport (EIS), which will provide elite athletes with a top-class training environment (national network, quality facilities and equipment, expert coaching, sport science and other training support for England's international performers of the future).
	 • **City of Manchester Stadium**—Within days of the Games' closing, the athletics track will be dismantled (transported to Birmingham to be used for the 2003 IAAF World Indoor Championships in Athletics) and the ground level lowered by six metres to convert it to a 48 000 seat professional football stadium. Manchester City Football Club (MCFC) will become the main tenant of the stadium, taking on the responsibility for the facility repair and renewal as well as the operational risk. The money raised from MCFC rent (linked to a percentage of ticket sales) will then be reinvested in the Sportcity site development (facilities and programs). The community will be able to use the stadium for at least 100 days per year.
	 • Local community and sport clubs will be able to use all other Sportcity facilities.

Manchester Aquatics Centre	*Facility features* • Provides the competition venue for the swimming, diving and synchronised swimming competitions • Only complex in the UK with two 50-metre pools (the competition one capable of adjustment through a retractable floor; the training one is for those on the world-class programs. Sited beneath the main pool, it includes adjacent state-of-the-art science, research and medicine facilities), a competition diving tank, fitness centre and dance studio • Seats 3000 people *Funding* Total project costs—£32 million (Sport England Lottery Fund of £22 million) *Use after the games* • In the longer term this facility will offer a community leisure pool, development programs and a world-class venue for swimming events

Sources: Guardian Media Group (2002); ILAM (2002); Sport England (2002).

understood best by initially relating them to a component of time, as it can be argued that every sport event and facility progresses through various sequential phases from conception to completion.

In the XVII Commonwealth Games scenario, it was the event that largely drove the new facility management schedule. (It is worth noting that this is not always the case, as many facilities are built first and then aim to attract sport events; see the Manchester Evening News Arena example.)

Transferring for the moment from the actual to the theoretical, it becomes necessary to introduce the typical project lifecycle for both a sport event and a newly built sport facility. Please note that 'typical' does not necessarily imply applicability to all situations. Certainly in the sport sector, where there is a considerable range of diversity of projects, there appears to be no common agreement as to the phases or the terminology used to describe each phase. The important point to grasp is that lifecycle models are an attempt to simplify the chronological and developmental process of managing projects—to integrate both general and specific planning requirements across a time-driven management context, so that succeeding activity can be better prepared for and cost-effectively managed.

As a useful starting point, Emery (2003) provides the following basic event lifecycle model that can be applied to the typical major sport event environment (Figure 2.1). This lifecycle model emphasises that there are three discrete phases—pre-event, event implementation, and post-event—each constituting a self-evident boundary of time and involving further substages. Such a model, which includes the dynamic generic management processes of planning, organising, leading and evaluation (Chelladurai 1985), can equally be applied and adapted to any type of sports event. But for the purposes of this chapter it will be elaborated on and applied to the Manchester Commonwealth Games setting.

Figure 2.1 Lifecycle stages and core management processes of managing major sport events

Stages	1. Pre-event			2. Event	3. Post-event	
Sub-stages	(a) Idea and feasibility	(b) Bidding process (if required)	(c) Detailed planning and preparation	(a) Implementation	(a) Clear away	(b) Feedback
Core management processes	← PLANNING → - →					
	← ORGANISING → - - - - - - - - - - - - - - - - - - →					
	← LEADING →					
	← (Formative) EVALUATION (Summative) →					
Time line	➤					

Key:

← Start of Management Activity   → End of Management Activity   - - - - Management Application

Source: Emery (2003).

1. Pre-event management stage

The first and longest stage of the lifecycle, often involving up to 90 per cent of the total event duration (Emery 1997), normally requires the majority of the resource investment spend, and typically can be subdivided further into the three substages highlighted in Figure 2.1.

(a) Idea and feasibility

This substage is vital, yet is barely considered in any depth by the amateur sport event organiser. In practice, the decision whether to host a sport event or not is often based on a personal and political whim rather than any careful appraisal of the project merits (Emery 2002). However, with the escalating costs involved in hosting events as well as the greater levels of accountability experienced in all sectors of the sport industry, clarification and justification of any resource investment should now be regarded as the norm. Any organisation wishing to host a sport event, whether from an internally or externally generated idea, should be able to justify it on the basis of the strategic fit between present and future organisational competence as well as environmental need.

As developed in Chapter 3, this means that the feasibility of the idea should be objectively appraised via analytical techniques, and via comparison with organisational selection and sanctioning criteria as well as competitor offerings. The purpose of this process is, as suggested by Wearne (1989, p. 34), to ensure:

> that sufficient work is carried out to reduce the uncertainties to acceptable levels. Within the procedure, expenditure is sanctioned in one or more stages to produce increasingly more reliable statements of viability. Thus the decision-making authority has the opportunity of reviewing the proposal as it progresses through defined stages before taking a final commitment decision.

In the case of the 2002 Commonwealth Games, pre-event independent feasibility studies were commissioned by both MCC and Sport England. Such feasibility studies helped to identify the respective organisation's short- and long-term performance targets, the likely costs and risks attached to these measures, as well as providing the information to determine the degree to which the organisations chose to be involved. It is quite possible that the outcome of this event substage will determine the project closure. This was exemplified with Sheffield City Council, which pulled out of the national bid to host the 2002 Commonwealth Games just one day before the submission deadline.

(b) Bidding process

Bidding is not an inevitable process, although it is commonly required when seeking to host internationally recognised sporting championships, such as World, European and Commonwealth events. Where bidding is required (as was the case in the Manchester Commonwealth Games), the local organiser is likely to experience increased resource commitment and greater levels of bureaucracy and uncertainty at each stage of the organisational, national and international approval process (Emery 2002). Ironically then, it could be considered to be a business venture where many organisations may start the race but where realistically there is only one winner. As there are rarely any benefits for second place, it could be argued that Manchester City Council's strategy of focusing on world-class sport events to rejuvenate the city constituted a very-high-risk strategy, particularly in the light of two failed previous Summer Olympic bids (1996 and 2000).

Sport events involving a bidding process additionally place the winning host in the role of a 'time-bound' franchisee, unlike many other cases, where the sport event is created by an individual or organisation and is hosted at the same venue each year. This latter type of annual sport event, which still requires the respective national governing federation's permission to host the event, includes the Wimbledon Tennis Championships, local athletic road races, and invitation rugby tournaments. Regardless of the nature of the sport event, successful implementation is possible only through the event organiser's meticulous attention to planning and preparation.

(c) Detailed planning and preparation

Once such permissions have been granted or candidature confirmed and a full commitment has been made to stage the event, the in-depth planning and preparation substage can begin. Planning, establishing the terms of reference (future ends), and the systems/means of achieving them, should begin the moment the event is initiated. This then, as highlighted in Figure 2.1, has a tendency to pervade all elements of the lifecycle. As more projects fail through bad planning than for all other reasons combined, it is likely that the planning and preparation substage will consume the lion's share of the allocated event resources. As Watt (1992, p. 14) explains:

> It is always a little dangerous to select one management function rather than another, but in terms of event organisation, it would appear quite legitimate to select planning as the prime factor of success ... Planning is so valuable because it reduces uncertainty; focuses attention on goals and produces unity of purpose; makes for efficient operation; and ensures appropriate control systems are established.

In essence, the core management process of event planning attempts to maximise positive impacts and to counter potential negative impacts through astute awareness and practical intervention activities (Bowdin et al. 2001). It is considered to be so fundamental to the nature of any type of sport event and facility management success that it will be discussed in considerable depth in Chapters 4 to 8 of this book.

Organising

The second core management process initiated in the pre-event stage of event management is that of organising. According to Watt (1992, p. 25), this entails determining:

> the activities to be accomplished towards achieving the end objectives; the gathering together of these activities into relevant structures; and allocating the achievement of objectives, through these activities, to the appropriate groups or individuals ... [Organisation] provides the framework within which individuals can co-operate together to achieve what they could not achieve on their own.

Being inextricably linked to planning, organising can be seen to be about creating synergy, and hence optimising the effectiveness and efficiency of goal achievement while minimising coordination costs. The difficulty of managing this process in the event management environment lies in the finite nature of the event; the complexity of the stakeholder involvement; as well as the human resource demands that peak at the implementation stage of the event. As highlighted in Table 2.1, M2002 was the organisation created to manage the event at the local level, and in terms of staff numbers it grew by more than 300 per cent in one month to implement the event; six months later the organisation was completely dissolved.

As a temporary, flexible organisation operating in a very dynamic environment, this multi-agency partnership potentially provided all the ingredients for a coordination disaster. Furthermore, organisation theory would suggest that such an environment demanded an organisational structure of low centralisation, job specification (horizontal and vertical), and formalisation. Paradoxically, local authority organisations are usually the drivers of major sports event local organising committees, yet they are historically characterised by functional bureaucratic cultures, the very opposite of what the event environment demands in theory.

For successful event management, this dichotomy obviously needs to be resolved, to create the many features cited for effective event organisation. Torkildsen (1999), for example, suggests that this should include:

- clear objectives to which all parties are committed;
- a highly respected coordinator of calibre and authority;
- a synergistic organisational structure, with discrete units for specific tasks;
- team effort, positive attitudes and enthusiasm;
- efficient formal and informal lines of communication; and
- coordinated effort, with no overlap or wasted time and resources.

Leading

From such a listing, it is apparent that one of the keys to successful event management is effective leadership, which must facilitate all stages of the event lifecycle. This constitutes the third component of the core management processes, and entails balancing the performance needs of the task, team and individual according to the event demands encountered. Achieving the task obviously dominates the desired behaviour of business activity, although human relations theorists draw attention to the importance of the team and comprehension of personal needs, particularly in light of the sport event scenario involving such a high percentage of their workforce as volunteers.

Given the previously established complexity of the event environment, it probably comes as no surprise that the role of the event leader is commensurately onerous, being multidisciplinary as well as multidirectional. Figure 2.2 illustrates the envisaged multidirectional role of the M2002 leader utilising Briner, Geddes and Hasting's (1996) classification system.

This model additionally highlights the potential accountabilities of leaders, at both organisational and individual levels, and can be linked directly to Meyer's (2002) 'purposes of performance measurement' model as presented in Figure 2.3. (As Chapters 10 and 11 will further develop the concept of performance measurement, only a concise synopsis of the model is presented here.) In briefly explaining this model, Meyer (2002, pp. 30–1) elaborates:

> the look ahead, look back, motivate, and compensate purposes of performance measures are placed outside the organizational pyramid because they are common from the

Figure 2.2 The role of the Manchester 2002 Ltd leader

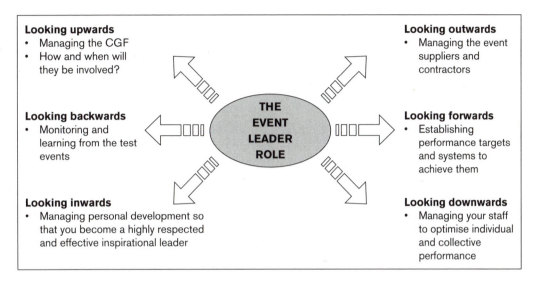

Source: Adapted from Briner, Geddes and Hasting (1996, p. 17).

Figure 2.3 The seven purposes of performance measurement

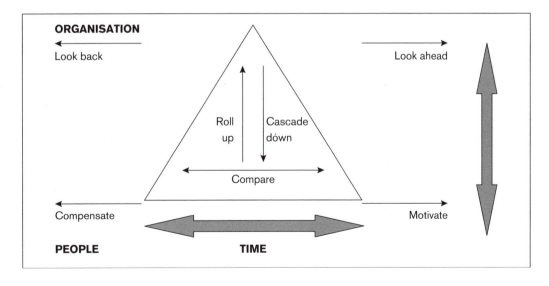

Source: Adapted from Meyer (2002, p. 31).

smallest and least formal to the largest and most organized firms. By contrast, the roll-up, cascade down, and compare purposes, which become significant as firms grow in size and complexity, are placed within the pyramid because they are the artifacts of organization ... look ahead and look back are placed at the peak of the pyramid because measures having these purposes gauge the economic performance and past accomplishments of the firm as a whole, whereas motivate and compensate are at the bottom of the pyramid because measures having these purposes motivate and drive the compensation of individual people.

Clearly, event leaders at all levels of the operation must have the ability to establish the leadership style(s) of 'best fit' determined by the event substage, the leader, the subordinates, the task and the specific goals of the organisation.

2. Event implementation stage

The second key stage of the proposed event management lifecycle is implementation. In major sport events, Emery (1997) identified this stage as typically involving about 1 per cent of the total project duration and more than 95 per cent of the workforce numbers. This is obviously the culmination of and justification for all previous work. As the prime indicator of event performance measurement it requires little explanation here, but will be developed more fully in Chapters 6 and 7. The ideal event, in essence, will be the one that leads to total satisfaction of all internal and external stakeholders—a memorable experience, run in a smooth, safe and enjoyable manner, in which all parties would wish to be involved again. According to Tork-ildsen (1999), this means a 'professional' presentation of the event, where class, flair and imagination are truly evident; and this becomes possible only if the pre-event stages have been thoroughly planned, prepared, rehearsed and executed. Whereas rehearsal, execution and evaluation are relatively easy to achieve in most sport operational management contexts, this is more difficult to practise in the unique environment of managing one-off major sport events. This is not to say that it is impossible to achieve. For example, in the Manchester Common-wealth Games situation, the sport facilities and systems were tested and evaluated through the hosting of other events, such as the World Track Cycling Championships in 1996 and 2002, and the national Aqua-Pura Commonwealth Athletics Trials held six weeks before the Common-wealth Games. There was even a spectator-attended final dress rehearsal of the Games Opening Ceremony held just two days before the actual ceremony. Obviously the key celebrities and fire-works displays were omitted so as not to spoil the surprises of the official event; but of particular interest were the spectators who attended this ticketed event: dress rehearsal tickets were prima-rily sold through the event volunteers, just for their friends and families or for the other event volunteers not specifically involved in the Opening Ceremony. To the volunteers this acted as an exclusive perk, creating considerable perceived added value, while to the event organisers it pre-sented a final opportunity to refine the operational plans and systems of the event, as well as yet another income stream and promotional activity to sell the official merchandise.

(a) Controlling

As with any aspect of sport performance, even the most perfect plan will not guarantee event success without some form of control. The interactive nature of people with their environment means that many uncertainties exist on the day of the event, and this is where performance measures need to be continually monitored and controlled. Monitoring, or 'formative evaluation', should take place throughout the event and not just during the implementation stage. For example, M2002 is likely to have monitored sponsorship procurement and ticket sales in the pre-event stage; security problems such as unattended baggage, drink and hooligan problems, and accreditation issues at the implementation stage; and evaluation questionnaire returns at the post-event management stage.

To eradicate risk and prepare for emergencies in the event implementation stage, key stakeholders are typically involved in many of the preceding substages of the event. This permits personal involvement and utilisation of appropriate expertise in the agreement of respective role(s), task integration, and the formalisation of important communication and control practices that span the entire lifecycle of the project. At the implementation stage of the event, Bowdin et al. (2001, p. 171) suggest that:

> Control consists of making sure that what happens in an organisation is what is supposed to happen. The control of an event can range from the event manager simply walking the site and discussing daily progress with staff, to implementing and monitoring a detailed plan of responsibilities, reports and budgets.

In large events such as the Commonwealth Games, a control centre is minimally established. Through closed-circuit television and radio communication, the event and facility multi-agency managers control the event through instantaneous communication with each other as well as their respective support staff. Control in this sense is about continuous monitoring of performance against planned activity, and its relationship with other management processes is reported by Cole (1999, p. 225) to be as follows:

> if planning represented the route map for a journey, then organizing represented the means by which one could arrive at the chosen destination. We can now add that controlling ensures that the travellers know how well they are progressing along the route, how correct their map is, and what deviations, if any, they need to make to stay on course.

3. Post-event evaluation stage

In some events this final stage overlaps with the implementation stage. For example, many world marathons start their clear-away processes literally minutes after the last runner starts the race.

(a) Clear-away

The clear-away substage does not relate just to returning the facility to its former glory: it refers also to the important exit of spectators, participants and other stakeholders from the event. The final memory of an event must not be spoilt by long delays and traffic jams due to the full volume of traffic leaving the facility at the same time. This is unlike the start of an event, where people typically arrive over a three- to four-hour duration. This substage is therefore as important as any other, and requires considerable depth of planning, organisation, leadership and evaluation.

(b) Feedback

Post-event feedback is often referred to as 'summative evaluation', and in the major sport event environment this normally equates to anything up to 12 per cent of the time involved in the event lifecycle (Emery 1997). Given the significance of all types of evaluation (performance measurement) on future learning, this will be elaborated on in more depth in Chapters 10 and 11. Suffice it to say that evaluation appears too often to be associated with negative connotations, such as coercion and blame, rather than the positive aspects of a continual learning process. Only when evaluation is interpreted as constructive feedback by all relevant stakeholders will it be possible to begin to achieve the long-term aim of continually improving the efficiency of people, units and hence the organisation. In the case of the Manchester Commonwealth Games, summative evaluation included a 500 000 word post-games report that was written to extend the legacy of sport event management both internally and externally. In the same way that the Sydney Olympic Games informed the practices of the Manchester Commonwealth Games, the Manchester practices were used to inform event management of the 2004 Athens Olympic Games as well as other events held in Manchester or the UK. In this way, such findings can begin to develop yet another event lifecycle, but more importantly enhance and professionalise the event industry of the future.

To recap: the purpose of applying the lifecycle concept to any project, in this case a sport event, is that it helps management to focus more specifically on the demands of each phase of development, clarifying the logical sequence and relationship between the interrelated components. However, the concept needs to be applied and intelligently adapted to the individual stakeholder circumstances.

Furthermore, and regardless of stakeholder perspective, management should place the lifecycle concept in context, meaning for example that it should consider its more strategic needs (such as the Games legacy) as well as other aspects of its portfolio. Sport organisations rarely operate as single-project entities, and in experiencing a multi-project environment they need to carefully consider the overlapping lifecycle demands of managing a portfolio of activities over time.

Such are the resource demands of some stages of sport event management that the lifecycle concept often includes many other projects and, in turn, their own lifecycles. From the perspective of Manchester City Council, subprojects requiring completion before the event implementation stage are likely to have included the bidding process, the Opening Ceremony, and obviously the building or adaptation of new venues.

Given the focus of this text, let us now apply the lifecycle concept to a 'new build facility' environment, but obviously not in the same depth as the event example. Drawing on the previous lifecycle terminology and the marketing lifecycle concept, Figure 2.4 illustrates an application to the facility environment—this time including financial details.

From Figure 2.4 it is apparent that the proposed stages can still be divided into three similar phases—pre-facility (conception and development), implementation (operation), and post-facility (termination) stages—from which seven substages can be identified. As many similarities exist with the event management lifecycle, these substages will not be elaborated on here but will be covered in more depth in subsequent chapters. An important difference to highlight between the two lifecycles relates to the component of time. While facility

Figure 2.4　Lifecycle stages of facility management

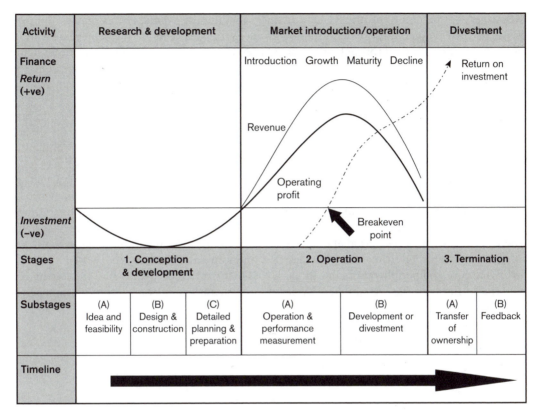

Source: Adapted from Kerzner (2001, p. 82).

projects are likely to consume significant capital budgets, their lifecycle duration and hence earning potential is usually over a much longer time frame than that of an event. Events by their very definition may be one-off activities, whereas sport facilities are often built for a minimum operational period of 10 years or, in some cases (e.g. Lord's Cricket Ground), more than 100 years of use. But in both facility and event applications it is important to realise that the early phase of development assumes considerable cash flow availability. As highlighted in Figure 2.4, the earliest return of investment and breakeven point is likely to occur in the implementation/operation stage of the lifecycle. Where short-term or political motives drive the project, and financial appraisals are superficially administered, 'white elephants' sometimes remain, which can become an embarrassing reminder to all of ineffective management. Examples of this might include the facilities of the Montreal Olympic Games in Canada (which are still being paid for more than 25 years after being built); or more recently the Millennium Dome in London, which despite being closed since the end of 2000 was still costing taxpayers almost £300 000 per week in 2003 as an unused empty building (Moss 2003).

A systems approach to facility and event management

Regardless of the nature of involvement in sport facilities or events, each organisation possesses its own unique purpose and attempts to measure its success by the achievement of its goals. These are achieved through an ongoing interaction with the organisation's general and specific macro-environment. As illustrated in Figure 2.5, effective sport management can therefore be explained by each organisation (the grey area) obtaining and utilising inputs from its environment, and implementing systems (referred to as conversion processes or throughputs) to produce and discharge outputs (services and short-term objectives) and outcomes (impacts and long-term aims) into the environment. This is known as systems theory, and is increasingly being used to understand the many complexities of sport facility and event management performance measurement.

Understanding this systems model places in context the interlinked core management processes that have been discussed here. More importantly, it establishes the framework of internal and external performance measurement that will be developed in Chapters 10 and 11. From Figure 2.5, it can be seen that each sport organisation operates in an open systems environment, with each external and internal subsystem dynamically influencing one another.

In effectively delivering the Manchester Commonwealth Games, the whole system—involving core and peripheral organisations across many different layers—had to be managed to achieve the high-risk yet publicly declared performance indicators. From a Manchester

Figure 2.5 Organisational systems and relationships

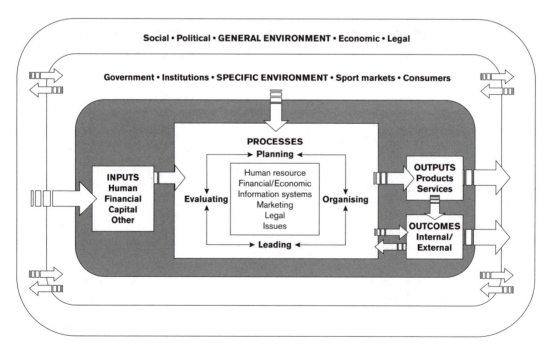

Source: Adapted from Soucie and Doherty (1994).

2002 Ltd perspective, successful management from the outset thus implied establishing a closely knit or loose coalition of multiorganisational partnerships to achieve collective goals. The complexity of this situation is nowhere more apparent than in the key milestone of the Games' Opening Ceremony. Here the local organising committee had one opportunity to demonstrate to the world that it had coordinated a diverse range of projects—the 63 000 mile, five-continent baton relay, the volunteer recruitment and training program, the building and establishment of the numerous operational systems of the City of Manchester Stadium—to achieve the minimal quality performance standards of the Commonwealth Games Federation.

Key drivers of event or facility management success

In such a complex, uncertain and accountable environment, the M2002 team needed to clearly identify their priorities, as well as those inputs and processes that they had most control over, if they were to fulfil their performance requirements. In particular, this meant identifying the key drivers of project success. From the project management literature this is summarised in Figure 2.6.

The outer ring in Figure 2.6 represents some of the key influences on the decision makers; the inner ring identifies the golden triangle or project drivers for successful management— namely, the essential and critical performance measures of quality, cost (human or financial)

Figure 2.6 Project management environment

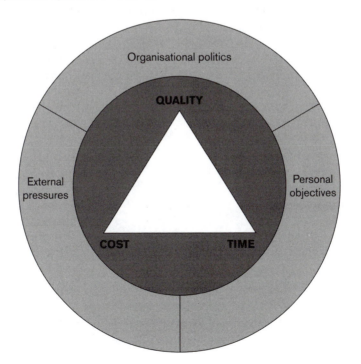

Source: Adapted from Briner, Geddes and Hasting (1996, p. 5).

and time. Interpreting this model from a sport event or venue management perspective, it is argued that each project or subproject needs to establish its goals and key performance requirements from the outset. Dependent on the unique demands of the project, the individual stakeholder perspective and the lifecycle development phase, one of the project drivers is likely to dominate management actions and become the primary limiting factor for success. Table 2.5, and the subsequent commentary, illustrates the diversity of sport scenarios and highlights the management implications and typical trade-offs encountered to maintain a balance of requirements across a project's lifecycle.

Scenario 1 in Table 2.5, for example, is driven by the notion of time, given that the Queen's Jubilee 'anniversary' was an immovable date. If the project was behind schedule, the only options available to management were to reduce the quality of the event or facility (e.g. shorter Opening Ceremony or cheaper facility signage) or incur greater costs (e.g. employ more people and equipment, or pay overtime) to meet the deadline. Scenario 2, on the other hand, was heavily influenced by financial resource constraints that directly affected the facility quality and timing. If the project costs escalated from the original estimates, the project manager could decide to reduce the quality of the synthetic pitch/surrounding area or postpone the project finish date until such time as the additional finance became available. Scenario 3 is particularly important for management to comprehend because external threshold performance standards must be achieved before the project can be implemented. For example, it is not

Table 2.5 Sport project diversity and management implications

Scenario	Brief project description	Project driver	Management implications
1	XVII Commonwealth Games	Time	• The date of the event cannot be changed, as it is the Queen's Golden Jubilee anniversary. • The only variables that can be altered are quality and cost.
2	Synthetic pitch of a local voluntary hockey club	Financial cost	• Maximum expenditure is likely to limit management options. • Time and quality decisions are dependent on availability of financial resources.
3	City Half-Marathon Road Race	Quality	• Without adherence to the appropriate legal safety standards and sport technical requirements, the event simply will not take place. • Cost and time can be altered to achieve the required quality criteria.
4	Private health and fitness club	Hybrid	• No key driver of the project from the outset. • Time, cost and quality can be played off against each other.

uncommon for pop concerts that include temporary structures to be issued a safety certificate just one hour before the doors open, due to additional work being completed to fully comply with the safety panel's conditions. The alternative option to this potentially higher cost could mean postponement or cancellation of the event, which equally would create additional management problems, bad publicity and further costs. Finally, Scenario 4 presents an example where management had more freedom in which to make decisions. Here the private health and fitness club project could be phased with building developments or membership packages, or conversely include a new opening date if the image and quality of the establishment was paramount to its success.

Clearly, the components of this triangle (project drivers) are seen to be interdependent, where a change in one is likely to influence another to restore the project equilibrium. The intention of management is therefore to establish an appropriate balance between the elements of quality, cost and time at any particular stage. This may vary throughout the project lifecycle as the key driver reaches its ultimate limit.

The very nature of many sport event management environments—namely, a finite activity with just one opportunity to get it right—often means that the component of time should always receive considerable attention. Technical facility specifications are usually controlled by international governing federation and building legislative standards and finance by the commonly used techniques of budgeting and cash flow forecasts. But how commonly are time management techniques and sanctions endorsed in the sport event environment? This is particularly important because, as Torkildsen (1999, p. 471) suggests: 'The event, unlike the normal ongoing program, is speeded up and delivered within a short space of time; this concentrates all the advanced planning and actions into specific hours and moments.'

Previous reference to the event lifecycle further reflects the nature of time, which has direct implications for the style of management adopted to achieve the designated performance output. For example, whereas activity in the early phase of the project may have demonstrated a democratic management style of involvement and empowerment, health and safety quality requirements one day before an event are likely to require an autocratic management style of operation.

The analysis of the Manchester Commonwealth Games shows that managing sport events and venues can be a particularly complex project to undertake, as unique environments of multiorganisation hierarchical partnerships and temporary involvement are often encountered. The management experience can be highly rewarding and, on occasion, very frustrating. To minimise the latter and maximise the former, there is a need to be astutely aware of the individual and holistic demands of each stage of the project, to fully understand the relationship between inputs, processes and outputs, and to recognise that organisational integration is paramount to successful event and facility management.

Summary

The central message of this chapter, which will be reinforced through subsequent chapters of this text, is that informed practice needs to be based on a clear understanding of the local operational context as well as on an insightful and appropriate breadth of awareness of management processes, systems, tactics and techniques. As conceptual awareness and clarity are fundamental to operational success, this chapter has provided the broad analytical frameworks for planning, organising, leading and evaluating a facility or sport event management performance. Through applying the lifecycle concept and systems theory of analysis to the multi-partnership complexities of contemporary sport, it is possible to simplify the real-world experience and be better able to manage the relationship between inputs and performance outputs or outcomes at any particular moment. Whereas lifecycle analysis highlights the important link between the present and the future, systems analysis provides the more immediate micro-management focus on the key drivers of operational success. In the case of effective and efficient sport facility or event management, the key to success, regardless of project scale and scope, could be said to be dependent on balancing the constraints of quality, cost and time within the unique and complex environmental demands of both internal and external political pressures.

Case study

Time–cost–quality and their relationship to planning, leading, organising and controlling at the Athens 2004 Olympic Games

The management functions of planning, leading, organising and controlling are central to the success of any event. Errors and oversights in each of these management functions will inevitably negatively affect at least one, and perhaps all, of the key drivers of event success—namely, time, cost and quality.

Irrespective of its position as the world's premium multi-sport event, history reveals that the Olympic Games is beset by myriad planning, leading, organising and controlling difficulties. Take for example the 2004 Games in Athens. The lead-up to these Games was characterised by all sorts of problems. For example, artefacts of great cultural and historical significance were uncovered during the excavation necessary for the building of some important event infrastructure (e.g. roads, facilities, train lines). Not only did the careful removal of these artefacts from harm's way result in time delays but their very presence resulted in the redirection of train lines and thus further delays as new routes were planned, designed and built. Several facilities, most notably the main Olympic stadium, fell behind schedule, and some important test events (e.g. Greek Athletics Championships) were held in less than satisfactory conditions as a consequence.

So considerable were the construction delays that the IOC and various international sport federations expressed their concern on several occasions. These worries, spread by the media, left the world wondering whether Athens would be ready on time and whether the Games would go ahead. Greece's reputation plummeted and Greek communities around the world cringed each time another negative story hit the news stands.

The public image of the Athens 2004 Organising Committee (ATHOC) was so poor that it was exploited by the Smiths snack food company in an Olympics-themed advertising campaign for its new 'Mediterranean-flavoured' crisps. Greek construction workers were seen enjoying the snack rather than working on the incomplete Olympic stadium. The advertisement showed the construction workers snacking in the foreground as athletes competed behind them on a dirt track, with one unfortunate runner tripping over a wheelbarrow!

In addition to the spiralling costs associated with infrastructure falling behind schedule came the costs arising out of the perceived need for extra security after the terrorist attacks on the United States on 11 September 2001 and the series of coordinated bomb attacks on Madrid trains on 11 March 2004. Already sporting a hefty security budget, ATHOC members scrambled to upgrade security measures to protect the Games. With the global community on the verge of terrorism paranoia, security expenditure doubled to $US2.4 billion, nearly four times that for the Sydney 2000 Olympics.

For the Athens Olympics, as with most sport events, it was never an option to change the time of the event. Thus the event's budget (already enormous in the initial planning stage) was compromised. So too was the event's quality, for while venues were complete to the point where the Olympic events could go ahead on time, the finishing touches of landscaping and painting were for some venues left undone. Other venues had more major construction problems. For example, there was no roof over the pool. Swimming's spectators, officials and athletes were forced to bake beneath a hot Athens sun as temperatures regularly reached 35°C and above.

Despite the cost and quality problems associated with the Athens Olympics, however, it is impossible to arrive at the conclusion that the Games were a failure. After all, events did run on time, world records were broken, new heroes were created, spectators rejoiced, and sponsors and broadcasters profited. Thus event success is often driven by factors other than time, cost and quality, and these factors will be discussed in greater detail in Chapters 10 and 11. However, Greece may well feel the negative fallout of the Games' time, cost and quality problems for years to come. Notwithstanding Athens' array of world-class sport facilities, given the last-minute scramble to start the event on time will the world have faith in Greece's ability to host other major events? And will the Greeks rejoice if the budget blowout from $US2.5 billion to almost $US7.3 billion means they will be paying off the Games for years to come?

Q. Describe how problems with each of the management functions of planning, leading, organising and controlling contributed to the time, cost and quality problems identified in this case.
Q. How could ATHOC have planned, led, organised and controlled differently so as to have eradicated, or at least minimised, the time, cost and quality problems?

3

Planning new sport facilities and events: feasibility analysis and market research

Chapter focus
Structure, size and trends in the sport facility and sport event sectors
Key success factors of operating sport facilities and running sport events
Developing new sport facilities: feasibility analysis
Developing new sport facilities: design and construction issues
Developing new sport facilities: preparing facility management infrastructure
Operating the new sport facility: attracting events
Operating the new sport facility: preparing event management infrastructure
Attracting customers: marketing the sport facility and the sport events
Running the sport event: event operations
Measuring facility and event performance: a scorecard approach to success
Measuring facility and event performance: impact on and for stakeholders

CHAPTER OBJECTIVES

In this chapter, we will:
- Demonstrate the importance of and need for feasibility studies.
- Explain the components of a feasibility study, including:
  - market research
  - environmental analysis
  - competitive analysis
  - consumer analysis
  - geographic analysis
  - legal and regulatory analysis
  - financial analysis.
- Outline how to undertake a feasibility study.
- Show the relationship between feasibility studies and the strategic planning process.

The need for feasibility studies

According to the preliminary feasibility study commissioned by the national committee responsible for preparing Hungary's bid for the 2012 Olympic Games, the country will have to invest somewhere around $US16 million on the bidding procedure. In addition, the report, which cost $US1.6 million to produce, highlights the developmental requirements in order to meet Olympic standards. For example, Budapest would need to construct about nine new covered stadiums, each with a capacity of 15 000 spectators. Locations would have to be found for 22 'special' sport events like mountain biking and sailing, each of which with their own specific needs, equipment and viewing configurations. An Olympic village capable of supporting 16 000 athletes and officials is also required, along with hotel accommodation for another 18 000 people. All of this will have to be built on a site of no less than 600 hectares. The report further speculates on the economic impact of the Games on the city. It is proposed that the Olympics could increase Hungary's GDP by up to 0.5 per cent. Final calculations are still needed to reach more definitive estimates of the economic costs and benefits of hosting the Games. The feasibility study results should help determine whether Hungary will pursue the Games at a development cost of billions in the hope that its investment will yield substantial returns.

Performed correctly, there is no more useful tool for the prospective facility or event manager than a feasibility study. Up to 5 per cent of the total budget allocated to a new project should be invested in its planning activities, the first of which is the feasibility study. This may account for as much as 20 per cent of the budget allocated to planning activities, as it yields the critical information concerning whether the project should proceed and, if so, in what form. While this might seem a large chunk of the budget required for a state-of-the-art stadium, it is much better to 'waste' a few million on a feasibility study than spend a few hundred million on a stadium that can never pay for itself or on an event that requires enormous capital investment. This approach is succinctly captured in the commentary of a recent report by the UK Culture, Media and Sport Parliamentary Committee (2001, p. 15):

> The staging of international sporting events must be seen as a means, not an end. Public support for the staging of events must be justified by proper analysis of the extent to which events are an effective means towards other ends, both sporting and non-sporting. The staging of events cannot be justified simply by vague assertions about national prestige.

There has always been one problem with great new ideas for both sport and recreation events and facilities: more often than not, what people want to buy is not the same as what is being sold. Any product, including events and facilities, is only as good as its ability to provide a recognisably useful addition to an individual's experience. It is easy to assign usefulness, but the harsh reality is that useful means that someone is prepared to pay for it. Naturally, in some cases this 'someone' is the public sector, such as local, state or federal government. However, these bodies also expect a bang for their buck. Each facility and event must return at least as much as it costs, either in financial terms or in its utility to the community. This is tempered by the realities of the Western world. Few facilities or events are so important to communities that they warrant full funding without any user-pays component.

The demand for new facilities is driven primarily by growth in the number, type, size and attendance at sports and entertainment events. The need for a redeveloped sport facility is often a function of a region's physical suitability and the nature of its usage. This means that those undertaking a feasibility study need to be aware of the complexities to be juggled in coming to a determination about the properties of a proposed facility or event, its location and what its potential users might want. Often, there is not as much overlap as might be hoped. In other words, feasibility studies often find that the needs of the users, the broad expectations of public authorities and the profit hopes of private partners are not the same. The pivotal dimension in any decision making remains consistent, however. Planning is predicated on sound information, which must be acquired through careful market analysis and the collection of consumer data. A clear link may be observed between the aspects of strategy, planning, market analysis and research, and feasibility. A feasibility study is a critical beginning to the planning process, because of the following factors (Government of Western Australia 1995):

- It determines whether a community or owner can afford to build and operate over a period of time.
- It radically decreases the risk of failure.
- It specifies the best fit of features of the facility or event to its prospective users.
- It is the first stage of balancing competing demands on facilities in an objective way.
- It identifies the revenue and expenditure opportunities and burdens that need to be factored into the capital and operational phases of the project.
- It begins to highlight the most appropriate management structures and marketing strategies required for the facility or event.

The feasibility study is the first serious stage of activity in the development of a sport facility or event project. It provides a comprehensive analysis of the costs and benefits of the proposed project, including a full consideration of its economic, social, cultural and political implications. The results of the feasibility study should determine the fate of the project. However, a positive result in a feasibility study is not a guarantee of success; it is merely a statement of risk: the more positive the results of a feasibility study are, the less the risk in proceeding with the facility or event. In the event that the project is deemed an acceptable risk, the feasibility study should provide much of the background information and analysis that is essential to the full planning of the project. Feasibility studies are decision-making tools, but they still require some interpretation. In addition, they can rarely be completed in less than several months. It is worth taking the time to complete them properly, however, because although they contribute only 5 per cent of a project's total costs, the results of the feasibility study and planning process can determine as much as 65 per cent of those costs, as illustrated in Figure 3.1.

A feasibility study is the first time in a project's development that all the pieces are put together to see whether they can perform in unison technically and with anticipated economic outcomes. Another way of looking at it is that feasibility is concerned with the fit of alternative solutions to a clear set of problems. Almost every facility or event disaster has been preceded by a feasibility study that assured its success. How can this be the case? The answer is simple: many studies are not undertaken correctly or are unduly influenced by the political agendas of stakeholders. This chapter provides the information needed in order to understand the feasibility process and to make informed judgements about the veracity of studies. We first outline the necessary strategic scoping that begins the study process. We then explain

Figure 3.1 Savings potential of planning

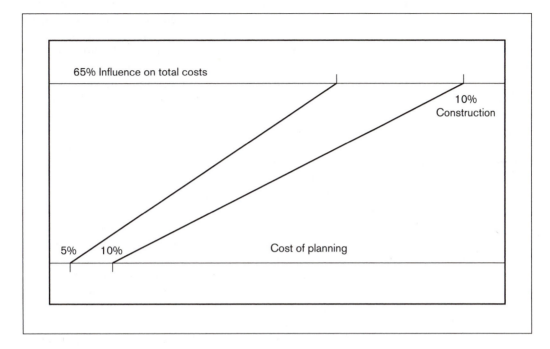

how to go about stakeholder analysis and market research and analysis. The chapter culminates in sections concerning the geographic, legal and financial aspects of feasibility.

Strategic scoping of the event or facility project

The essential first task of the forthcoming facility or event project is in the determination of its scope. This requires a statement of exactly what the project entails, its objectives and how it is to be achieved. Fundamental agreement on the philosophical foundations of the project is therefore paramount. For example, is it driven by a community need or is it simply an opportunity to be seized by a private provider seeking a profitable return? Subsequently, the industry or marketplace in which the project will compete needs to be considered, along with the products and services to be offered and the potential users of the project. Ultimately, these uncertainties must be resolved in a project 'charter' that reflects the mission and objectives of the stakeholders involved.

The size of the required task comes to light during this scoping process. More often than not the project is larger than anticipated. For example, consider the magnitude of constructing a new 18-hole golf course. Going from dirt to sculptured land is a massive task. It is not unusual for up to 500 000 cubic metres of dirt to be moved, including the excavation of a lake or several bunkers and the planting of hundreds of trees.

The measurement of feasibility can be considered from a number of angles, ranging from the purely financial to the largely intangible social benefits for the users. Thus, the return on capital investment and the profits that a facility or event can generate are only part of the picture. This is not to say that feasibility is not subject to an ultimate financial imperative. Simply stated, the money has to come from somewhere, and there are few facilities or events that require no ongoing financial support once the structure has been built or the initial event has been conducted. In practical terms, there are more facilities and events that, when measured exclusively on financial returns, are economic burdens than there are those that deliver a net return. We must therefore be as clear as possible on the purpose of the project before an analysis of its feasibility can be undertaken. If, for example, we are concerned with an event that is to be run for the cultural benefit of a region, it may be inappropriate to constrain its feasibility to purely financial indicators. A sound analysis will always reveal the financial situation unambiguously, but it should also highlight any non-financial benefits that might be worthy of the costs involved. The difficulty comes when users want a facility or event but are either unprepared to pay for it in entry fees or they consider the fees too high. Other benefactors, usually bolstered by public funding, are then necessary to make the project a reality. These benefactors are rarely altruistic. They, like any stakeholder group, covet agendas that might be as wideranging as the acquisition of political favour or the promotion of specific cultural values. Not all motivations can be justified economically, or even rationally. For example, the primary motive for constructing some football stadia in the United States (using public monies of the city) is to attract a professional franchise to the city. Professional football franchise relocations are not unusual, as a consequence of the desire of clubs to capitalise on favourable lease arrangements. Cities substantiate their decisions on the basis of a combination of the enhanced economic impact that accompanies a professional football team—a measurable value, and the social benefits that collective support of a football team brings—an immeasurable value.

In order for scoping to be completed, all stakeholders need to be consulted. While this is understandably a lengthy process, it is far less onerous than the management of important groups that perceive themselves as marginalised after the project is under way. It is a sensible investment to ensure that all stakeholders are identified and their perspectives solicited. As with all large projects, those conducting the feasibility study have the added complication of determining not only who the stakeholders are and what they overtly seek but also what might be part of their 'hidden agenda'. Some of the objectives of stakeholders will almost certainly be contradictory. These issues must be worked through before the project proceeds. If these differences cannot be resolved, it goes without saying that the project is not feasible. It is probably worth noting that most feasibility studies report reasonably high economic risks, but do not discourage decision makers from proceeding with the project on the basis of other benefits implicit in the project's completion. In other words, many stakeholder groups are married to the idea of proceeding before any objective data arrive, and these expectations are usually communicated to the feasibility team.

Scope management is primarily concerned with the definition and control of what is or is not included in the project. It encompasses the processes needed to ensure that the project includes all the work required to complete the project successfully. The processes of scope management interact within the context of the scope of the product and the project. *Product scope* refers to the features and functions that are to be included in a product or service. Completion is measured against these requirements. *Project scope* refers to the work that must be done in order to deliver a product with the specified features and functions. Completion is measured against the plan. The processes, tools and techniques used to manage project scope are a key focus for success.

There are two distinct phases associated with scoping in any situation. The first—*defining the project*—occurs through developing a charter, and is critical to project success. If the parameters of the project, including its goals and desired outcomes, rationale for its initiation and the constraints to be imposed, are incorrectly defined or unclear, then the project is heading for the dangerous realms of ambiguity. Without a charter, projects cannot establish a clear direction for their activities and are almost certainly heading for disaster.

The second phase—*planning the project*—has two component parts. Component 1—scoping the project—takes the outcomes set out in the charter and uses them to determine the project activities and deliverables. It looks broadly at the viability of the project. The scoping approach is essentially a process in which a series of interactions occur with various stakeholders, through discussions, review of documents, and meetings, to clarify, define, obtain information or persuade others. Often, the drafting and redrafting of documents towards an agreed position results from this process. Component 2—defining the project plan—involves detailed plans for what to produce (interim and final deliverables), what resources (human and other) are required, and how to go about producing the deliverables within the constraints established. The process of definition should account for the strategic goals of the organisation, including all the possible management concerns (financial return, market share, public perception etc.). Historical information gleaned from previous projects can assist at this stage, as well as the implementation of sophisticated modelling techniques (i.e. decision models, decision trees, software packages) or expert judgement or consultation in order to manage the process. Following an extensive process of clarification and definition, a charter is produced that clearly defines the project's parameters.

The project charter

This is the authorisation for the project manager to proceed with the project, and gives the authority to use organisational resources for the project. It is sometimes referred to as the *project brief*, the *mission* or the *terms of reference*.

The charter describes the objectives, deliverables (products or outputs) and customers of the project, as well as the customers' expectations for the final deliverables. The charter should cover the business need or product description that is being addressed.

Content included in the charter should reflect the following key areas:

- *Title page*—provides the project name and identifies the project owner and owner's representatives. The date signifies the beginning of the project.
- *Introduction, overview or background*—gives a brief description of the project. This should include the business need, problem or opportunity, and the events leading to the formulation of the project.
- *Goals*—provide the larger picture of what the project is aiming to achieve.
- *Deliverables*—are the outputs of the project: a good, service, process or plan, designed to satisfy customer needs and requirements.
- *Key stakeholders and resources*—represent the people or organisations that have either influence or interest in the project.

- *Constraints and assumptions*—reflect factors that may limit the scope or viability of the project and are related projects, corporate policy, risks etc. that will affect the outcome.
- *Planned approach*—states how the project will be conducted, indicating main areas of activity, resources required, and steps in development.
- *Authorisation*—involves senior management signing off or giving written approval before proceeding with the project.

Planning the project

The first phase involves developing a written scope statement to act as the basis for future project decisions. This reflects in broad terms what is to be done, when and how. It focuses on the key considerations of time, cost and quality. A written scope statement will identify the project deliverables at each stage of the project, also the project objectives outlining the criteria that must be met for the project to be considered successful. Objectives must include at least cost, quality and schedule measures.

The implementation of an *action plan* is the next phase in the scoping process. The action plan looks at the various activities and tasks that may be required to complete the project successfully. It identifies who will carry out the activities and when the activities will be completed.

Within the framework of the tasks to be completed in order to achieve the objectives of the project, a *work breakdown structure* (WBS) is generated. This is a graphic representation which defines activities down to tasks and subtasks, which are then more easily organised, costed and managed, and against which time and material resources are allocated. From this point, the detailed requirements specification is more readily achieved. A WBS becomes the launching pad for the next phase of activity, namely research, and is constructed primarily with the following information:

- objectives of the project from the charter;
- identification of major activities leading to each objective—the phases of the project;
- identification of tasks leading to each phase; and
- development of detailed specifications for each work package, comprising such components as objective, deliverables, responsibilities, schedule, cost estimates, resource requirements.

Market research

Market and competitor analysis

We have established that scoping the project is necessary before the feasibility team can begin gathering data. A sound starting point for this data acquisition phase is with the simple economic principles of supply and demand. In the first instance, we must consider the available marketplaces that might be entered, including the other facility or event players that these contain as well as the consumers that constitute those markets.

The prospect of entering the planning process for a new sport facility can be quite intimidating. When committing to a capital-intensive and subsequently risky process like constructing a new facility or organising a new event's infrastructure, it is critical to have a thorough understanding of the dynamics of the different markets that the proposed facility will cater for. In the context of planning new sport facilities, we will overview here the market analysis process by distinguishing between four components: industry analysis, external environmental analysis, consumer market analysis, and competitive analysis.

Industry analysis

When the idea to build a new sport facility or develop a new event is born, the first things that should come to the minds of the policy makers and planners are the issues of competition and demand. These two must be confronted early in the feasibility study because the viability of the project is directly dependent on the levels of competition and consumer demand.

An industry, as a collection of producers of similar goods or services, can be very attractive if few organisations are competing in it. In an industry that is very competitive it is hard to earn profits. For the facility operator or event manager, it is important to gather data about the industries in which they seek to establish a presence before further resources are committed. Events in terms of their properties and offerings, and facilities in terms of their physical features, need to be designed and constructed to accommodate the opportunities identified. It makes little sense to choose to operate in unattractive industries.

Defining the industry

In Europe, for example, the majority of stadia need to accommodate the needs of the principal spectator sport, soccer. Therefore, the collection of elite soccer-producing organisations (as a spectator sport) can be defined as the soccer industry. From the perspective of the financiers of facilities, in this case local or regional governments, an analysis of this industry is important before any further planning pertaining to a new facility takes place. Examples of other industries that might require investigation include popular elite sporting leagues, the international events and concerts industry, and the major sporting events industry. Also important are the intended beneficiaries of a facility or event. The World Cross Country Championships held in Belfast in 1999 illustrate the sporting benefits an event can bring to a community. The Championships enabled 4000 young people from 100 primary schools to participate. A superficial analysis of other international events may be a starting point in this case, but for community sport the emphasis is on whether the facility or event will meet a need.

Market analysis scope

The scope of the market analysis depends on the anticipated reach of the facility or event—that is, from how far away the potential customers are likely to travel. Market analysis when planning a new stadium for the local soccer club playing in the second division and competing in the regional soccer industry needs a completely different perspective from that when planning a new facility for Manchester United soccer club, which competes in the global soccer industry. A widely used tool for analysing the competitiveness of an industry is Porter's competitive forces model.

Applying Porter's competitive forces model

Porter's competitive forces model is presented in Figure 3.2, which describes the *five forces* that facility and event planners should review when examining competition and the attractiveness of an industry. This model can be applied at different levels of analysis. For example, it can be used to assess the competitive forces between different sports operating in the sport industry as whole. One can also analyse the competition between different sporting leagues.

The five forces include the threat of new entrants, bargaining power of suppliers, determinants of buyer power, the threat of substitute products, and the intensity of competition between existing firms within an industry. Quite often, attractiveness of an industry is measured by profit potential, which is not always the principal goal of sporting organisations. For example, the number and location of teams in geographic (metropolitan) markets requires a feasibility researcher to assess the attractiveness of a market. Shilbury et al. (2003, p. 22) remind us that:

> other questions indicative of industry attractiveness might include: Is the economic base of a city or region large enough to sustain one, or more than one team? How many other professional sports already exist in this market and what other recreation and leisure pursuits are potentially competing for disposable income?

The first force concerns the **intensity of competition** within an industry. In the case of a soccer league, the number of teams and their location is the first example of intensity of competition. Melbourne, Australia, hosted two professional soccer clubs. The Melbourne metropolitan

Figure 3.2 Porter's competitive forces model

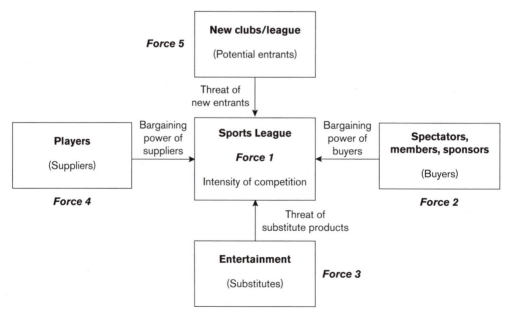

Source: Adjusted from Porter (1985).

market consists of approximately 3.7 million inhabitants, so there should theoretically be sufficient consumers for two soccer clubs. But beyond the soccer market the industry competition intensifies as a result of the presence of other sporting codes (e.g. Australian Rules football, with nine teams in the metropolitan market) seeking sponsor dollars, spectators and members. Shilbury et al. (2003, p. 23) observe that, within sports leagues:

> exit barriers have remained very high. This highlights the peculiar economics associated with sports leagues. Tradition, emotion and club loyalties often over-ride economic deficiencies experienced by some clubs, explaining why it has not been so easy to achieve a better geographical balance of teams competing in these national leagues.

From an event's viewpoint, decreasing competitive intensity may not be a matter so much of changing locations but of changing scheduling. In some cities, however, the sporting events calendar is so cluttered that new events inevitably face considerable competition.

Intensity of competition deals with the supply side of the economic equation. In the simplest of terms, the fewer competitors fighting for the same consumer dollar, the better the chance of a feasible enterprise. Another way of defining the competitive intensity revolves around what is known as the area of dominant influence (ADI). A term commonly used by the broadcast media, ADI refers to the number of people who can be reached through major broadcast channels. This is relevant to events in particular, where broadcasts need not be confined to the geographical zone in which they are physically being staged. As a result, competition intensity needs to be viewed in light of the nature of the product offering.

The **bargaining power of buyers** constitutes the second force. The buyers are those parties who express interest in consuming the goods and services offered by facilities or events. These are the consumers of sport, personal and corporate. In sporting terms, there is often a practical limitation given the finite number of teams located in each area. Attendance, membership, and sponsorship (and TV) revenues provide most sporting clubs with their main sources of income. If buyers are powerful enough to force prices down, demand higher quality and play competitors off against each other, they represent a competitive force to be considered by facilities and events. In other words, the bargaining power of buyers grows with the number of options they have to switch to other facilities or other events. Of course, this is a complex issue, particularly when factoring in the power of the buyers of television rights and the fact that fans will tend to be loyal to clubs (or specific events), not facilities. The greatest source of bargaining power is found with sponsors looking for the best sponsorship opportunities from facilities or events. Sponsor bargaining power increases as the number of clubs based in a market increases. Sponsors also are not solely dependent on sporting clubs: they can choose to invest their sponsorship dollar in non-sport properties, which in turn strengthens their bargaining power in the sport industry. Bargaining power is considered strong when buyers or consumers have a strong influence on the nature and thus price of goods and services offered.

Another major force affecting the sporting industry is the **substitutability of products**. In other words, are there other recreation and leisure activities that offer 'substitute' benefits for those provided by participation or spectatorship in sport (in this case, spectatorship in soccer)? According to Shilbury et al. (2003, p. 23):

> it is this force which provides the greatest range of competitive forces for a sports league. Under the broad heading of 'entertainment' a variety of products have the

potential to attract the consumer's money normally available for leisure pursuits. These might include other sports, the movies, videos, and the theatre. A major determinant of the strength of these potential substitutes is the switching costs associated with each product.

Switching costs refer to the financial and psychological cost of switching from one brand to another, and if these costs are low consumers will become susceptible to substituting a product from one organisation for the (similar) product of another. For many sporting clubs and events brand loyalties are high, whereas they are low for facilities. Many sport consumers have supported a team for all of their lives. The psychological association with a sport or club is often far more important than economic considerations. This means that particular sporting events, like a Formula One Grand Prix, grand slam in tennis or major golf tournament, can be the recipients of significant brand loyalty. If the venue for any of these events were to be moved, then so too would the consumer loyalty. Facilities therefore need to be cautious in making any assumptions about their place compared with established sports or events. Substitutability is considered high when many different facilities can be used for the same event, or when many events can fulfil the needs of buyers.

The **bargaining power of suppliers** in an industry increases with the ability of these suppliers either to form a united front or to become singularly important to the industry players. In sporting leagues, the major suppliers are the players. Recent examples of attempts to change the power of suppliers relative to sporting leagues come from the USA, where NBA (basketball) players and MLB (baseball) players went on strike to negotiate better employment conditions (salaries). Player associations, unions and player agents boost the bargaining power of players in that they allow players to combine their individual bargaining power to a united effort, threatening the league with 'non-production' action in the process. According to Shilbury et al. (2003, p. 24):

> bargaining power of the players has the potential to erode industry profits via their salary demands, rather than what it costs to procure players from specific suppliers. In their quest for the ultimate prize, a premiership or championship, clubs often accede to the demands of high priced athletes explaining why the sports economy is often regulated via the use of salary caps.

Facilities can often take the role of suppliers in the sport industry. They must fight for the opportunity to host events by providing the most attractive leasing or hosting arrangements. The bargaining power of suppliers is considered strong when few other options are available to event owners.

The **threat of new entrants** refers to the likelihood that new facilities or events will spring up to compete for the same consumers. This, of course, is a normal occurrence in business, but it is less frequent in sport. For example, leagues have the potential to decrease market share of existing clubs or, worse, to make existing clubs fold or merge. It can also lead to falling league profits if a new entity attempts to set up a whole new (rival) league. In Australia during the mid-1990s, Rupert Murdoch's News Ltd established the breakaway 'Superleague' (Rugby League) competition, enticing existing clubs and players in the Australian Rugby League's competition to defect to Superleague. Murdoch ignored contractual obligations of players and clubs, which eventually led to a court case that was lost by News

Ltd, at least on paper. Murdoch, however, almost overcame the barriers to entry, the structure and product offerings of the established Australian Rugby League (ARL) competition. In the end, access to players and clubs proved a difficult barrier to overcome, but Superleague and the established ARL competition now jointly operate the National Rugby League competition. The same issues affect all established events and facilities. During the feasibility process, the study should ascertain whether further new entrants are likely to join the competition, in addition to the new event or facility being proposed. If we were focusing on a new recreational facility proposed for a local community, we would be interested in the likelihood that another facility would consider the market attractive enough to enter. There is a high threat of new entrants in markets that are underserviced or where certain niche services or goods are absent.

An industry analysis delivers the feasibility researcher a wealth of information about the specific products and markets in which the proposed facility or event seeks to operate. Depending on the five competitive forces, feasibility researchers can obtain a clearer picture about the viability of a new project and the potential contribution of operating in a particular marketplace delivering particular goods or services. The outcome of this analysis should be an assessment of the attractiveness of the prospective project as measured by competitive forces. It should also begin to make clear where the strategic opportunities lie for a new facility or event in terms of the functionality desired in a new facility or the experiences sought during an event.

External environmental analysis

The analysis of the external environment, also called the macro-environment, of an organisation deals with those trends or 'need' changes that not only have an impact on one body (in this case the new facility or event) but also influence operations of most organisations in the vicinity. The analysis is aimed at identifying important changes in the macro-environment that might influence the operation of organisations or provide new opportunities for business.

External environmental analysis scope

As previously, the scope of the environmental analysis depends on the definition of the industry. In the same way as the planning of a new stadium for the local soccer club playing in the second division determines the scope of the industry analysis, so it does for the external environmental analysis. Competing in the regional soccer industry is more likely to lead to the identification of domestic trends and consumer needs than when competing in the global soccer industry, which clearly requires a global scope of external analysis. The different environments to consider for this analysis are briefly described in the next section.

DESTEP analysis

DESTEP is the acronym for demographic, economic, sociocultural, technological, ecological, political, the six environments that need to be considered during macro-environmental analysis. Some examples might be useful in understanding the importance of this form of analysis. For the feasibility researcher it is important to know what is likely to happen to the demographic constitution of the population in the geographic target market of the facility or event. If the average age of the world or region's population is steadily rising, this is likely to affect consumers' profile in years to come. If an important part of the facility's target market (or financiers) consists of groupings of people in a certain geographic region of the world, but the economic prospects for that part of the world look grim, this is likely to influence the bottom line sooner or later. Similar examples are easily found for the other variables, like changes in community attitudes towards violent sports (sociocultural), the incorporation of the Internet in all aspects of life (technological), the growing global conscience about maintaining a healthy natural environment (ecological), the free flow of labour, money, goods and services in a regional area (economic), and the government policy of supporting elite rather than grassroots sport (political).

These examples emphasise the importance of taking both an external and an internal view of the new project. It cannot be assumed that the facility or event will thrive in isolation, ignoring the bigger picture of what is happening in the world surrounding it. Feasible projects have teams that anticipate the future and incorporate it in their design in order to exploit opportunities and counter threats when these arrive.

Consumer market analysis

Following the examination of the competitive forces and the macro-environment in which the proposed facility or event will be placed, a closer look at the people who make up the potential markets of the new facility may begin. The consumer market analysis deals with those people (including sponsors and corporate guests) who are most likely to attend events at the new facility and the motivations governing their behaviour. Facilities and events can position themselves in several markets in order to maximise their revenue opportunities. For example, the feasibility study conducted for the University of South Alabama (USA) to determine the viability of its desire to field a Division One football team identified three potential markets. First, the higher education market offers the opportunity to entice students to attend matches and reinforces the appeal of the campus environment. Second, the commercial market provides opportunities for general public attendance, sponsorship, media exposure for the university and a positive community profile. Finally, the competitive athletics market presents opportunities to encourage other university supporters to attend home matches or athletic conferences hosted by South Alabama.

An industry can be understood as a collection of producers or sellers of products, where markets can be seen as the collections of people who buy these products. The people in the soccer market buy the soccer product from producers in the soccer industry. The local soccer club will attract only regional customers, whereas Real Madrid or Arsenal are likely to attract customers from all over the world. In the same way as the industry definition determines the scope of the industry analysis, so does the market definition determine the scope of the market analysis. Along similar lines, the people in the market for major sporting events are not the same people as those in the market for soccer. So in this case, from both a product and geographic perspective, the feasibility researchers have to become involved in a number of different market analyses. Market analyses can range from simply describing the size and attractiveness of a market to in-depth data collection through interviews and focus group research, followed by mass consumer surveys, aimed at obtaining very detailed information about the consumer behaviour of people in those markets.

Market analysis is a vital activity when planning a new facility or event, particularly because construction of a facility is such a capital-intensive and irreversible activity. The size of potential markets, how much people in those markets are prepared to pay for a range of products, where they reside, how they can be reached, how they can be motivated to buy, their interests and ambitions in life, and how much money they are likely to have in 10 years' time, is all information that planners need in order to optimise the physical design and construction of the facility. Market analysis will also deliver data that inform management how to accommodate activities to be hosted by the facility for which there is a genuine and financially healthy demand in the marketplace.

Demand is affected by the amount and quality of other events or facilities offering the same product(s) in the area. Research concerning the competition is therefore paramount. This competition may even go beyond the same goods or services. Alternative leisure, recreational or sporting activities also need to be considered.

Demand is further determined by the existing population in the geographic catchment in which the facility or event is placed. Associated with this is the fact that demand is driven by growth. The building of new facilities needs to be justified either by an increase in the size of the catchment zone the facility is said to represent or by an increase in population density within the zone. For example, the feasibility study conducted by the City of Orillia in Ontario, Canada, designed to establish the need for a new multiuse recreation facility, examined predicted trends in population growth until 2031. The implication was that the new multiuse centre had still to meet the needs of the population for a lifecycle of around 30 years if it was to be feasible. One way of calculating needs is on the basis of supply ratios. Orillia, for instance, calculated that one tennis court for every 4000 residents was a ratio that had seemed appropriate in the past and should therefore be maintained.

In some circumstances, where the facility houses potentially high-profile international events, it is important to consider overseas as well as domestic demand. Clearly, for local events, research in nearby regions should be undertaken. (We consider the geographic analysis in greater detail later in this chapter.)

An estimate of the amount of usage or attendance the proposed facility or event is likely to attract is essential in consumer analysis. There are several ways to undertake this. The most straightforward is simply through direct consultation with the potential user groups. Surveys can be used to ask what specific facilities, programs and services these would use, how often they would be employed, when they would be used and how much the user groups would be prepared to pay for use. This is the **consultation** method. A second is the **comparison** method. This involves using an existing facility or event that is comparable to the proposed one as a benchmark for estimates of demand and interest. This approach works best when similar products are being compared for a marketplace with similar demographic characteristics. It is useful to benchmark against the existing competition, but it is dangerous to expect similar outcomes, given that the existing facilities and events are established and that the proposed one will more probably take some of their market share as well as attract new customers. A third method is known as the **participation** approach. This requires the examination of participation rates categorised according to demographic features. This information can be applied to the recreational or sporting products that are being offered. A final option is known as **trend analysis.** This method reveals consumption patterns across a range of facilities and events in an attempt to establish a trend that should continue into the future. Naturally, the best approach to forecasting demand involves the use of several or all of these methods in the hope of establishing the most reliable picture possible. Any method may need to be undertaken for each of the target groups anticipated to be users of the facility or event.

Competitive analysis

A market analysis in isolation makes little or no sense. When a market turns out to be very attractive, there will probably also be a lot of competition for a share of that market. In other words, we need to perform a competitive analysis to get a clear picture of how attractive a marketplace really is. The first step towards a competitive analysis we presented earlier, through the application of Porter's five forces model. The competitive forces analysis requires a basic insight into how many competitors operate in an industry, and how easy or difficult it is to enter or exit the industry. Building on this knowledge we can take the next step.

Organisations mostly choose to operate in a certain marketplace. Based on their own market analysis they decide whether they have the capabilities, ambitions and resources to justify entering a market and working towards obtaining a share of that market. To that end, what feasibility researchers define as the market they wish to operate in determines who the main competitors are for the future facility or event. If they want to operate in the regional soccer market, their main competitors are smaller regional facilities that can accommodate the needs of a local soccer team; it makes little sense to look any further than, say, the domestic competitive environment. For the feasibility researchers of Telstra Stadium (formerly known as Stadium Australia) at the site of the Sydney 2000 Olympics, however, it was important that they consider operators of major stadia in Sydney, Melbourne, Brisbane, Adelaide, Perth, and even in New Zealand and parts of Asia. Because of the sheer size of Telstra Stadium, facility planners could not afford to operate exclusively in the domestic marketplace. In an attempt to make their stadium viable they have been forced to attract international events and compete with venues that operate similar-sized stadia in the South Pacific region. Examples of competitive analysis techniques, apart from Porter's five forces technique, are: conducting a SWOT analysis for each competitor (in particular determining their weaknesses and the threats they are facing), benchmarking other companies pertaining to issues that can deliver competitive advantage, market share analysis, maintaining a competitive intelligence system (collecting and compiling files with competitors' information), and the construction of a GE matrix or a perceptual map to determine an organisation's position relative to competitors.

In order to feel reasonably secure that a facility can be operated viably but, more importantly, to move into a position of marketing dominance through detailed knowledge of competitors' marketing tactics and strategies, facility planners have to perform competitive analysis. Based on the findings from a five forces analysis, competitors need to be identified, their strategies and objectives need to be assessed and their strengths and weaknesses exposed, in order to determine their most likely reaction to the movements of other operators in the industry.

Outsourcing versus in-house market analysis

In some cases project managers will do parts of the market analysis themselves, leaving the more complex or less sensitive parts of the analysis to specialised feasibility research companies. For example, a competitive analysis is likely to be outsourced, for the simple reason that relatively independent researchers are more likely than the organisation itself to be able to collect useful data on competitors. On the other hand, the macro-environmental analysis can often be done without having to access people in industries or markets. Because they concern macro-trends, the information for these analyses is often readily available in nationally or internationally commissioned research projects, and is either for sale or available through government agencies, universities or libraries.

Timing and cost issues

The timing and cost of research affect the schedule and costs of the total planning and construction project. The longer it takes to obtain industry or market information, the longer it is before construction can commence. This in turn can affect the cost of the project, especially when it involves international finance (through fluctuations in the money market). The more research is outsourced, the faster results can be delivered, as the different analyses can run in parallel. However, outsourcing research is expensive. In the end, facility planners need to prioritise their research needs based on the relative importance of the scope of the research. Which industries are more important? Which markets are more important? Is the domestic perspective more vital than the international perspective? Do we need broad-based or very specific information? Answers to these questions determine who gets the job, how much the job will be worth, and how much time can justifiably be spent on it. This information can also be used to help narrow the geographic possibilities.

Geographic analysis

Earlier, we noted the feasibility issues from both an industry and market perspective. It was shown that the scope of (parts of) the market analysis always relates to the geographic distance of potential customers to the facility: the broader the scope, the bigger the geographic area to be incorporated in the market analysis. Geography, in other words, is important when considering the new facility's or event's potential customers. In this section, customer and operational issues of geography like location, transport philosophy and capacity, cost of ground, construction and labour, climate, the natural environment, and development of tourism will be introduced as part of the feasibility equation.

Location

To some extent the real estate cliché that there are only three principles determining the market value of properties—location, location and location—holds true for the positioning of a sport facility or event. The fact that (in the majority of cases) a building cannot simply be picked up and taken to another geographic area makes the decision of where to build it in the first place an influential one. The 'location' decision drives further decision making and perceptions (from occupants and potential customers) about the new facility, such as how to get there (easy), visual attractiveness of surroundings, availability of essential services (e.g. shops, recreation, suppliers), cost of construction and maintenance, and subsequently the production costs of services delivered through the facility. Often, if the initial location proposed is too small, it is not worth building a reduced version of the facility. For example, the average size of a street skateboard park is around 3000 square metres. A smaller facility will have limited diversity and flexibility, which in turn will diminish its usefulness. Smaller sites are also more likely to compromise flow patterns and cause safety problems. Larger sites are better because they can encourage not just skateboarders but also BMX riders and bladers.

From a community and local and regional government perspective, some other issues of location need to be considered. For example, how does the proposed facility fit into the government's overall site development plans? What is government's role in directing new facility developments to areas of unused, reclaimed or derelict locations, in its role as city, not facility, developer?

Transport philosophy

Considering available locations for the new facility immediately poses the question of how people will get there. City locations offer the benefit of existing and extensive transport infrastructure, but the downside is the heavy traffic and congestion common to 'downtown' city areas, like those which frustrate sport fans on their way to the relatively new Staples Center in Los Angeles.

Train, tram or metro access to downtown areas is often of excellent quality. Access by car, on the other hand, requires extensive parking areas, land that in city areas is very expensive or has already been used for office or residential developments. Suburban or country locations for new facilities or events offer the benefits of easy access by car and plenty of parking spaces, but access by public transport is impractical. It may even be difficult to get approval from local government, as the anticipated social and economic benefits of the proposed facility or event may not in their eyes outweigh the social costs of air, noise and visual pollution. On the other hand, it might be government that is championing the new event or facility, in which case some local residents may complain, and finding suitable contractors might be difficult.

Transport capacity: population and catchment areas

Although the consideration of how many people live in the surrounding areas of the anticipated location comes close to what has already been looked at in the market analysis, a closer look from a geographic perspective is justified. For example, while in the market analysis we would focus on the buying behaviour of people concerning the products on offer through the facility, in the geographic analysis the emphasis needs to be on issues of travel, such as travel time, access to transport systems, willingness to travel, and transport capacity considerations related to the size of the catchment areas the facility is likely to serve. Can and will people travel the distance at a different level of comfort? Feasibility researchers must determine whether existing transport infrastructure is sufficient, and whether there are opportunities to work with the government or private transport operators to upgrade the number of available services.

Cost of land and construction

The cost of land is a function of the attractiveness of the location. As a rule of thumb, one can assume that the closer a facility or event is to the largest cluster of potential users—the central business district of a city—the higher the cost of the land to be built on and the more expensive the leasing of existing facilities for events. The same rule can be applied to the number of suppliers of services and goods in close vicinity to the facility: the more there are of them, the more expensive the land. In areas where there is fierce competition for space, the demand for construction labour will probably also be higher. From a government perspective, the question needs to be raised whether indeed the ground can be used for sport facility developments. Are such developments to the benefit of the majority of the community, or should the expensive ground and labour be used for other community purposes (e.g. building an extension to the city hospital, including extra parking spaces)?

Climate

Climate as a geographic issue can be defined as a macro-variable, in that for local or regional feasibility researchers climate will not vary enough to be a consideration. However, the choice whether to build a new stadium in either Florida or New York to accommodate a new football franchise is dependent on climate. With the ever-increasing service and comfort expectations of modern-day sport spectators, the constant humidity of the South would require the incorporation of cooling systems—and a roof covering all the seats, given the frequent tropical thunderstorms. In New York the likelihood of freezing winters might suggest the inclusion of a retractable roof and heating systems. In general, average rainfall in particular geographic regions will necessitate incorporating simple or advanced drainage systems, especially when the grass is not artificial and gets heavy use throughout the year.

Natural environment

The natural environment has been an issue of great debate in relation to the planning and development of sport facilities throughout the world. Stadia in particular, because they are such large constructions, are sometimes considered visually unattractive or even pollutant to the natural surroundings. In some cases they also take up space that was public parkland before the development. Facility developments in the French Alps for the 1992 Albertville Winter Olympic Games attracted negative media coverage when a new bobsled track was carved through an unspoiled mountain area, destroying the natural environment forever. Sydney 2000 Olympic Games organisers made sure that even in their bid documents they strongly communicated the fact that the site developments would take place at a polluted, deserted, derelict swamp area in the outer suburbs of Sydney. Reclaiming and redeveloping the area for the Sydney community was used as a spearhead public relations exercise, emphasising a 'green' Olympic commitment. Confirmed in the city development plans of local governments around the world, blending new facility developments into the 'natural city environment' features highly on the political agenda.

Development of tourism and business

Because sport in general attracts substantial attention from the media (Mullin, Hardy & Sutton 2000), the opportunity to create exposure through a sport facility is present at local, regional, national and international levels. More recently, city marketers have realised that bringing major sporting events to a city can result in wide publicity for the host city (and host facility), creating a flow-on effect of people wanting to come and visit the city and the stadium. In 1993, KPMG Peat Marwick undertook a study into the impact of the 2000 Olympic Games. It concluded that during a 10-year period (1994–2004) the Olympic Games had the potential to contribute $A7.3 billion to Australia's gross domestic product. The study also revealed that, of that $A7.3 billion, benefits would spread across a wide range of industries, including manufacturing ($A1.15 billion), retail trade ($A1.2 billion), personal services ($A1 billion), finance ($A990 million) and construction ($A370 million).

Facility planners attempt to optimise the location of proposed facilities with several critical issues in mind. First, does the facility blend into the scenery of the city in a way that it can be used for television or photographic purposes? Second, can the facility be readily incorporated in the standard 'tourist route' through the city, not taking visitors too much out of their way? Finally, can the facility be used for a variety of events (multi-purpose), including business meetings or conferences, one-off tourist events, and other major events that are likely to attract visitors from other geographic regions to the city?

As with all components of a feasibility study, the hard decisions culminate at the financial end of the process. It is essential to consider the location of a speculated facility or event in light of an economic equation. For example, the nature of the facility or event will determine its revenue opportunities and its expenditure obligations. This is a formula that can vary considerably with scope and location. Organisers of an event designed for a television audience do not need to think so seriously about being located somewhere inconvenient for commuters. Stadia designed as much for live attendance as broadcasting, where gate receipts are paramount, do have to consider such factors as parking and accessibility to public transportation. Naturally, the more attendees at an event, the higher the revenues that can be anticipated in ticketing, food and beverages, and merchandise. But these convenient locations come at a price premium.

Parking can be another significant revenue generator for stadia. The provision of large-surface parking lots can encourage commuters. For this reason, some stadia end up in locations further from central business districts because they can significantly augment their revenues by 'forcing' spectators to drive. Some stadia have been deliberately positioned away from existing public transport in order to capitalise on this revenue opportunity. This is a risky proposition, however, and should not be pursued without careful consideration of the opportunity costs. For example, in cities where public transport systems are adequate or where roads are poor, the strategy will only force people to stay away. It also has the effect of reducing the type of spectators who attend to those who have access to vehicles. This may be an acceptable strategy in the Western world but is less sensible in countries where cars are not so readily available. As parking can yield a margin of up to 40 per cent due to its limited maintenance requirements and the limited costs associated with the collection of entrance fees, the ideal facility would have a balance of parking and access to public transportation.

In summary, the most influential factors associated with the selection of a site for a sport facility or event are those related to design, accessibility to customers and participants, the size of the geographic catchment (the market size and potential), climate, marketability, and potential occupancy or utilisation rates. All of these factors have revenue potential and inherent costs which must be weighed against each other. As with all aspects of project management, feasibility is a function of time, cost and quality. The perfectly located facility or event may be possible, but it will come at a price. If price is compromised, so too is quality, which might result in reduced opportunities for multi-purpose usage. Better quality takes longer to construct and organise.

Legal and regulatory analysis

In Chapter 7, we go into detail on risk management and legal issues. At this stage we will simply make a few general comments. There are a number of critical legal, statutory and regulatory issues that need to be considered before the event or facility becomes a committed project. Many of these are items to be added to the projected costs of the project. The following checklist of questions should assist in this task:

- Will government approval (local, state or county, federal) be required? Assuming that it can be obtained, are there any fees or taxes associated with the activities proposed?
- Which licences will be required for the activities proposed, both during preparation and construction and during events?
- Will insurance be required, and at what cost?
- Are there any patents and intellectual property rights for design and ownership?

The requirements are locally specific. For example, in many states in the USA, drilling a well for water that more than 25 people will be using requires regulatory approval and the payment of a several-thousand-dollar fee. The legal costs associated with staging a major event can be considerable. The feasibility study conducted to support the Canadian bid for the 2010 Soccer World Cup includes budgeted items amounting to several million dollars for insurance and the legal costs for establishing commercial, venue and local authority contracts.

Financial analysis

A financial feasibility analysis is a comprehensive study of all the potential and existing factors that may affect the likelihood of financial success of a proposed facility or event. Like all feasibility constituents, such as geographic and market analysis, the data obtained from the financial analysis are used to determine whether the development should be pursued, revised or abandoned. This section highlights three principal questions that must be resolved in order to complete a reliable financial feasibility analysis. First, how much money is needed in order to satisfactorily finance the facility's design and construction or the event's organisation? Second, where is the money going to come from? Third, do the benefits outweigh the costs from a purely financial perspective? Specifically, we consider the sources available for funding facilities and the subsequent implications of each possibility. In addition, we discuss the financial ramifications of operational, technical and schedule feasibility.

While at the feasibility stage it is impractical to precisely calculate design and construction or organisation costs, it is nevertheless essential to develop preliminary estimates. Expenses incurred during the design and construction phase are reviewed in Chapter 4, and collectively provide a comprehensive summary of the items to consider. The important decision at the feasibility stage is to determine approximately how much money will be required in order to plan and build the facility or lease and administrate the event. Pedantic decisions about specific architectural configurations are unnecessary at this point, but the broad strategic purposes of the facility or event need to be determined. In addition, some preliminary operational calculations are required in order to satisfy lenders and stakeholders. While it is logical to begin by calculating the amount of money required to develop and construct the facility or hire the personnel required to organise an event, the amount of money *available* for design and construction will ultimately provide the boundaries for specific decisions. Thus, the amount of money desired will be dependent on the funding available. Almost every project manager is forced to compromise their idealised design as a result of the limited financial resources that accompany the implications of certain funding strategies.

Project costs

Design and construction costs

Chapter 4 provides a detailed checklist of design and construction elements. For the purposes of a financial feasibility analysis, it is necessary to develop estimates of these elements. Further, if development is to be undertaken in phases, distribution of costs per phase should be identified. Costs should also be calculated at a macro-level using broad, generic categories that can readily be understood by non-architects. Typical headings may include: land acquisition, site preparation, permits and temporary facilities, road system, power system, communication system, water system, sewerage and drainage, fencing, buildings, parking, landscaping, and architecture and engineering. A good example of the range of capital costs can be seen in the feasibility study undertaken to establish the economic wisdom of a Canadian-hosted Soccer World Cup. In order to provide sufficient infrastructure, the need for significant upgrading of nine existing facilities and the construction of one new stadium was identified. The maximum level of capital expenditure was estimated at $C165.5 million. Cost areas typically included improvements to the pitch, scoreboard, temporary seating, permanent seating, roofing and amenities. For the event manager, the initial costings will revolve around the lease or hire of the appropriate site to host the event. From there, operational costs will have to be calculated, particularly taking into account the staff requirements before, during and after the event.

Project financing

Funding composition

The composition of revenue to finance the design and construction of facilities has far-reaching implications for the financial feasibility of the project and its scope. The importance of where the money comes from is often underestimated in feasibility studies. Typically, all that is relevant is whether the money is going to be available at all. In reality, however, the ramifications of the choice of funding arrangements are substantial, and will affect the financial feasibility of the facility or event for the rest of its operational life. The most common funding approaches are considered below.

Private funding

Few facilities or events have the luxury of exclusive private funding, where an individual, group, company or consortium (group of companies) provides the full financial resources for their design and construction or operations. Obviously, the capital required to build even a small recreational facility can easily run into the tens of millions. Although events do not have the burden of heavy capital investment, they can require significant sums of money well before any return is yielded. For example, international events like the World Masters Games or the Gay Games need staff working all year around, even though the event itself lasts only a few weeks. Even larger events, such as the Olympics, Commonwealth Games and the World Cup of soccer, have substantial staff numbers working over the four-year cycles in which the events are run. Many events also demand significant alterations to the host facility. Where substantial, these are made at the expense of the event rather than the facility. For example, a multi-purpose arena might provide an indoor tennis court one night and a basketball court the next without unduly raising the hiring price; events such as motorcross or extreme sports are normally faced with much greater costs. In some instances (e.g. a street circuit motor race) massive changes need to be made to the venue, including the addition of signage and protective barriers. These changes are made at the event's expense. So while only the largest international events cost as much as a new facility's construction, most events are not inexpensive, nor do they require staff only for the event's actual performance.

The advantages of private funding are that all profits are returned to the owners, as well as the decreased likelihood that the stakeholders will seek competing or non-complementary goals. The disadvantages are that private ownership necessitates significant investment in a non-current asset, which is difficult to convert readily into cash for other projects, and that it forces all risk squarely on the owners.

Government funding

Government funding may come in several forms, and is accompanied by numerous conditions. Like all creditors, the government will lend money to finance a facility if it perceives sufficient reciprocal benefits. Governments tend to provide funding for three reasons. First, as its core stakeholder is the general community, government tends to be interested in facilities that can provide generic, low-cost services to the general public. Many governments assume some responsibility for furnishing necessary sport and recreational infrastructure. In the extreme, a government may supply the entire resources for constructing a facility. The same holds true for events that a government deems to have benefits relevant to its constituency. For example, cultural festivals are often supported by public money. While this can be great news for event entrepreneurs seeking to minimise their risk, it is also likely to minimise their profits. Many local governments or councils in Australia, New Zealand and Europe finance the construction and operation of sport and recreation facilities.

Second, governments may see a proposed facility as a prudent consolidation of cash assets that may provide an attractive return. As with any investment, the government would expect its share of the profits and, like any shareholder, would demand a voice in the facility's or event's policy and operation.

Third, the government may assess the venue or event as a possibility for providing a significant economic stimulus, in either or both of its construction and operation. With this scenario, it may provide financial support on a short- to medium-term basis in order to reap the economic and social benefits. The advantage of this support is that financial resources are more likely to come at a discount; the obvious pitfall is that these will inevitably have to be repaid.

Governments may become involved for any one or a combination of these factors. Other options are more complicated and reflect agreements between government, communities and sometimes corporations. General obligation bonds, for example, work well when the facility or event is at least a partially government-owned project. In this agreement the local community, in the form of its local government, finances the facility or event, and recovers its investment slowly through operational profits and local taxes. Several other methods have been employed, many of which use a unique configuration of tax funds, grants, private investments and in some cases donations, student fees, institutional contributions and public subscriptions.

Corporate funding

Private organisations may be enticed to provide a share of the funding necessary to design and construct a sport facility or support the planning and operational phase of an event until the first revenues arrive. Companies may become involved in financing for three chief reasons. First, the company may seek to provide a facility within which to deliver its own products or services or its own major event. This is essentially a method of vertical integration. For example, a sport organisation may wish to construct a facility that can be used to house its own events: the Australian Football League has taken this approach with the state-of-the-art Telstra Dome in Melbourne. The relationship can also work the other way around: for example, a facility might independently organise events to help contribute towards better capacity utilisation. Many larger multi-purpose arenas not only solicit the interests of event promoters but also operate their own event departments, which develop and run new events. Clearly, their margins in these events are excellent because of the fixed venue costs. Most facilities, however, do not seek managing events as their core business. Alternatively, a television network may supply money for a stadium in order to secure exclusive rights to televise the hosted activities. Or a company may contribute to a sport facility's construction in order to obtain advantageous associations as well as carefully positioned exposure. This sponsorship option may include naming rights to the facility and advertising and signage space around the facility, including the scoreboard (sponsorship and marketing is explored further in Chapter 8). Second, companies may commit financial support for no other reason than as an investment opportunity. Sometimes this comes in the form of joint ventures between the real estate developers involved in different aspects of the project. For example, some might specialise in hotel or night club developments, and can be enticed to invest in a new facility.

A third option is to raise money by selling portions or shares of the facility to the general public. This has rarely if ever been attempted with sporting events, although in theory the idea has merit for the same reasons that it works with a facility. The only troublesome issue is that the legacy of an event does not have the same tangibility as that of a facility. Larger events companies, rather than any single event, have been publicly listed. The mechanisms governing company 'floats' are sophisticated, varying from country to country, and will not be discussed here.

Public funding

It is important to consider the implications of raising money through selling shares to the public. The great advantage is that the revenue need not be repaid, and may be invested in the capital works of the facility without worry about interest repayments. However, public shareholders are demanding, and will expect the prompt payment of dividends and an increase in the value of their holdings, which are exposed to the vagaries of international money markets and volatile economic perceptions. In addition, public companies are subject to weighty regulations governing accountability and policy making. Some facilities attempt to circumvent the complications associated with public share offers and pre-sell reserved seating and other limited services such as memberships for life. While this approach can provide much-needed revenue during the early life of a facility, it tends to contribute insubstantially to the overall funding, and can limit essential operational income. One variation is seat preference bonds, offered to individuals or corporate groups, allowing them the exclusive privilege of buying season tickets or tickets to significant games, events or even days during an event in the best viewing positions, prior to their release for public sale. Public funding to assist elite performance can bring dividends that are just as tangible as those from staging events. Lottery funding is widely recognised as having played a crucial role in the success of the British teams at the Sydney Olympic and Paralympic Games.

Borrowings

Typically, many prospective facilities and events are forced to consider borrowing money. There are a number of critical issues associated with debt financing that must be understood before deciding on the financial feasibility of the facility or event.

Variable versus fixed loans

Naturally, the first consideration before borrowing money is the interest burden it demands. The relative implications of variable and fixed interest rates should be assessed as part of a financial feasibility study. Variable interest rates are lower on a current basis, but are also subject to volatile movements. Fixed interest rates, while higher, allow the borrower to 'lock in' interest expenses over the term of the loan. As variable rates are controlled by the market and can move unexpectedly, they are more difficult to define in the feasibility equation. Convention recommends conservatism, but this obviates the chance of discounted rates.

Equity requirements

Lenders are mainly concerned about risk. If they perceive the likelihood of being repaid their money with high interest, then they will look favourably on a project. However, they will seek to assure themselves that if the facility can no longer meet the payments, they can recover their money through the sale of the facility and property. Equity represents the proportion of the facility's value that is owned by the facility. In other words, borrowers prefer to lend money to facilities that have accumulated some of the property and structure's equity, which can pose a problem for facilities that are seeking to borrow 100 per cent of the value of the property and finished structure. This is one of the reasons why events have more difficulty in acquiring loans: they rarely have anything tangible to return to a bank until after the event is run and gate receipts, sponsorships and broadcasting rights (if there are any) have been cashed in full.

Amortisation

Amortisation or depreciation is the process of decreasing the value of the facility on the balance sheet over time. Amortisation takes into account the theoretical effect of time on the life of a facility's structure, inbuilt equipment and fittings. It is important to calculate the amount that may be legally removed from the value of these assets because they can have a significant impact on the net profit of a facility. For example, amortisation is recorded as an expense, and can therefore be used to offset total revenue. The outcome can be a substantially more favourable tax burden, which must be accounted for in order to assess financial feasibility. Again, events without ownership of tangible assets are not hit with the concern of deteriorating facilities, but neither can they yield tax benefits from them.

Debt-service ratios

When dealing with significant sums of money, most lenders impose rigorous requirements for borrower liquidity. This is often determined by calculating the ratio of existing and anticipated funds available for debt-service payments due the lender from the borrower. In simpler terms, lenders might expect that for each dollar that is owed to them, the borrower has a minimum of one and a half dollars, either already collected or expected to be collected, available to pay. This would represent a debt-service ratio of 50 per cent. The lower the ratio, the more feasible the project. This often poses a problem for events, which have no source of revenue until they are run. As a result, the more successful events have managed to smooth out their cash inflows by signing up sponsors early or by pre-selling television rights that provide injections of funding during the planning phase of the event.

Working capital and liquidity

Allied to the notion of debt-service ratios are working capital calculations. Lenders impose provisions for borrower liquidity, which is determined by the availability of current assets. Working capital can be determined by subtracting current liabilities from current assets. Providing the result is sufficient to comfortably cover debt payments, the facility or event may be considered feasibly liquid.

Management team

Some lenders use subjective criteria to evaluate project risk. Lenders are expected to carefully scrutinise the skills and experiences of the management team that will supervise the design and construction as well as operation of the facility or event.

Collateral and security

Most lenders require some amount of collateral in order to satisfy themselves that the loan will ultimately be repaid, irrespective of circumstances. Collateral expectations may range from the minimum, anticipation of complete loan repayment, to the maximum, the opportunity for the first mortgage to the financed assets and other property. Lower collateral expectations make for a more feasible project.

Contractor requirements (penalty incurred for late finish)

When new construction or renovation is proposed to lenders, most will impose their own requirements in terms of architect and contractor experience and construction contracts. It is essential to identify these requirements so that they can be built into the costs of the facility construction or the development of the event infrastructure. Contractor requirements imposed by lenders do not necessarily lead to a less feasible scenario. In fact, in most cases, although these impositions are constricting, they tend to be in the best interests of the facility or event owners.

Market appraisal

Some lenders will ask the borrower to engage an independent assessor to demonstrate that there is sufficient demand for the facility's services. Others will require only that an appraisal of the market value of the property and facility be undertaken. The costs of these services must be included when determining financial feasibility. In some instances, it is the process of market appraisal that stimulates the feasibility study. Almost without exception, lenders will not provide financial support without a feasibility study showing a favourable result. Occasionally lenders commission their own feasibility studies when they believe the ones provided by facility or event owners to be excessively optimistic. In truth, this is a sensible practice for lenders, as many feasibility studies are not as independent or conservative as they should be.

Financial projections

Under the broad banner of financial projections fall four essential dimensions: economic, operational, technical, and schedule feasibility. Each has an impact on the overall financial feasibility of a project. *Economic feasibility* is concerned with the economic impact of the facility, and is principally concerned with whether the outcomes of designing, constructing and operating a facility outweigh the costs. For example, the Canadian Province of Alberta was awarded the 2005 Winter Goodwill Games. A study undertaken by the feasibility committee showed that staging the event would directly generate a minimum $US160 million economic impact. This benefit is principally a legacy of the facilities developed for Calgary's hosting of the Winter Olympics.

Economic impact may be calculated in a number of ways, but the most common method is to undertake a cost–benefit analysis. The simple consequence of a cost–benefit analysis is an estimation of the total financial costs involved in developing the facility as well as the future financial gains. If the gains or benefits are clearly greater than the costs, then the facility may be considered economically feasible. Economic impacts are difficult to identify precisely, and are subject to myriad assumptions and valuations, including the quantification of intangible benefits. For example, it may be appropriate to consider the effects of holding a major event in a particular region on employment in the area, or the cumulative effect of purchasing huge quantities of building materials on the related industries.

Economic impact depends on facility or event size, (multi-)function, location, usage rates, quality, profile of events, and experience of key staff. Often, sporting events will channel 'new' financial flows into a region, and (as explained later) these flows then multiply into additional work opportunities and taxation points. Economic impact projections can play a significant role in feasibility studies if the event has been proposed with the justification of economic value-adding to a region. Events in particular should be viewed with caution when net economic value is predicted. For example, while the 2000 London Marathon generated over £63 million in economic activity and the 1999 Rugby World Cup generated £83 million for the Welsh economy, Sheffield City Council, which subsidised the World Student Games in

1991, has a continuing annual debt burden of £22 million from the cost of providing facilities. However, there are fewer hallmark events organised or major facilities constructed in any given region than there are community-targeted facilities or events. These smaller projects are not measured in terms of economic value-adding, but rather against other less tangible and financial indicators.

Ultimately, an economic feasibility analysis should provide a range of estimates that explain the financial implications of developing and operating a facility. Operational revenues and costs should be investigated at this point to determine *operational feasibility*. Investors will expect to be provided with return on investment (ROI) figures. The ROI indicates the amount recovered as a percentage of the investment. For example, an ROI of 10 per cent means that for every dollar invested, a yield of 10 cents is returned. In general, an ROI of greater than 10 per cent per annum is considered outstanding.

ROI figures must be substantiated by rigorous financial forecasts, which are typically presented in the form of projected financial statements. Anticipated revenue and expenditure should be developed in the form of a budget, including a breakeven analysis. The breakeven analysis demonstrates the point at which revenues equal expenses as measured by sales. Thus, for sporting events, a certain number of ticket sales correspond to collective revenue that covers all fixed and variable costs up to that point. This analysis is essential to sport facilities and events. Assets and liabilities should be approximated in a balance sheet and cash flow predicted in a cash-flow statement. In order for economic feasibility to be exhaustively considered, financial statements for the first five years of construction and operation should be completed.

The *technical feasibility* of the facility also has financial ramifications. Technical feasibility refers to the relationship between design and construction, where the difficulty of building the facility to meet its specified purpose is examined. Technical feasibility may be established by answering certain questions. Is the necessary technology available, and at what cost? What are the legislative and taxation requirements for this project? Can the designed quality be delivered feasibly with available materials? These questions are often asked for events as well. Often, specific sporting activities must be able to be undertaken within facilities that were not originally designed for such a purpose. Technical feasibility must be considered for new events to ascertain whether there is an appropriate location for them. A good example is indoor equestrian events, which require not only particular configurations of equipment but also large quantities of dirt and facilities for horses to be stabled during the event, and for their riders and owners to be accommodated in close proximity to the horses. An equine-friendly facility should have jumping equipment, scoring software and scoreboards, and a public address system.

Finally, the financial consequences of *schedule feasibility* must be accounted for. In the first instance, the probability of construction completion on time will influence the final financial feasibility of the project. Issues to consider in determining this probability may include control over timing, externally imposed deadlines and windows of opportunity, contractors and their track records, and the political landscape. Naturally, the greater the probability of completing the project on schedule, the greater the likelihood of no negative financial pressures and of an improved feasibility outlook.

Operational financial projections

The basic tool for financial planning is the budget, which is a prediction of an organisation's financial arrangements, usually for the coming year. As well as being a valuable administrative tool, the budget can be important when communicating with members and customers, particularly if there is a need to justify higher fees and charges, or to assess the financial implications of new development initiatives. The purpose of a budget is to provide a systematic estimate of future revenues and expenses organised by time and activity. It also provides a procedure for monitoring, controlling and evaluating an organisation's financial resources. Below we introduce the budgeting process, which needs to be undertaken during the feasibility stages in order to ensure that the new facility or event is operationally viable once it opens its doors to paying customers.

Elements of a budget

There are three principal components of a budget: total revenue, total expenses, and profit. We look at each of these briefly here in order to explain the aspects of facility or event operations that need to be considered to determine feasibility.

Total revenue

The total amount of revenue earned is the foundation of any budget. Common revenue sources for sporting facilities and events include gate receipts, venue hire charges, broadcasting rights, sponsorships, signage and endorsements, memberships, catering services, equipment hire, food and beverage sales, merchandise, gaming machines, government grants and subsidies, parking fees, vending machines, publications, bar trading, social functions, rent on leased premises, investments and asset sales. Projections for each of these items need to be made over at least a five-year period. For example, a city undertaking a feasibility study to underpin a potential bid to host the Olympic Games would need to estimate the revenues it could expect from a number of key sources. To begin with, it would calculate the Organising Committee for the Olympic Games' (OCOG) share of broadcasting revenue paid by the International Olympic Committee (IOC). The IOC will transfer a total of $US2.35 billion from broadcasting to the OCOG's revenue until 2008. The analysis may even factor in the possibility of receiving a share of profits earned by NBC (the US broadcaster until 2008) or EBU (the European broadcaster until 2008) if a certain volume of sales is reached when the rights are on-sold to other broadcasters. Next, the study would determine a reasonable projection for marketing revenues, including sponsorship and merchandising. For instance, in Sydney, licensing fees were about $US44 million of its $US500 million total merchandising revenue—around four times the merchandising revenues associated with the Super Bowl. Then, ticketing revenues would be estimated. In Atlanta and Sydney, gate receipts contributed nearly one-quarter of the OCOG's budgets. Last, other 'special' revenue opportunities would be included, such as Olympic commemorative coins, postage stamps and lotteries.

Total expenses

Total costs include fixed and variable expenses. Fixed expenses remain unaffected by the amount of activity and revenue a facility or event may generate. For example, the interest payments on a loan taken for the construction of the facility will not vary depending on how many people attend a particular event or how much revenue is acquired through the sale of television rights. Fixed expenses, therefore, must be discharged at the same rate over a standard period, irrespective of the nature or health of a facility. Common fixed expenses for sporting facilities and events include rent, interest, 'core' personnel, and licences and permits. A college football program in the United States can expect to incur expenses for the football program itself, in the form of personnel, scholarships, equipment and operations; support systems costs, in the form of support personnel, supplies and equipment; and facility costs, in the form of infrastructure for training and competition.

While fixed expenses remain static, variable expenses are directly affected by the level of activity the facility or event experiences. For example, merchandise costs are directly affected by the number of items that are sold. The more merchandise sold, the greater the purchasing costs. Similarly, food and beverage costs and extra casual staff salary costs will rise proportionately with additional levels of consumption. Other common variable expenses for sporting facilities and events include cleaning, maintenance and repairs.

Unfortunately, to complicate matters, a large range of 'semi-' or partly variable expenses are typical for sporting facilities and events and make budget development more troublesome. These semi-variable expenses have both fixed and variable components. For example, in some countries a telephone bill includes a standardised cost for the rental of the handsets and a variable cost dependent on the volume of calls. For the purpose of accurate budgeting, it is advisable to break semi-variable expenses into their constituent parts, and identify them as either fixed or variable costs. The fixed element represents the minimum cost of subsiding the activity or supplying the product or service. The remaining variable component will be affected by the level of activity, which must be estimated accordingly. Examples of semi-variable costs include leased equipment, utilities and office supplies. Like revenues, each of these costs must be itemised with projections over a minimum five-year period. Completing financial forecasts is extremely time-consuming because it forces feasibility planners to determine everything associated with a facility or event's operation, including products offered, prices, human resource requirements, information system and other technological needs, marketing activities, legal compliance, purchasing and logistics, ongoing research and development, and leadership and management.

Profit or surplus

Careful consideration must be given to constructing realistic and appropriate profit projections. On the one hand, the total profit must be adequate to make the operation of the facility worthwhile for its owners; on the other, it must be sufficiently modest to ensure competitive pricing to encourage additional custom. It is also unrealistic to expect that lenders are going to support a facility or event that does not return a reasonable dividend; on the other hand, lenders will have difficulty believing projections that demonstrate immediate and easily acquired profits. Furthermore, all projections need to be supported by the data collected earlier in the feasibility study, during the market and competitive analysis phase. This ensures that projections are credible and based on objective data, rather than on the whimsical guesses of the project manager. Past trends, inflation and the conventional assumption of conservatism (under project revenue and over project expenditure) are relevant issues to remember. Experienced project managers will also insist that at least 10 per cent of the budget for the construction and development phase be allocated to 'contingencies'. This accounts for unforeseen occurrences, where the budget has 'blown out'. There are always unforeseen expenditures, and this contingency budget rarely goes untouched.

A financial feasibility analysis should examine three issues. First, the costs associated with designing and constructing the facility should be estimated. Second, the quantity of financial resources available for the project must be established and the implications of the funding arrangements clearly understood. Finally, financial projections should be calculated that unambiguously demonstrate whether the benefits of the project outweigh the costs. Operational feasibility comes down to budgetary projections.

Summary

Feasibility, as we have dealt with it in this chapter, forms the basis for the ongoing strategic planning of an organisation. From this viewpoint, the activities and analysis that are undertaken during the feasibility study are not 'one-off' ideas but rather are essential analytical techniques for the ongoing assurance of viability and prosperity. Nevertheless, in order to get a new facility or event off the ground it is essential to scope the project first, culminating in a project charter against which the rest of the feasibility study is benchmarked. Next, a comprehensive market and competitive analysis must be performed to provide the objective data concerning the machinations of supply and demand, or competition and consumers. Legal issues also need to be studied to be certain that no legal barriers obstruct the development of the facility or event. Finally, with all of these data, the financial feasibility of the project can be evaluated. If, after this process has been completed, the project remains attractive, it may be started with as much confidence of success as can reasonably be anticipated. However, a positive result in a feasibility study is not a guarantee of success. It is merely a statement of risk: the more positive the results of a feasibility study are, the lower the risk in proceeding with the facility or event.

Case study

The Volvo Ocean Race stopover

The Volvo Ocean Race is the premier around-the-world sailing event, pushing both sailors and yachts to their limits. Held every four years since 1973/74, the world-class event has one of the highest global profiles in sailing. The race track follows the traditional routes of old clipper ships, including those feared for their savage storms and icebergs.

Starting in Spain in November and finishing in the Baltic States the following June, the 2005/06 yachting marathon has 10 'legs'. Between each leg are the stopovers and pitstops in different countries. Traditionally, these stopovers have enabled crews to snatch a few days' rest, restock supplies and make any necessary repairs to their vessels. However, a rule change for the event, specifically one introducing in-port racing, will keep the crews extra busy during their stopovers. A day of in-port racing during each stopover will provide the local public and media with an up-close sailing spectacle as the yachts and their respective crews battle it out over challenging short courses. The in-port races will be fiercely contested, as they account for approximately 20 per cent of the overall race's points.

The second and longest stopover is in Melbourne, Australia, from 19 January to 12 February. The 25-day stopover period encompasses four weekends, each dedicated to a particular theme or activity. The first weekend will celebrate the arrival of the yachts in Melbourne. Australia Day (Australia's National Day) celebrations will take place on the second weekend. The third weekend will be taken up with the 35 nautical mile in-port race in the northern half of Port Phillip Bay. The final weekend will see Melbourne say farewell to the yachts and their crews, wishing them all the best for the next, arduous leg of the race. In addition to the more formal activities associated with each weekend, there will be a range of festivities and activities, possibly including a Summer Boat Show, Blues and Music Festival, Tall Ships and Super Yachts Display, Food and Wine Festival, and Twilight Symphony Concerts.

The stopover location will be Waterfront City at Docklands, located a 20-minute sail up the Yarra River from Port Phillip Bay and a 10-minute walk from the Melbourne central business district. Docklands is a newly developed and thriving residential, business, shopping, entertainment and café precinct. As well as being home to the yachts, their crews, and the crews' respective friends, partners and families, Docklands will be home to an event operations centre, media centre, maintenance area, corporate hospitality facilities and medical centre. Together, these will form the hub of the stopover—that is, the Racing Village.

Located only a few kilometres downstream from the Racing Village towards Port Phillip Bay is the Port of Melbourne, one of Australia's largest and busiest ports, servicing approximately 3200 ships every year. The Port of Melbourne Corporation (POMC) oversees port operations. Two of the POMC's most important customers are terminal operators P&O Ports Ltd and Patrick Stevedores, which between them handle 70 per cent of the freight passing through the Port of Melbourne. Yachts competing in the Volvo Ocean Race will share the same channels as the ships that need to load and unload their cargo at the Port of Melbourne. The yachts will also need to share the Docklands Port area with many river-cruising tourist operators. Furthermore, Melbourne's boating community is expected to use these channels more than it normally would, as the very presence of the yachts and the stopover festivities will encourage extra boat traffic in Docklands.

When the yachts participate in the in-port race they will be utilising a part of Port Phillip Bay that is typically used by leisure craft, windsurfers, jet skiers and the local ferry service. Moreover, the same area houses Station Pier, which is used by the Star of Tasmania, a ferry service between the states of Victoria and Tasmania, as well as by cruise liners.

Hosting the Volvo Ocean Race stopover will inject an estimated $A26 million into the state of Victoria's economy. The Victorian Major Events Company (VMEC), a government-backed events corporation whose primary purpose it is to attract major national and international events to Victoria, played a considerable role in attracting the event to Melbourne, a city not traditionally recognised as a sailing city. Once the stopover was secured, the state set up the Melbourne Stopover Organising Committee (MSOC), a local organising committee. The MSOC will work with the UK-based event owner, Volvo Event Management, to run the Melbourne component of the event.

Three different types of sponsors are involved in the event: namely, the race sponsor (for the overall event), the port sponsors (for each stopover), and the syndicate sponsors (for each yacht). Volvo is not only the race sponsor but is also its owner. The Australian company Waterfront City Holdings, local government authority, VicUrban and the Victorian state government are the port sponsors for the Melbourne stopover. Numerous other organisations have come on board as syndicate sponsors.

The stopovers, such as the one in Melbourne, can be considered events in their own right. As with any event, the Melbourne stopover has numerous stakeholders, many of which have been mentioned here. The stopover stakeholders were identified early in the planning process, with the support of several of them (e.g. local and state government) being essential to bidding success.

Q. Some of the Melbourne stopover stakeholders have contradictory objectives for the event.
Identify some stakeholders that you think might have contradictory objectives.
- *Describe these contradictory objectives.*
- *What would be the impact on event planning, event operations and overall event success if these contradictory objectives were not resolved?*
- *How can the MSOC resolve or manage these contradictory objectives?*

Q. There are several groups in addition to the event stakeholders that will be affected by the planning and hosting of the Melbourne stopover.
- *What are some of these groups (not all directly mentioned in the case study)?*
- *How will they be affected?*
- *How can the MSOC resolve or manage any negative impacts?*

4

Developing new sport facilities: design and construction issues

Chapter focus
Structure, size and trends in the sport facility and sport event sectors
Key success factors of operating sport facilities and running sport events
Developing new sport facilities: feasibility analysis
Developing new sport facilities: design and construction issues
Developing new sport facilities: preparing facility management infrastructure
Operating the new sport facility: attracting events
Operating the new sport facility: preparing event management infrastructure
Attracting customers: marketing the sport facility and the sport events
Running the sport event: event operations
Measuring facility and event performance: a scorecard approach to success
Measuring facility and event performance: impact on and for stakeholders

CHAPTER OBJECTIVES

In this chapter, we will:
- Move from broad facility considerations/analysis to specific design decisions.
- Consider the importance of stakeholder involvement in design planning.
- Discuss multi-use flexibility in design planning.
- Consider a range of design features.
- Review the temporary facility as an events option.
- Discuss the importance of the building brief.

At this point in the book we have outlined a range of broad, pre-development and event considerations for sport facility and event managers. This chapter takes the manager into the next phase of facility development—the final design and construction specifications. In many ways this is both the most exciting and the most important phase in sport facility and event management. Many of the decisions made now are largely irreversible, and are likely to have a significant effect on the project's overall success. Having said that, this stage allows managers to incorporate their own vision and ingenuity into the project, and as such presents a stimulating challenge.

Up to this point, a need has been identified in the marketplace, key success factors outlined, and feasibility analyses and market research conducted. We now consider moving the project into the next stage, and converting that research into a 'tight' building brief that meets the project's desired outcomes, providing the blueprint for a high-quality facility. We commence with an overview of the design and construction process. This will include a rather extensive discussion of the more vital elements of this process, such as continued community consultation and site selection. Following the design brief we will introduce some major design features, culminating in a discussion of sport-specific regulations and specifications. We conclude with an overview of a number of operational and service considerations and the optimisation of secondary spend areas and architectural identity.

The design and construction process

According to the publication *Better Places for Sport*, jointly published by Sport England and the Commission for Architecture and the Built Environment (2003), there are 10 key success factors to consider when planning, designing and constructing a sports facility:

1. strong client leadership;
2. best-practice benchmarking;
3. developing a clear, detailed brief;
4. selecting the right team;
5. implementing sustainable objectives and practices;
6. ensuring a match between the project and context;
7. implementing integrated procurement strategies;
8. ensuring client sign-off at key stages;
9. making realistic financial commitments; and
10. providing sufficient time for design.

This suggests, broadly speaking, that systematic planning, careful program management, detailed documentation and cooperative team–stakeholder relationships are the keys to developing a successful building solution.

The primary task of the project initiators (referred to here as the client) is to translate the needs of the facility into a detailed strategic and then design brief. The needs of the facility are derived from business, customer, human resource, environmental, community and legislative concerns. In the early design and conception phase, generally a small number of people make far-reaching decisions that will affect the future efficiency and effectiveness of the facility. The key at this stage is to make decisions with the most complete information (de Groot et al. 1999), gathered through systematic research and consultation.

Even at this early stage, it is valuable to avoid a situation where the design and construction team operate in a fragmented manner. A construction consultant may add significant value to the design process. The design and construction process should be structured to facilitate collaboration between clients, designers, users, legislators, advisers, engineers and contractors. Different members of the design and construction team have different agendas, and are often contracted separately with individual profit expectations. Architects, for instance, have been criticised for valuing design aesthetics well above cost, while structural and mechanical engineers have been criticised for making provision for safety and maintenance access at the expense of aesthetics (Locke & Randall 1994). Disciplinary (quality) fragmentation within design and construction teams has been worsened by tightening time and financial constraints on all industries. It is the pivotal and challenging role of the project manager to facilitate an integrated approach, where interdisciplinary disputes can be successfully negotiated. Once the project manager and design team have been appointed, they will coordinate the subsequent stages of design and construction, which are broadly summarised in Table 4.1.

Continued community and customer consultation

As we have already indicated in Chapter 3, an estimate of the amount of usage or attendance the proposed facility or event is likely to attract is essential in the analysis of potential consumers. We have outlined several ways to undertake this, and the most straightforward way we have identified is simply through direct consultation with the potential user groups. In the context of establishing a design and building brief, this process can be extended. The process of consultation with the major stakeholders of a facility will, in that regard, yield significant benefits. Broadly speaking, it will help to ensure that the design of the facility meets the needs of the community. If the needs of the community are adequately met, then the facility has the potential to secure an ongoing customer base and operational cash flow. In addition, collaborating with the project's stakeholders provides the opportunity to positively resolve any conflicts between the needs of the facility managers and those of the community. Although collaboration can be criticised by some as delaying decision-making processes, in the long run it represents the best method for garnering community ownership of the facility, and for overcoming conflicts that could otherwise halt the project altogether.

Nessen and Blank (2001) provide an excellent example of tapping into the energy and expertise of community stakeholders in a US skateboard park. The park designers decided to go beyond the 'token' gesture of inviting local skateboarders to a public meeting in order to hear their views. Instead, they opted for a model of greater involvement, where skateboarders were invited to participate in a committee with the right to voice an opinion on everything from site selection to design. Nessen and Blank (2001) suggest that the right to voice their opinion comes hand in hand with the responsibility to work within the team. The skateboarders were expected to positively collaborate with the other community stakeholders (such as local residents), research and design the park layout, as well as provide manual labour.

The apparent simplicity of such schemes belies both their importance and the regularity of their omission. Such an omission can have serious drawbacks for any facility. For example,

Table 4.1 An overview of the design and construction process

Stage	Details	Personnel
Conduct research	• Market research • Needs analysis • Feasibility study • Establish budget and funding alternatives	External consultants
Develop a strategic brief	• Includes development plan • Informed by business plan • Indicates the business case • Project constraints (budget, time plan)	Client (initiators of project)
Seek board approval		
Submit funding applications		
Tender for and appoint project manager	Earlier appointment of the project manager can yield significant benefits	Project manager Client
Select a site	• Continued community consultation • Comparative analysis of sites • Site and soil surveys • Site optimisation analysis • Site layout • Site access and services	Project manager Surveyors Engineering consultants
Develop a design brief	• Summary of strategic brief • Design aspirations • Operational needs of facility • Performance needs of facility • Lifecycle plans for facility • Planning brief • Project management systems	Project manager Client Consultation team: facility staff, community representative, Construction consultant
Tender for and appoint design team	Consider external evaluation of tenders for objectivity	Project manager External consultants
Negotiate design response and develop detailed design brief	• Increased detail for all sections of initial design brief • Revised cost and time plan • Detailed drawings • Building specifications	Project manager Design team Construction consultant
Develop building brief and fit-out brief		
Tender for and appoint constructions contractor	Evaluation criteria include: • costs • ability to comply with brief • licences and registrations • technical expertise • financial capacity • timing • logistics • procurement planning • obtain planning consents, including the right to appeal	Project manager Design team Construction consultant
Tender for and appoint subcontractors		Contractor
Construction		
Develop operating brief		

designers may miss an opportunity for input on cutting-edge trends, and the ability to create a sense of community ownership of the facility is lost. Such ownership feelings can be linked to such issues as usage and vandalism.

Site selection

As observed in Chapter 3, the *real estate cliché*—that there are only three principles determining the market value of properties: location, location and location—also holds true for the positioning of a sport facility or event. The fact that (in the majority of cases) a building cannot simply be picked up and taken to another geographic area makes the decision of where to build it in the first place an important one. The 'location' decision drives further decision making. In a nutshell, the selection of a site for development should represent a win–win for all concerned—facility managers, the local community, potential customers and the relevant government bodies. It should also be appropriate for the building application in terms of site and soil composition. In other words, as with all stages of the planning, construction and design process, a collaborative and inclusive approach will ultimately yield the most successful outcome. But what does a win–win mean in practice?

In terms of the facility managers, a win–win would primarily mean that the facility is located in the hub of potential customers identified through the market research component of the feasibility analysis. The site will ideally be accessible to these customers through a public transport infrastructure, adequate public roads and parking facilities. The existence of other sport and recreational facilities in the vicinity is another important consideration, as it is undesirable to compete with similar facilities in the same area for the same customers. Given these conditions, the facility is most likely to receive patronage. This, of course, will supply the ongoing income stream required for the facility to be economically viable. Cost management may further be facilitated by considering the location of existing services to the site, such as electricity, gas (where applicable), water and mains drainage, and existing roadways.

For the prospective customers, transport accessibility is also a win. At the same time, the aesthetic wishes of these customers and the local community may influence the choice of site. Local residents, for instance, may not look favourably on the installation of a facility that blocks the sun from their backyard vegetable patch, nor on one which they believe contradicts a dominant architectural style that characterises their neighbourhood. The planning of the facility layout may help to combat these issues, with the careful placement of parking, open park space and screening vegetation.

Local community, as well as environmental groups, may be concerned with the potential environmental impact of the choice of site. In today's society, developers and facility managers are increasingly expected to be good custodians of the environment. A prominent example of this issue affecting the choice of site is Homebush, the Sydney 2000 Olympics site in Australia. In the planning and design phase of development, a colony of endangered frogs was identified. Environmental groups successfully campaigned for the preservation of the colony. The location of building structures and roads was redesigned, and the immediate area of the colony was transformed into picturesque parkland.

As representatives of the local community, local government is likely to be concerned with the issues of local residents. In addition, it will be required to consider such issues as historical zoning classifications on any sites in question.

In response to the needs of local communities and their governing bodies, there has been an increasing trend to locate new venues in underprivileged areas or disused industrial sites. This is particularly true for larger, international-standard facilities that have suffered in the past from being located in areas where they have received little use after an international event. The new weightlifting stadium for the Athens 2004 Olympics, for example, has revitalised a disused quarry in a low-income suburb (Hope 2003). Other Athens 2004 sites include stadiums at Liosia and Galatsi, home to large communities of immigrant workers, to whom the developers have left a positive legacy after the games (Hope 2003). The Homebush Bay area of the Sydney 2000 Olympics famously transformed an industrial waste and slaughterhouse site into a trendy new suburb. Although the Sydney Olympics site was criticised by some as failing to exploit the unique aspects of Sydney, such as the harbour (McGuigan 2000), others have praised the attempt to add value to a less salubrious area.

To summarise, the choice of site for facility development should generally consider 11 issues:

1. consultation and collaboration with all stakeholders;
2. pedestrian, public transport and vehicle access;
3. geographic placement in relation to potential customers;
4. current servicing to area by other sport and recreational facilities;
5. aesthetic impact of proposed building structure;
6. environmental conservation;
7. zoning classifications;
8. site and soil surveys;
9. site topography;
10. site history, boundaries and ownership; and
11. existing services (electricity, gas etc.).

Having obtained input and 'buy-in' from community stakeholders, particularly with regard to the selection of the building site, we are now in the position to consider the different elements of the design and building brief.

The design and building brief

As with any architectural construction, the ultimate goal of a sporting facility is to be used, not merely observed. In other words, form should follow function. The design team should have an intimate understanding of how the facility will be used, when it will be used, who will use it, how it will be maintained, how it will be administered and the many different kinds of equipment and services that the facility will house. For example, a stadium that needs to allow 50 000 spectators to flow into and out of the stands will need to incorporate different access features from those of a recreational pool facility that services 2000 people per day. In addition, factors such as the budget, local regulations and the aesthetic needs of the immediate vicinity will have a strong bearing on the design. The issue of regulations, in particular, is a complicated area. Sporting facilities are subject not only to national building standards and specifications but also potentially to the requirements of national and international sporting federations in order to allow the organisation of international sporting events and competitions.

This, therefore, represents the kind of information that should be provided in the form of a design and building brief. The brief should also establish the processes for evaluating and modifying the design to ensure that it accommodates the needs of all stakeholders. In other words, the design brief should provide a clear picture for the designers of the needs and limitations of the project. The greatest testament to the creativity of a design team will ultimately be their ability to create an aesthetically 'appealing' design within these myriad logistical, financial and political constraints.

A comprehensive design and building brief should therefore include information on the following parameters:

1. Introductory summary
   1.1 Summary of strategic brief, including mission, vision and objectives of the facility
   1.2 Overview of commissioning organisation(s) and key stakeholders
   1.3 Policy and funding context of the facility
2. Design aspirations
   2.1 Desire/tolerance for innovation
   2.2 Strategic branding concepts
   2.3 Local and/or sport-specific features to be highlighted
   2.4 Expectations of design quality
3. Project limitations
   3.1 Budget (as informed by feasibility research)
   3.2 Time scale and development deadlines
   3.3 Local ecological and community issues
4. Operational needs of the facility
   4.1 Facilities and space required
   4.2 Internal space arrangements
       4.2.1 All primary and secondary spend areas
       4.2.2 Staffing and administrative spaces
       4.2.3 Media, technology and broadcasting spaces
       4.2.4 Maintenance needs
       4.2.5 External spaces (parking, landscaping)
   4.3 Specific user and staff needs (as determined through market research and consultation)
   4.4 Technology requirements
5. Performance requirements of the facility
   5.1 Sport-specific regulations
       5.1.1 Individual sport requirements
       5.1.2 National and international competition standards
   5.2 Government standards
       5.2.1 Building codes
       5.2.2 Sport playing surface and space codes
       5.2.3 Occupational health and safety
       5.2.4 Accessibility
       5.2.5 Services/energy efficiency
   5.3 Environmental sustainability
       5.3.1 Materials

      5.3.2   Sustainability
      5.3.3   Unique ecological issues

6. Lifecycle plans for facility
    6.1 Life expectancy of facility
    6.2 Planned schedule for refurbishment/development (e.g. 5–10-year cycle)
    6.3 Potential future uses and flexibility needs

7. Planning brief
    7.1 Site information
        7.1.1   Site and soil surveys
        7.1.2   Boundaries
        7.1.3   Ownership
        7.1.4   Topography
        7.1.5   History
        7.1.6   Urban context
        7.1.7   Pedestrian and vehicle access
        7.1.8   Car parking and public transport
        7.1.9   Services in situ
    7.2 Plans and other relevant documents included

8. Project management and monitoring mechanisms
    8.1 Anticipated configuration of project management team
    8.2 Process for reviewing and negotiating design proposals
    8.3 Specific kinds of experts or consultants to be involved in decision making

Ideally, the design team will respond to the above information with careful analysis of the options, constraints and costs. Providing designers with sufficient funding to explore a number of alternatives at this stage may yield longer-term benefits with regard to problem resolution and design quality. Design responses should include a cost and deadline program. Design responses will be presented to the project management team in the form of a report, in addition to outline specification drawings and potentially actual or virtual models. The opportunity should then be taken to creatively negotiate any alterations required before a more detailed brief is drafted. The detailed design brief will include the above information with further detail on all levels, for example details of products and materials to be used. For this reason it is advisable that building and construction experts be involved in the decision making at this early stage. In addition, the following should be included:

9. Additional detailed brief information
    9.1 Revised program plan
        9.1.1   Costs
        9.1.2   Deadlines
    9.2 Specialised sports surface materials and equipment
        9.2.1   Outdoor turf and track surfaces
        9.2.2   Indoor playing surfaces
        9.2.3   Specialised illumination
        9.2.4   Seating
        9.2.5   Scoreboard

Major design features

Some of the features of the new facility are more important than others, principally because the major design features affect the core products of the facility directly. In this case capacity decisions and playing surfaces are important, and we discuss them below as the major design features.

Capacity and capacity allocation

To state the obvious, estimates of spectator capacity should be arrived at only after substantial consideration in the market research and feasibility stages of planning. Once determined, the anticipated spectator capacity of a facility has a huge impact on the overall size of the structure. However, the expected capacity of a venue is a much larger design issue than merely determining size. Maximum capacity projections have an enormous impact on other design features, such as access doors and ramps, choice of seating, support columns and bracing for the stands, spectator views of the playing area, merchandising and amenities, the need for media and broadcasting facilities, also optimising secondary spend and architectural identity.

Designers of large-capacity stadiums, in particular, must creatively explore how to accommodate vast numbers of spectators while minimising logistical problems and establishing a unique architectural presence. Two recent stadium developments exemplify this achievement. The ballpark of the Baltimore Orioles baseball team has achieved this by creatively rearranging traditional seating design to realise a 67 000 seat capacity (Brake 2002). The corners, which offer the least desirable seats, have been notched out. Through these notches the outer layers of the stadium are constructed from translucent glass. This gives the spectators a greater sense of place, while passing pedestrians can not only hear but also see the excited crowd. To compensate for the lost seats, the stands have been extended at the 50-yard line, covered by a unique canopy that contributes to better lighting and sound system uniformity.

Similarly, the construction of the CGMI Field, home to the New England Patriots football team in Massachusetts, has accommodated a 68 000 seat capacity with an unusual design (Aveni 2001). An open area has been established at the north end of the stadium where seats would normally be located. To compensate, the main concourse is designed to be unusually high, reaching up to 21.8 metres. Typical storey heights of facilities range from 7 to 8 metres, whereas the CGMI Field boasts 12-metre storeys. The opened north end enables spectators to enjoy an unobstructed view of the field when entering from the concourse or club level.

Outdoor playing surfaces and turf

The selection of the playing surface presents venue managers with significant trade-offs that can render decisions far from 'clearcut'. Like their indoor equivalents, outdoor surfaces can be selected from a range of artificial options or grass. There is, by and large, no one product solution that is applicable to any one venue. Different sports have different surfacing needs, while the vast array of products available confuses the decision even further. The unique climatic conditions in different countries may also influence the decision-making process.

With regard to outdoor surfaces, the debate between natural and artificial options remains heated. While artificial surfaces can be praised for their durability and stability, they have also been criticised due to their initial expense, safety, and the replacement costs occasioned by their finite life span (Weber 2002). In contrast, a natural grass field can last a life-time if installed with an appropriate sub-base and serviced by an appropriate maintenance program. However, natural grass can succumb to wear and tear as well as weather conditions such as drought and heavy rain.

While outdoor synthetic turfs may have their critics, after an intensive two-year evaluation, the American NFL team 'The Buffalo Bills' installed a new synthetic surface in May 2003. The evaluation period involved visiting sites, reviewing field studies and consulting other teams, and trialling the product for a season on half of the field. Numerous major European soccer federations, including the English Football Association (FA), the Spanish Football Federation, the Belgian KBVB, the German DFB and the Danish National Soccer Federation, utilise artificial grass pitches for their training centres. Other facilities, including those of the Seattle Seahawks and the Australian Institute of Sport, also utilise artificial turf surfaces.

One outdoor playing area where natural surfaces are not an option is of course the athletics track. While the choice of surfaces for this area is limited to synthetic ones, there is such a plethora of artificial options that the decision remains complex. Generally speaking, artificial track surfaces can be installed using a variety of materials including liquid urethane and sheet rubber (Weber 2002). Indoor tracks are often constructed using the sheet rubber approach, while the liquid plied surface approach is more common for outdoor surfaces (Weber 2002).

Technology continually contributes to improved design in artificial surfaces, but it is also radically improving maintenance systems for natural grass fields. This is because, away from the athletics track, natural grass still has its supporters. The field of the Denver Broncos' new stadium, for instance, features a unique underground maintenance system (Gonchar 2001). Polyethylene tubing that contains 70 per cent water has been installed 10 inches (22 cm) below the surface to maintain the grass roots at a constant temperature. In addition, the soil is oxygenated and excess water removed through a vacuum air-conveyance system.

Technology is also offering hybrid natural–synthetic turf surfaces, in an attempt to maximise the benefits of each system while minimising their respective weaknesses. A hybrid system, for instance, is now installed in the stadiums of Dutch soccer team Feyenoord, Real Madrid, Liverpool FC, Tottenham Hotspur FC and the Denver Broncos, among others. The system involves injecting over 20 million artificial grass fibres approximately 20 cm down into the natural grass pitch. The artificial fibres then constitute approximately 3 per cent of the total surface. As the natural grass grows, its roots intertwine with the artificial fibres, which anchor them and enhance the stability of the surface. The manufacturer suggests that the enhanced stability of the system enables heavy use of the turf, allowing multiple games and events to take place without destroying the surface.

Table 4.2 Issues to consider for facility turf requirements

Parameter	Issues to consider
User profile	• Sporting codes and activities • Intensity of use (frequency and duration) • Pattern of use over time • Age of users • Level of user performance (e.g. club, national) • Training use • Non-sport use (e.g. temporary car parking) • Future expansion of use
Budget	• Initial outlay • Maintenance (labour and equipment) • Replacement or major works
Site survey	• Soil composition and drift • Topography • Natural site drainage • Local ecology • Expected local weather and rainfall patterns • Site history
Maintenance	• Recommended schedule • Mowing, aeration, fertilisation, irrigation, seeding and pest control • Specialised equipment and training

When the decision about choice of turf surface is being taken, it is imperative to undertake extensive research, particularly given the broad range of systems available. Research should include site visits, referral to long-term users, examination of published research and on-site testing. This will enable the decision makers to construct a more complete picture of the product performance, maintenance requirements and safety issues. Extensive thought and planning is required to make the installation of turf a successful investment in the long term. The parameters that should be explored are presented in Table 4.2.

The guidance notes provided by Sport England's *Natural Turf for Sport* provide a detailed introduction to natural turf construction and maintenance issues for soccer, rugby union and league, cricket, hockey, tennis and bowling.

Indoor playing surfaces

The choice of floors for indoor surfaces will be heavily influenced by the requirements of the sport to be played on the surface. Where a number of sports are to be accommodated within one area, the final choice of flooring is likely to be a compromise for all codes concerned. Larger-scale facilities may have the financial resources to overcome this problem by installing flexible flooring systems. The Vodafone Arena, for example (part of the Melbourne Park complex in Australia), accommodates a 250-metre velodrome circuit, which can be covered by retractable seating stands (10 800 retractable, removable seats) in order for other events to be staged, such as basketball, Australian Open tennis or concerts.

Each sporting surface will need to fulfil certain sporting performance requirements. These can be measured using sophisticated methods, and must conform to the regulations for activities to be played on the surface. All sports will require the surface to be level and consistent, so as not to interfere with play. More specifically, the sporting performance requirements include provision for the ball–floor interaction and the person–floor interaction. For example, ball–floor interaction requirements include such properties as the spin, angular and vertical rebound characteristics of the floor. With regard to the person–floor interaction, most sports will require a degree of friction to prevent slipping but enable controlled sliding and free foot movements. Shock absorbency is another person–floor interaction variable. Even the humble community facility must consider national standards when selecting flooring surfaces for indoor sporting applications. Most countries now have standards in place regulating the degree of impact absorption that should be offered by a floor surface used for sport. These may include provision of a flooring surface that offers point elasticity (deflecting shock at a specific point of impact) or area elasticity (deflecting impact over a wider area). Some of these performance requirements are further explained in Table 4.3.

Sport England's guide, mentioned above, includes the performance parameters and British standards relevant to a wide variety of sports (Sport England 1999). The document also outlines useful information regarding types of indoor sport surfaces and the related construction methods. The materials and construction methods used for indoor surfaces vary greatly. Materials range from timber in a variety of forms (strips, blocks, composite

Table 4.3 General performance requirements of indoor sporting surfaces

Performance requirements	Property
Ball–surface interaction	• Spin characteristics • Angular rebound • Vertical rebound • Velocity change of ball
Person–surface interaction	• Traction coefficient • Slip resistance • Peak deceleration • Slip-resistant when wet or dusty • Allows controlled foot movement
Durability	• Abrasion resistance • Fatigue resistance • Low-temperature impact resistance • Spike resistance • Resistance to indentation
Environmental resistance	• Critical radiation flux value
Maintenance	• Ease of cleaning • Tolerates spillages of a range of liquids
Other	• Sustainable sourcing of timbers • Light reflectance value of 40%–50% • Visual contrast with floor marking system and walls.

Source: Adapted from Sport England (1999).

boards and composite tiles), sheet floors (rubber, vinyl, linoleum and composites), in-situ polymerics (prepared and laid on-site without joins), and textiles (felt, heavy woven fabric, velour and specialised carpets).

According to Sport England, sheet materials are generally inappropriate choices for multi-use areas unless they are combined with a support system that provides areas with elastic qualities to conform to the relevant sport standards. Similarly, the in-situ polymeric systems must have appropriate mechanisms to ensure area elasticity, such as support systems or synthetic meshes. Textile surfaces tend to be specialist surfaces for specific sports activities, such as weight training, gymnastics and aerobics, as well as temporary facilities (Sport England 1999). In other words, textile surfaces do not generally lend themselves to multi-use scenarios.

When using timber, moisture and expansion control mechanisms must be implemented. A damp-proof membrane must be installed between the subfloor and wooden floor, supplementary to that required by building regulations. In addition, a perimeter expansion gap must be provided to allow for lateral movement due to changes in humidity. The floor installed may also have specific ventilation requirements recommended by the manufacturer (Sport England 1999). Installation of subfloor heating or other facilities may be considered for the void between a subfloor and top floor surface, with provision for access panels. However, this should be thoroughly discussed with the floor manufacturer to ensure that any resulting heat and humidity do not interfere with the performance of the floor materials.

The choice of surface materials may also bear on the choice of marking system used. PVC tape may be appropriate for temporary surfaces, while painted or inlaid lines are used for permanent surfaces, depending on the base material. Markings must be accurately laid within a small error margin (generally 0.1 per cent) to comply with competition regulations (Sport England 1999). National sporting commissions may provide details regarding the recommended colours and widths of lines used for the different sporting codes.

Sport-specific regulations and specifications

Next to the consideration of more generic major issues, the design specifications need to take into consideration the regulations pertaining to a range of (sometimes smaller) sports. In other words, the facility needs to be designed from a multifunctional perspective, especially if this means that not much more design and construction money needs to be spent on accommodating a range of smaller sports. Activity spaces should be planned to accommodate the recognised dimensions and specifications for the sport that (potentially) will be played there. This may include requirements for the height of ceilings, the width and length of playing surfaces, the location of floor markings, and depth of pools. Regulations for community club participation may differ from national and competition standards.

Liaison with the relevant provincial, state and national sporting associations, in addition to government sports councils or commissions, will yield significant benefits in the planning stages. Not only will these sources have the capacity to advise on regulations, but they may also be able to offer wider expertise regarding the facility design and construction process. Sport England, for instance, publishes a number of documents to aid developers of community sports facilities. The documents, many of which are available through its website, include advice on disabled access, community hall design and considerations for using natural turf.

Roofing

Unlike many other types of buildings, sport and recreation facilities do not necessarily require complete roofing coverage. Whether a roof is required depends largely on two factors: first, the types of activities and events the facility will host; and second, the prevailing climate around the site. For instance, big-budget stadiums that are designed for use as large-scale concert venues and sporting fields often capitalise on open roofing. This is particularly useful if natural grass turf is installed, given the benefits of natural sunlight and precipitation. If inclement weather is a feature of the location, a fixed or retractable roof requires consideration.

An example of a fixed, open roof within a new international facility is the Daegu Stadium in South Korea, co-host to the 2002 football World Cup with an overall maximum capacity of 70 000. The dramatic, crescent-shaped roof structure was constructed from glass fibre membranes stretched across tubular steel arches. However, beyond the aesthetic appeal of the roof, the structure accommodates many practical features. The shape covers 70 per cent of the visitors' stand, with minimal supports that block vision. Thus, while South Korea's weather is generally hospitable to an open roof design, the 70 per cent coverage provides additional security and visitor comfort in case of bad weather.

The retractable roof has become a widespread feature in many big-budget stadiums in temperate climate zones. The Seattle Mariners' home field, for instance, is a 47 000 seat capacity grass field with 13 000 tonnes of roofing that takes 20 minutes to unfold (*Mechanical Engineering* July 1999). The design and construction of a retractable roof is obviously complex and expensive. Basic issues to be considered include the number and dimensions of retractable sections, the design of the structures that will contain the retracted sections, the wheel and rail system, logistic controllers to provide precise speed control, and staffing levels required to open and retract the roof.

Despite the popularity of the retractable roof, it is not necessarily appropriate for all conditions. In Sapporo, northern Japan, the climate makes a retractable roof impractical. Architects have designed an immense dome, without columns, that envelopes a natural grass soccer field. To maintain the grass, a pneumatic system moves the field outside to expose it to sunlight (Kubany 2002).

Smaller-scale club or community recreational facilities are obviously faced with different demands when considering roofing options. The retractable roof is here not only financially impractical but generally unnecessary. In these cases roofing choices will be influenced more by practical and financial needs than by impressive design mechanics. It is important to remember that the roof will function as more than a simple cover to waterproof the structure. The roof and ceiling cavity may also need to contain service infrastructure, such as temperature control vents and electrical conduit, and to accommodate the safe passage of service personnel. If air-conditioning systems are not possible within the budget, the choice of roofing system can allow for ventilation and temperature control, particularly for such facilities as indoor pools (Scott 2000). Acoustic linings can be considered for both walls and ceilings to facilitate sound absorption and control. The design and construction team should be able to provide recommendations regarding appropriate reverberation times for different sound frequencies. Ceiling colour should encourage the reflection of light back down to the playing area while minimising glare. Exposed ceiling and roof structures should be designed with few junctures and surfaces in which balls could become lodged.

Special building requirements

The function of some sporting and recreation facilities may necessitate the consideration of special building requirements. Indoor swimming facilities, for instance, must contend with such factors as rusting, vapour and moisture, and need a vapour barrier not only within the walls but also in the roof. Metals chosen for ducts should have an appropriate coating system applied to ensure that expensive and awkward repairs are not required in the future. Similarly, the metals used for beams, joints, trusses, stairs and seats should be chosen for their resistance to rust and corrosion.

Another example of special building requirements occurs in regions where seismic regulations are in place. The New England Patriots stadium in Foxboro, Massachusetts, needed to account for this variable. The design incorporates a framing system that results in biaxial bending, which is counteracted by cruciform columns. Splice plates connect deep trusses to the columns; during an earthquake these splice plates yield to ground motion before the trusses and columns. Seismic regulations also required the designers to consider the location of expansion joints, as swaying structures are not permitted to come into contact with them during an earthquake.

Determining the need to address special building requirements is important in the research and planning stage. Collaboration with building contractors, designers and government agencies on this point is therefore essential. Networking with managers of other facilities may also yield valuable insight.

Operational considerations

A number of operational issues need to be specifically considered from the perspective of design and building specifications. Provisions such as amenities and offices, traffic flow to and from the facility, holistic approaches to designing for maximum safety, storage and energy efficiency need to be considered first before we take a more specific look at service considerations.

Amenities

Provision of amenities should be made for male, female and special-needs customers. Reference to local building standards will outline the minimum number of facilities required based on expected capacity, as well as specifications with regard to layout. A common ratio used in the industry of female to male toilets is 3:1. Unisex access will be required to nappy-changing facilities and nappy disposal. Mechanical air-extraction units are necessary for toilets, changing rooms, kitchens and showers. A variety of options for hot water can be explored, ranging from individual water heaters to a multi-point heater and from storage systems to continuous supply. The choice of system will have implications for the cost of installation, type of pipes installed and ongoing utility costs.

It pays to consider indoor as well as outdoor access to change facilities. This enables control of traffic flow, minimisation of maintenance and cleaning in passageways, and helps to reduce the risk of falls on wet corridor surfaces. Concealed entrances to changing rooms are essential and, surprisingly, often overlooked. The amenities area is likely to be a high-access and high-maintenance area. Careful planning for customer flow in and out, customer queuing, ease of refilling soap and toilet paper as well as ease of cleaning will yield longer-term efficiency.

A pivotal consideration for the design of amenities is provision for customers who may have special needs, such as the elderly or disabled. Wheelchair-accessible toilets (and showers, if these are provided) require attention to many essential features, including:

- an adequate door width to allow the wheelchair to pass through;
- a door-opening mechanism that can be operated from a wheelchair;
- a stepless floor;
- an adequate circulation space that allows a wheelchair to enter and manoeuvre next to the toilet and basin;
- an appropriate height of toilet (usually higher than 'standard' toilet bowls);
- installation of grab rails at appropriate positions to aid customers in getting onto and off the toilet;
- an appropriate height of sink to allow access to a person seated in a wheelchair (usually lower than 'standard' sinks);
- space to allow the wheels and footplates of the wheelchair to slide under the sink;
- an appropriate mechanism for turning the tap on and off; and
- appropriate heights and positions for other items such as hand driers, toilet roll holders, mirrors, and doorknobs and locks.

As noted before, occupational therapists can provide expert consultation on access planning, particularly for elderly or disabled customers.

Administrative offices

Once the facility is officially opened, it is the administrative and operational staff who will form the lifeblood of the facility. It is at this stage that the ability of the infrastructure to support the administrative functions comes into question. In the worst-case scenario, operational and customer satisfaction difficulties can ensue if the needs of the staff are not accommodated.

As noted by Scott (2000), the provision of amenities such as a staffroom for breaks is an important consideration in facility design. While such an area is not a primary area for customer spending, it provides vital support to the staff, enabling them to better service and satisfy customers. Scott (2000) suggests that the provision of an adequate space for resting, changing clothes and completing paperwork aids in recruitment and retention. Staff will also require easy access to control systems for the facility, such as lighting panels, public address systems, temperature control systems, security and safes. Accommodating technology such as wireless systems may also be relevant to enabling staff to operate the facility optimally. (In Chapter 5 we deal more extensively with the operational structure of the facility management organisation, and discuss the types of staff needed to successfully run a sport or recreation facility, and the types of space they need to optimise their working environment.)

Traffic flow and access

Compliance with the relevant government standards for access to public spaces should be sought. These standards will outline the minimum requirements for physical accessibility to all areas of the building, including consideration for customers with disabilities. Areas for consideration include external access (pathways, stairs, railings, ramp gradient ratios, door width and door openings, hallways, height of reception windows), as well as access to toilets and showers.

The access pathways into a facility are not a mere ancillary feature. They are, in fact, the main arteries of the building. It has even been suggested that the design of a sports stadium is, in effect, the design of ways into and out of the facility (Canter, Comber & Uzzell 1989; Frosdick 1997). Provision for disabled users is a legal requirement. This, in addition to indications that slips and falls are a major cause of facility accidents, means that ramps are often preferred over stairs. Signposting and a logical, unidirectional pathway will aid traffic flow, particularly when confusion is caused in cases of emergency. Non-slip, easy-to-clean and even surfacing will further maximise safety and maintenance.

Safety design issues

The area of safety and risk management is significant and complex, and the many aspects of this area are discussed often in this book. Here we will introduce some of the broad safety and risk issues, noting the need for an integrated, ongoing strategic approach to safety management that includes expert consultation. In each country there is specific legislation pertaining to safety in sports and entertainment facilities as well as events, and subtle differences may be noted internationally.

Consistent with a systematic and strategic approach, a safety advisory group or committee should be established to consult on safety-related issues. While this is obviously pertinent to the facility when it is operational, there are advantages to using this kind of expert consultation in the design and construction phase. In addition to representative(s) from the facility, including security, occupational health and safety, and operational or building control officers, the committee will benefit from including representatives from sport-specific licensing authorities or emergency services (Frosdick 1997).

It will be the role of this committee to ensure the development, implementation and review of the safety policy and procedures. This will include ensuring that the facility complies with relevant legislation, conducting risk and safety management audits, and implementing procedures and developing other safety strategies as required in the context of the specific facility. All staff should be regularly trained in emergency procedures, the use of emergency equipment, evacuation procedures and pre-event checks. First-aid-trained staff and a core of emergency services workers (depending on the facility and event size) should be considered. Adequate provision of public address systems, fire detection systems, standby power, security surveillance cameras and control room, emergency communication, clear signage and entrance security are some of the essential elements of a safety plan (Highmore 1997). Frosdick (1997) recommends that stadium safety design should be considered as being composed of four zones, each zone having specific safety concerns. These zones are presented in Table 4.4, with our own addition of zones 5–7.

Frosdick (1997) goes on to suggest the major safety issues present in each zone, with a particular emphasis on risks associated with spectator behaviour at UK football matches. He suggests that in zone 1, the activity area, the pivotal issue is the prevention of spectator invasion. This can be addressed through physical barriers as well as such other mechanisms as security or police presence, warning signs about law infringement and education programs.

Table 4.4 Safety zone classifications

Zone	Stadium area	Safety classification
Zone 1	Activity area	Temporary safety zone
Zone 2	Viewing area	Spectator zone
Zone 3	Circulation area	Temporary safety zone
Zone 4	Outside stadium	Final safety zone
Zone 5	Staff access areas	Employee safety zone
Zone 6	Player areas	Player safety zones
Zone 7	Maintenance zones	Employee safety zone

Source: Adapted from Frosdick (1997).

It is well known that physical barriers must be designed carefully, so as not to cause additional danger to spectators. Staffed emergency exit gates are another pivotal consideration.

Safety in the viewing area, zone 2, can be aided by ensuring unobstructed views for all spectators. This will have implications for the design of roofing, seating and pavilions as well as other features such as lighting poles, scoreboards and goals. Varying sports may require different viewing configurations (e.g. athletics as opposed to rugby), which may need to be accommodated through creative or flexible design solutions such as movable seating systems. The principle here is that conditions that encourage spectators to remain seated will contribute to spectator safety. Standing areas obviously cannot fulfil this requirement, but if they are planned it is important that they not be positioned in zones where they are subject to pressure from crowd surges or high densities of spectators. Alternatively, standing areas can be restricted to non-spectator zones (e.g. food and beverage consumption zones) to minimise the potential for inter-spectator agitation.

Circulation zones, zone 3 in Frosdick's (1997) classification, are largely composed of the natural access and exit pathways to and from the facility. Natural human behaviour in crisis situations will lead spectators to try to exit a facility in the same way they entered it. A logical consequence of this knowledge is that the most 'natural' exit points of a facility are critical when planning for (emergency) circulation zones. Lots of people need to be able to leave the facility in a short time without being exposed to the danger of being crushed in the moving masses. Circulation zones can therefore also be considered to include entry gates and foyers where adequate safety screening measures may be required, such as bag checks and metal detection devices. The use of ticketing design to discourage forgeries can contribute to the overall safety plan, effectively eliminating the danger of overcrowding in certain areas of the stadium.

The area external to the stadium, zone 4, has been addressed to some degree in the discussion surrounding site location. Ease of vehicle access to and egress from the building, particularly during peak times, can influence pedestrian safety and the ability of emergency services to enter or exit the facility. Generous access to public transport will enable better safety management for the simple reason that it solves another part of the 'crowding' problem. Only because the organisers of the Sydney 2000 Olympic Games ensured virtually continuous transport by train away from the Olympic Park at the peak of the program could several hundred thousands of people obtain a seat on a train within 40 minutes of the finish of the event they visited. Finishing times of events were further planned to enable the train station to deliver its maximum transport capacity of 50 000 people per hour.

There are other risk areas within a sports facility that are not mentioned in Frosdick's (1997) model, given that it relates primarily to *spectator* safety. Employee access areas, maintenance worker/contractor and player zones must also be considered. For example, the playing surface needs to be prepared as a safe working environment for professional athletes after the facility has hosted a rock concert in the main arena. In addition, there are safety issues to be considered during the construction process. The tendering process should ensure that contractors provide evidence of adequate experience, health and safety policies and procedures, a hazard identification system, as well as liability and employee insurances.

Energy efficiency

The introduction of energy efficiency measures during the facility planning process has the potential to provide both environmentally friendly outcomes and significant cost savings. The lighting of sport facilities, for example, has received considerable attention because of its capacity for 'bottom-line' benefits. Providing for optimal natural light in indoor facilities and installing automatic dimming systems are examples of such considerations. Kennedy (2000) considers some lighting and efficiency issues for outdoor fields, including the use of metal halide lamps for sports fields and the importance of the positioning and height of and material used for light poles.

Other diverse considerations arise when planning for lighting-based energy efficiency measures, such as television broadcast requirements, making a comprehensive plan a considerable task. And lighting is but one element of facility energy efficiency planning, which may include heating, cooling, water treatment, turf maintenance, and cleaning issues. Energy efficiency planning is therefore a highly specialised and complex component of successful sport facility design and construction, but one that has the capacity to influence the facility's fortunes significantly. Cost savings can be enormous, and the political and personal benefits of designing an environmentally supportive venue are also significant.

Energy efficiency is a goal that will affect other services, including temperature control. Avoidance or minimisation of the use of air conditioning can be achieved through the careful planning of ventilation. Intensive night ventilation, for instance, can be applied to cool down the thermal mass (particularly exposed ceilings) of the building. Insulation of the building envelope is another important parameter to be exploited. Innovative architectural design can also improve the 'natural' ventilation capability of the facility. For example, the Sydney 2000 Dunc Gray Velodrome won an award for ecologically sustainable design, largely as a result of its innovative passive ventilation and natural day-lighting system, which dramatically decreases its dependence on electrical energy consumption. The ventilation system is designed in a way that during hot summer days the natural flow draws in colder air from underneath the facility, sucking the air through ventilation holes in spectators' seats and releasing hot air through the roofing system.

Increasingly, (building) authorities are setting minimum energy efficiency standards that builders are required to meet. A commitment to a specified level of energy efficiency (such as a star rating), with consideration of greenhouse gas emissions and appliance use, may well put a sport facility in a position of world best practice, providing a marketing opportunity to put the facility 'on the map' and fix it in the minds of consumers. Energy efficiency standards should be made explicit to the design and construction team, and should become part of the building brief.

Storage

Scott (2000) makes the observation that although it is often said you can never build too much storage, storage facilities are inevitably the first casualties of budget cuts. While storage spaces cannot be converted into primary spend areas, they are a vital support system. The capacity to adequately store equipment and supplies ensures that customers will have unimpeded physical access to service areas, increasing satisfaction and reducing occupational health and safety risks. In addition, adequate storage should enable staff to access equipment without requiring inappropriate manual handling risks, such as awkward and heavy lifting. Doors to the storage area must be wide enough to enable passage of the largest items of equipment or furniture that need storage but also regular movement to event-designated usage areas. Fireproofing may be required for the storage of certain items, such as plastic foam mats, as well as a smoke detection system.

Storage planning is best undertaken with advice from those who are going to utilise stored items on a day-to-day basis. If prospective staff have not been identified or hired at this stage, consultation with staff from similar facilities will deliver significant operational knowledge that can be applied when day-to-day operation is commenced. Fundamentally, equipment and furniture storage should be directly accessible from the areas they service. Generally, an open-plan area with flexible shelving will accommodate most needs, particularly if floor and wall markings delineate areas for large items. Lockable compartments are also worth considering for specialised equipment or clubs' assets—also storage for customers' prams/push chairs, baggage, coats and lost property, preferably close to the entrance area.

Storage facilities should be planned for cleaning and maintenance equipment. This should be equipped with shelving, appropriate lockable cupboards for the storage of chemicals (as indicated by local occupational health and safety regulations), as well as hot and cold running water and large sinks.

Service considerations

Having taken care of broader operational issues, we can now take a more specific look at design considerations that relate to optimising service delivery to customers. Issues such as seating, scoreboards, lighting, parking/transport, media/broadcasting, child care and temperature control all have a direct impact on (end) consumer satisfaction levels, and can largely be prepared for in the design and building stages of the facility.

Seating

Issues to be considered when selecting seating options include cost, visual impression, ergonomic features, durability, ease of maintenance, and coordination with overall construction. Whether the seats are to be used for a corporate box or for public access stadium seating will, of course, dramatically affect these variables.

Durability can be facilitated by the use of corrosion-resistant materials, flexible plastics to prevent snapping, plastics that minimise UV radiation damage, and features to minimise opportunity for vandalism. Other characteristics (particularly in stadium seating) may include ventilation holes and full back support to prevent the intrusion of feet from spectators seated behind. The ease of removing seats can also be an advantage in instances where it is required to replace damaged seats or to attach new sponsorship logos.

In addition to these variables, the choice of seating may be affected by more unusual features that are designed to delight the venue's customers. The materials and design of seating in the Denver Broncos' stadium, for instance, were chosen in part to enhance the stomping noise of spectators during a game (Gonchar 2001).

Scoreboards

The scoreboard needs of the local basketball club and those of a state-of-the-art international-standard stadium are worlds apart. The greatest difference, perhaps, is the potential for the mega-stadium to broadcast streaming vision, such as replays and advertisements. However, both ends of the facility spectrum should consider the scoreboard as one of the prime spaces for sponsorship exposure. This is one of the locations where spectator gaze is guaranteed. The scoreboard at the Baltimore Orioles' baseball field takes on the form of a sculptural object, and as a consequence is marketed as being more attractive for sponsorship (Brake 2002). In the case of large stadia where games are televised, the promotion of sponsors may require complicated arrangements with broadcasters serving their own corporate interests. In the case of the local club, the scoreboard provides an outstanding opportunity to garner support from local business.

Lighting

The lighting system for a facility includes three broad elements: the daylight system, the artificial system, and the controls. Maximising natural lighting facilitates energy efficiency, as previously mentioned. However, an artificial system and associated controls must still be selected. Evaluating artificial lighting options for a facility involves the consideration of disparate issues. For example, energy efficiency, uniformity of illumination, luminaire type, radiation of heat, placement and type of lighting poles, specialised broadcasting needs, visual comfort, initial and ongoing costs, as well as ease of cleaning and replacing lamps, may all play a part in the lighting decision.

Fortunately, technology is helping to ease the decision-making process. Lighting innovations now allow for enhanced illumination at lower cost, particularly when compared with traditional incandescent lighting. Metal halide lamps, for instance, are a form of high-intensity discharge lighting. Metal halides emit more than five times the light of incandescent lights without producing intense heat (Kennedy 2000). Metal halides also have superior colour rendition, which is particularly important for televised events. (After all, the Redbacks would not want to look more like 'peachy-backs' under high-pressure sodium vapour lamps.) According to Weber (2002), broadcast-quality lighting usually requires a minimum of 75 foot-candle lighting, as opposed to the 50 foot-candle lighting for non-broadcast purposes.

Uniformity of lighting coverage is another important consideration in lighting design. Better lighting coverage leads to an enhanced uniformity—in other words, no dark areas. Uniformity can be measured as a ratio of the brightest to the darkest area of a field: the lower the number, the better. Greater lighting uniformity can be achieved by determining the best horizontal and vertical angles for all of the lights. Computer programs are now available to aid in this process. Using different lighting patterns, including patterns that combine wide and narrow beams, can further decrease dark areas.

The position, height and use of appropriate material for lighting poles can also have an impact on whether the field is adequately illuminated. Kennedy (2000) suggests that wooden poles, for example, may warp and require the lights to be re-angled as often as annually, making metal poles a more attractive option. The height of the poles needs to accommodate the variety of activities that will be played on the field, for example illuminating not only a hand-thrown football but also the high trajectory of a baseball or cricket ball. With pole positions, it is usually better to avoid obstructing spectator views by placing them behind bleachers. Installing lighting poles adjacent to bleachers will limit future options to extend seating.

Lighting infrastructure is a consideration even in smaller-scale sports fields, as well as the large state and national facilities. High school sports fields, for example, particularly in the United States, and regional competition centres are increasingly addressing the need for night-time illumination. The initial investment may be substantial, but the resulting boost in participation and revenue balances the scorecard (Weber 2002). Lighting is also important in car parking areas, for both safety and security. Time-clock or sensor controls will be required for all external illumination.

Sport England (2001) provides a summary of typical parameters for illumination and temperate control of community-based sports facilities (Table 4.5). While this is not provided as a rigid guide for planning, it emphasises the complexity of illumination, ventilation and temperature control systems through the different areas of a facility. Numerous factors may further influence the levels required in a specific facility, such as local regulations, competition specifications, and the standard temperature range in a given region.

Parking/transport

Increasing ease of transport access to a venue is an important factor in encouraging repeat customer patronage. For large state and national projects it can also yield benefits in terms of environmental management. The Sydney Olympics site, for instance, is serviced by a rail system that can handle 50 000 people per hour, terminating at the award-winning Olympic station (McGuigan 2000). The timetabling of trains can obviously cater for the reduced demand post-Olympics, and reflects the need for collaborative partnerships with the transport providers.

Accommodating a temporary demand for parking is an issue faced by designers of facilities that are home to one-off or even annual events. The major site for the Salt Lake City Winter Olympics 2002 created a temporary parking lot and drop-off area, now being restored to its natural state (Lewandowski 2002).

Media/broadcasting

Beyond the logistics of space and accessibility, accommodating the broadcasting and media needs of a facility demands consideration of significant technological issues. At the time of writing, high-level sports and entertainment venues were addressing the need to install wireless technology to allow for high-speed connection between media personnel and their outlets and publishers. In addition, major sport events organisers are concerned with providing

Table 4.5 Summary of typical parameters for illumination and temperature control for community facilities

Facility area	Temperature (°C)	Illumination (lux)	Air change (rate per hour)
Main hall	12–20	300–400	1.5–3.0
Secondary halls	18–21	300	1.5–3.0
Lounge	21	200	
Foyer	18	200	
Office	21	500	
Bar	21	100–200	
Bar store	10	100	
Kitchen	18	500	20
Equipment store	10	100	
Toilets/change rooms	20–21	100	6–10

Source: Sport England (2001).

impressive display screens for spectators and VIPs, as well as facilitating state-of-the-art coverage by commercial and pay-TV providers.

The installation of wireless technology for sport event photographers represents one of the latest media advances. Sydney's Telstra Stadium, for instance, completed the installation of wireless technology for photographers in May 2003. The system used wireless LAN products based on the IEEE802.11b worldwide standard, running at 11 Mbps. Traditionally, photographers were forced to transmit their digital files after the game, which is often a time-consuming process. Wireless technology now enables the photographers to transmit their images instantly to their photo editors, while the game is still in progress. The photo editors are able to provide immediate feedback to the photographer, potentially resulting in improved coverage and higher-quality images.

The installation of broadcasting technology is usually a consideration for large stadia (including college stadia in the United States) and sporting events that occupy a temporary space. The technical requirements for this infrastructure are in a constant state of flux, and demand a great deal of flexibility and negotiation by facility and event managers. The Fosters British Grand Prix, for example, has attempted to remain ahead of the game. It collaborated with technology providers CT Screenco in order to service the 2003 track with 17 giant video screens, ranging from 30 to 40 square metre displays. Many of the screens are new-generation, self-elevation mobile displays, which are mounted on masts and therefore minimise the logistical difficulties of installing large structures. In addition, the VIP and hospitality areas were serviced by 6–12 square metre screens.

Establishing and maintaining a capacity for broadcasting involves a partnership between the facility, the broadcaster and technology providers. The physical spaces required for on-site broadcasting include a studio or commentary booth, production control room, communication and control apparatus bays, a VT hall for editing of vision, off-tube booth, dressing room, editorial and production offices, and secure storage for cameras. The technological requirements, however, usually demand a flexible and collaborative approach, given the pace of innovations in this area.

Childcare facilities

The provision of, or access to, childcare or crèche facilities becomes an issue of increasing importance with facilities of growing size. The local football club is unlikely to consider this factor, given the nature of its use, but community-based recreational facilities, as well as large state and national facilities, often need to consider the childcare needs of their staff and customers. For example, a facility that plans to attract 30–40-year-old women to a fitness program must consider the likelihood of the customers' need to accommodate young children. Larger employers may include child care as a component in their staff benefit and equal opportunity programs.

Consultation with a state or national child safety information service may provide invaluable information on the physical design of the space, but the design of a physical space for crèche facilities is only the first step in this complex service area. The operational considerations of a childcare facility are substantial, with government regulations often detailing such requirements as training and accreditation, occupational health and safety, and staff-to-child ratios. In some instances a facility may be able to accommodate these needs by establishing a relationship with a local childcare facility, without establishing its own service.

Temperature control

Surprisingly, the need for heating and cooling is often overlooked, due to budgetary restrictions. It is false economy to ignore provision of these control systems and expect that they can be accommodated at a later stage. Like all areas of construction and infrastructure, technology is continually extending the options available to facility managers. Engineering advice is invaluable in this area, as careful planning of natural ventilation can contribute significantly to cooling systems and therefore add to energy efficiency. Options for heating include underfloor systems, as well as ducted warm air and radiant panels. Insulation levels that create a well-sealed building envelope are essential. The location of master controls is another important consideration. (Energy efficiency issues surrounding control of temperature have already been discussed.)

Secondary spend areas

From the perspective of the sport facility manager and the sport event manager, areas for secondary spend are essential to the commercial success of the venture. Other avenues towards revenue maximisation need to be fully exploited, especially when the facility operators have only limited access to the revenue pie that is represented by event broadcasting rights. It will come as no surprise that how a facility is designed, taking into consideration how people (staff and customers) move through the facility, will determine where customers are most likely to spend money. Hence, service providers need to be located to present customers with opportunities to buy.

Merchandising

The scope of merchandising facilities should directly reflect the anticipated spectator capacity calculated for the sport facility. Small, community facilities can usually accommodate merchandise in the front reception, which minimises space and staffing requirements. The dedicated shopfront, the temporary merchandise tent and roaming sales staff are three additional options used in medium to large facilities. Market research conducted at the pre-design stage should determine *how*, *where* and *what* potential customers will purchase. Like other secondary spend areas, such as food and beverage, merchandising may offer possibilities for outsourcing.

Food and beverages

Like many operational services, food and beverage facilities are increasingly likely to be commercial services provided by external companies that have successfully tendered for the privilege. The tendering process should be commenced well before construction in order to allow the successful company to collaborate with the design and construction teams. Infrastructure and design needs may be unique to the provider. The type of food and beverages available should reflect the needs of the customer as determined in the planning phase. Focus groups, for example, can be used to elicit ideas for the prospective facility users about the produce they are most likely to buy, and under what conditions. This approach can potentially be delegated to the service operators as part of the tender process, and will increase the likelihood of customer loyalty. However, it is important not only what people like to eat and drink but also when, how often and why they leave their seat to buy food or drinks. This behaviour varies dramatically across a range of sports. For example, the US baseball leagues offer frequent 'time-out' opportunities for fans to leave their seat to get some food: it is part of the tradition of watching baseball to eat hot dogs and drink beer with friends in the stands. Soccer matches, on the other hand, offer few opportunities to leave the action because of the continuous play and few goal-scoring occasions. Stadium developers in the US based Major League Soccer have started to build food and beverage stands facing the field of play in order to allow spectators to continue viewing the action while buying food and drinks. In other words, smart design, where designers and builders have put themselves in the customer's seat, leads to increased secondary spend.

Architectural identity

In order to put the new facility on the marketing map and position the facility in the minds of consumers, 'localising' a facility, be it a temporary or permanent venue, will greatly enhance the architectural identity of the place.

Localising a facility

Localising a facility design can be a useful adjunct to the overall marketing plan. This can be achieved by the use of unique design elements reflecting the character of the city, district or country. Used as a promotional tool, a strong architectural identity can facilitate media coverage, local community pride and even international attention.

Preparation for the 2004 Olympics in Athens included the development of a localised facility for the weightlifting competition. A concrete amphitheatre was built in a disused quarry in Nikaia, a low-income suburb of Athens. The 'House of the Weightlifters' is the world's first purpose-built stadium for a sport that does not usually attract much attention. The $US34 million complex was designed to echo the amphitheatres of the ancient Greek and

Roman world, with a spot of natural light falling on the athlete through a circular gap in the stadium's roof, and panoramic views of western Athens—from the rocky Aegaleo Mountain, to Acropolis hill and the Parthenon.

Similarly, the Denver Broncos' new $US384 million, 76 000 seat stadium has been injected with the Denver spirit, thanks to its horseshoe-shaped design that opens towards the mountains. The upper seating bowl takes an undulating shape, mimicking the profile of the mountains as well as conveying the idea of a saddle. The designers have even enhanced the ability of fans to make 'Rocky Mountain thunder', the deafening rumble designed to intimidate the opposition teams. This was achieved by selecting specific seating units where the 'rakers' and 'stringers' supporting each seat were sized to accommodate the frequencies created by stomping and rhythmic dancing.

The temporary facility

Temporary facilities are increasingly being considered as an option where research suggests that usage levels will not support a facility beyond the scope of a finite event. Major sport events are in some cases being managed like a travelling circus, with organisers erecting temporary event structures that reduce costs and improve location flexibility.

Architects, for instance, have presented a series of temporary options as part of London's bid for the 2012 Olympic Games. This is based on the understanding that a 20 000 seat capacity swimming pool is not needed in London. The temporary options include a 50-metre pool built on a football pitch, and a 'floating pool'. The former option would involve the digging up of the stadium to allow a temporary pool to be inserted, with a temporary, helium-filled roof. A smaller, permanent pool would then be built adjacent to the site for warm-ups. The floating pool could be towed to a site and anchored alongside an onshore grandstand. After the games, the tank could be towed to another location and reused. Again, a permanent but smaller pool could be constructed next to the location and used by the community after the Olympic event.

Lewandowski (2002) states that the construction of major facilities for singular events is particularly worrisome, with the world 'littered with Olympic sites that were used for a month and then, effectively, abandoned' (p. 86). The cross-country skiing facility developed for the 2002 Salt Lake City Games serves as an example of how to avoid this problem. Extensive planning has been invested in transforming the site into an ongoing legacy for the local community. A legacy foundation has been established to facilitate this, aiming to attract as many different demographic groups as possible to ensure the ongoing viability of the site. Examples of the programs they have pioneered include a school-based skiing program that attracted 6000 students in its first year of operation. Off-season sees the day lodge being used as an information centre, as well as a venue for horse and bicycle rentals. Athletes can also use rollerskis over a paved, three-kilometre section of the course.

Facility development for the 2004 Athens Olympics also attracted interest in temporary design. Options for demountable designs were explored, such as facilities that could hold 15 000 spectators for sports such as boxing. While these kinds of structure have the advantage of being fast to erect, their construction includes the use of PVC (as well as metal and recycled components from the Millennium Dome), and may therefore raise questions about environmental sustainability.

The temporary facility also means temporary infrastructure. Portable seating, mobile lighting trucks, catering, and technology for live screening of the event represent the tip of the iceberg. The 2003 UEFA Champions League final had to tackle these problems when it transformed the area outside the stands into an impressive, tented hospitality village for the major sponsors. The area boasted a complete relay distribution that provided guests with live action and looped highlights of previous rounds, together with pre- and post-game statistical information. The venue was themed and marketed as Old Trafford's 'Theatre of Dreams'.

Summary

The emphasis of this chapter has been on the planning, design and project management aspects of facility development. Clearly, there are myriad specific building and construction issues that are beyond the scope of this book. We therefore emphasise the need to collaborate and seek expert consultation throughout the design and construction process. As the client, the initiator of the project needs to understand the broad logistical, political and conceptual issues, and to receive advice from experts. The client does not need to know how to install a retractable roof. What the project requires is a team capable of successfully negotiating the inevitable difficulties that will arise during design and construction. The team developing the new Denver Broncos stadium, for instance, faced challenges due to land acquisition delays. Because different parcels of land became available at different times, the project was unable to continue in the traditional sequence, where each project subcontractor works progressively around the field, race-track style. Instead, the stadium was constructed in the form of eight mid-rise buildings, the different sections being built from the ground up as the land was acquired.

Case study

Designing and building the Manchester Aquatics Centre

Having considered significant background information regarding the 2002 Manchester Commonwealth Games during the case study in Chapter 2, the opportunity to build on and enrich that knowledge is utilised here. On this occasion we specifically consider the design and development of the Manchester Aquatics Centre, as described by Bill Stonor in his article 'The design of Manchester Aquatics Centre' (2001). A brief description of events surrounding the development of this particular facility provides a meaningful introduction to the subsequent discussion regarding facility design and construction.

Following the City of Manchester's successful bid for the 2002 Commonwealth Games, it was apparent that the existing aquatic facilities were inadequate to host the event. The five water sports events (swimming, diving, water polo, synchronised swimming and synchronised diving) required an international-standard venue, while the local community would benefit from a new recreational pool facility. In other words, the resulting project necessitated balancing the 1 per cent needs of the two-week Commonwealth Games with those of a 99 per cent community legacy. The project also involved coordination between three bodies, the Manchester client, the Amateur Swimming Federation of Great Britain (ASFGB), and Sport England. Having employed a specialist group to undertake a feasibility study, select a site and determine a budget, the city attempted to move systematically towards the development of a detailed designer and building brief that satisfied these at times competing needs.

The decision was made to capitalise on an existing international facility located less than 40 miles from Manchester, therefore limiting the size requirements of new developments. The existing site, known as Ponds Forge, was earmarked to remain the premier international spectator pool in the United Kingdom. As a result, the facility development in Manchester did not need to accommodate regular international events, and could be designed at 75–80 per cent of the overall size of Ponds Forge. Obviously this facilitated substantial savings, not only on initial capital investment but also with regard to ongoing maintenance.

Flexible use of the pool was facilitated by the installation of movable floors in both the main and diving pools. In fact, as of 2002 the Manchester Aquatics Centre boasts the world's largest area of movable floors within any one facility (1360 m^2). This enabled the water to meet the FINA depth standards (2 m for the standard pool, 5 m for the diving pool), as well as accommodating recreational use in shallower water. Temporary seats were also erected over a third pool, the 250-metre permanent shallow leisure and fun pool with two flume rides, which was otherwise not required for the Games. This helped to overcome the 1 per cent versus 99 per cent equation of spectator requirements. In other words, while the Commonwealth Games required a capacity of 2500 seats, general capacity requirements were estimated to be in the realm of 1250 seats. As a result, only 1250 permanent seats were planned, with an additional 1250 temporary seats used for the Games.

The facility design incorporated café and fitness and health areas, and a crèche, all of which would be accessible from the main pool hall and its spectator gallery, so that they could be used as support spaces for the Commonwealth Games (press room, VIPs and officials etc.). An entrance foyer, changing rooms, administration offices and heating, ventilation, electrical and water treatment plant rooms were also included in the facility design.

Before answering a number of questions, please consider the following information:

- **design and construction budget**—£22 million (includes pool building, external works, equipment and infrastructure);
- **location**—a prominent, central location was selected between three universities, two of which provided adjacent sites to maximise the space available (UMIST and Manchester Victoria University);
- **the tender process**—following completion of the design, tenders were sought for a contractor; evaluation criteria included costs, supplier resources, key staff and organisational skills. The design team and contractor cooperated in seeking tenders for construction, finishing and servicing suppliers. The contractor then formulated, negotiated and took responsibility for a final, fixed cost before the commencement of work;
- **major community stakeholder organisations**—the City of Manchester, Manchester

Victoria University, UMIST University, Manchester Metropolitan University, the Amateur Swimming Association of Great Britain, and Sport England;

- **facility dimensions**—basement 3500 m², ground floor 5500 m², upper level 3000 m²;
- **major design criteria**—a strong architectural presence on Oxford Road; sensitivity in terms of materials used and effect of total building mass on neighbouring facilities (including UMIST business school and a cluster of residential blocks);
- **major design resolution**—the design was made to coalesce with neighbouring facilities, by using stone from the same quarry as was used for the business school as the major cladding material. The graceful curve of the roof mimics the contour of a wave, and ensures that the maximum height is achieved for the highest diving platform without unnecessarily dominating the landscape;
- **special design features**—although standard in major national training centres, a system was installed in the diving pool to release large bubbles during training. This cushions the impact of the diver, which aids in injury prevention;
- **energy efficiency**—high insulation levels minimise the need for artificial temperature control. The wave-like roof greatly minimises the open space that would have been created by a traditional geometric design, thus curtailing problems from control of temperature and atmosphere. The control of the pool atmosphere is further enhanced by a cleansing and recycling system;
- **water treatment**—given predictions that the shallow water pools would be subjected to the heaviest leisure use, two water treatment systems were installed: first, the customary sand-bed filtration system was used, with the addition of an ozonation system, which minimises necessary chlorine levels; second, partial ozonation was installed in the 50-metre training pool, together with a value system to enable the 2-metre deep water to be occasionally flushed with ozonated water;
- **layout**—the facility is designed according to a simple floor plan. This maximises the ability of customers to access different zones, makes emergency and evacuation plans straightforward, and facilitates ease of staff transfer within the building;
- **completion of works**—completion of works occurred 10 weeks ahead of schedule and approximately two years before the 2002 Commonwealth Games;
- **appointment of management**—the management team was appointed three months before completion of the contract.

Source: Adapted from Stonor (2001).

*Q. Considering the basic design and construction issues arising from building modern-day **multipurpose** sporting facilities, how would you rate the Manchester Aquatics Centre in terms of its ability to cater for a range of events?*

Q. Knowing that aquatic facilities rarely deliver a profit to their owners, what would you have focused on when designing the facility and briefing the builders on the critical aspects of construction?

Q. Are there any design features that you would consider to be vital in order to maximise the facility's multi-purpose flexibility? In that context, who would you describe as the Centre's most important customers?

5

Developing new sport facilities: preparing the facility management infrastructure

CHAPTER OBJECTIVES

In this chapter, we will:
- Introduce the concept of organisational structure.
- Discuss the dimensions of organisational structure.
- Overview the key staff functions for sport facilities.
- Discuss the processes of staff performance and remuneration management.
- Discuss the issues relating to outsourcing facility management labour.
- Discuss the issues relating to occupational health and safety.

Ultimately, it is people who will do the job

Chapter 4 has brought us to the point of having established a well-designed, soundly constructed and aesthetically appropriate facility. However, it remains an empty building that needs to be fitted with human infrastructure in order to fulfil its intended purposes. The staff of the facility is charged with the tasks of managing the physical space, physical structures, as well as the services and events that occur in the facility.

The staffing needs of a facility will be driven by a number of factors. These include the objectives of the organisation, its service quality philosophy and its structure. The service quality philosophy of the facility operator, for instance, will drive staffing needs, such as minimum qualifications and full- versus part-time appointments.

In this chapter we will overview the range of management functions that are specific to the preparation and operation of the sport facility. Moreover, we will not take the perspective of one specific facility type: rather, we will aim to overview functions that relate to major arenas, public sport facilities, temporary event sites, and public/private health and fitness facilities. Rather than providing one organisation chart, this approach will ensure that we consider a wider range of functions, allowing you to pick and choose and apply a chart to your specific facility context.

Organisational structures

Today's highly competitive, global marketplace has seen a proliferation of many different styles of organisational structure. As observed by Graetz, Rimmer, Lawrence and Smith (2002), in order to be profitable, organisations must now function flexibly, with high market sensitivity and a participative work environment. In order to perform in this responsive and competitive manner, sport facility operators must evaluate the most appropriate organisational structure to adopt. This involves not only establishing structure and locations of responsibility but also ensuring that the appropriate procedures, resources and staff skills are in place to support the organisational structure.

The traditional hierarchical structure has been criticised in recent times for lacking market responsiveness and discouraging human resources from maximising their potential within an organisation. Closely linked to the hierarchical model is the functional structure, a rigid, highly formalised organisational composition. This structure is based on the idea of organising according to specialised areas such as sales and marketing, finance and human resources. It suggests that an organisation should be structured according to different functional areas, hence the label 'functional structure'. While the functional approach facilitates efficiencies within each work function, the overall structure has been criticised for lacking responsiveness and flexibility.

The divisional structure represents an attempt to relax the rigid formalities of the functional structure. Separate divisions or departments are established to manage differing goods, services or even regions, which represents geographic divisionalisation. Each division is serviced by its own units (e.g. finance or personnel). This configuration offers the advantage of allowing increased responsiveness within each division, but one obvious drawback is the duplication of resources within departments and the loss of specialisation.

The matrix structure represents an effort to combine the efficiency of the functional approach with the responsiveness of the divisional composition, while encouraging subordinate employees to participate in decision making (Graetz et al. 2002). A matrix structure is often used in organisations that deal with many non-routine tasks and where relationships and responsibilities constantly change in order to meet the needs of the particular project at hand. Reporting relationships are vertical (the traditional hierarchy), for example, to a functional manager in finance or marketing; and horizontal, to what is often a project manager. As can be appreciated, the project manager deals with all the functional specialists across the project (left to right), whereas the functional manager deals with all the functional specialists across all projects (top to bottom). Predictably, the main criticism of this model is due to the increased likelihood of conflicts in lines of authority and responsibility, but it may not come as a surprise that many event organisations use matrix structures to manage the diverse needs of the event.

A more recent paradigm in organisational structure is the networked organisation, or the 'loosely coupled system' (Limerick & Cunnington 1993). Essentially this model aims to dismantle barriers between divisions by establishing small, networked units where relationships are the key consideration. Depending on the resources and skills a work project requires, different units may operate autonomously or pool resources as a project team. In other words, it is a form of project-based organising, as opposed to organising based on structure. Of course, there are many different ways in which a networked organisation may configure itself (Graetz et al. 2002). For example, the organisation may still operate with centralised planning and formal, hierarchical lines of responsibility and thus resemble a traditional pyramid structure in many ways. Alternatively, the networked structure may be more 'truly' networked, in other words decentralised and flexible with strong horizontal rather than vertical communication. This structure, of course, is of particular relevance for event-organising organisations, as these require high levels of 'on the spot' problem-solving flexibility, in both preparing and hosting the event.

Innovations in organisational structure

Although many forms of managing and organising have evolved in the recent past, this does not mean that the hierarchy has ceased to exist at all. It is perhaps more accurate to suggest that the hierarchy is one element of a complex organism with other, equally important elements playing vital roles. Graetz et al. (2002) suggest that the 'emphasis is no longer on structure and control, functional hierarchy, size and scale, costs and efficiencies, decision-making and planning, but on relationships and processes, collaboration and inclusion, flexibility and boundary spanning, creativity and change' (p. 154).

In other words, these changes in traditional organisational arrangements represent a shift in emphasis from organising around structure to organising around processes and relationships. Ghoshal and Bartlett (1995) suggest that three core processes, rather than structure, underpin successful management in today's knowledge economy. These are encouraging initiative (an entrepreneurial process), linking and maximising competence (an integrative process), and managing downsizing and regeneration (a renewal process). Similarly, Kanter (1996) advocates the use of three key strategies—namely, building synergies, establishing alliances, and encouraging 'streams' of new information—in order to establish an organisation that is responsive and competitive. *Synergies* operate best in environments with a flatter organisational structure (less hierarchical), where employees have greater involvement in workplace decisions and processes encourage integration across functional departments. Developing *strategic alliances* refers to building collaborative relationships with other organisations, such as suppliers to whom the organisation has outsourced non-core services (Whittington, Pettigrew, Peck, Fenton & Conyon 1999). The establishment of *new information streams* refers to the building of formal communication lines that ensure that new ideas do not become 'lost in the system'. In summarising the observations made by Kanter about the newly emerging organisational form, Graetz et al. (2002, p. 142) state the following:

> It is person not position centred, emphasising expertise and relationships rather than power and status . . . it is concerned with developing best practice through diversity, creativity and innovation, not specialisation and repetition; it is results rather than rules oriented, encouraging its people to experiment and take risks; it recognises and rewards individual and group endeavours, not rank or position; it operates and finds opportunities through its range of intra- and inter-organisational networks, rather than relying on formal structures and channels of communication (and, in this way, seeks to expand rather than restrict the flow of information); and is renewal rather than stability oriented, continually seeking to leverage new opportunities and empower its work-force, rather than pursuing ownership and control.

Once again, in service-based industries such as sporting events, where the delivery of the event service is a one-off opportunity to impress the customer, a rigid control-based organisational structure would restrict event employees in their ability to optimise the service experience. Free-flowing information combined with an empowered ability for most staff to 'act on the spot' are characteristics of a structure in which customer satisfaction can be optimised.

Whittington et al. (1999) evaluated the management practices associated with organisational innovations in 450 large and medium-sized European companies. Specifically, they noted changes in management practices that occurred across three organisational design dimensions:

Dimension	Management practices
Structure	1. Delayering (reducing layers between highest and lowest levels of management)
	2. Decentralising operational and strategic decision making
	3. Project-based organising (collaboration, cross-functional teams)
Processes	1. Increased vertical communication (reinforcing the hierarchy in the context of delayering and decentralisation).
	2. Increased horizontal communication
	3. Information technology infrastructure investment (facilitating vertical and horizontal integration)
	4. New HR practices (organisation-wide mission building activities, team-building, increased horizontal communication channels, organisation-wide workshops)

Dimension	Management practices
External boundaries	1. Increased outsourcing (particularly in large and 'knowledge' based sectors) 2. Developing strategic alliances 3. Downscoping (moving from unrelated to related diversification)

Developing the HR structure in a sports facility: staffing functions

Having established the broad parameters around which a sports facility organisation may be structured, it is important to determine its specific staffing requirements. Broadly speaking, each functional area of the facility will require specialised human resource skills. Table 5.1 provides a general overview of (some) staffing functions, including management, administrative, customer service and maintenance considerations. Some key considerations of the personnel expertise required for each function are listed in Table 5.1.

Outsourcing and contract management

Before we outline the broader functions that staff in a sport facility have to fulfil, it is important to briefly discuss the issues of outsourcing and contract management (of which a practical application will be presented in the case study at the end of the chapter). Many industries and, hence, organisations in those industries have gone through a cycle of rapid economic growth and expansion, then into economic decline and rationalisation or even downsizing. The latter process in particular often leads to the question: What is the core business of the organisation? This is an important question, because it makes management of the organisation focus on what it does best, and on which areas it is most likely to be successful and thus profitable in. If the answer to the above question leads to the observation that a lot of 'non-core business' is being conducted 'in-house', the issue of potentially outsourcing that part of the business becomes an important business consideration. In order to successfully outsource parts of the non-core activities of the organisation, well-defined specifications need to be established; equally importantly, when the business is brought to the open marketplace for tender, the successful tenderer needs to be monitored in order to ensure high-quality provision of outside services.

The process of 'competitive tendering', for example, security or catering contracts in a sport facility, first ensures that 'specialist' providers compete against each other to provide the sport facility with the best and most cost-effective service package. Competitive tendering also provides the range of tendering organisations with the stimulus to constantly review and upgrade their service offerings in order to remain competitive. This benefits the professionalism of the industry as a whole. As the outcome of a successful tendering process, a comprehensive and specific contract will be drawn up between sport facility management and the outside provider in order to have a clear and agreed overview of service specifications and the requirements of both parties involved, allowing for quality monitoring and continuous improvement.

There are, of course, a variety of ways in which to contract the full range of non-core services. The past two decades have seen a growing emphasis on the benefits of outsourcing,

Table 5.1 Summary of key staffing functions for sport facilities

Staffing function	Critical considerations
Executive	Board of directors and executive management; expertise in strategic management, corporate law, risk management, performance management
Finance	Bookkeeping, payroll, computerised account-keeping expertise, goods and services tax reporting, asset management and depreciation, company taxation, budgeting, financial analysis, auditing, annual report preparation, strategic accounting advice, performance management
Administration	Programming, contract management, secretarial/personal assistance, media liaison, front desk/reception management
Human resources	In-house/contractor expertise in legal obligations of employers, occupational health and safety, industrial relations, recruitment, retention, performance management, incentive schemes, training
Marketing	See Chapter 8
Event management	See Chapter 7
Maintenance	Grounds and parking, engine room, machinery, pool, water management, fitness equipment, utilities, media technology, security systems, turf management
Cleaning	Customer and staffing zones, shower and bathroom facilities, major event cleaning (turnaround between events), health and safety standards/obligations
Catering	Quality and variety of food and beverages, in-house/outsourced split, corporate box services and policies, health issues
Security	Standard operations, special events, crowd management, vandalism, alcohol policies, law enforcement policies and collaboration with police, risk management
Program delivery	Fitness, personal training, learn to swim, aerobics, in-house sporting competitions etc.
Ancillary customer service	Ticket/box office, retail and merchandising, relationship/communication with outside ticketing agency

in tandem with trends towards privatisation and tender management. Indeed, outsourcing offers the facility a number of key advantages, including higher levels of service specialisation and decreased complexity of internal human resources. The reduced levels of staffing and specialist management expertise needed naturally articulate into lower fixed staffing costs, and the fixed costs of service delivery are known at the signing of the contract.

However, it is also important to recognise the drawbacks inherent in the outsourcing model. Higher variable costs for service delivery are likely, as well as higher administrative demands for contract management. The process of service specification and tendering, for instance, requires specialised expertise. In addition, drafting of a contract, including duration, terms of renewal, and conditions such as costs, profit sharing, incentives and alliances, must be performed. Further disadvantages include the relinquishment of control over service quality on implementation of the contract.

Given the delicate balance of advantages and disadvantages afforded by outsourcing, not all functional areas of the facility will be served best by the approach. The decision to contract for services is obviously complex, and is aided by considering some key principles. As noted before, current best practice suggests that organisations should focus on their core competencies, rather than look towards diversification (Graetz et al. 2002). It is thus the non-core activities that tend to be considered for outsourcing (such as the event-cleaning services, as presented in this chapter's case study), rather than essential management and primary service delivery. Areas such as cleaning, security, catering, and major project work or maintenance may be most successfully outsourced.

Human resource management systems and processes

Establishing and maintaining a human resource infrastructure within a sport facility goes far beyond identifying the staffing roles that are necessary for the facility to function. Human resource management is now recognised as a strategic tool for the maximisation of organisational performance (Guthrie 2001; Huselid 1995). Beyond establishing thorough recruitment procedures, it involves establishing performance management systems, reward systems, incentive schemes, and mechanisms for identifying and fulfilling training needs. The human resource function of a facility will also need to consider the organisation's legal responsibilities to its employees, as well as remuneration and benefits policies, how to approach industrial relations matters and occupational health and safety management.

Recruitment and selection

The recruitment and selection of appropriate personnel, with suitable experience and qualifications, will help the facility to fulfil its objectives. Recruitment, as a process, begins with identifying the organisation's human resource needs, and ends with the receipt of applications. It is at this point that the process of selection commences.

To maximise the success of the recruitment process, the job must be clearly defined. This is achieved through the process of job analysis and design. Job analysis and design requires the systematic evaluation and documentation of the job content, work methods required, and the reporting relationships that will support the employee and facilitate appropriate communication mechanisms (Maund 2001). Job description and job specification documents can be drafted after conducting the job analysis. The job description should outline the job title, duties and responsibilities, organisational relationships, reporting relationships and work conditions (Stone 2002). The job specification, on the other hand, documents the parameters, skills, abilities, qualifications/training, work experience and knowledge that a potential incumbent must possess in order to perform the job description.

Once the job has been identified and defined, the decision needs to be taken as to whether internal or external recruitment is appropriate. It is important to note that some geographic regions and specific industries will be subject to laws regarding accepted procedures for internal and external recruitment. Internal transfer and promotion can offer a number of advantages, including lower recruitment costs, intimate knowledge of the employee's work capacity, reduced orientation needs and improved morale among existing staff. Of course, it should be noted that internal recruitment can bring disadvantages, such as promotion of personnel beyond their maximal capacity, limited opportunity to introduce new perspectives and skills, as well as the potential for conflict among existing employees applying for the position. In the case of sporting events it is common industry practice to 'event-hop'. For example, numerous professionals who worked for the Sydney 2000 Organising Committee were subsequently recruited by the 2002 Commonwealth Games organisers, and some moved directly to the Athens 2004 or Beijing 2008 Olympic Games.

In the case of a new facility, the option to recruit staff internally does not usually exist at this point. Recruiting from external sources may therefore be necessary, bringing with it different advantages and disadvantages. The new sports facility may go about recruiting externally through a number of different mechanisms, including advertising, employment services, recruitment consultants and search firms.

The selection of appropriate employees cuts training needs, and there is a reduced likelihood of turnover and such other problems as job dissatisfaction, absenteeism and poor performance. Good selection practice is more likely to occur when relevant legislation has been observed (e.g. equal opportunity and affirmative action laws), the right match of job description to job specifications has been identified, and a selection policy clearly outlines a systematic selection process. The selection process should clearly outline the role of participants, such as management, human resource personnel and external consultants, in the decision-making process. It should also overview the selection steps and techniques to be used, such as screening mechanisms, type of interview, use of psychological and aptitude tests, and background investigations.

Performance management systems

Performance management can be defined as a set of processes for measuring, assessing and providing feedback on the progress of individuals and the organisation towards stated objectives. Benefits of performance management systems include optimisation of employee performance, improved mechanisms for accountability, higher employee motivation (Anderson 1996), and the capacity to drive and reinforce change (Locke, Shaw, Saari & Latham 1981).

Generally, performance management can be thought of as a cycle or feedback loop incorporating a number of key elements (Newton & Findlay 1998). These elements include the setting of clear objectives, performance management methods, evaluation mechanisms, and identification of needs for modification. Performance management at the organisational level will be dealt with in Chapters 10 and 11. Each of the factors at the level of human resource management is explored further in Table 5.2.

While a number of variables contribute to the success of a performance management system, the overall match between the system and the organisational objectives, as well as acceptance of the system by employees, are arguably the most pivotal. Obviously a performance management system is implemented to achieve a goal, and it is therefore vital that this outcome contribute to the overall objectives of the organisation. Similarly, a program is more likely to be successful if representatives of all levels of the organisation are involved in its design and implementation. Employees are more likely to participate in a system that they understand, and that offers positive outcomes for both themselves and the organisation. As a result, successful performance management systems contribute to employee development and career management, in addition to succession planning. This process becomes more complex in event organisations that are characterised by relatively short-term committed staff in combination with a high percentage of part-time and sessional employees.

Rewarding performance

The reward system within an organisation is concerned with facilitating its desired outcomes through positive reinforcement. Remuneration is a key element of the package, but other

Table 5.2 Elements of the performance management process

Performance management elements	Factors for consideration
The setting of clear objectives	Derived from organisational strategy, set for department as well as individual workers
Management methods	Communication of objectives, supervision, mentoring, coaching, reward systems, salary benchmarking, design and delivery of training
Evaluation mechanisms	Review match between outcomes and objectives, performance appraisal systems, ranked and weighted competencies, feedback loops between individuals and organisation
Modification and feedback	Identify need for new behaviours, training needs to fill gap between objective and outcome, identify appropriate rewards to encourage changes, set new objectives and goals (feeds back to first step)

factors may play a role, such as recognition, opportunities for participation and challenge, professional development and career progression. Employee remuneration is an essential organisational function that not only underlines the values of the organisation but can also help fulfil its objectives (Stone 2002). The remuneration system, for instance, can reward high levels of job performance, facilitate employee satisfaction, and reward desired behaviours and ideas including service innovations. Not only is remuneration a key feature of the overall reward and performance management systems, but it can be used to leverage change and to reward desired outcomes.

Remuneration

Compensation objectives should be established after careful consideration of the overall objectives of the organisation and of the human resource function. Compensation objectives may be to observe legislative requirements, attract and retain a core of quality staff, motivate employees towards improved performance, provide fair and reasonable compensation, remain competitive within the industry and ensure an appropriate level of return on investment (Stone 2002). In the sport, entertainment and event industries, it has been quite common to be paid considerably less for the same or similar work than in other industries. Part of the reason for this is the inherent attractiveness of working in the major sporting event industry. Many people are willing to give up financial rewards and trade them in for the privilege of being part of, and hence associated with, the high-profile, exposure-generating events and their stars. In other words, to be working in the sporting event industry for many people is a reward in itself, which to a certain extent compensates for being paid less money.

Once the compensation objectives have been established, the operational specifics of the remuneration program can be developed (Stone 2002). Here, the job analysis, mentioned under the heading *recruitment and selection*, provides management with the first level of information required to determine appropriate compensation for each role. From this starting point, both internal and external equity should be established.

Internal equity should be established for each role within the organisation. This can be achieved by evaluating the worth of each role to the overall organisational structure and objectives. A variety of methods exist for conducting this kind of analysis, ranging from relatively simple ranking systems to more complicated (and less subjective) systems that aim to compare positions based on measurable job parameters.

External equity should also be explored, not only through complying with legislated award levels but by way of understanding wider industry and competitor practices. Matching the results of these internal and external equity surveys should establish salary ranges. In other words, through evaluation of the job worth within the organisation and the job worth within the external labour market, as well as establishment of a competitive market position, a job pricing outcome will ensue. Of course, once established, the salary system must be administered, monitored and audited (Stone 2002).

Other incentives

In today's society a remuneration package means more than salary. Additional employee benefits must be provided by law, including minimum levels of superannuation, leave entitlements, worker's compensation cover and smoke-free work environments (depending on the legislation relevant to different countries and industries). In the context of sport facility management this has led to situations where smoking is banned in the whole facility, even when the facility is an outdoor venue. Banning smoking in public facilities takes into consideration the perspective not only of the organisation's employees but also of its customers. Other benefits may be considered at the discretion of the employer, guided by the objectives and philosophy of the organisation, such as fringe benefits, child care, health care insurance, life and permanent disability insurance, and employee assistance programs such as counselling. Again it can be noted that employee access to valuable tickets for high-profile events can significantly contribute to a sport facility employer being favoured by high-quality staff. Overall, these employee benefits form a significant component of the organisation's overall compensation costs, and require specialised human resource skills and knowledge to administer.

Identifying and fulfilling training needs

The training and development function of the human resource program plays a vital role in improving organisational performance, and in enhancing the career development of individuals. In order to fulfil these roles it is vital that the program be aligned with the organisational objectives and with employee performance through the performance management system. In this way the corporate goals of the facility are supported, and the behaviours required of individuals to achieve them are facilitated.

To ensure a cost-effective and successful training program, a systematic approach should be taken. This should involve the logical steps of needs analysis, program development and implementation (see Figure 5.1), and finally evaluation (Stone 2002).

A needs analysis should determine the specific training needs of the organisation, including the specific skills or knowledge, where in the organisational structure these are required, and who requires them. Stone (2002) suggests an 'organisation, task and person' model for evaluating training needs. The internal environment of the organisation, including its culture and overall objectives, will influence the kinds of skills and knowledge that are required of and considered appropriate for employees. In addition, the external environment of the organisation may indicate the need for training through legal, social or technological changes.

Figure 5.1 Performance appraisal and training needs

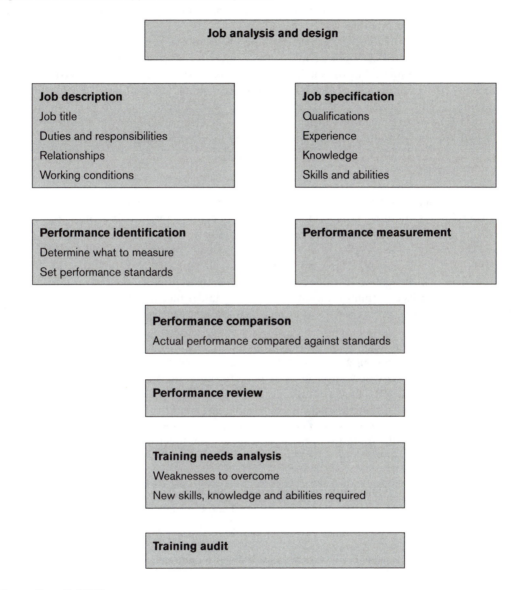

Source: Stone, R. (2002).

The 'task' component of Stone's 'organisation, task and person' model indicates the skills and abilities required by the incumbent or potential employee. The process of job analysis and design, indicated in the section 'recruitment and selection', will contribute to an understanding of task components and competencies. Finally, the 'person' variable of the model indicates how an employee is actually performing the job requirements. The outcome of evaluating each of the 'organisation', 'task' and 'person' variables should be a comprehensive set of behavioural objectives for the training effort. Behavioural objectives are clearly stated goals that can be measured. A comprehensive behavioural goal will include a series of elements, as depicted in Table 5.3.

It is evident from Table 5.3 that the training program will flow logically from a clear set of objectives. Also, the development and delivery of the training program should consider not only the content required but the methods and learning principles to be employed.

Finally, the effectiveness of the training program should be evaluated. Evaluation may determine whether knowledge was learned, skills were gained and job performance was improved. The program can be further evaluated to determine whether the attainment of the skills and knowledge translated into the realisation of organisational objectives.

Legal responsibilities

All aspects of managing the human infrastructure of a sporting facility are now moderated by a complex system of legislation, different in every country or state. It is obviously beyond the scope of this book to detail the specific legal obligations of organisations in every state, region and nation of the world. It is useful to emphasise, however, that legal obligations for the employer are complex. This complexity stems, in part, from the number of different sources from which legal obligations are documented, in addition to the relevant documents' size, density and legal terminology. Once again this underlines the imperative to hire qualified human resource professionals to ensure that breaches in legislation do not arise from ignorance.

As mentioned, the legal obligations of employers come from a range of different sources. These can include common law precedent, arising from court judgements of specific cases, as well as statutory law generated in both federal and state parliamentary forums (Stone 2002). National and state awards outlining the obligations of employees are also common, and usually include conditions such as minimum pay, hours of work, types of leave and appropriate termination processes. These awards may be generated and reviewed by industrial relations tribunals. In addition to these sources, employer obligations can be outlined in the contract of employment, and through enterprise bargaining mechanisms in certain countries.

Other aspects of employment that may be regulated by legislation include personal income tax, payroll or company tax, goods and services taxes, occupational health and safety,

Table 5.3 Elements of behavioural objectives for training programs

Who:	Indicating the personnel who will be receiving the training program
Given what:	An outline of what will be delivered in the program, including content, learning principles and tools, motivation tools, assessments
Does what:	A statement indicating what the person(s) receiving training will be able to do on completion of the program
How well:	An indication of how the performance of the person(s) receiving training can be measured after the program to determine if it has been successful. This may include completion of a knowledge test, or ability to perform a task to a specified standard
By when:	Indicating the timeline of the program

equal opportunity, antidiscrimination, sexual harassment, superannuation requirements, maternity and parental leave, annual leave and long-service leave.

Industrial relations

The term 'industrial relations' essentially refers to the relationship between employers and employees through their representative unions, mediated by an industrial relations court or tribunal. The function of industrial relations tribunals is not only to encourage observance of relevant legislation but to arbitrate disputes that may in turn generate new or altered legislative requirements. Generally, negotiations centre on such items as rates of pay, hours of work, penalty rates, suspension and termination procedures, disciplinary procedures, leave entitlements, special allowances and other employment conditions. Although the nature of union presence varies from country to country, and between industries, union influence is probably more significant in most Western and first and second world nations, and particularly in large organisations and industries. The need to accommodate union presence in employee negotiations is likely to be critical to the success of the day-to-day running of a sporting facility.

There are a number of different formats that direct industrial relations negotiations may take. These may include consent award, over-award and collective bargaining negotiations (Stone 2002). Consent award negotiations, for instance, occur when the employer and union negotiate directly with one another and reach agreement within parameters set by the relevant government industrial relations body. Over-award negotiations occur when unions attempt to negotiate directly with employers to exceed the pay rates and conditions set down in an award, on the understanding that awards set a minimum rather than maximum requirement. Collective bargaining can take many forms, but essentially refers to employer–union negotiation on all issues of employer–employee relations.

Given both the reality of and complexity in industrial relations issues, the sporting facility must have access to human resource expertise. It is the role of the human resource manager or consultant to fully understand the legal obligations of the facility and to manage industrial relations negotiations.

Occupational health and safety

Managing the complex occupational health and safety (OHS) needs of an organisation is fundamental to providing employees (Nankervis, Compton & McCarthy 1993), and indeed customers, with physical and emotional security. Today, organisations must negotiate a complex array of legislation in order to understand their obligations and establish appropriate policies and procedures.

Potential occupational hazards include both physical and psychological considerations, and can encompass a range of hazards:

- *physical hazards*—thermal stress, noise, vibration, ultraviolet radiation, fire, electrical and machinery hazards; work practices arising from problems with manual handling, ergonomic and overuse problems;
- *chemical hazards*—poisons, toxins, corrosive substances, irritants, sensitisers, explosive/ flammable materials and asphyxiants;

- *biological hazards*—e.g. animal and plant material containing micro-organisms such as viruses, bacteria and fungi;
- *psychological hazards*—from cultural, interpersonal and organisational factors, as well as work practices.

In order to effectively manage the risks presented by these factors, a comprehensive policy and procedure system is required. Generally, the occupational health and safety policy should identify the following information:

General policy statement

- Duties and responsibilities of employer and employees
- Declaration of employer's intention regarding provision of safe and healthy working conditions
- Indication of commitment to consultation with employees, consultation of experts
- Relevant legislation for state/country
- Compliance of policies and procedures with legislation

Mechanisms for risk analysis

- Indicating consultative processes with employees
- Indicating provisions for consulting experts
- Indicating consultation with relevant government agencies and other pertinent sources of information
- Use of appropriate audit tools

Allocation of responsibilities

- Indicating clear lines of communication
- Defining roles and accountability of management structure
- Indicating means for allocation of human and financial resources
- Indicating means of determining OHS priorities

Statement of procedures

- Provision of information and training
- Dealing with problem areas
- Effective inspection and maintenance of facilities and equipment
- Managing introduction of new facilities, machinery, equipment, substances and processes
- Dealing with identified hazards
- Ensuring safe systems and methods of work

Mechanisms for monitoring evaluation

- Indicating how and by whom policy and procedures are to be monitored
- Indicating mechanisms and responsibility for evaluation

Before we take a closer look at preparing the facility for the first event to be hosted, which includes setting up a human resource structure for managing the event, in Chapter 6 we will first consider the process that involves attracting the events in Chapter 7.

Summary

The structure and processes of managing organisations have changed significantly over the past few decades. The hierarchical model of management has ceased to be the overriding determinant of organisational functioning and has moved towards being one element in the mix. New-generation thinking suggests that organisations are able to perform more responsively and competitively when structures are 'flatter', organised around project teams, and when decision making is decentralised. Processes that enable networking, and that empower employees to develop relationships, take risks and innovate, are processes that encourage contemporary organisations to flourish. It has also been observed that organisations today are seeking to develop strategic alliances with other organisations in order to leverage resource utilisation, and to collaborate closely with suppliers to which non-core services are outsourced.

The organisational configuration that is established for a sporting facility will influence the subsequent staffing profile. Generally speaking, each functional area of the facility will require specific staffing expertise. General functional divisions include: executive, finance, administration, human resources, marketing, event management, program delivery, maintenance, cleaning, catering, security, program delivery, box office and merchandising. The mode of delivery for these services may vary from permanent to casual and from full-time to part-time. In addition, the organisational philosophy may support outsourcing of certain functions, on a contract or consultation basis. Given the delicate balance of advantages and disadvantages afforded by outsourcing, current thinking suggests that it is most appropriate for non-core activities.

Managing the human resource infrastructure of a sport facility requires a comprehensive and strategic human resource program. This should include consideration of recruitment procedures, retention policies, performance review systems, incentive-based reward schemes, and mechanisms for identifying and fulfilling training needs. Further, the human resource infrastructure must be able to negotiate a complex array of legal obligations, including occupational health and safety regulations.

Case study

Outsourcing facility and event cleaning services

To be the best and most environmentally aware provider of cleaning and waste management services to venues and events on a global basis.

This is the mission of Cleanevent (2003), an Australian company based in Melbourne, with international contracts in the United States and the United Kingdom. Established in 1987, the company provides cleaning and waste management services to venues and events, specialising in what it calls venue *presentation* and waste management *consultancy* (Masters 2003). It has cemented a reputation as the global leader in event and venue cleaning (Kelly 2002).

Cleanevent's client list is indeed both impressive and long. It includes premier sporting events such as the US Tennis Open, Wimbledon, the Daytona International Speedway, the 2002 Winter Olympics in Salt Lake City, the Super Bowl, the Sydney 2000 Olympics, the Australian Formula One Grand Prix and the Australian Motorcycle Grand Prix. In fact, in the USA alone, Cleanevent reportedly services 60 per cent of NASCAR events and 40 per cent of Indycar races (Masters 2003). Cleanevent also boasts contracts for some of the world's most famous home-ground stadiums, including Legends Field, Florida (the spring training facility for the New York Yankees), Highbury Stadium (home of the English premier league football club Arsenal), as well as its second NFL stadium in Jacksonville, Florida (home to the Jacksonville Jaguars).

The organisation is estimated to deliver 25 per cent of its business in Australia, 55 per cent in the USA and 20 per cent in the UK (Masters 2003). However, this balance changed in 2004, when Cleanevent delivered on its Athens Olympic contract. The contract has been estimated to be 50 per cent bigger than the Sydney 2000 deal, which saw Cleanevent collect 8500 tonnes of waste over the full period (Masters 2003). The Athens contract is reportedly worth $A55 million, requiring 1.2 million hours of labour (Masters 2003).

Publicly, Cleanevent attributes its success to two key factors. It has established a commitment to service quality, featuring high standards of cleanliness and timeliness (Masters 2003). Second, it has established systematic protocols and procedures to ensure that these standards can become a reality (Daniel 2002). Service quality, according to the company, involves delivering responsive service during events to maximise patron safety and satisfaction, in addition to providing rapid post-event cleaning, thus allowing venues to program events in close succession (Masters 2003).

According to Craig Lovett, chairman and founder of Cleanevent, however, the organisation is ultimately successful because it sees its primary service as logistics, not cleaning. The 2000 Sydney Olympics, for instance, was an enormous undertaking, with turnaround times of 45 minutes or less to clean a 110 000 seat stadium (Savage 2000). In Lovett's own words: 'it's got nothing to do with cleaning, it's got all to do with logistics—right people, right place, right equipment, right attitude, right time' (Savage 2000). Clearly, the approximately 4500 staff worldwide cannot deliver on Cleanevent's promises without thorough planning, detailed logistical support, and well-executed tactical responses (Industry Search 2001–03; Masters 2003). Lovett explains: 'I liken myself to a football coach. You can't change the way the players are going to play on the field. All you can do is give them the right attitude, the right equipment, the right thought, perhaps a game plan for them to go out and deliver' (Savage 2000).

The success of Cleanevent, growing from a $A16 000 investment in 1987 (and despite financial difficulties in Australia in 2001), is therefore attributed to its development of appropriate policies and procedures (Daniel 2002). According to

Lovett, the organisation has grown thanks to its ability to build systems and structures, as well as through creating the right tools to monitor and manage business operations (Daniel 2002). The Cleanevent Management System is one such tool, a proprietary software system that enables the company to plan, monitor, manage and report on all aspects of the business (Daniel 2002).

Apart from its commitment to service quality, timeliness and logistical effectiveness, Cleanevent's success may be attributable to other important factors. The company has established itself in a relatively new niche, thanks to the phenomenon of outsourcing non-core services. In the early 1980s, sport and entertainment facilities did not consider contracting external providers for their cleaning functions. Cleanevent entered the arena at the pivotal time, when organisations began to consider the potential benefits of outsourcing non-essential services. One of these potential benefits is service specialisation, which is a feature that Cleanevent has maximised. The company services only sport, entertainment and exhibitions, becoming expert in fulfilling this niche, while leaving facilities such as factories, high rises and warehouses to other players (Masters 2003).

Furthermore, Cleanevent has made its services more attractive to event and facility managers with its policy on environmental responsibility, which incorporates a strategic alliance with Visy recycling. This approach clearly finds a competitive advantage, given the increasing community pressure to run environmentally responsible events.

Finally, the organisation implements a marketing strategy to maximise its exposure and brand recognition among the general public and hence its clients. Cleanevent has actively sought naming rights and sponsorship deals with sport and entertainment events, such as its three-year naming rights sponsorship of the IRL Infiniti Pro Series event at Nashville Superspeedway, now the Cleanevent 100 Infiniti Pro Series race (Kelly 2002).

Q. Argue why it would be beneficial for an event such as the Athens Olympic Games to outsource event cleaning rather than setting up an internal structure to take care of this vital aspect of organising a multitude of sporting events.

Q. From a human resource management perspective, what are the top five issues that you can think of when largely depending on a part-time or casual workforce? Consider the issue of delivering the highest possible quality of service to your customers.

Q. If you were put in charge of organising the Olympic Games in Beijing in 2008, what are the top three services that you would consider outsourcing rather than keeping in-house? Justify your answer.

6

Operating the new sport facility: attracting events

CHAPTER OBJECTIVES

In this chapter, we will:
- Outline the role of the facility and event manager in attracting events.
- Identify the distinguishing features of the bid process.
- Consider the requirements of a bid application document.
- Develop the management lifecycle phases of a sport event and facility from the perspective of the initial bid through to the evaluation of that bid.
- Identify the relationships between key actors in the event bidding process.

Getting a piece of the action . . .

The process of attracting major events to a particular location, whether these events represent sporting, cultural or arts activities, has received widespread attention over the past decade. This attention extends to a variety of influential and interested parties, from political figures and community members through to major corporate interests. Support has been generated from within whole countries (and even continents) to secure the FIFA World Cup finals, while individual cities compete for the right to host an Olympic Games, initially against other cities within the same country and ultimately against cities from other nations. Even regions compete against each other for the right to host a multitude of smaller festivals and events. The rewards on offer to the region, city or country that wins the right to host these events can be vast, ranging from the generation of significant economic upturn, enhanced employment opportunity and infrastructure development, through to the boom in tourist visits that can accompany these events. The interest that is created through the attraction of major events to a community extends to key groups ranging from the sport governing body and the facility manager, relevant community interest groups, the media, politicians, government departments and the building and construction industry, to name but a few of the organisations involved. No individual or group in the community remains unaffected by the intrusion that these events bring with them.

This chapter will discuss the business of attracting sport events, both large and small, and the impact hosting events has on the sport facility manager, who is seeking to ensure that events can be held at his or her venue, and the sport event manager, who is seeking to attract and host a high-quality event. Incorporated in the analysis will be the impact that attracting events has on all major participants and the arising relationships that are essential in their formation from within the communities that host them.

Changing boundaries for attracting events

Developing an interest in being involved in hosting major events has not been without its negative moments throughout history. The 1984 Summer Olympic Games was awarded to the only host city that applied, Los Angeles. Much of the negativity associated with hosting an event such as the Olympic Games at the time was a result of the parlous financial state that Montreal saw itself plummet into as a result of hosting the 1976 Games. Even in 1999, the situation of attracting a host city for a major sporting event saw Melbourne emerging from a possible three-host city contest to being the only city left standing in its bid to host the 2006 Commonwealth Games. There are significant economic, political, technical and social consequences associated with bidding for and ultimately hosting major events. These consequences affect a broad range of community groups, which ultimately affect the capacity of an application to host major events to proceed.

As stated in Chapters 1 and 2, stadia in the current generation are increasingly incorporating multi-purpose facilities and audience-friendly environments. The influx of a corporate and entertainment culture within the facility and the movement away from being purely a home ground for one particular team requires today's facility managers to assume the role of successful capacity management strategists. Managing a weekly fixture list over the course of a structured league season is of vital importance to the facility manager. Increasingly important is managing the 'downtime' or 'structural wastage' associated with a facility. (These concepts will be discussed in greater detail in Chapter 7.)

The influx of other sporting and entertainment events into the facility management calendar has become an increasingly significant consideration facing the facility manager. The requirement to attract new customers to the facility, both spectators and event operators, places additional burdens on the facility manager. (The opportunity to develop new markets, increase signage and sponsorship exposure, while also adding to the corporate and membership rights, will be examined throughout Chapters 6 and 7.)

New attractions can present new difficulties and burdens. The need to clean the facility for a completely new event to be held on the following day, removing or relocating signage, changing and adjusting flooring and seating, ticketing and security, among other considerations, all place significant strain on the facility and the facility management staff. Coupled with the operational issues associated with hosting a variety of events and competitions is the problem of ensuring that the facility presents sufficient grounds to be considered suitable to host these events in the first place. If the facility is presented as part of the city infrastructure during the bid application, then the city must be in a position to undertake this responsibility while (more importantly) also being supportive of the bid. Equally, a facility manager may seek to bid to host events in the facility's own right, again being mindful of the total application process.

An additional critical role played by the facility in attracting events is that of providing a clearly developed infrastructure framework. This infrastructure is vital in supporting the event bid team in convincing event owners that the city or country can meet the demands associated with hosting the event. Vital to the success of any event bidding process are facilities of an adequate standard to meet the scrutiny of minimum (international- or national-level) tournament requirements. Facilities must be able to provide a suitable competition platform, which must include a playing surface of appropriate standard, areas for participants and officials to prepare and warm up, and the capacity to cater to a range of spectator and media needs.

As well as the facility infrastructure elements essential to a successful bid application, the event bidding team is responsible for presenting city-related infrastructure options such as accommodation, transport, and food and beverage outlets. Coupled with the enormous range of infrastructure delivery requirements is an ever-increasing range of economic, political, social and technical opportunities that must pass the scrutiny of the event owners in order to convince them that the event can be both successfully managed and staged. The event bid team must bring together an often diverse range of people and community groups in order to meet their obligations to the event owner, and as a result must develop a clearly defined bid application document. All of these core components for inclusion in a bid application document will be examined throughout this chapter.

Attracting events

There are a number of key issues surrounding the process of attracting events. Events are of particular importance to specific groups within the community for a multitude of reasons. (These reasons are presented in the section on bidding considerations.) The attraction of events can be developed from the perspective of the community (comprising the country, region or city) and of the facility itself. The facility must attract events in order to remain a viable and profitable business entity in its own right. The community attracts events in order to generate economic turnover, tourism and interest in the region. The type of events that are attracted by both community and facility groups range in their size, structure and global importance.

Events can extend to a broad range of activities, from sporting fixtures through to unique cultural performances or even national celebrations. This broad definition of what constitutes an event was provided by Getz (1997, p. 4), who referred to events by their context as 'one-time or infrequently occurring event outside normal programs or activities of the sponsoring or organising body'; or, from the point of view of the event organiser or customer, as 'the opportunity for a leisure, social or cultural experience outside the normal range of choices beyond everyday experience'.

Bowdin, McDonnell, Allen and O'Toole (2001) further characterised events according to their size and scale. Size and scale reflect a significant feature in generating interest within groups seeking to bid for the right to host events. Common categories can be determined and aligned with events that often involve a bidding process. These events can be termed mega-events, hallmark events, major events or local events. The events can also reach across a range of sporting, business or cultural fields in terms of their potential attractiveness.

Mega-events are those events that are so large that they affect whole economies and reverberate in the global media. They often reflect a significant and competitive bidding process. Events within this category include the Olympic Games, FIFA World Cup and Commonwealth Games, largely representing activities that produce high levels of tourism, significant media coverage and economic benefits, and bring a distinct level of prestige to the host.

Hallmark events are those events that become aligned with a city or nation to the extent that they gain widespread recognition and awareness, becoming synonymous with the name of the place. They represent (Hall 1989, p. 4):

> major one-time or recurring events of limited duration, developed primarily to enhance the awareness, appeal and profitability of a tourism destination in the short and long term. Such events rely for their success on uniqueness, status, or timely significance to create interest and attract attention.

The Carnival in Rio, the Wimbledon Tennis Championships and the Melbourne Cup are classic examples of hallmark events, providing identification with a place, developing tourist visits and embracing a strong sense of local pride.

Major events are of significant size and interest that they can attract tourist visits and media coverage and produce economic benefits. Many top sporting events—world championships such as the World Swimming Championships, or international competitions such as the Formula One Grand Prix—fit into this category and are increasingly sought after and bid for by national sporting associations or governments.

Local events are smaller but are of sufficient local interest and benefit to a smaller city or regional community. These events can still represent significant tourism and economic benefits, and foster local pride in a township or region. The Stawell Gift professional foot race, run at Easter each year in rural Victoria, Australia, is an example of this type of event.

Given their significance and size, major events are usually at the centre of highly competitive bid processes. These bid processes can be influenced by strong interest from key communities or by interest from within the facility itself.

Attracting events into the community

Attracting events to a country, city or region reflects a conscious planning process, whereby specific rituals, presentations, performances or celebrations are conducted to mark special occasions or to achieve particular social, cultural, government or corporate goals.

Getz (1997) argues that all community and destination areas should formulate event tourism plans in order to realise tourism potential through communications, packaging, and other forms of assistance and cooperation. Putting in place a destination vision enables a community to define a long-term major development process that can shape it for many years. The key areas that can be affected by the successful attraction of events to a community include (Getz 1997):

- creation of a favourable image of the 'place';
- attraction of an increased number of foreign visits (and their yield);
- expansion of the tourist season;
- improvement of tourist infrastructure;
- stimulation of repeat visits;
- development and improvement of management and infrastructure needed to attract events;
- development of sports, arts and culture within the community; and
- maximisation of benefits and impact on the community.

The attraction of events that will have an impact on the community is an important feature of the input of city councils and local and federal governments. The input of key city or government decision makers plays a critical role in the attraction of events. The support that these bodies can engender from within business groups, the public and the media will often result in a successful outcome.

Attracting events to the facility

The broad emphasis on events predominantly reflects the event attraction process from a holistic viewpoint, encompassing the broad range of potential applicants comprising interested parties representing such groups as the country, the city, politicians, and sporting organisations. The involvement of these groups is instrumental (and influential) in the success associated with attracting events. However, one of the core groups associated with this process includes key facilities. Facilities are crucial in presenting infrastructure support for a bid, and the presentation of a substantial facility option as part of a bid can only enhance the way in which the bid is received. Equally important to the facility's being included as an infra-structure support dimension of a bid application is the fact that in certain cases the facility must present itself on its own merits to be considered as a host venue for major events.

The process of including a facility in the bid application is a significant consideration. This process extends to the bid team's including the facility in the bid application, while ensuring that the facility views the attraction of key events to the community as a key require-ment. Equally important is the ability of the facility to attract events of a suitable nature. This capacity to attract events represents a vital aspect in the success of the facility. There is a case to be made for the facility manager's becoming a successful event bidder, in much the same way that a city or a sporting organisation might be. The event bidding process descriptions provided throughout this chapter extend to the facility as event bidder, as much as they do to a host city or sporting organisation as event bidder. It is worth taking a brief look at the facility as an event attraction in its own right, however.

There are a number of key issues that surround the facility when bidding for events. A facility will often be referred to as an 'infrastructure asset' in many bid application documents used for attracting hallmark events or mega-events. The facility here should be featured in these bid documents, with the support of a formal contractual agreement. The bid may refer to the 'outstanding' facilities that already exist in the city, to highlight to the event owner the level of infrastructure in place. This process is integrated in the bid especially where the facility has some community or local government ownership or affiliation.

The facility manager in the position of managing a community or government asset must consider all its obligations to its existing tenants and competitions, while considering the demands associated with hosting an event that has been attracted to the city. Referring to the facility as an infrastructure asset in the bid document brings with it many issues connected with the facility's existing tenants, who might already be contracted to play in the arena.

The arrival of a major event could well disrupt these fixtures—this coupled with the effect on existing agreements and introduced obligations, such as signage removal or relocation, or even the requirement for a removal of all signage (as is the case for the Olympic Games, where there is no signage allowed in the stadium). Other issues can arise with respect to existing members or season ticket holders, existing (or even conflicting) naming rights obligations between the stadium and the event, and existing catering and pouring (food and beverage) rights obligations.

For a facility to schedule a regular set of fixtured competitions or events—often ensuring weekly obligations which can then be disrupted by the attraction of a once-only specialised event—requires significant negotiation, goodwill, and support from all parties involved in the process. The event bidding team must obtain the support of the facility, which in turn needs to ensure that the staff are well informed and receptive to hosting a new event. The facility manager presents the facility favourably to all customers and visitors, while being adequately compensated for the new event. This is not always a simple operation, and the outcomes can often require intense negotiation.

An example of this occurred during the 2003 finals series for the Australian Football League competition and National Rugby League competition. The Sydney Swans AFL team was set to play a home finals game at the Sydney Olympic Stadium (Telstra Stadium), which was also a potential home base for the Canterbury Bulldogs NRL team in its finals game. Neither team had utilised the stadium as its official home base, but both had played some competition games at the stadium during the season. If the finals panned out as anticipated, the Canterbury Bulldogs were booked in to play at the stadium at 5.30 pm on a Saturday evening, with the Sydney Swans to play at 7.30 pm the same evening. This presented a significant dilemma to the facility operators, it being impossible to host two different football competition finals on the same night. The potential crowd support for the Bulldogs was anticipated to be 30 000. The Swans support was predicted to be 70 000 (the facility can accommodate approximately 80 000). Fortunately, the Swans' first final win was against all expectations, meaning they received a bye in the next week of finals, ensuring that their home final would be one week later than anticipated and thereby alleviating the fixturing dilemma.

This example displays the way in which the facility manager can be placed in a compromised position by demands from a wide range of groups. Each of the clubs wants to ensure it maximises the outcome, as does each respective league governing body. The facility is attempting to maximise its attendance while retaining each club as a future tenant.

Conceptualising the event bidding process

There are numerous considerations to take into account when applying to host events. Gaining access to an event may require the submission of a formal bid document and presentation to support the bid application. This submission may be provided to an event owner and may involve development of a standard contractual agreement to cover a particular period of time.

Much of the existing information available on the value of hosting hallmark events has focused on the staging of the event and the post-event analysis. There has been limited insight into the preparation of a bid and the submission of the bid documents. Information available in these areas mainly focuses on technical requirements, such as location, equipment, facilities and personnel. The underlying factors that improve a bid organisation's chance of securing an event, such as community support, the support of media and the formation of relationships, have been largely neglected in the literature.

A successful bid is one that addresses the technical (facilities, budget, location), support (personnel, transport, accommodation) and cultural (entertainment, television, ceremonies) elements (Wilkinson 1988). The International Olympic Committee (IOC) has a number of criteria for the bidding process, which include controlled lobbying, evidence of government and community support for a bid, and a wide range of candidature documents highlighting the technical capabilities to stage the event. These elements are in turn supported by a visual presentation. (The process of bidding to host the Olympic Games is presented in detail in the section on bid application documents later in this chapter.)

Given that the limited research available stresses the need for technical competency in a successful event bid, an important question arises. If two bids are identical in technical aspects, how does one city succeed over another in gaining the rights to stage the event? It appears that there are other factors beyond the purely technical components that play a critical role in the selection process. McFarlane (1992, p. 4) suggested that the Adelaide bid for the 1998 Commonwealth Games was 'risk free, offering all the necessary infrastructure to ensure [the event's] success'. However, one of the reasons given for the bid being unsuccessful was 'a failure to accurately gauge the intensity of the third world sentiment within the Commonwealth'. The result was that Kuala Lumpur overwhelmingly won the rights to stage the Games (40 votes to 25).

McGeoch and Korporaal (1994) pointed out that the IOC Evaluation Committee gave Melbourne (1996 bid) a good report on its technical capabilities and venues but, again, an Australian city failed to secure this prestigious mega-event. Booth and Tatz (1994a) proposed that other factors came into the equation, such as Melbourne's location in the southern hemisphere, the combined distance and time problems, and again the issue of lobbying or systematic cajoling. Booth and Tatz (1994b, p. 6) noted that 'while technical competence and financial viability are two obvious selection criteria, neither is *the* determinant'. A broader range of factors needs to be considered when wanting to make a successful bid for a sporting mega-event.

Bidding considerations

There are a number of important criteria that need to be considered when bidding for major events. For a bid to be considered, these criteria (as identified by the event owners) must be met. Many event owners, such as the IOC, have specific guidelines that must be adhered to by the bid committee as part of lodging a bid. Ingerson and Westerbeek (2000) originally presented these criteria as mandatory requirements of a formal bid application. The criteria, reflecting a qualitative analysis of the viewpoint of key event bidding experts, are listed as:

- political—process, policies, government support, political stability;
- economic—economic potential, financial stability and ability to fund;
- media—local, global media support and image;
- infrastructure—location, accessibility, transport and pre-existing facilities;
- technical—communication system and technical expertise;
- sociocultural—image of the city and community support;
- building relations—influencing decision makers, spending time in contact, and accessing people in key positions;
- bidding brand equity—having key power brokers and a bidding presence;
- commitment—full-time bidding and starting early;
- guaranteed added value—product knowledge and research capacity;
- legacy—generation of goodwill and benefit to community;
- bidding experience—established networks and understanding of important aspects;
- bid team composition—mix of youth and experience and good team selling skills;
- creative statistics—present credible event specific information;
- business environment—ability to attract businesses to the area; and
- competitive environment—an understanding globally of other bidders and events.

The capacity to distinguish a bid application was recognised by Crockett (1994, p. 13), who stated that cities bidding for events 'need to get smarter about the bidding process'. There is a limited supply of hallmark status events and an increased demand for events worldwide.

The criteria identified by Ingerson and Westerbeek (2000) are by no means exclusive, nor exhaustive. For every bid there are a variety of considerations perceived as being an important part of the bidding process. For example, Athens being granted the right to host the 100-year anniversary of the Olympic Games in 1996 was seen as a strong emotional reason to win the bid. However, the bid was unsuccessful, with the winning host city being Atlanta, because of 'an impressive marketing campaign on the International Olympic movement using a wonderful youth-friendly lobby team' (McGeoch & Korporaal 1994, p. 34). Therefore, in comprehending the complexity of the bid process, it is necessary to identify the whole range of criteria that may be important when wanting to bid for a hallmark event.

Westerbeek, Turner and Ingerson (2002) extended the research of Ingerson and Westerbeek (2000) by developing the bid criteria through a quantitative analysis of the views of 135 event experts. The results of this study identified key success factors for bid teams:

- *Accountability*—presents the reputation, legacy components, technical expertise, and facilities of a host city.

- *Political support*—presents the stability and economic contribution, as well as government support for a city.
- *Relationship marketing*—presents key relationships, whether political or event decision-oriented, in support of the event.
- *Ability*—presents the sport-specific technical expertise, equipment and event capabilities of the bid team.
- *Infrastructure*—presents the accessibility, transport infrastructure and community support for the event.
- *Bid team composition*—presents the level of support, mix of personnel and selling capacity of bid team officials.
- *Communication and exposure*—presents the city's capacity to develop media exposure opportunities and capacity for communication systems to support the bid.
- *Existing facilities*—presents the current facilities available, construction dates and accommodation capacity.

The key success factors highlight those elements required within the bidding framework in order to achieve success. The capacity of the bid team to appreciate and understand what is required (i.e. essential) in order to achieve a successful bid outcome is presented in the factors identified. The key features considered important in the bid process are developed under the following subheadings.

Political and economic features

Political criteria encompass the processes and policies of the local, regional or national governments in support of the bid. Government involvement in securing events is increasingly being seen as a critical attribute, and the strength of government support can be observed by the level of spending on infrastructure and capital works going towards attracting events to the city. Political support is important from the perspective of securing vital resources (financial, physical, human resources) as well as the political and financial stability of the city and country in relation to the formulation of (longer-term) government policies that will clearly contribute to the quality of the event. It is important for government representatives to be able to show the potential economic contribution of the event to the local economy, thereby generating considerable community support for the event and boosting the popularity of the politicians involved.

Added to this political environment is the way in which events have become unique entities to attract to a region investment from business visitors coupled with spending of non-business visitors. Major events are invariably linked to large and wealthy corporations as well as governments, due to the range of economic benefits that can accrue. The economic benefit associated with events is aligned closely to the tourist return that these events can generate directly through attending the event and through promoting the host region as a place for future visits.

Communication and exposure (media) features

Communication and exposure reflect many city marketing issues incorporating the reputation of the city as a major tourist destination and the communication and information technology (IT) systems that are in place, ensuring national and global media exposure of the event. The importance of media involvement in the event itself is identified as being essential to creating interest in a destination and attracting future visits and investment. Obviously, widespread communication and exposure are important to both the event and the host city, both looking to enhance the brand equity of their 'properties', and this process will largely benefit from high-tech communication systems being in place.

Infrastructure and existing facility features

Infrastructure is the physical evidence of venues, accommodation and transport systems for staging an event. A well-integrated infrastructure can reduce costs, improve spectator and athlete convenience, and provide long-term benefits for the community after the event has gone. Attention to the infrastructure requirements of an event enables the event organiser to convince the event promoter that the event host has the capacity to successfully host the event personnel and competition activities. The visual and architectural attractiveness of the facilities, coupled with the location representing sufficient population size in the catchment area of the event and strong community support for the event, ensures that the event will be visited by many people.

The pre-existence of established high-quality facilities includes the availability of overnight accommodation (for key groups such as spectators and participants) in the host city/region and a range of established facilities. Provision of facilities that will have long-term use for the community and sustainable business revenue as tourist attractions, training sites or operational venues following the event is paramount. Poorly conceived or dated structures lessen the longer-term viability and the short-term interest in selecting a city to host an event.

Ability and technical features

The ability to stage the event reflects the high level of management expertise demanded in the organisation of such an event. Sport-specific technical expertise, the event management (administration) expertise, the event equipment available, and the ability of the event organisers to fund the event (public and private) are all base requirements that directly relate to the actual event being hosted. The ability to organise an event is evidenced by a solid track record in organising similar events.

The primary means of showing the event organiser a city's competency to host an event is through its technical presentation. Great emphasis is placed on a detailed technical analysis by the bidding city, because this creates such a visual image of the success of an event. Technical elements include such features as competition and non-competition facilities, event location, proposed budgets, personnel (including staff knowledge as well as experience), equipment, and other resources that contribute to the successful staging of the event. A site visit adds to this technical bid process. An event promoter sees the ability of the event organising team as a critical service in the decision to award the bid team the right to host the event.

Bid team composition features

Bid team composition develops the importance of a mix of talent on the bid team. This is particularly relevant in ensuring that the bid team is regarded favourably by key decision makers. A mix of age and experience, men and women on the team, and strong personal selling and networking skills of bid team members (relationship marketing) ensure that a wide variety of skills and approaches are available to tackle a range of complex tasks. Bidding experience and bid team composition reflect the need to recruit, train and develop individuals with specific bidding skills. Ingerson and Westerbeek (2000) identified that experienced bid members bring essential knowledge and networks to new bid committees. Visible proof of product experts (i.e. former athletes, high-profile board members) is needed to establish further credibility with event owners. Here the bidding organisation also needs to show it has established external support (e.g. corporate and from regional politicians).

Accountability features

Accountability deals with the dependency relationship event bidders have with event owners and the public(s). It links the psychological and community effects to the ability to generate goodwill for the event through the legacy the event leaves behind. Event bidding organisations are accountable to the public in relation to the need to show where tax money has been spent and how the local community will benefit from the event being held in its city. Event bidders can prove they will be accountable by showing they have an established and recognised presence in the marketplace as a bidding organisation, a strong reputation (as a city) in hosting successful (sporting) events, and by showcasing a broad range of excellent sporting facilities. Accountable practices present to the event promoter and the various stakeholders in the community and political circles the capacity of the event organising team and the city to deliver on the critical elements of the event. The event organiser is in a position to convince the event promoter that it has sufficient expertise and procedures in place to ensure a successful event.

Adding to accountable practices, the city's culture and its community members are an important consideration in securing an event. Given that public funding supports many events, it is necessary that a bid incorporate the local community. When choosing to host an event, the character of the residents and their desire to support the bid must be taken into consideration.

Relationship marketing features

Relationship marketing reflects the relationships and 'friends made' between the key parties in the bidding process. A good relationship with politicians and having people with sufficient influence and positional power to support the event organisers' bid are seen as crucial influences on the event promoter. This is supported by general relationship marketing theory, which maintains that building and enhancing interactions with key stakeholders (decision makers) can develop long-term satisfaction and mutually beneficial partnerships.

The more skilled bid team members are at relationship marketing, the greater the strength of the partnership that is being built and the more likely interactions will be favourable for both parties. Bid teams (cities) must show a commitment to the cause (event)— either through continual bidding for a range of hallmark events, as Manchester did at both Olympic and Commonwealth Games levels, or with infrastructure and public support, as Melbourne has achieved by building a range of international-standard facilities.

Aligned with this relationship marketing process is the capacity to build brand equity, which is best illustrated 'if the bid organisation's name is immediately recognised, and brand identity can be leveraged' (Ingerson & Westerbeek 2000, p. 248). Guaranteed added value and legacy become important criteria for consideration within this brand building. As part of the determination of the value they are offering, bid committees need to consider the perceived value from various stakeholder perspectives. For example, the facilities, improved infrastructure, business opportunities or the development of sport are common examples of the legacy an event delivers to the city's occupants. For the event owner, an attractive (popular) host city coupled with a successfully staged event will give the organisation prominence on the world stage and attract future (attractive) bids for its events.

Finally, creative statistics reflect the ability of event bidders to present event (organising) specific information (e.g. projected spectator numbers, potential profit) in such a way as to support the merits of the bid and the benefits of a particular community hosting the event.

Each criterion identified can be reflected on as being more or less important, depending on the circumstances of the bid, the critical significance and the size of the event. Ingerson and Westerbeek (2000) found that excluding specific criteria may lead to incomplete bid preparation and evaluation. The criteria presented here differentiate the competing bid application documents, in terms of the number of possible bidding organisations, the strictness of conditions stipulated by the event owner, and the host bidder capacity to meet all infrastructure demands. Certain bid criteria include those features which may not be essential to win a bid but which can substantially enhance the bid proposal. Event bid committees may concentrate their strategies on all or some of these elements to distinguish their bid from other competitors. These strategies are highlighted in the next section, which introduces bid application requirements.

The bid application document

A successful bid application demands significant time, energy, financial and personnel resources in order to ensure that it meets the standards and criteria required to achieve success. While the key success factors identified previously are of crucial importance in achieving success, the final application must represent a document which identifies and supports the required components that are requested by the event owner. Here we examine some of those crucial components, via an in-depth analysis of the IOC bid application prerequisites and then a brief look at the way in which this process can be adversely affected, through a review of the Salt Lake City bid for the 2002 Winter Olympic Games. What follows is an analysis of the bid process that emerged from the bid reforms and initiated the bid procedures required for the 2008 Summer Olympic Games.

Successful bid application documents obviously need to attend specifically to the requirements as defined by the event owner. The submission needs to examine all required aspects and present the necessary information in a clear and concise manner. The IOC, reflecting on the quality of the bid, advises that the basics be placed ahead of the glitz and glamour of significant personalities. As stated by Jacques Rogge, President of the IOC, in an interview concerning London's bid for the 2012 Olympic Games, 'we are not impressed by big names . . . We are not going to be impressed with former sport stars or current ones. We are living with them all the time, they are our bread and butter'. Rogge indicates that the essential elements of a bid are security, the comfort of athletes, a good Olympic village, good sports venues and good transport to bring them back, followed by an urban and sporting legacy (*The Telegraph Sport*, 2003, p. 1).

The IOC has a manual for candidate cities bidding for the right to host the Olympic Games. This document requires the submission of information via a 'candidature file', representing a master plan for organising the Games. Each bidding city is presented with a questionnaire containing 18 themes with 149 questions to which the city must respond, and a model candidature file that shows the city how to present these replies. The concept that surrounds this process ensures that the candidature committee is saved unnecessary work, effort and expense while ensuring that the information provided to the IOC can be easily and objectively analysed and compared (IOC Candidature Acceptance Procedure 1999).

The 18 themes represent aspects that would be considered in a wider forum beyond that represented purely by the requirements of the IOC. These are attributes that can be applied to any bid application document (excluding perhaps the specific event activities in the Paralympic Games information). Each element should be carefully considered and relevant aspects identified in order to enhance the bid application document. While specifically stated to represent the requirements of the Olympic Games, the crossover into other sporting events is clearly evident. The 18 themes are briefly examined here.

Eighteen themes

National, regional and candidate city characteristics

This aspect provides the event owner with information on the political, economic and social structure and stability of the country. The jurisdiction, responsibility and prerogative of the country, including the general public opinion, is monitored.

Legal aspects

The legal elements associated with hosting the Olympic Games are identified and covered, reflecting an understanding of the Olympic Charter, the Host City Contract, the Candidature Manual, the process of the conditions governing the use of the Olympic symbol, and procedures and undertakings.

Customs and immigration formalities

Entry and immigration regulations are identified along the lines of authorising entry into the country for accredited Olympic officials, ensuring access and work accreditation where required so that these officials can undertake duties in preparation for the Games. Coupled with this aspect is the guarantee to import, use and export, free of customs duties, the goods necessary for the successful celebration of the Games.

Environmental protection and meteorology

The Olympic movement supports and commits fully to sustainable development, endeavouring to contribute to the protection of the natural environment. Issues such as architecture, reuse, restoration and protection of habitats, handling of waste and consumption as well as air and water quality are given particular attention.

Finance

Financial guarantees and economic effects need to be determined and reported to clearly describe the way in which the city will manage the Games and construction. Budgets reflecting the sources of revenues and expenditures, capital investments and cash-flow fore-casts need to be outlined.

Marketing

Olympic marketing includes all aspects of private financing, such as broadcast rights (radio, television, Internet, WAP), sponsor and supplier programs, licensing programs and ticket sales, as opposed to financing from the government by means of grants. In conjunction with discussion with the IOC Marketing Department, the candidate city must outline ways in which it can support and/or enhance the marketing program.

General sports concept

The sports that constitute the Games program must be fixed seven years beforehand. The planning and strategy relating to general sports organisation is detailed and presented. This includes reference to the sports schedule, timetabling for the sport-program, ceremonies, competition sites, test events, participation statistics, equipment, and sport-specific logistics.

Sports

Each individual sport that is represented in the Olympic Games presents a series of technical management elements that must be addressed, including questions relating to competition sites, training venues, officials, and media sites, construction and work schedules, venue capacity, and weather patterns that may affect competition.

Paralympic Games

Specific to the Olympic Games, the host city provides the infrastructure and equipment for the Paralympic Games, with support for 4000 athletes and 2000 team officials.

Olympic village

The Olympic village presents a place where up to 16 000 athletes and team officials are able to prepare for competition without being disturbed or distracted by media, visitors or spon-sors. Design and architecture, including scale diagrams and room plans, should be presented.

Medical and health services

The city's health and medical system should be described in terms of medical resources, hos-pitals, doctors, medical expenses and reported epidemiological risks, including arrangements that will be put in place for the Games.

Security

A safe and secure environment should be presented in a discreet but efficient manner. The infrastructure to be considered should reflect the information-gathering mechanisms, overall general security for the village and venues, relevant plans for emergencies, risks and control procedures, security for transport, public services and crime management.

Accommodation

Accommodation includes presenting an inventory and method of securing rooms and tariffs within the city for the 'Olympic Family', officials, media and athletes. This list should include number of rooms, quality of rooms, allocation of accommodation types and guarantees on room rates.

Transport

Effective organisation of the transport system can ensure the success of the event. Demand for transport will extend to the Olympic Family (including athletes and officials), media, Games staff and spectators. Transport questions are divided into four areas: (1) offer relates to transport infrastructure; (2) demand relates to transport data, principles and logistics; (3) concept develops the offer and demand; and (4) planning and management presents the processes involved in meeting potential demand.

Technology

Technology identifies the requirements for pre-event preparation and implementation in IT and technical areas. This relates to timing, results processing, accreditation, ticketing, recruitment of volunteers and media circulation of information. All IT requirements are identified, ranging from systems development through to integration and operations.

Communications and media services

The communications function requires management of the media and clear communication with local communities, authorities and all other constituents. Media operations and services extend to two key components, representing the international broadcast centre (IBC) and the main press centre (MPC).

Olympism and culture

Worldwide cultural and educational programs need to be developed in order to promote the Olympic spirit within the country hosting the Games. The traditions of the host country should be reflected, and protocols and practices established surrounding such ceremonial events as the opening and closing, medal and welcoming ceremonies.

Guarantees

A list of guarantees is required that clearly identifies what the host is able to support and fulfil.

The above list of items is extensive and relevant to the preliminary requirements of the IOC. It is clear that most items would appropriately match those sought by other event owners.

The differentiating factors would largely be reflected only in the size of the event. A smaller, single-sport activity might not require the extent of information on all 18 areas of that required by the Olympic movement, but the requirement for the key attributes should be considered as a minimum when developing a bid application document.

Wilkinson (1988) supports this bid application information process through inclusion of aspects referring to:

- *technical elements*—represented by the site of the event, facilities, budget, proposed dates, promotional plans, critical path, presentation aids and evaluation;
- *support elements*—represented by personnel services, local government approval, role of the city/community, transport services, accommodation, availability of officials, media facilities, special services;
- *cultural elements*—represented by the city or locale, television coverage, ceremonies, demonstrations/displays, cultural program, evaluation/guidelines and final report.

These items for consideration are similar to the list of Olympic Games requirements previously outlined. A bid application document should, as a minimum, consider these requirements and include those that are relevant to the event owner. The inclusion of as many of these factors as possible presents the bid in the most comprehensive manner. At the end of this chapter, two case studies are presented that deal with different issues in relation to a proper and ethical bid process.

The event bidding lifecycle

Within the framework of the project lifecycle introduced in Chapter 2, coupled with the fact that a bid application is largely representative of a two-part lifecycle (the bid and post-bid outcome), it is important to look at the bidding process taking into account the lifecycle associated with it. Ingerson and Westerbeek (2000) identified a seven-stage process contained within the event bid procedure, with criteria ranging from the formation of a bid committee to a post-event analysis. The bid process has evolved into a lifecycle with a clear time frame from conception to announcement, and ultimately implementation through to evaluation of the actual event.

The initial stages in the bid process represent the identification and gathering together of a group of people (phase one: formation of the bid committee) who will represent the key stakeholders of the city, state or region in preparing and planning for the bid. These people will create a bid team that will identify the key elements and attributes that must be presented to the event owner. The bid team will be formed early in the process and will undertake the task of preparing the bid (phase two).

The bid preparation phase will involve various steps in acquiring knowledge about the bid, ensuring that the documentation meets the requirements of the event, through to establishing contact with key partners and officials. This preparation process will culminate in a submission of the relevant bid documents, lobbying of key decision makers (phase three), and ultimately a decision announcing the success or failure of the bid (phase four).

Most references to bidding identify phase four as the final element of the process, whereby the achievement of a final outcome concludes the bidding phase. Reality suggests that if the bid is successful, then particular components of the bid process will extend into the remaining phases connected with the event itself. The preparation, hosting and post-event phases will ultimately require some input from the bid team or relevant partners to ensure success. This is due to the initial commitments that have been made during bidding being a distinct part of the process. If the bid is unsuccessful, then the bid team completes its work and the process ends.

Ingerson and Westerbeek (2000) presented the seven phases of the bid process with very much a linear approach. In this mechanistic overview of the process, there is a distinct starting and end point. The linear approach is rigid and inflexible, with no two bidding activities being declared alike. Emery (2002) criticised this linear approach to the bidding lifecycle, a position supported by Ingerson and Westerbeek (2000), who stated that the bid process really should be seen as cyclical, crossing the boundary between one event and the next.

The optimum bid process as cyclical is depicted in Figure 6.1, and bid organisations will become more successful when repeating this cycle. In phases one to four, the bid team forms and then creates and submits the bid application. If the bid is successful, phases five to seven incorporate the remaining stages of the event development, while including the aspects and people connected with the bid.

At this point the bid process is essentially over, and bid personnel may move to inclusion in the planning and running of the event or move on to the next task, in either another activity or another bid application. If the bid is unsuccessful, it can be argued that the process enables the expertise already in existence within the bid team, and the knowledge gleaned

Figure 6.1 The cyclical bid process

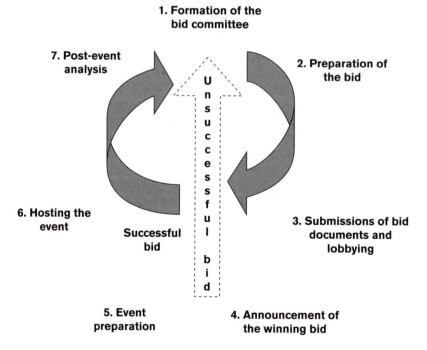

Source: Adapted from Ingerson and Westerbeek (2000).

from bid documents, to be redeployed for future bid applications. The establishment of key government event agencies such as the Victorian Major Events Corporation, whose job it is to identify major events and support the bid application process, reflects the cyclical approach, whereby expert bid application teams and personnel are created. These teams will regroup, add expertise and bid for future events. Whether the bid application is successful or unsuccessful, the outcome will be recreated and the formation of a team with key knowledge and expertise in bidding will remain intact.

Reflecting on the bid application lifecycle, it can be seen that the process of bidding for events is not a simple one-off, hit-or-miss technique, but one which involves a great deal of thought, a gathering of key teams and expertise, and a process of improvement and development of the approach and techniques adopted by a bidding community. This approach is crucial to identifying a best-practice approach to bidding for key events and activities.

Within the bid lifecycle framework presented, coupled with the factors required to achieve success and the bid application document inclusions, it makes sense to form event networks that are equipped to deal with or, even better still, integrate all the recurring elements. The formation of a network that includes groups from a wide range of all the involved parties, who represent interests that range from political, host city, the media, the community and the facility, all of which obviously present a key contribution towards achieving a successful bidding outcome, is a further requirement to ensuring success in any bid application.

Network relationships in the event bidding process

The growth and professionalisation of events has meant that these now serve a multitude of agendas, reflecting government objectives, regulation, media requirements, sponsor needs and community expectations, among others (Bowdin et al. 2001). A number of stakeholders are present in the event, all with various needs and conflicting demands. The success of an event can be achieved through the way in which these needs and demands are balanced. The event bidding process is also faced with this range of stakeholder expectations.

With this diversity of stakeholders, there are a number of ways in which the event bidding team can be presented and structured. Different structural types such as simple organisations, functional or divisional groups, matrix organisations, networks as well as other configurations are examined in more detail in Chapter 5.

Although event bidding teams may be formed with particular structures that suit one of the above possible types, it is worth looking at the network aspect of the event bid team process in more detail. This is because major events predominantly epitomise a virtual corporation in which, though relationships may be ongoing, they remain more informal, less structured, and thus more dependent on consistent performance to ensure recontracting in the future. Some events can be seen as an extreme form of virtual organisation because the participants come together, literally, only once a year to stage the event and then immediately part ways until the following year (Erickson & Kushner 1999). At the more extreme end, the participants come together once and then disband the organisation completely (which occurs with the Olympic Games). This virtual corporation relationship is true of event bid committees, where the level of interdependence of partners is substantial, with organisations coming together to support and enhance the bid, ensuring a high degree of resource and competency sharing. After the bid process these organisations disband the relationship formed and develop or seek new arrangements.

As for events, it is clear that these involve a comprehensive network of partners as a key requirement for success. Erickson and Kushner (1999) posited a typology in which the relationship types present in an event network were developed. The event network represented a focal (dyadic) relationship between two principal actors: a primary relationship involving participants with direct ties to the dyad partners, a secondary relationship representing organisations that influence each other in their relationships with a dyad partner, and a tertiary relationship relevant to only one dyad member.

The focal relationship exists between the key partners in the network, usually represented by the event bidder and the owner (promoter) who owns the event on behalf of groups such as the sport-governing bodies including the IOC or FIFA. Equally, an event agency such as IMG might own the event. The network begins to emerge through the decisions of this event owner in seeking tenders for the right to host the event. These tenders may extend to a facility directly, or to a host country or other like partner. The result of this 'host-seeking' tends to be the formation of several bidding teams that become responsible for establishing committees. Ultimately, the event owner will narrow down several potential networks to identify the one with the successful bid. The other focal partner in the dyad then emerges as event host, and will initially begin at the other end of the core focal relationship as event bidder. This network partner might represent such groups as the facility, the sporting organisation or the community.

This basic relationship is one in which initial administrative power rests largely with the event owner. The event owner is in the position of deciding on the successful bid applicant. The event owner determines where the event will be held and can set the rules by which the final choice will be made (as shown in the IOC application document example previously).

Given that there exists this significant administrative imbalance in the focal relationship, the bidding team is required, almost by default, to present a highly specialised network of relationships to the event owner. In order to strengthen its position, the event bidder must seek to enter into relationships with other organisations in order to provide resources and ties that will benefit its bid. The event-bidding partner must seek to become attractive to the event owner, not only as a result of the bid team composition and technical expertise gathered but especially through the micro-network of other already established relationships that it is able to offer to its partner.

Incorporating the key success factors identified by Westerbeek et al. (2002), internally the bid team can maximise its composition through the inclusion of key experts in order to convince the event promoter that there is sufficient expertise and capacity within the bid team to successfully develop the requirements relating to the event. Technical expertise reflecting equipment and staff knowledge is an important element in the bid presentation. Externally, the bid team can develop political support and access to major infrastructure projects in support of the bid. The introduction of these key resources through relationships with key individuals and organisations strengthens the relationships that the bid team is seeking to form with the event owner.

Primary relationships associated with the event bidding team clearly emerge when analysing the network process. These primary relationships often include the integration of the event owner and event bidder into groups such as the national sporting organisations (NSOs), state sporting organisations (SSOs) and even event participants. Primary connections enable enhancement of the focal relationship. For example, a bid team forming an alliance with organisations representing athletes such as players' unions or athlete management companies would do so in order to strengthen its organisation with high-profile identities to place its bid at the forefront in political, media and profile terms.

Secondary connections, involving links between key dyad partners, can also be formed. Secondary relationships can be represented through such groups as sponsors and the media. The capacity for these groups to develop relationships within and across boundaries is an important process in the development of a successful bid. Local media brought in by the event bidder and international media brought in by the event owner may represent such a secondary relationship.

Media and sponsor groups representing the local community have a clear role to play in their tertiary relationship with the bid team. Positive involvement of the media will have an effect on the communication and exposure that a bid team receives. The media can enhance the support from community and consumer groups and deflect any animosity presented by special-interest groups with anti-event sentiments.

Finally, tertiary connections may be introduced to the network. These are network relationships critical to the success of the public event but handled by only one dyad member. The connection is made to a participant, perhaps external to the event, who remains a member of its original micro-network only. The new participant may never join with any participant in the opposite network. Contacts with the government or local community may take this form of connection.

Tertiary relationships reflect the formation of close ties with potential allies. These ties could occur in the form of relationships with key politicians, sponsors, city officials and media, whereby people with sufficient influence and power to support the event organiser's bid are identified. These groups reflect the relationship marketing factor identified by Westerbeek et al. (2002). The capacity to have a good relationship with these groups can be seen as a crucial influence on the event promoter. Being accountable ensures that the support required by these groups is provided in association with the bid.

A secondary tertiary connection (termed the T2 relationship) has been inserted to represent participants who have a relationship with a tertiary network member that affects the network process but is clearly not a direct network partner in the sense of having a direct link to one of the focal network partners. An example in this instance may be a local government organisation interacting with a specific community group on an event-specific issue (e.g. noise pollution at a Formula One Grand Prix event). This issue is presented to the local government organisation rather than the focal network member.

Given the expense involved in establishing facilities and putting on an event, and the public risks involved in delivering the one-off final product, the total risk to event participants is magnified far above levels generally considered in standard network theory. Consequently, the circumstances involved in putting together a network for a public event will provide even stronger incentives to prospective participants to seek out partners with extended track records in such events (Erickson & Kushner 1999). An example of the event network is presented in Figure 6.2.

Convincing the event promoter that the host city has the necessary infrastructure for the event to be successfully held in that city plays an important role in the success of the bid. In the network, the relationship between the city (or host) and the existing infrastructure that it provides and the bid team is an important component. The link in the network between the event team and facility management is clearly identified here.

A strong relationship is of significance during the period of the bid in order to ensure that all parties are fully supportive of it. The greater the support between all parties in the

Figure 6.2 Network relationships in the bidding process

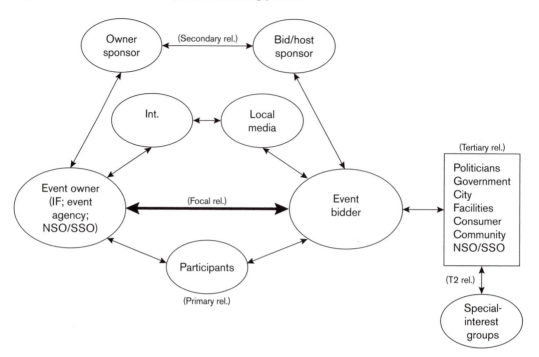

network, the more influence the bid team will wield on the outcome. It is clear that the integration of network partnerships, coupled with a knowledge of the key factors supporting successful bidding outcomes, can enhance the host's bid application to an event owner, thereby building the potential host's case for selection.

Summary

This chapter has introduced the complexities associated with the bid application through emphasising the considerations that must be taken into account by facility managers and event bidders in the bid application process. This bid application process is clearly a cyclical one in which the members of a bid team must ensure that they themselves have sufficient expertise and experience, coupled with support in the form of other personnel, whether political, media or general community support. Added to this must be a suitable infrastructure already in place and the capacity to present all of this information in a way that will make the bidding organisation appear attractive to any decision makers. There are a number of key issues that face the bid team in presenting information, but the critical components surrounding political support, contracts and obligations, finance and financial management, safety and security, stadia and support infrastructure, media, accreditation, ticketing, sport support services and community support services must be covered in order to present and develop a successful bid.

Case study 1

Bidding for favours—the Salt Lake City bid for the 2002 Winter Olympic Games

> The intense competition to host the Olympic games, coupled with the multi-billion dollar enterprise that results from winning that competition, have exposed the weaknesses in the Movement's governing structure and operational controls. (Report of the Special Bid Oversight Commission 1999, executive summary.)

In late November 1998, a report appearing in the Salt Lake City media alleged that the daughter of a late member of the IOC, René Essomba, had received educational assistance from the Salt Lake City bid committee. The subsequent investigation into this matter by the Salt Lake Organising Committee (SLOC) revealed that the bid committee had established a financial assistance program, described as an 'NOC Support Program', aimed at developing countries. This program was reportedly established following the close loss experience by Salt Lake of the 1998 Winter Olympic Games, which were ultimately awarded to Nagano.

Subsequent investigations revealed that payments had been made, *inter alia*, to or for the benefit of members of the family of several IOC members, and that other payments had been made to or for the benefit of persons designated by IOC members and charged to the program. Additionally, it appeared that cash payments dating back to late 1991 or early 1992 had been made to some IOC members (Report of the IOC *ad hoc* Commission 1999).

Following the revelations of improper bidding practice, the Board of Ethics of SLOC (1999) was charged to investigate allegations of impropriety in connection with the Salt Lake bid committee's efforts to win the bids for the 1998 and 2002 Winter Olympic Games. This report identified many irregularities associated with each of the bids in respect to the interaction, expenditures and gift endowments made by a bid city. A number of recommendations were made at this time, predominantly concerned with the enforcement of rules governing interaction between bid cities and IOC members reflecting expenditures and the provision of gifts and support to key NOC or IOC programs.

In March 1999 a Special Bid Oversight Commission reported that for change to occur, it needed to begin from within the IOC. The broader culture of improper gift giving in which candidate cities provided things of value to IOC members in an effort to buy their votes was prevalent within the organisation. The culture was found to flourish through the closed nature of the IOC and the absence of any ethical or transparent financial controls and operations. The findings indicated that there was a transaction involving a giver and a taker, but that the taker triggered much of the demand. The Commission reported that the selection process should be free of improper influence on IOC members and should be made instead on the basis of which city could best stage the Olympic Games.

Case study 2

Bidding ethically—bidding for the 2008 Summer Olympic Games

Following the damning reports and inquiries into the bidding process for Salt Lake, the IOC expelled six members in March 1999, a number of members were issued with serious warnings, a Reform Commission was set up and an Ethics Commission assembled.

Coupled with these governance and organisational reforms, the bidding process was examined and new procedures introduced. This process involved amendments to Rule 37 of the Olympic Charter, which refers to the election procedure for a host city for the Olympic Games and the Winter Olympic Games. The amendment to Rule 37 included the introduction of a two-phase host city election procedure. Phase 1 presented a candidature acceptance procedure to be conducted under the authority of the IOC executive board. This process involved the proposing of a host applicant to the IOC by its respective NOC. Each city nominated by the NOC would be considered an applicant city for a period of 10 months before being accepted by the IOC board as a candidate city. The applicant city must now present information to the IOC board through submission of a questionnaire. Assessment by a working group of external experts and IOC administration members will cover technical criteria, government support, public opinion, general infrastructure, security, venues, accommodation and transport. Through this candidature acceptance procedure, the IOC executive board determines which cities are to be accepted as candidate cities.

Those accepted as candidate cities go through a second phase, during which they are required to submit a candidature file to the IOC. These files are examined by an evaluation commission, which also makes inspections of the candidate cities before issuing a report. Based on this report the IOC executive draws up a list of candidate cities to be submitted to the IOC session for election. The evaluation commission comprises, among others, representatives of the International Federations and National Olympic Committees, IOC members, representatives of the IOC Athletes' Commission and International Paralympic Committee, as well as IOC experts. This group undertakes one evaluation visit to each candidate city.

Within the candidature acceptance procedures are guidelines of adherence to the ethical practices and a number of rules of conduct for a candidate. These rules involve: the designation of an independent expert (auditor) and information about this person to the IOC ethics commission; promotion which does not display the Olympic logo; Internet sites for information only; and limitations on the international promotion of the candidate. The organisation of receptions, exhibitions and meetings to promote candidature at international events within or outside a candidate city's country is prohibited, as are gifts, and any visits by the evaluation commission will be programmed accordingly. Other visits by IOC members will not involve any promotion by the candidate, aid programs to other NOCs must be declared, and promises and commitments must only be given if they can be fulfilled.

These measures have been initiated for bids relating to the 2008 Olympic Games and beyond. With particular reference to the 2008 candidature, the IOC executive board adjudged five cities as candidate cities, and the evaluation commission assessed each city on the basis of the 18 themes within the risk assessment framework. This approach was undertaken in an attempt to identify any risks that could occur in the period up to and including the Olympic Games. Osaka, Paris, Toronto, Beijing and Istanbul formed the five cities, with the commission rating three bids as excellent and in which only minor deficiencies were identified (all of which could be resolved before 2008 by an efficient Games organisation). The cities of Paris, Toronto and Beijing were considered able to organise an excellent Olympic Games in 2008. The five cities were drawn from the original list of 10 applicant cities, which included the five candidate cities plus Bangkok, Cairo, Havana, Kuala Lumpur and Seville.

Final voting for the host city was undertaken in July 2001, when Beijing was selected after polling 44 votes in the first round (Istanbul 17; Osaka 6; Paris 15; Toronto 20). Osaka was eliminated and Beijing polled 56 votes in the second round (Istanbul 9; Paris 18; Toronto 22).

Q. Having looked at the key success factors of event bidding in this chapter, how important do you think the 'relationship marketing' component of the bidding process is relative to, for example, ability to organise the event? Justify your answer.

Q. Knowing the economic and possibly social importance of attracting major events to a city or region, which do you feel are the most important stakeholding parties in the process of deciding whether the event can justifiably be hosted by the region? Consider the less powerful stakeholders, such as the local community, when you formulate your answer.

Q. Do the owners of the world's biggest sporting events have local responsibilities? What are the benefits that global events can deliver to the regions that host the events?

Q. Outline the top five most important steps towards securing an event that would attract at least national-level media coverage. Justify your choice.

7

Operating the new sport facility: preparing event management infrastructure

CHAPTER OBJECTIVES

In this chapter, we will:
- Highlight the complexities of preparing for a facility in event mode.
- Outline the requirements for a successful facility and event project management structure.
- Identify the distinguishing features of contract management as applied to a sport facility.
- Identify the distinguishing features of risk management as applied to a sport facility or a major event.

If you build it, they will come . . .

The Alfred McAlpine Stadium in Huddersfield, UK, was built between 1991 and 1994. Its design description portrayed a facility that would act as a social oasis, capable of attracting future investment into leisure and retail developments on the site. Built to house Huddersfield Football Club, on a 50-acre site, there was a strong emphasis on meeting the national requirements for British football stadia. The initial design for this stadium was for a temporary function, including two stands that would house all club and maintenance and service facilities. Inclusions within these two stands were designed to enable commercial facilities to coexist, with the view that these commercial operations would aid in funding future developments. The stands could accommodate and host conferences and meetings, with hospitality suites capable of being transformed into hotel rooms on non-match days. Public amenities included an indoor swimming pool, council offices, a health club and hotel, which had been designed into the perimeter of the stadium (John & Sheard 2000).

Not content with just building a facility that could accommodate the 30–40 'home' games of a perennial lower-division football team in the English Football League, the facility design and construction was planned with a community 'legacy' in mind. Such a multi-purpose facility puts the onus on the facility management team to ensure that both access and operations meet demands emerging from within the community. Not only will this facility host a football team, but it will have to ensure that members of the public can gain ready access, members of the business community can access and utilise the amenities, and spectators can view an array of major events in comfort, and with suitable services.

Preparing for the event

The facility is built, staff are in place to run the facility, and now the facility is ready to host its first event. This moment reflects the outcome presented by the feasibility study and through the design and construction process. The first event may involve the competition game of a host sport tenant, or a special event that has been foreseen in the planning process. Hosting the regular home fixtures of a tenant, who may pay rent to the facility or who may be an owner of the stadium, places the facility in a slightly more enviable position than that faced by the facility manager who must attract a range of events without relying on a sequence of regular fixtures. A critical consideration, no matter what the circumstances faced, is that the facility manager must seek to maximise the usage of the facility in order to make it pay. Where multi-use operations have been built into or are expected of the facility, then there is an expectation that a wide range of events will be forthcoming to the facility. The facility manager must respond to this condition of operations and must seek to maximise usage through attracting events.

If the conditions surrounding the facility involve no permanent tenants, or there is a lack of fixed activities through the major spectator sport leagues, then the facility must present itself as a viable option for attracting other forms of entertainment. These options might range from a variety of sport, arts or cultural activities through to some radical approaches to meeting the entertainment demands of consumers. The facility manager must be mindful of the elements that reflect ownership conditions, tenancy conditions, government demands, accessibility of the region to events, size of the facility, services that are offered, dimensions of the arena surface, current sponsorship or licensing agreements in place, to mention just a few of the wide-ranging usage responsibilities.

The earlier description of the Alfred McAlpine Stadium in Huddersfield identifies the multi-use capabilities that are becoming a more common requirement of service delivery. Throughout this chapter, we outline concerns surrounding preparation for events in the facility. We discuss the considerations that must be made both by the facility manager and by the event manager in order to ensure that successful outcomes can be achieved. We identify those aspects that will ensure success, such as operational, marketing, financial and staffing issues. From these issues emerge contract and risk management responsibilities that will also be addressed.

No matter what emphasis is placed on ensuring that facility managers follow up on the identified issues, there is no point in the facility manager working alone in preparing for the event without input from those responsible for running it. Equally, if event managers simply assume that an event will be run successfully without their ongoing input and double-checking the facility, they are likely to find that things do not go according to plan.

The facility in event mode

The preparation of events from the perspective of production and staging is not dissimilar, whether viewed from the position of the facility manager or from that of the event manager. Critical to either perspective is the attention to detail that is required. Every aspect pertaining to the event must be considered and designed to meet the needs of every relevant stakeholding group. The quote from Graham, Goldblatt and Delpy (1995, p. 43), 'Gather as much information as possible. You can never ask too many questions and if you assume that you know what your client is talking about, you may find yourself in big trouble', never rings more truly than in the case of event management operations.

All events held within a facility have similar lifecycle and organisational elements. These elements can be categorised in very different ways depending on the event itself, but all must be considered in order for an event to be successfully coordinated and operated through a facility. For ease of reporting, the categories have been identified within the phases of concept and planning, operations, and post-event. Remember, these phases reflect the actual running of the event within the facility, and are not aligned to the phases necessary in the feasibility, design and build aspects that have already been outlined.

Concept and planning phase

The concept and planning phase requires all the details surrounding the event to be identified and enacted by all parties. Meetings between facility management and event management should be conducted with the conditions and requirements being clearly outlined. If a special surface is required to be in place for the safe conduct of the event, especially if it is mandated for compliance with international guidelines, then this must be clearly understood. For example, the sand used for indoor beach volleyball events is of a particular salt-free consistency (Graham et al. 1995). The requirements associated with this 'floor' type must be clearly advised to the facility management, which must ensure that it is readily available and that it can be laid over the existing surface. Added to these conditions is that the costs associated with this surface must be included in the relevant negotiations. All necessary logistical elements should be identified and determined, with solutions outlined at this stage in proceedings. Ensuring that this is done will result in a relatively stress-free event.

Aspects for consideration during the concept and planning phase include:

- *Event date/usage schedule.* The event date must be identified early, with arrangements made to ensure the facility is available for that date. The facility will have bookings with tenants and special contractors that may extend years in advance. It is necessary to identify the availability of the facility with sufficient lead-time to ensure that a booking can be made. This date should be checked and double-checked to ensure there are no problems at a later date.
- *Information exchange.* It is crucial for the efficient management of an event that the parties responsible for running the event meet with facility management and exchange ideas and information. There may be the opportunity for the facility experts to provide a better way of achieving the event objectives, given their experience in running similar events. Equally, the event organisers will be better placed to ensure that their wishes are met if there is a consistent and regular exchange of ideas.
- *Research.* The more knowledge that all parties have about the event, the operations and support available, the better placed event organisers and facility managers will be to ensure a successful outcome.
- *Negotiation.* Each party involved in the event will be keen to maximise their respective outcomes. Negotiation will occur during the contracts phase. It is important that this process result in a fair outcome for all parties, otherwise there is likely to be resentment and the potential for a less than desirable effort put in by the aggrieved parties. Once negotiations are finalised, it is important that all parameters be included in contract negotiations.
- *Contracts.* A standard contract between the facility and event organisers should be drawn up and enforced. It is important that this agreement clearly state what each party will deliver. There is no point in coming back to the facility to request that they open up the pressroom after the event if there was no mention of this in the original agreement. All conditions and requirements should be identified during the information, research and negotiation stages and included in the contract.
- *Budget development.* The development of the budget should coincide with the other phases. The facility may have different policies associated with its hiring charges, depending on the type of event and the number of spectators in attendance. This may involve an initial flat-fee charge and then a percentage of the gate receipts over and above this, once the spectator numbers rise above a certain limit. Again, the specifics need to be clearly outlined and recorded in the contract. There may also be costs and charges associated with special requirements for flooring, concessions, sponsor signage, merchandise, ticket sales and many other elements connected with overall operations.
- *Retail policy/rates.* This element connects with those previously mentioned, in which there needs to be clear agreement between all parties on policies around sales and the way in which the income from sales will be distributed.
- *Staff selection.* The staffing of the facility and the event need to be clearly delineated. The event staff should be responsible for ensuring that the activities surrounding the event are managed and coordinated, while the facility staff should ensure that those aspects connected with the facility are clearly identified. Again, this should appear in and be clearly agreed on in the conditions of the contract.

A significant level of financial and economic success is dependent on the successful implementation and management of the core aspects identified here in the concept and planning phase.

Operational phase

The operational phase occurs at the completion of the planning phase and is when activities surrounding the event begin to occur. The facility moves into operations phase, ensuring that patrons have access to all required services. The event organisers ensure that the event activities are undertaken in a smooth and efficient manner.

Aspects for consideration during the operational phase include:

- *Promotional/PR campaigns undertaken.* Advising people of forthcoming events promotes both the event and the facility. This process can occur in conjunction with the event, in conjunction with sponsors or stakeholder groups, or independently. Whatever the approach, at the very least as a courtesy, all promotional activities should be agreed on by the parties involved. The facility and event management teams should approve the way in which their facility is included in any promotional materials or publicity campaigns.
- *Ticket sales and box office operations commence.* Establishment of a ticket sales regimen occurs at this time and ticket sales for the event should begin. Again, as with promotional campaigns, all parties should agree on the policy surrounding ticket sales. This should include whether sales will be made available to the public at the facility or only through agents. At the very least, answers to queries and access to information should be readily available through both the facility and event agency.
- *Facility preparation occurs.* At this stage all activities relevant to the event should occur, such as the checking of access to specific facility areas, of correct surface conditions, equipment checking and erecting, facility cleaning, and monitoring of concessions and merchandise.
- *Concessions and catering commences.* The purchase, supply and storage of all food, beverages and merchandise occurs to be ready for sale to patrons.
- *Parking.* Conditions associated with parking, including athlete and officials and VIP parking, should be identified and determined. Remaining conditions for spectators should be identified and clearly communicated to patrons.
- *Signage.* All sponsor and directional signage conditions and requirements must be enacted at this stage. Facility and event staff should be fully aware of the requirements for placement and maintenance of specific directional signage at the venue, as well as the conditions for placement of sponsor signage. This is especially important if the event signage is to override or replace current facility sponsor signage.
- *Media/communications.* Clear access, location and equipment services need to be provided for the media. The provision of fax machines, phones and computer connections is an important requirement at this point. Media access to the arena needs to be clearly delineated, as does access to the participants.
- *Spectator facilities engaged.* All requirements for the comfort of spectators need to be checked and rechecked to ensure that sufficient rest rooms will be available, access to concessions runs in a smooth and orderly fashion, and supplies for the expected number of attendees are adequately met.
- *Emergency services enacted.* Emergency plans and procedures should be known by all staff, and policies and procedures implemented.

- *Cleaning initiated*. The facility should be cleaned ready for spectators and participants, and clean-up should occur as soon as practicable following the event.
- *Maintenance monitored*. Ongoing checks should occur of the facility and equipment utilised to ensure a safe environment for all spectators, participants, staff, players and officials.
- *Safety and security implemented*. Staff responsible for security should be integrated into key areas of the facility, be fully equipped and accessible through the communication mechanisms in place.
- *Administration activities in place*. Clear guidelines and activities reflecting financial management, staffing and operational aspects of the event should be in place and enforced.

Post-event phase

The post-event phase is concerned with the evaluation and clean-up activities. All activities associated with the event will have concluded, spectators and participants will have departed and the final undertakings need to be initiated.

Aspects for consideration during the post-event phase include:

- *Box office termination*. Final arrangements for auditing box office operations need to be made to ensure that the correct financial and administrative outcomes are achieved and reported on.
- *Event settlement*. The facility and event management teams must ensure that all contractual obligations have been met, final spectator numbers tally and all agreed costs are finalised.
- *Clean-up*. The phase of clean-up and dealing with a number of maintenance aspects requires a thorough assessment of any damage to the facilities and equipment, to ensure that payment for such damage is covered by the party responsible.
- *Evaluation*. An evaluation of procedures, operations and outcomes should be conducted, including a review of aspects for future improvement, to ensure that all parties are satisfied with the activities undertaken.
- *Staff redeployment/severance*. Staff should be redeployed to a new event, transferred or paid out for their services. Any volunteer staff appointed to assist with the event should be thanked and rewarded for their involvement.

Attracting events to the facility

Once the planning, operational and evaluation phases have been considered and mechanisms put in place to cater for the activities required, the facility is ready to begin hosting events. Crucial to this aspect of hosting is the creation of an environment in which the facility can attract events. Circumstances surrounding the facility, such as design, location, capacity, leasing arrangements and staffing, are all critical elements for an event manager to consider when seeking a venue. The facility manager has to ensure that the facility is relevant to meet the needs of the event manager.

The facility manager must consider the fit of any event from the perspective of spectator and tenant needs, the frequency of event hosting requirements, and the capacity to run the event in an economically viable manner. The modern theme of developing stadia with more multi-purpose practices in mind places pressure on the facility manager to be more than just a specialist basketball, baseball or football operator. The stadium must be able to be transformed with short lead-times from a football park to a rock venue. The Telstra Dome at Docklands in Melbourne, a fully functional 52 000 seat arena with retractable roofing, has been transformed from a football stadium to a cricket oval to a World Wrestling Entertainment (WWE) ring to a concert venue in the space of a few days. This capacity to cross seasons (football is traditionally a winter sport, while cricket is played over summer in Australia) and entertainment options (sport and music) makes it a highly sought-after arena by event owners and promoters.

Being able to attract events results in good cash flow while displaying a versatility and capacity to accommodate, a feature attractive to key event decision makers. The capacity to accommodate a variety of events limits the downtime experienced by the facility. But being able to meet a variety of tenant and entertainment options, often at short notice, has a potential downside. Hosting too many events can affect the competition surface for major sporting tenants. This can detract from the desirability of the facility for future tenant agreements. On the positive side, an abundance of interest in events being hosted by a particular facility can reduce wastage (i.e. times when the facility is not in use). A suitable balance must be achieved. Maximising usage is a crucial consideration for facility management, and must be viewed from the perspective of capacity management (wastage) and scheduling issues.

Effective capacity (wastage) management

Capacity management is the process of measuring the amount of work scheduled and then determining how many people, machines and physical resources are needed to accomplish this work. There exists within this framework an assumption that there will be capacity surpluses or shortages, and that the way in which these are managed will affect the organisation's profit (Watts 1999).

One core issue in capacity management is the identification and elimination of wasted resources. A key aspect associated with wastage in the facility management area is idle capacity. Watts (1999) presented the structural waste associated with a hypothetical sport stadium, highlighting obvious wastage components with the ground facility utilisation. Wastage extends largely to the physical facilities surrounding the ground, functions, seating, equipment utilisation and office utilisation aspects of the stadium. The crucial aspect is how to maximise utilisation and minimise wastage.

Table 7.1 lists those aspects that should be monitored by facility management in order to minimise wastage and keep the facility operating at maximum output. The approach taken to minimise wastage needs to be carefully considered on the basis of what can physically be undertaken by the facility management. It will not be physically possible for a major spectator stadium to operate 24 hours a day, 365 days a year. Facility management must look at maximising usage while maintaining profitability. If closing the facility down for one event in a particular week presented a more lucrative opportunity to the facility management than booking a number of smaller events during the same time period, then the facility would be best served by lying idle for the week, to host only the one event. Equally, facility management must question whether operating the facility for only a small number of spectators attending an event is in the best interests of the facility.

Table 7.1 Examples of structural waste

Resources	Total capacity	Utilised capacity	% Waste
Ground facilities	8760 hours pa*	3000 hours pa	66
Function facilities	8760 hours pa	2500 hours pa	72
Seating capacity	40 000 seats	25 000 seats	38
Ground staff	1750 hours pa	1000 hours pa	43
Grounds equipment	8760 hours pa	1000 hours pa	89
Office staff	1840 hours pa	1500 hours pa	18
Office equipment	8760 hours pa	1500 hours pa	83
Management	2400 hours pa	2400 hours pa	0
Supplies	bought as req'd	100%	0

* pa = per annum

Source: Adapted from Watts (1999).

Scheduling/timing of events

Closely related to the concept of capacity management is the requirement for scheduling events within the facility. Although scheduling has been discussed in previous chapters, it is worth briefly revisiting the concept from the perspective of scheduling events. This is a critical area for an event manager, and it must be taken into consideration within the constraints of the entire facility calendar.

In order to maximise the usage of the facility, facility management must put together a clear timeline of availability. Obviously, all the known events within a particular period can be included in this event calendar. These known events will include competition games of permanent tenants as well as special prebooked activities. The calendar of known events can then be assessed in line with opportunities that may arise to attract other events that are known to be available or potentially forthcoming. Scheduling of events is crucial to the success of any facility. Events generate revenue and exposure, which in turn have the ongoing effect of membership generation and media interest formulation.

An event schedule pro-forma is presented in Table 7.2. This pro-forma includes the identification of the major sporting league commitments as part of the arrangements for a hypothetical multi-purpose, 30 000 capacity stadium within one year of its operation.

Table 7.3 presents a further list of possible future events that could be staged at the facility. As an exercise, one could identify and determine which events (selecting from the current and potential event schedule) could be considered part of a viable event schedule. Consideration should then be given to the opportunity costs of including one event over the other in the facility schedule as well as the costs of altering league commitments.

The first stage of this process should include conducting an assessment of the facility's current calendar, noting strengths and weaknesses in its programming, including possible opportunities and threats that need to be considered. This analysis will lead to a justification of current event scheduling. Key information reflecting on the individual events—such as lead-time, cost range, breakeven capacity, profit margin, ability to attract alternative events, and date of scheduling—must be considered and used to eventually justify either hanging onto certain events or replacing them with other potential events at the same time of the year.

Table 7.2 Event schedule pro-forma (current agreements)

Event	Jan	Feb	Mar	Apr	May	June	July	Aug	Sept	Oct	Nov	Dec
Int'l cricket one-day series	10–14	22–23	3				8–11					
Domestic cricket one-day series	4–6 18–21	8–10	7–9									
AFL football			18, 1, 9, 25									
VFL football			28	1, 2, 9, 16, 30	7, 8, 15, 23	4–6, 13, 20, 26, 27	3, 17, 18, 25	2, 11, 12, 26	3, 9, 11, 13, 18			
Domestic rugby union									30	8, 11, 14, 21, 28	5, 12, 19	
Concert/ entertainment bookings			14–16		3–5			4, 18–20			21–25	26

Table 7.3 Event planning schedule (future interested parties)

Event	Jan	Feb	Mar	Apr	May	June	July	Aug	Sept	Oct	Nov	Dec
Soccer int'l	7–9					23	31					
Domestic/club cricket competitions	4–6 18–21		7–9							12–16	18–22	18–22
State (AFL) football finals			20–23						22–24, 29–30			
Domestic soccer league + finals	12	18, 25	7, 14, 21, 28	12	1							
Int'l rugby union (+ super league comp.)		12, 19, 25	8, 22	1, 14, 22–24	20–23	8–12						
Concert/ entertainment booking opportunities	11–16		1	9–12						15–22		

The final yearly schedule needs to reflect a longer-term outlook, in which ongoing tenant relationships could be maintained, new relationships could be developed further and old ones could be severed. An annual breakdown and a longer-term analysis of events and tenants can then be identified.

Event impact summary

The impact of all events held at the facility should be assessed following each event. This assessment should take the same form as that of an economic impact assessment: it should identify the financial impact of the event on the relevant parties, as well as the customer impact. The latter is a report on the number of people attending the event and relevant circulation/flow outcomes associated with those attending. The report on the flow of patrons should cover all aspects of entry/exit, rest room accessibility, concession stall lines, supplies, cash flow, and some form of monitoring of customer satisfaction.

Structure for effective operations

Organisational management reflects the management philosophy surrounding the facility as well as the staffing (see Chapter 5), servicing and event management components. The quality of management and service staff can determine the ability of the facility to attract and retain tenants and supporters, ensuring profitability and income for the facility owner and a successful venture for the event owner. Organisational management reflects the development of an organisational structure incorporating all key staffing requirements, contract versus in-house management needs and staffing needs components.

The management structure can be dissected into its core categories, representing financial and economic success, the responsibilities of facility management, and policy and financial control. These core categories have largely been identified and discussed earlier in this chapter through the planning, operational and evaluation phases, but it is important to consider how facility or event management processes are structured in order to achieve the best possible outcomes. Understanding the required tasks ensures that the facility manager can respond to organisational management needs. Included in this structural approach is the critical element of determining activities that will be contracted out and activities that will be conducted in-house. (This aspect is considered in the next section in greater detail.)

Organisation structure is important, and enables the key divisions within a facility to be clearly identified. Facility operations managers have a variety of departmental responsibilities, ranging across areas such as engineering, event coordination, security, maintenance and housekeeping. They must possess suitable knowledge of budgeting, cost control, methodology, negotiation and motivation in order to complete their job effectively.

A pro-forma organisational chart is presented in Figure 7.1. Although this chart does not do justice to the broad range of divisions that would occur within a facility or event, the inclusion of two key functional areas of maintenance and merchandise sales, one being maintained by facility management as an in-house arrangement and one as a contracted activity, makes for ready discussion. Whether either or both of these functions should be undertaken by the facility itself or by another specialist contractor is the first question. Will there be economies of scale associated through incorporating a contract approach? Will there be a level of specialisation achieved by appointing a contractor to deliver a particular outcome? Will the appointment of a contractor reduce the need for full-time appointments to the facility (thereby reducing wastage as already identified)? Identifying the different divisions, and their reporting pathways, within a facility or event management structure is an important initial stage. Determining whether these divisions will be integrated into operations in an in-house or contracted capacity is the next important consideration, and is examined in more detail later in this chapter.

Staffing the facility for events

Staffing the facility is a very important process. The facility manager needs to ensure that the recruitment and training procedures undertaken follow appropriate legislative guidelines, while ensuring that the best-qualified personnel are employed. Key management areas, support personnel requirements and casual versus full-time appointments need to be determined. The technical skills of staff are a key attribute for success, and the capacity to manage and coordinate a wide range of operational activities with facility staff and contract staff is a significant factor in the staffing process.

Staffing the event

The requirements for staffing faced by the event manager are not dissimilar to those experienced by the facility manager. There are issues of contract versus full-time appointments, recruitment, training and deployment. The event manager, similar to the facility manager, may deal with large numbers of casual appointments, but there may also be a large number of volunteers appointed to support the event operations. These people must fit the needs of the event, with clearly identified roles and responsibilities.

Figure 7.1 Sample organisational structure for a sport facility: separating in-house and contract operations

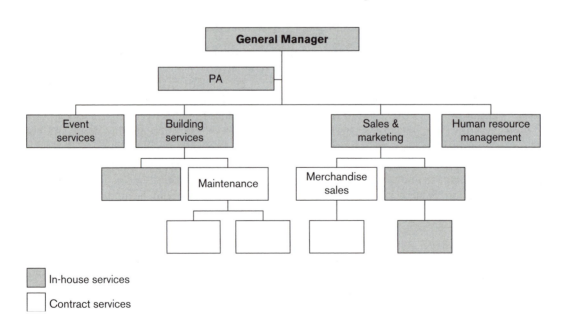

From event management structure to venue management structure

The parameters of the event structure circumscribe the requirement for facility-dependent events to move from an event-related structure to a venue or facility-oriented structure. This is particularly crucial to those large events that operate from large spectator facilities. The Sydney Olympic Games in 2000 operated along these lines. During its early planning phase, staff were appointed in event-specific roles with a clear emphasis on planning and preparing for the broad requirements associated with the event. As the event date moved closer, many of these same staff were relocated to the facility in which their events would be held, to work more closely with the facility management staff. Many of the roles undertaken were closely aligned to facility staff. The Sydney Organising Committee for the Olympic Games (SOCOG) staff were responsible for checking and double-checking with the facility staff to ensure that the facility was clean and ready for the next day's competition, that the playing surfaces adhered to international standards, that the spectators were located in their assigned seats with the minimum of fuss, that the athlete areas were clean, accessible and available at the required time, that the media had access to required equipment and accredited areas, that concessions were supplied to meet demand and so on.

Many of these activities were performed by the facility management through its regular staffing arrangements, but the event organisers undertook extensive checks to make the event run smoothly. After all, the event management was responsible for the smooth running of the event. If anything went wrong with the event, media and spectator dissatisfaction would be targeted at the event managers. The facility might also be criticised, but not necessarily so severely. Event managers must move into a venue management role prior to the event being run, to ensure the smooth operation of a large facility-dependent event.

Contract management

Contract management presents a management tool that enables the facility to manage the areas of sales, service, equipment and maintenance. The use of contract services, as outlined in Chapter 5, helps management to better control the costs, responsibilities and liabilities involved in operating a facility. Contract services can range from a simple one-area agreement in which, for example, merchandise services might be provided through to the more complex arrangement of contract management applying to the entire facility.

Contract management decisions usually reflect the determination of performance standards and associated costs that relate to key operational activities. Expensive equipment involving a large capital investment may be better employed through a contract provider than through purchase. Equally, a large catering firm might bring significant economies of scale in purchasing and catering management, not to mention a wide range of experience and expertise, and might therefore provide a better option than that of any in-house arrangement.

In Figure 7.1, the organisational chart has four divisional areas associated with the facility management structure. Across the whole structure, some divisions will be contracted out or managed in-house. One such area, merchandise sales, is presented as a contract opportunity only. The other, maintenance, is presented as an in-house management operation.

Given the approach to retain maintenance as an in-house operation, the facility management must see that appropriate personnel (numbers as well as skills) are appointed to meet the required tasks. Having contracted the area of merchandise sales out to external expertise, the facility manager must ensure that the appropriate controls and standards are applied. Contracts for service must be enacted and management should meet and coordinate on a regular basis with the contractor to check that quality controls meet agreed standards.

Having contractors provide certain services implies that a contract will be in force over an agreed period of time. Contracts should clearly stipulate the obligations of all parties included or named in the contract. This can create a dilemma if an event owner using the facility does not wish to deal with existing contractors. For example, the event owner may refuse to have its merchandise sales undertaken by the facility's contractor. Here, the facility may have to compensate its contractor for not being the official supplier of merchandise at this particular event. Ideally, these additional costs will be negotiated with the facility hirer. This situation also often arises with sponsor signage and food and beverage concessions, when a one-off event hires the venue but requires a 'clean' venue and that existing signage and caterers give up (sell) their facility rights for this one event. The reverse of this situation could also become a solution, where for example existing beer or soft drink suppliers of the facility are granted exclusive rights to provide the beverages at the one-off event. In the end, the important thing is that the facility manager attempts to meet the demands of the event hirer but is also mindful of existing agreements with other contractors.

Risk management

Risk management reflects the potential for exposure to harm. The most common problem experienced by sport facility managers is minimising financial loss and liability exposure resulting from injuries to patrons. The primary goal of risk management is to reduce the possible losses and exposure to danger, harm or hazards.

The exposure of an activity to risk is its exposure to uncertainty of outcome. Due to this uncertainty of outcome, risk must be managed or it can have devastating consequences. The approach to risk management in sport facility and event management should be considered an integral part of good management practice. Risk management is the terminology applied to the method of identifying, analysing, assessing, treating, monitoring and communicating risks associated with any activities, functions or processes faced by facility or event managers (Hughes 1998).

The facility or event senior management team is responsible for defining and documenting their policy for risk management. This policy should clearly reflect the organisation's goals and strategic context. The approach should incorporate the following principles relating to risk (Hughes 1998):

- organisation's rationale for managing risk;
- objectives for and commitment to managing risk;
- links between the policy and organisation strategic plan, including the range of issues applicable;
- guidance on what may be regarded as acceptable risk;
- who is responsible for managing risk;
- support available for those responsible for managing risk;
- level of documentation required; and
- plan for reviewing organisational performance with respect to risk.

Briefly outlining the above elements, the organisational context or rationale relating to risk should reflect the range of financial, operational, political, social, legal and market aspects that will be affected by the occurrence of a risk-related event. Criteria should be developed against which risk is to be monitored. Risks should be identified, analysed, assessed and treated as required. Incorporated into this monitoring process is the development of risk management personnel and the ongoing evaluation and redefinition of risk factors.

Some of the common risk areas in sport facility and event management are identified below. There are the various injuries sustained by athletes, which may be in part attributable to the competition surface; the injuries sustained by spectators at Association Football stadia (e.g. as a result of some of the infamous English stadium disasters in the late 1980s and early 90s); the Monica Seles stabbing incident at a tennis tournament in Germany; tit-for-tat political disputes over attendance at Olympic Games in Moscow 1980 and Los Angeles in 1984; and the Munich air disaster in 1958, in which many of the Manchester United football team lost their lives. These are all incidents that have exposed sporting organisations to a significant degree of risk. The key is how those organisations responsible for running sporting events manage these risks and other occurrences. Aspects relevant to risk in sport facility and event management include (but are not limited to):

- sport participation itself
- spectators
- legal issues (legal liability, contracts, insurance)
- athlete protection
- loss prevention
- storage
- accreditation
- facilities/equipment/property
- hiring
- training
- transport
- safety/security
- environmental factors (natural events)
- economic circumstances
- political circumstances
- management activities and controls
- human behaviour
- terrorism.

The sport facility or event manager must clearly assume responsibility for and be prepared for risk. There are many aspects related to this level of preparedness, which include the following:

- Constantly update and review risk management plans.
- Undertake emergency 'drills' to ensure that all staff understand and know how to react to an emergency.
- Ensure that key personnel are familiar with all requirements and aspects associated with the risk management plans and procedures.

- Constantly refine strategies and incorporate new technologies and methods of risk management.
- Clearly determine a chain of responsibility and ensure that all staff are aware of the requirements. Key managers *must* be immediately notified of an emergency or crisis situation, regardless of the time of day or night.
- Expertise needs to be recognised and experts included in risk management policy development and support when an emergency arises. This expertise should reflect medical, legal and financial knowledge as well as operational expertise where appropriate.
- Reviews and recommendations should be documented, regularly updated and acted on.
- All incidents should be reported on and practices and outcomes reviewed.
- Senior management must have a clear knowledge of the requirements and procedures and be immediately informed of any emergency that arises. This is particularly important, as they will often be identified by the media for comment.
- Those directly involved in the emergency need to be debriefed immediately after the incident, and need to understand the actions required and the reporting of those actions.
- Staff should be briefed on the emergency as soon as possible after the incident so that they are aware of what has occurred. This should extend to ensuring that they are aware of what is being done about the situation.
- The media will most likely be interested in the incident and the organisation should have a clearly identifiable spokesperson, who is well briefed and able to present a sufficiently developed organisational response with updates available as news comes to hand.

Figure 7.2 displays a brief pro-forma outline of the approach that might be undertaken in developing a checklist for a first aid risk treatment policy for a small event. There clearly exists a framework within which the facility or event manager has knowledge of what occurred prior to the event. Aligned to a standard operating procedure (SOP) form for medical risk (displayed in Figure 7.3), the risk is at least acknowledged and therefore able to be dealt with.

The process of risk management, in order to be effective, involves understanding five key components. These components are:

- recognising risk (identification)
- analysing risk
- assessing risk
- treating risk
- monitoring risk (creating standard operating procedures to manage risk).

Each of these components is examined in detail in the following sections.

Risk identification

This phase is where the facility must discern the various risks that could potentially cause loss to the facility. Some of the risk types applicable to the sport situation have already been identified. Primary and secondary factors need to be considered when identifying risk, and reflect those aspects which are directly attributable to the daily operations of the facility (primary factors). An example of this is where a security staff member forcibly removes an intoxicated spectator, or an athlete injures themselves, slipping when entering the arena. Secondary

Figure 7.2 Checklist example for treating risk through adequate first aid policies for a minor event

Is a stretcher provided on site?   ☐
Is the stretcher location known to the participants?   ☐
Is a qualified first aid attendant present?   ☐
Is a telephone available for emergency use?   ☐
Are emergency telephone numbers known?   ☐
Have the first aid kit stocks been checked?   ☐
Is ambulance access provided?   ☐
Is emergency first aid equipment available?   ☐
Is an appropriate recovery facility available?   ☐
Do first aid personnel know location of the hospital?   ☐
Are first aid personnel adequately trained?   ☐
Do the first aid personnel have qualifications?   ☐

factors are those events that again affect the facility but not during the actual event or directly involving athletes, spectators and staff during the competition. Secondary factors represent those outcomes that are largely external to the direct operations of the facility. The components of weather, event or activity type, patron demographics and facility location are the types of secondary factors that prevail.

Risk analysis

Having identified possible risks to the facility or event, there needs to be analysis into which risk factors have potentially the greatest effect. These risk factors should therefore receive priority. The level of risk is analysed through combining estimates on the basis of two criteria, namely the severity of the loss and the likelihood of occurrence. A matrix of frequency (likelihood) to consequence (magnitude) of loss should be set up. Table 7.4 displays a matrix for determining the level and consequence of risk.

The risk assessment matrix displayed in Table 7.4 is a 5×5. Alternatives include a matrix in a 3×3 or even a 7×7 format. The crucial elements are to determine the likelihood or frequency of loss against the consequence of these losses and then apply the outcomes to potential risks that have been identified in the identification phase. This chapter's case study presents a framework for applying this particular type of risk matrix.

Risk assessment

Following the identification and analysis of risk, it is important to compare the level of risk found during the analysis process with previously established risk criteria and then decide whether risks can be accepted. If the risks fall into the low or acceptable categories, they may be accepted with minimal further treatment. These risks should be monitored and categorically

Table 7.4 Risk assessment matrix: likelihood/frequency vs consequence

| Consequence | Likelihood/frequency | | | | |
	A: Almost certain	B: Likely/ frequent	C: Moderate	D: Unlikely/ infrequent	E: Rare
1. Catastrophic	Avoid	Avoid	Shift	Shift	Shift
2. Major	Avoid	Avoid	Shift	Shift	Shift
3. Moderate	Shift	Shift	Shift	Shift	Keep & decrease
4. Minor	Keep & decrease	Keep & decrease	Keep & decrease	Keep & decrease	Keep & decrease
5. Insignificant	Keep & decrease	Keep & decrease	Keep & decrease	Keep & decrease	Keep & decrease

Level	Descriptor	Description
Likelihood		
A	Almost certain	Event is expected to occur
B	Likely/frequent	Event will probably occur
C	Moderate	Event should occur at some time
D	Unlikely/infrequent	Event could occur at some time
E	Rare	Event not expected to occur
Consequence		
1	Catastrophic	Death, huge financial loss, catastrophic impact on operations
2	Major	Extensive injuries, major financial loss, major impact on operations
3	Moderate	Medical treatment required, financial level of loss, significant impact on operations
4	Minor	First aid treatment, some financial loss, minimal impact on operations
5	Insignificant	No injuries, low financial loss, no effect on operations

reviewed to ensure they remain acceptable. If, however, the risks do not fall into the category of being acceptable, they should be treated using one or more of the possible treatment options.

Risk treatment

The treatment stage takes the matrix from the assessment stage and develops strategies for avoidance, transfer of risk, or internal procedures for managing the risk. These risk treatment views reflect on whether to avoid the risk completely or to keep the risk and attempt to reduce its impact. The Australian Standard for risk management recognises six major treatment options, as outlined below (Hughes 1998).

Avoid the risk

The event or facility manager makes a conscious decision not to proceed with the activity at all. Risks should be avoided when they cause a high degree of loss and occur often. The facility should consider the possibility of not hosting the event at all if there is the possibility of large monetary loss.

Accept the risk with support financing

The risk is accepted within the organisation itself and the organisation diverts some funds to cover expected risk-related occurrences.

Reduce the likelihood of occurrence

Taking proactive measures to minimise risk occurrence can ensure a lower-risk environment. For example, ensuring that the facility is designed to be a slip-free zone for spectators given any climatic conditions will reduce the likelihood of falls and potential lawsuits.

Reduce the consequences of the occurrence

This is again a proactive measure, in which the facility or event management reduces the impact or severity of injury through their actions. For example, removing wire fences at football grounds in the United Kingdom meant that people may gain access to the field but are less likely to be crushed against a barrier.

Transfer the risk

This involves another party bearing or sharing some part of the risk. The combination of severity and frequency (likelihood) may not be large enough to warrant avoiding the risk. It may, however, be large enough to cause substantial monetary damage to the facility. The solution is to transfer the risk to an organisation that is willing to take the risk. This may occur through the drawing up of special conditions within contracts or taking out insurance. Many facilities now require the event owner to provide sufficient legal liability coverage for injury to spectators, thereby sharing some of the costs associated with risk.

Retain the risk

The facility manager can keep the risk and attempt to decrease the amount of loss or risk that could occur. In the matrix, risks that are kept and decreased are those that have a very low potential for loss. The facility manager should ensure that proper precautions are taken to decrease the occurrence of and monetary losses associated with the risk. This can be accomplished through the use of documentation and implementation of standard operating procedures.

Risk monitoring

Risk monitoring involves the ongoing assessment and continual evaluation of possible risks and attention to new emergent risks that may affect operations. Few risks remain static, and factors and circumstances will change regularly. The sport facility and event manager must be aware of ongoing changes and reassess each risk accordingly (and regularly).

Risk monitoring should include the development of relevant manuals and standard operating procedures for risk. Information concerning treatment and decisions emerging from all risk situations should be documented in order to achieve the best possible approach and outcomes. Relevant information relating to key areas includes:

- development of maintenance charts;
- ongoing assessment of the level of care;
- regular staff training and planning;
- drills (emergency) undertaken and practised regularly; and
- reporting systems introduced and monitored.

Ideally, a risk management or emergency procedures (disaster plan) manual should be established that identifies crucial areas of concern. The manual should extend to incorporating methods of dealing with the media in times of crisis that may emerge in a risk-related situation. The monitoring process should be reviewed on a regular basis in order to ensure that risks are adequately covered and regularly evaluated for frequency and loss outcomes. One of the approaches to risk monitoring is to create a standard operating procedure.

Standard operating procedure (SOP)

The development of strategic plans for minimising risk sees the formation of the SOP. The SOP is a set of instructions giving detailed directions and appropriate courses of action for given situations (Farmer, Mulrooney & Ammon 1996). These plans should be developed for all

Figure 7.3 Standard operating procedure for an on-site spectator injury

Injured spectator details:
    Name: _____
    Address: _____
    Contact numbers: _____
    Email: _____

Injury details:
    Description (type) of injury: _____
    _____
    Time/date of injury: _____
    How did the injury occur?: _____
    Explain the circumstances surrounding the injury: _____
    _____
    Was anyone else injured?: _____
    Location of injury: _____

Witnessed by:
    Name: _____
    Address: _____
    Contact numbers: _____

Attended to by: _____
Treatment undertaken: _____
_____
Name of manager incident was reported to: _____

recognised risks, except for those that will be avoided. Plans should be developed even for risks that have been transferred, as this will ensure that claims are reduced and insurance premiums can then remain at manageable levels. A standard operating procedure sample form for a spectator injury is identified in Figure 7.3.

Summary

This chapter has introduced the complexities associated with a facility moving into event mode. The requirements associated with hosting events can be complex and diverse. It is not a case of simply building the facility and waiting for events to come and take care of themselves. The facility manager must properly present the facility to the event owners, must schedule events to maximise usage and minimise wastage, while also ensuring that facility operations are not compromised. Furthermore, managing events in the facility requires the integration and implementation of contracts with a variety of service providers as well as with the event owner, which is a contract partner in its own right. There is also a key management requirement that risks be identified and managed. All of these elements place the facility and event manager in a position to maximise their operational efficiency and achieve success.

Case study

Assessing risk for a major event

The task of identifying and categorising risks associated with a major event is an extremely important one. Understanding the risks associated with an event, and analysing, assessing and then treating those risks, can make the difference between a trouble-free or troublesome event.

Given the basketball event description below, a risk assessment matrix (5×5) should be developed. Table 7.5 presents a 5×5 matrix pro-forma that can be applied to considerations of risk surrounding this event. All relevant events that can be foreseen, relating to both event and facility circumstances, should be identified to the facility and event managers and analysed in terms of severity. The list of possible risk areas broadly covers sport participation itself, spectators, legal issues (legal liability, contracts, insurance), athlete protection, loss prevention, storage, accreditation, facilities/equipment/property, hiring, training, transport, safety/security, environmental factors (natural events), economic circumstances, political circumstances, management activities and controls, human behaviour, and terrorism. Q. *Your task is to identify all the potential risk management factors that need to be considered in order to plan for this tournament. Once identified, these factors should be put in order of severity. Four possibilities are already included. Identification of potential risk factors and severity associated with the risk:*

- *political/diplomatic environment (B2–4)*
- *athlete protection (C3)*

- *athlete transportation (D3–4)*
- *spectator safety (B2–3).*

Refer to Table 7.4 for a framework for assessing whether to avoid, shift, or accept these risks.

Table 7.5 Risk assessment matrix: likelihood/frequency vs consequence

| | Likelihood/frequency | | | | |
Consequence	A: Almost certain	B: Likely/ frequent	C: Moderate	D: Unlikely /infrequent	E: Rare
1. Catastrophic					
2. Major		Political/ diplomatic			
3. Moderate		Spectator safety	Athlete protection		
4. Minor				Athlete transportation	
5. Insignificant					

Event description: the preparation is being undertaken for a six-nation basketball tournament to be held in Melbourne (15 000 capacity stadium) on 5–16 June 2008. The invited teams include Australia, China, Chinese Taipei, Croatia, Yugoslavia and Russia.

8

Attracting customers: marketing the sport facility and the sport events

Chapter focus
Structure, size and trends in the sport facility and sport event sectors
Key success factors of operating sport facilities and running sport events
Developing new sport facilities: feasibility analysis
Developing new sport facilities: design and construction issues
Developing new sport facilities: preparing facility management infrastructure
Operating the new sport facility: attracting events
Operating the new sport facility: preparing event management infrastructure
Attracting customers: marketing the sport facility and the sport events
Running the sport event: event operations
Measuring facility and event performance: a scorecard approach to success
Measuring facility and event performance: impact on and for stakeholders

CHAPTER OBJECTIVES
In this chapter, we will: • Identify a variety of facility and event customers by way of a typology. • Stress the importance of identifying and understanding the different needs and wants of various customers. • Discuss the facility and event product within a services marketing framework. • Describe facility and event marketing strategy in terms of market segmentation, targeting and positioning. • Describe some tools to help you maximise service quality and customer satisfaction and thus facilitate customer retention. • Explore the challenges of resource commitment and coordination associated with multiple marketing stakeholders.

Kotler, Brown, Adam and Armstrong (2004) define marketing as 'a social and managerial process by which individuals and groups obtain what they need and want through creating and exchanging products and value with others' (p. 8). Central to this definition are needs and wants. The needs and wants of facility and event organisations are in general quite limited, with one of the more obvious being revenue generation. However, the needs and wants of customers span several different types, and their identification can be a complex task. But before we turn our attention to uncovering these needs and wants, it is critical that we identify exactly who a facility or event's customers are. Kotler et al. (2004, p. 167) list five types of customer markets:

1. *consumer markets*—individuals and households that buy goods and services for personal or household consumption;
2. *business markets*—organisations that buy goods and services for further processing or for use in their production process;
3 *reseller markets*—organisations that buy goods and services in order to resell them at a profit;
4. *government markets*—government agencies that buy goods and services in order to produce public services or transfer these goods and services to others who need them;
5. *international markets*—overseas buyers including consumers, producers, resellers and governments.

Consumer and business markets, in both the domestic and international sense, are the markets of greatest relevance in the context of facility and event management. It is important to include international buyers as an important customer group, as many facilities such as Wembley Stadium and Madison Square Garden host international events and have international consumers and international business partners.

Consumer market customers can be divided into two broad categories, namely spectators and participants. The spectator category includes (a) people who place their 'bums on seats' in venues all over the world to watch an event unfold, and (b) those individuals who, whether by choice or necessity, spectate 'at a distance' in front of the television, via the Internet, or by radio. In contrast to remote spectators, participants must be present at the facility to consume the participation product. That is, the swimmers need to be in the pool in order to swim, the lacrosse players must get themselves onto the field to throw, run and catch, and the ice-hockey players need to hit the ice to skate.

Business market customers include (a) event owners and promoters that hire out a facility, (b) television or radio networks that broadcast the event, (c) Internet companies that deliver the product online, (d) sponsors that seek an association with a facility or event for the purpose of promoting their own organisation and its products, and (e) corporate box/suite holders, who may or may not also be sponsors.

The different customer markets just introduced for event and facility organisations are depicted in Figure 8.1. It should be noted that several additional classification criteria, such as 'international—domestic', could be added to this classification schema. You are encouraged to select a facility or event you are familiar with and to both identify which customer types exist for it and list specific examples of these customers. You are also invited to contemplate the classification of corporate suite/box customers. That is, how do they fit into the typology?

Figure 8.1 The facility and event customer typology

Customer type					
Business			Consumer		
			Spectator		Participant
Broadcaster	Sponsor	Event owner/ promoter	At-venue	TV/Internet radio	
Event					
Facility					

The way in which a facility or event should be marketed depends on the customer market of interest (i.e. consumer or business), the smaller segments within these two broad domains (e.g. spectator or participant), as well as the even smaller segments within these categories (e.g. live-at-venue or television). That is, marketers must use different strategies to attract and retain the various customer groups depicted by the facility and event customer typology. This is because different types of customers often have very different needs and wants.

Customer needs and wants

An understanding of customer needs and wants is key to understanding marketing and is thus a precursor to effective facility and event marketing. Kotler et al. (2004, p. 8) define human needs as 'states of felt deprivation' and wants as 'the form taken by human needs as they are shaped by culture and individual personality'. In other words, wants are needs in a specific product package. For example, people *need* to spend time together and they *want* to do that at a sporting event. Marketers therefore have most influence on 'creating' wants.

From the perspective of the individual consumer, there are many types of needs and wants that can be satisfied by sport spectatorship and participation. Participating in sporting events can, for example, meet an individual's need for health and personal development, whereas sport spectatorship can meet the needs for relaxation and escapism. Alternatively, extreme sport products can satisfy the thrill-seeking sport spectator or participant who wants an adventure-packed experience. The needs and wants of business customers can be understood in terms of organisational goals. A business relationship with a facility or event can meet, for example, a sponsor's need for certain sales volume and product awareness levels, and potentially even the sponsor's desire to become a market leader.

The needs and wants of customers relate to the reasons for their first trying and then continuing to buy certain products. That is, a customer's purchase reasons relate to the needs or wants he or she believes products will satisfy. Effective facility and event marketers have a range of product offerings at their disposal, in recognition of the different needs and wants of their various customer groups (see Table 1.2 in Chapter 1 for some examples pertaining to consumer products).

Although it is easy to define any product as simply something that people buy, many marketers prefer to think of a product as a 'bundle of benefits'. Indeed, marketing guru Theodore Levitt (1960, p. 53) was famous for this, claiming that people don't buy gasoline (i.e. what we'd normally think of as the product) but 'the right to continue driving their cars' (i.e. the benefit of the gasoline). In this light, products can also be thought of as 'problem solvers'. Likewise, customers don't buy merely a ticket to a sport event or facility but excitement, sociability and networking opportunities.

The facility and event service product

As well as conceptualising the various facility and event management products as bundles of benefits, it is important to conceptualise them as services. Hoffman and Bateson (2002) distinguish between the service product and the manufactured 'good' product by describing services as 'deeds, efforts, or performances' and goods as 'objects, devices, or things' (p. 4).

Services marketing is a particular type of marketing that emerged in the 1980s in recognition of the fact that services are very different from goods, and as such the marketing of services needs to be approached differently. The differences between services and goods are typically explained with reference to four unique characteristics shared by all service products—intangibility, inseparability, heterogeneity, and perishability.

Intangibility

Intangibility is the key distinguishing characteristic between services and goods. Moreover, it is from the service product's intangibility that its other three characteristics emerge. Intangibility refers to the product's inability to be touched and seen in the same way that other products can be (e.g. a tennis racquet, golf balls). As a deed, effort, or performance, a service is also an 'experience'. A key problem for facility and event marketers resulting from the intangible nature of services is the inability to store them—that is, perishability. Perishability of the service product is such a significant problem that it is a unique characteristic in itself (and will be discussed later).

Inseparability

Inseparability of production and consumption refers to services being produced and consumed simultaneously (i.e. in 'real time'), as opposed to being produced first and then consumed at a later date, as is the case with manufactured goods (a swimmer does not see the factory worker making the goggles he buys much later from his local retail sport store). With services, the customer and the service provider are both present when the service is experienced, and often other customers are present too (when you play a game of hockey, the umpires as well as other players are part of your hockey experience). The key marketing implication associated with service inseparability is that each of the parties present (i.e. the customer, service providers, other customers) can either enhance or detract from the service experience. (We will discuss a range of issues related to this later when we look at the sport servuction model.)

Heterogeneity

Heterogeneity refers to the variation in consistency from one service to the next. This inconsistency is largely due to the three parties present during the service experience (i.e. the customer, service providers, and other customers), as well as the fact that services occur in real time, as noted previously. Thus a key marketing implication associated with service heterogeneity relates to quality—that is, ensuring that customers receive consistent levels of quality from one service experience to the next. Unfortunately, when something goes wrong with the facility or event service the quality cannot be remedied *before* it reaches the customer. For example, when one of an event's long-term corporate customers and her accompanying guests are provided with the wrong tickets, they are effectively 'locked out' of the stadium until a supervisor arrives to fix the mistake. Because this mistake occurs in real time there is nothing that can be done to stop the impact it has on the customer. Instead, considerable effort needs to go into 'making it up' to the customer.

Perishability

Perishability refers to the fact that services cannot be stored (i.e. inventoried). Services cease to exist if they are not sold when they become available. An inability to store the service product inevitably results in the problem of matching supply and demand. For example, a football stadium with a capacity of 50 000 might achieve an average occupancy of only 70 per cent throughout the season but be sold out during the finals (a very common problem). Unfortunately, the facility or event marketer does not have the ability to store the unused seats from earlier matches and sell them later in the season when demand is high.

We have outlined the unique characteristics of services—namely, intangibility, inseparability, heterogeneity, and perishability. These characteristics, as well as their implications, need to be acknowledged by facility and event marketers and accommodated by using a services marketing framework when marketing their facility or event products. Those of you who would like to pursue further reading in the area of services marketing are referred to the texts of Hoffman and Bateson (2002) and Lovelock, Patterson and Walker (2004).

Marketing strategy

The aim of the chapter thus far has been to provide a framework within which to think about the marketing of facilities and events, as well as a foundation for the remainder of the chapter. We have offered several definitions and identified a variety of facility and event customer markets. The importance of meeting the many and diverse needs and wants of customers, as well as the need to conduct facility and event marketing within a services marketing framework, have also been emphasised. We now move on to discuss facility and event marketing strategy. For a sport-specific discussion of the marketing strategy process, we refer you to a book in the Allen & Unwin Sport Management Series, *Strategic Sport Marketing* by Shilbury, Quick and Westerbeek (2003).

Market segmentation together with target marketing and product positioning are central to marketing strategy, enabling an organisation to better meet customer needs and wants and thus simultaneously achieve its own objectives. The steps of segmenting, targeting and positioning, together with each of their two substeps, as discussed by Kotler et al. (2004), are explored next.

Market segmentation

1. Identify bases for segmenting the market

The first step in market segmentation is to identify *how* to break down the total market. Numerous types of segmentation criteria exist (e.g. demographics, psychographics, behaviours), with marketers often using them in combination (e.g. age and lifestyle). (Refer again to Figure 8.1 to see some of the ways in which the overall market for event and facility products can be broken down.) Some of the more specific variables that multi-purpose facilities such as the Sydney Olympic Park Aquatic Centre (the aquatics venue for the Sydney 2000 Olympics) might use to segment their consumer participant market include user group (e.g. individual, family, school), benefit sought (e.g. relaxation, fitness, rehabilitation), and preferred service (e.g. lap pool, leisure pool, fitness centre).

The choice of segmentation variables can vary greatly from one organisation to the next. What is important, though, is for the variables and thus resulting segments to be meaningful. For example, it makes good sense for a golf club to segment its participant market on the basis of employment status (e.g. employed versus retired), as it needs to balance supply and demand for both its weekend and its weekday product. It does not make sense for the same club to segment the market on the basis of ice-cream flavour preference, a variable that has no influence on golf consumption.

2. Develop profiles of resulting segments

After a market has been segmented, the resulting segments need to be studied and understood. That is, the facility or event marketer must develop a profile of each segment in order to get to know, or develop an understanding of, the potential customers contained in that segment. For example, having identified three business market segments of potential sponsors, an event organisation such as NASCAR will seek additional information on each segment (e.g. values, objectives, expectations, product range). In combination with the next step of the market segmentation, targeting and positioning process, an enhanced understanding of market segments enables a facility or event organisation to select the right markets. A compatibility of organisational values, for example, can be very important when it comes to targeting sponsors.

Market targeting

3. Develop measures of segment attractiveness

After the facility or event marketer has identified and profiled a variety of market segments, they must identify which segment(s) to pursue. This is because it generally makes sense for an organisation to strive to meet the needs and wants of *some* rather than *all* potential customers. Thus, the first step involved in target marketing is to measure each segment's attractiveness. Each segment can then be ranked according to its degree of attractiveness, based on such factors as size and growth potential, competitors (i.e. both current and potential), and the objectives and resources of the facility or event. In sum, these factors point to a segment's profitability, which is a popular means of segmenting the market. A sport and entertainment venue might give a high ranking to the baby-boomer concert-going market, as this is a large segment with substantial discretionary income. Moreover, this segment's preferred concerts (e.g. Bee Gees, Barbra Streisand) have lower operational costs (e.g. for stage production, security) than the under-25s concert market with its preference in performers (e.g. Eminem, Linkin Park, Christina Aguilera).

4. Select the target segment(s)

Once the ranking process described above is complete, the facility or event marketer can select the most attractive segment(s). The marketer may choose just one segment or several. As previously noted, facilities and events have a range of customers, and indeed product offerings, and will thus select several market segments. For example, among the 2003 Rugby World Cup's target markets for sponsors was the multinationals segment (e.g. Visa, Heineken), as well as the Australian companies segment (e.g. Bundaberg Rum, Telstra). Cup organisers also targeted the Melbourne and Sydney business segment for premium-priced corporate ticket sales, and the international sport tourist segment (e.g. the Irish, the English) for general ticket sales. As with the baby-boomer concert-going market noted previously, each of these World Cup markets would have been selected due to their attractiveness on a range of variables.

Market positioning

5. Develop positioning for each target segment

Following the identification and selection of the preferred target market(s), the facility or event marketer needs to determine the position his or her organisation and its products should occupy in those segments—that is, the consumer's perception of the organisation and its products relative to competing organisations and products. Creating and maintaining a desired position is a critical marketing function, as the position a product occupies in consumers' minds affects their buying behaviour.

Just as marketers can segment the market in a variety of ways, so too can they employ a variety of positioning strategies. The marketer's choice of positioning strategy should be based on competitive advantage—that is, the thing(s) customers believe (rightly or wongly) the organisation does better than competitors. When contemplating competitive advantage, it's important to pause for a moment to consider *who* a sport facility or event's competitors are. For instance, spectator sport is part of the entertainment industry, and consequently the sport facilities and events of interest to this book are in competition not only with each other but with non-sport-themed facilities (e.g. concert halls and exhibition centres) and their respective events. Moreover, major facilities and events often find that their competitors are hundreds—if not thousands—of kilometres away, and perhaps even in a different country.

A facility or event can be positioned based on its product attributes (e.g. a venue's closing roof), the benefits it offers (e.g. the family fun offered by a community sports carnival), and the class of user (e.g. teenagers for X Games). So, too, can the facility or event be positioned directly against, as well as away from, competitors. The Commonwealth Games and the Olympic Games are both major international and elite multi-sport events, but the Commonwealth Games are positioned as the 'friendly games', whereas the Olympics' position is more in line with being the 'best of the best', which is consistent with its motto of 'faster, higher, stronger'. Instead of employing single positioning strategies, facility and event marketers may choose to use a combination of them.

Certain positioning strategies will be more appropriate for certain organisations and certain products. As such, it can be difficult to think of one strategy as being superior to another. However, according to Kotler et al. (2004), some of the prime positions to occupy are best quality (e.g. premium seating), best service (e.g. corporate hospitality), lowest price (e.g. tickets), best value (e.g. season tickets), and most technologically advanced (e.g. in-seat game analysis, food ordering and communication tools).

Irrespective of the strategy chosen, what is important is that marketers determine the position they want their organisation and products to occupy rather than letting the market decide. That is, consumers will position a known product in their minds even without any prompting or manipulation on behalf of the facility or event marketer. However, as positioning affects customer choice and hence organisational success, it cannot be left to chance but must be managed instead.

Lovelock et al. (2004, p. 190) list four undesirable outcomes for those service organisations that fail to engage in positioning:

1. The organisation (or one of its products) is pushed into a position where it faces head-on competition from stronger competitors.
2. The organisation, represented by its offerings, is pushed into a position that nobody else wants because there is little customer demand there.
3. The organisation's service position is so fuzzy that nobody knows what its distinctive competence really is.
4. The service has no position at all in the marketplace because nobody has ever heard of it.

6. Develop marketing mix for each target segment

The final step in the market segmentation, targeting and positioning process entails developing a marketing mix for each target segment. Kotler et al. (2004) define the marketing mix as 'the set of controllable marketing variables that the company blends to produce the response it wants in the target market' (p. 109).

The marketing mix was traditionally referred to as the 4Ps of marketing (product, price, promotion, place). This mix has since expanded, particularly among service marketers, who now incorporate people, physical evidence and process in marketing strategy. Numerous texts discussing the marketing mix are available, so only a brief summary of each element is provided here. However, those who would like additional information on this topic are referred to the services marketing texts of Hoffman and Bateson (2002) and Lovelock et al. (2004), as well as to the sport marketing texts of Mullin, Hardy and Sutton (2000) and Shilbury et al. (2003).

*   *Product*—what is offered to the target market: that is, the good or service and its benefits.
*   *Price*—how much money the product costs the customer.

- *Promotion*—the communication of the benefits, or desirable characteristics, of the product to the target market via such means as advertising, personal selling, direct mail, sales promotions, public relations, promotional licensing and sponsorship.
- *Place*—often referred to in terms of distribution; the availability or accessibility of the product in terms of location and timing.
- *People*—the two groups of people that need to be considered and thus managed: namely, those who provide the product (i.e. the employees of the selling organisation) as well as those who consume it (i.e. the customers).
- *Physical evidence*—the tangible component of the product. The dominant piece of physical evidence in the context of facility and event marketing is the facility itself. Other pieces include scoreboards, staff uniforms, tickets and seating.
- *Process*—the series of steps by which the service is eventually delivered to the customer. The service process is a combination of 'backstage' (invisible to customer) as well as 'front of stage' (visible to customer) steps. (Later in this chapter we discuss the facility and event service process by way of the 'sport servuction model' and flowcharting.)

Each of the seven marketing mix elements must be consistent with the organisation's or product's desired position. In other words, each element must reflect this position. For example, if a yacht club has positioned itself as being of the highest possible quality then it also needs to ensure that its marina is second to none, its staff are impeccably dressed, highly trained and courteous, prices are at a premium to reflect quality, and so forth.

As well as being consistent with the positioning strategy, the marketing mix strategy must be consistent with the needs and wants, as well as characteristics, of the customers that the facility or event manager is trying to attract. As such, strategies to attract and retain consumer market customers need to be quite different from those needed to attract and retain business market customers. Imagine trying to attract a $500 000 naming rights sponsor for your facility or event by promising a free can of Coke and a hot dog, a strategy that can be quite effective in attracting families. Similarly, strategies designed to attract and retain participants must differ from those aimed at spectators. Refer again to Figure 8.1 to identify other customer groups that require variations in marketing strategy and hence different marketing mixes.

Marketing strategy constraints

Marketing strategy is constrained by many factors in addition to those pertaining to positioning and the needs, wants and characteristics of customers. Figure 8.2 identifies many of these constraints, as well as a range of possible revenue sources flowing into the facility or event organisation and a variety of expenses flowing out. The items included in Figure 8.2 by no means form an exhaustive list; they may also vary somewhat between facilities and events, and as to whether the model is viewed within the context of a particular event, season, or over several years.

Figure 8.2 shows that the extent to which revenue can be generated (i.e. a chief responsibility of any marketer) and money must be expended is very dependent on these marketing constraints. The design of the facility, for example, affects the amount of money the facility or event can generate in numerous ways: the larger venue, the greater the number of tickets that can be sold but the higher the initial capital outlay on building the venue (to say

Figure 8.2 Marketing strategy constraints

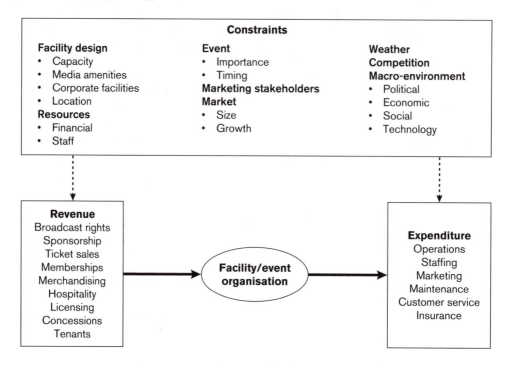

nothing of the considerably higher ongoing costs of such things as maintenance and cleaning). Perhaps most important though, in terms of the relationship between facility design and revenue generation, is whether the facility adequately caters to the media, as the media are necessary to promotion, sponsor attraction and satisfaction, as well the production of a successful television product.

A key role for the marketer is to ensure that revenue generation exceeds expenditure. Exactly how this is achieved is a real challenge, one that varies from event to event and between facilities. Compounding this challenge is that customer needs and expectations will continue to evolve and, while events can quite easily be changed to accommodate the whims of the market, the marketer must continue to work with the same building—that is, an inflexible 'bricks and mortar' structure which is not only incredibly difficult to modify in any significant way but always exceptionally expensive to do so. (You are encouraged to select an event or facility you are familiar with and to outline how several of the constraints depicted in Figure 8.2 affect revenue generation and expenditure.)

Attracting customers versus retaining customers

More often than not, marketing strategy focuses on attracting customers rather than on retaining them. This is evident for consumer markets as well as business markets. However, keeping customers is just as important as attracting new customers, particularly when you consider customers in terms of lifetime value. Calculating a customer's or group of customers' lifetime value involves calculating the financial worth of retaining them over a certain period of time (not necessarily a lifetime) and therefore their importance to the facility or event organisation.

Customer lifetime value, as a function of the costs of serving a customer and the revenue received from the customer over the particular time period, is expressed below.

Time period × (Revenue − Costs) = Customer lifetime value

For example, the lifetime value of a thoroughbred racing club member over a 10-year period might be $6100, whereby:

Time period = 10 years
Annual revenue = $890
Annual costs = $280

Not only does a facility or event forfeit the money that lost customers would have spent on the core product (i.e. $6100 in the racing club membership example) but it will miss out on the money spent on a range of peripheral products, such as food and beverage, parking and merchandise. It is also possible that lost customers will cause others to leave, making for an even greater loss in revenue. For example, fitness centre customers may each take one or two friends or family members with them when they leave for the services of a competing centre.

The ramifications for other types of facilities can be much more serious when you consider how a decrease in live-at-venue customers for the spectator facility may also result in lost business customers. Many sponsors, for example, want large crowds at the events and facilities they sponsor: a large crowd is a sign of success, and sponsors wish to be associated with this success. Also, these crowds are often part of the sponsor's target market. Therefore, a smaller crowd represents a reduced opportunity for the sponsor to promote its products, and for some sponsors a reduced opportunity to sell product as well. For example, a beer sponsor with exclusive pourage rights at a facility or event will sell less beer and hence generate less revenue when crowd size decreases. Broadcasters too prefer large crowds at the events they televise, as a large and enthusiastic gathering of fans contributes much to the event's atmosphere and thus the attractiveness of the sport TV product. It is the degree of attractiveness of the TV product that drives advertising sales, a network's primary source of revenue.

In addition to the current customers they could lose, facility and event marketers should concern themselves with the loss of potential customers. One of the most successful means of promoting services is positive word-of-mouth, and those customers that are lost because they were unsatisfied with some aspect of the facility or event service provided are unlikely to recommend it to friends, colleagues, families and other businesses. Indeed, these lost customers may actually spread negative word-of-mouth about a facility or event, actively deterring potential customers. Research shows that customers are much more likely to complain about products they find fault with, as well as the organisations that produce them, than to spread good news about those which satisfy them.

Although a convincing argument for retaining customers has been made, it is true that facility and event organisations often have the financial capacity to weather the loss of several and even hundreds of consumer customers. For example, any large facility such as the Millennium Stadium in Cardiff would not suffer too much if it attracted 69 000 spectators instead of its anticipated 70 000. This is not the case for business customers, as these customers are significantly fewer in number but contribute tens and hundreds of thousands (and sometimes millions) of dollars or pounds to the facility's or event's coffers. Retaining sponsors and broadcast partners is critical, given that these customers generate more revenue for facilities and events than do spectators.

The media are littered with stories of panic and financial woe of those events and facilities which have lost critical business customers. For example, early in 2001 the Australian Open, a premier international tennis event, lost Ford as its long-term naming rights sponsor. Months later, as the 2002 tournament drew steadily closer, organisers were still struggling to find a replacement for Ford. The Australian Open commissioned IMG in its search for a major sponsor, which secured the KIA car company at the last possible moment. What would have been the ramifications to the Australian Open if no major sponsor had been signed in time?

Strategies to retain customers

We have highlighted the importance of retaining customers, and that the easiest way to retain customers is to satisfy them. But what is it that makes a customer's facility or event experience a satisfying one? Essentially, customers will be satisfied when they get what they want, and all customers want quality!

The relationships between quality, satisfaction and retention are depicted in Figure 8.3 and have been well supported across a range of research contexts. Murray and Howat (2002), for example, found that sport and leisure centre participants' perceptions of service quality on a range of factors (e.g. staff, program, parking, child minding) influenced their satisfaction and in turn their repeat purchase intentions. Like Murray and Howat, Wakefield and Blodgett (1996) found that the relationships held true for spectators attending Major College Football and Minor League Baseball games. Their study revealed that the quality of the facilities (in terms of layout accessibility, aesthetics, seating comfort, and cleanliness) positively affected spectator satisfaction, which in turn positively contributed not only to the spectators' desire to return to the facilities but also to the length of time they desired to spend in the facilities. While the importance of retaining customers has already been stressed, customers spending more time at facilities and hence at sporting events is also an important factor. Essentially, the more time customers spend at an event, or in a facility, the more likely they are to spend large sums of money.

The relationships between quality, satisfaction and retention hold true also for business markets (i.e. event owners and promoters, sponsors and broadcasters). Moreover, the ability to serve, satisfy and retain one particular type of customer is related to the successful retention of another. For example, a quality facility or event that produces satisfied spectators or

Figure 8.3 The relationship between quality, satisfaction and retention

participants that keep coming back for more obviously contributes to the satisfaction and retention of event owner and promoter as well as that of sponsors and even broadcasters.

Sport servuction model

A useful tool for all facility and event marketers interested in maximising the quality of their services and hence customer satisfaction and repeat purchasing is Shilbury et al.'s (2003) sport-specific adaptation of the servuction model (Langeard, Bateson, Lovelock & Eiglier 1981), shown in Figure 8.4. The 'sport servuction model' depicts the different elements that constitute the facility and event service experience as well as how the service experience is created.

The sport servuction model can be divided into two parts—that which is visible to the customer (i.e. customer A), and that which is not. The visible part of the model comprises three components, namely the inanimate environment (the facility itself, including physical evidence), the staff (contact personnel and service providers), and other customers (i.e. customer B). The invisible part of the model, which should play a 'support' role for the rest of the model, comprises just one component. Although Langeard et al. (1981) referred to this component as the invisible organisation and system, in a facility and event management context it is more aligned with the traditional marketing department role, whereby event owners/promoters work together with facility owners/managers to plan and organise the event. The services (i.e. bundle of benefits) experienced by the customers come from each of the model components as well as the way in which they are synchronised, or coordinated.

Figure 8.4 Sport servuction model

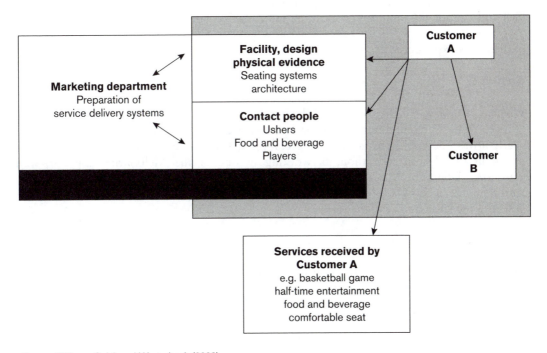

Source: Shilbury, Quick and Westerbeek (2003).

The association the sport servuction model has with the 'Service quality → Satisfaction → Retention' relationship discussed previously is that its visible and invisible components have the potential to positively as well as negatively influence a customer's service experience and thus affect the benefits he or she receives. Together with a brief description of each component, examples of the ways in which they may positively influence a facility or event customer's experience are outlined below. (You are encouraged, perhaps by reflecting on your own experiences, to identify ways in which each component might also negatively influence the facility or event experience, as well as develop solutions to eliminate these problems.)

Facility design and physical evidence

The non-living features that are present during the service encounter constitute what Langeard et al. (1981) referred to as the inanimate environment. In a facility and event management context this means the facility itself, incorporating non-physical elements like music, lighting and odours, as well as physical evidence such as scoreboards and staff uniforms. A centrally positioned and air-conditioned corporate suite complete with flat-screen television, Internet access, a top-of-the-range fit-out and well-stocked bar is an example of how the facility design and physical evidence can positively influence the corporate customer's experience.

Contact people

The contact that customers have with facility and event staff can involve a direct interaction (e.g. spectators handing their tickets to ushers or buying beer from food and beverage staff) or an indirect (remote) interaction (e.g. spectators being present to watch their team throw, kick and run, or the umpire signal a time out). Having fair and skilful umpires officiate at a volleyball grand final is an example of how contact people can positively influence the participant's experience.

Customer B

Whereas customer A is the recipient of the bundle of service benefits, customer B refers to all other customers present during customer A's experience. Sport facility and event products are nearly always publicly consumed (e.g. spectating at Daytona International Speedway, competing in the Boston Marathon, networking in one of the Melbourne Cup corporate marquees). Doing the Mexican wave, laughing, talking and cheering with fellow fans, the atmosphere created by a full house, are all examples of how other customers can positively influence the spectator's experience.

Marketing department

This particular component of the sport servuction model relates closely to management philosophy and incorporates various rules, policies and procedures, including the what, where, when, why and how of service production. A plethora of considerations—for example, membership eligibility criteria, the number of ushers and turnstile attendants employed at any one event, and dress codes—need to be addressed by the marketing department. A policy ensuring a streamlined and well-organised accreditation process, whereby the broadcaster's production crew are couriered their passes in a timely fashion, is an example of how the marketing department can positively influence the broadcaster's experience.

The sport servuction model has been presented as a useful tool for identifying several variables that constitute the facility and event service experience and hence influence the customers' perception of quality, their satisfaction and likelihood of purchasing the experience again. As such, the model can be used for quality improvement purposes. That is, the facility or event marketer can manage and integrate each component in the model so that customers receive the best possible bundle of benefits. Another useful tool in the pursuit of service quality, and one that is best used in conjunction with the sport servuction model, is flowcharting.

Flowcharting

Flowcharting is a means of identifying each step in the service process. Flowcharting originated in manufacturing, and was concerned with maximising the effectiveness and efficiency of the flow of raw materials through the production process. Bateson and Hoffman (1999) note how in the service sector customers replace these raw materials. Thus, sport service flowcharting is concerned with mapping the process of how customers interact with the sport servuction system and subsequently how their service experience is created.

Figure 8.5 is a simplified flowchart for the spectator sport service. The figure makes the distinction between the visible (i.e. front stage) and invisible (i.e. backstage) parts of the production process, demonstrating that a range of invisible-to-the-customer support steps are necessary for the service to be delivered. That is, behind each visible step is at least one invisible step. Moreover, it should be noted that several of the invisible steps are actually carried out by agencies other than the facility itself (e.g. the delivery of the mailed tickets by the postal service and the scheduling of additional trains by the public transport authority), resulting in the need for considerable interorganisational cooperation and coordination. (Many more steps could be included in the flowchart, such as staff recruitment and training, facility maintenance, and contract negotiation with suppliers, but a figure incorporating this additional detail would be far too large for this book.)

One of the particularly important functions of flowcharting in a services context is that it identifies the occasions on which customers interact with an organisation's staff. Each of these interactions represents a 'moment of truth', or an insight into the service organisation's ability to deliver a quality customer experience. It is often from these moments of truth that the customer's perception of quality is realised. Hence, effective human resource management, including recruiting the right people and providing them with superior training, is critical to services marketing and therefore facility and event marketing. The notion of moments of truth can be stretched to encompass a customer's interaction with any part of the facility or event, such as seating comfort, sight lines and crowding.

Each moment of truth is potentially a 'critical incident'—that is, an interaction that leads to either an extremely positive or negative experience for the customer. In other words, each step in the service process has the potential to generate customer satisfaction or dissatisfaction. Flowcharting is a particularly useful diagnostic tool, as it identifies where problems might occur in the service process. Lovelock et al. (2004, p. 50) specify that at each flowchart step marketers must ask three questions. First, 'What does the customer really want?'. Perhaps spectators want friendly turnstile operators and ushers who greet them with a smile and a 'Hello', or, contact personnel who just get people into the venue and to their seats as

Figure 8.5 Flowchart of the spectator sport service

Visible	Invisible		
Purchase tickets via ticketing agent	← Enter data	← Print tickets	
↓			
Receive tickets in mail	← Deliver mail	← Sort mail	← Post tickets
↓			
Catch train	← Schedule additional trains	← Liaise with public transport authority	
↓			
Purchase program	← Supply program sellers	← Print programs	
↓			
Undergo bag check by security staff	← Brief security staff	← Set up bag check areas	
↓			
Enter turnstile	← Test automatic scanners	← Open turnstiles	
↓			
Meet concourse usher	← Allocate staff	← Launder customer service staff uniforms	
↓			
Purchase beer and hotdog	← Food and beverage preparation	← Storage of food and beverage	← Purchase of food and beverage
↓			
Meet aisle usher	← Allocate staff	← Launder customer service staff uniforms	
↓			
Take seat	← Clean seating area		
↓			
Purchase team cap and scarf at half-time	← Storage of merchandise	← Purchase of merchandise	← Manufacture merchandise
↓			
Use restroom	← Clean restroom	← Fill toilet roll and soap dispensers	
↓			
Meet aisle usher for re-check of tickets	← Allocate staff	← Launder customer service staff uniforms	
↓			
Leave venue	← Open gates		
↓			
Catch train	← Schedule additional trains	← Liaise with public transport authority	

quickly as possible. Second, 'Where is the potential for failure at this step?'. Turnstiles that don't open on time and faulty ticket scanners are obvious failures at the venue entry step in the spectator service. Finally, 'What number and types of steps will best serve to optimise service delivery efficiency and standardisation, customer throughput and satisfaction?'. This will obviously vary greatly, depending on both the customer and the service.

It is interesting at this point to pause to consider where the boundaries of services lie—that is, where the service begins and ends, and thus the steps in the production process that should be included in a flowchart. Consider the flowchart depicted in Figure 8.5, which incorporates buying tickets from an outside agent (such as Australia's Ticketmaster 7) as well as public transport. Although the facility or event might have a contract with the ticketing agent, it has limited control over the quality of the service the agent provides its customers with, and no control over whether trains or any other means of public transport will serve its customers well. However, a customer's service experience and hence satisfaction judgements and likelihood of repeat purchase can be determined by such external factors. Facilities and events now outsource many services, including ticketing, security, food and beverage, and cleaning, and have consequently reduced their capacity to control quality. These organisations must ask themselves whether they have found the right balance between the economies of outsourcing and the high priority many customers place on these peripheral services being performed well.

The final point to make on flowcharting the facility or event product pertains to who should be involved in this activity. It is important that the marketer consult with operations staff, including those who have direct contact with the customer (e.g. ushers, receptionists), as these employees often have a more intimate customer knowledge, such as where customers typically experience problems with the service. Likewise, the marketer needs to include customers, not only for their knowledge of the service but also because it is the customer who needs to perceive the service as being of sufficient quality. Failure to include these parties in the flowcharting process runs the risk of designing a one-sided and thus not necessarily accurate or useful map of the customer's service experience.

Relationship marketing

Service quality, customer satisfaction and customer retention are central to relationship marketing, a form of marketing that emerged in the early 1990s and then quickly accelerated to a place of great significance within the marketing discipline by the turn of the century. Relationship marketing is concerned with building, maintaining and enhancing long-term customer relationships to the benefit of both customer and organisation. Although relationship marketing can be conducted within the context of numerous customer markets, in this book these markets will be restricted to those identified in the facility and event customer typology.

Relationship marketing evolved due to the realisation that in a highly competitive market it is often not enough to merely conduct transactions (i.e. one-off sales) with customers. It is becoming increasingly necessary to retain customers that will purchase from the organisation on multiple occasions. Thus, underpinning relationship marketing is a repeat purchasing or customer retention philosophy. Further underpinning relationship marketing is a 'win–win' philosophy whereby the objectives of both the customer and the service provider are met.

Despite the ready acknowledgement of the importance of customer repeat purchase and many an industry's acceptance of the relationship marketing mantra, it is important to note that facility and event organisations should not seek to develop relationships with *all* of their customers. According to Shani (1997), 'Relationship marketing centers on developing long term relationships with the organisation's best customers' (p. 11). Inherent in Shani's words is the notion that some customers are more worthy of relationship marketing efforts than others.

Which customers to develop relationships with

Like Shani (1997), McDonald and Milne (1997) recognise that some customers are more important than others. They recommend that marketers assess their customers' lifetime value (as discussed previously) and relative relationship strength (i.e. the customer's intangible, and often emotional, bond with the organisation) in order to determine which customers are the most valuable and therefore worthy of pursuing relationships with.

In order to better accommodate the facility and event marketing context, we have adapted McDonald and Milne's (1997) four-cell conceptual framework by replacing relative relationship strength with the extent to which the customer needs the service (i.e. degree of customer need) (see Figure 8.6). As with McDonald and Milne's model, the cells into which customers fall should determine whether a relationship is pursued, as well as the extent to which resources be expended on doing so. We have used thoroughbred racecourse examples in our description of each of the four customer groups. It is up to you to determine how the framework can be applied to different facility types (e.g. football stadia, aquatic centres), as well as to events.

- *Cell 1: high CLV and high DCN.* As with most sport facilities, some of a racecourse's most valuable customers reside in cell 1. Customers in this cell are business market customers, including sponsors, broadcasters, corporate box/suite holders, concession holders and bookmakers. Not only do these customers provide racecourses with substantial income, but racecourses in return provide them with the opportunities to generate their own income through the achievement of various business objectives. For example, broadcasters use the televised racing product to sell more advertising space, and concession holders sell food and beverage to race-day spectators. In other words, these customers are considerably dependent on the racecourses they do business with, a situation compounded by the fact that limited viable alternative suppliers typically exist for this customer group. Just as it is critical that racecourse management build and maintain relationships with its cell 1 customers, so too is it crucial that these customers reciprocate these relationship marketing efforts.
- *Cell 2: high CLV and low DCN.* In the context of racecourses, cell 2 customers are typically the club members, who often pay a considerable fee to enjoy the privileges of

Figure 8.6 Framework for allocating relationship marketing efforts

Degree of customer need (DCN)	**Customer lifetime value** (CLV) **High**	**Low**
High	**1**	**3**
Low	**2**	**4**

Source: Adapted from McDonald and Milne (1997).

reserved seating and premium views of the track. These customers expend their money not only on a membership but also on product extensions such as parking, food and beverage, and merchandise. However, while cell 2 customers do make substantial financial contributions, their need for the racecourse product is not critical, as the various benefits they derive (e.g. social, prestige, networking) can be obtained through a variety of other products. Racecourse management should employ relationship marketing strategies to ensure the ongoing financial outlay of cell 2 customers.

- *Cell 3: low CLV and high DCN.* Like the customers in cell 1 these customers have considerable need for the racecourse product, in either the 'live' or televised format. These customers are typically 'professional punters'—that is, customers who make their living (or at least try to) from gambling. Although many gamblers will lay a bet on just about anything (in Australia you can bet on anything from a Queensland cockroach to a Northern Territory camel), professional gamblers typically stick to the one or just a few types of betting, such as thoroughbred racing. Cell 3 customers who attend the racecourse spend more of their time and money on the bookmakers than on the services offered by the racecourse per se, and those who gamble at a distance through a betting agency don't even contribute a gate fee to the racecourse's coffers. Other than ensuring that adequate racecourse betting facilities are available, racecourse management should not embark on relationship marketing activities with cell 3 customers.
- *Cell 4: low CLV and low DCN.* Cell 4 customers attend the racecourse infrequently, and typically only when a major meet is scheduled. Often also 'theatregoers', these customers may not even be particularly interested in horse racing and will often bet 'just for the fun of it' or because betting is perceived as a quintessential part of the race-day experience. There is no better place to see cell 4 customers than at the Spring Racing Carnival in Melbourne, particularly on Melbourne Cup Day itself, when for many in attendance the racing is secondary to the fashion, frivolity and partying. Cell 4 customers contribute little financially to the racecourse over time. Their infrequency of attendance is evidence of their minimal need for the racecourse product, as is their lack of interest in pursuing a racing club membership. Relationship marketing resources should not be spent on this group of customers.

In summary, no facility or event organisation should blindly engage in relationship marketing activities with all customer groups. Instead, facility and event marketers are asked to carefully consider which of their customers are most worthy of the resource expenditure associated with relationship building and maintenance. Also important to note is that not only are some customers better suited to relationship marketing efforts than others—so too are some organisations. However, given the business customers that facilities and events typically have, as well as the fact that many facilities' customers are also members, most facility and event marketers should be engaging in at least some relationship marketing activities.

Multiple marketing stakeholders: the challenges of resource commitment and coordination

A fundamental question, not typically addressed by facility and event management texts and one related to the topic of relationship marketing in the context of business customers, is:

Who is responsible for marketing the facility or event? The answer to this seemingly straightforward question is largely dependent on whether the organisation that owns the event also owns the facility in which it must be run, and whether it will run and promote the event itself. However, with the exception of small and typically participation events, as well as some professional sport events (more often than not in the USA and the UK), most events are not owned, run, promoted and 'housed' by the one organisation. Instead, several different parties may be involved, each of which can play a marketing role.

Unfortunately, the multiplicity of parties involved in running an event and hence the larger pool of marketing resources and knowledge does not necessarily result in a more successful marketing campaign. Instead, and particularly in a professional sport context, it can be a challenge to get the various stakeholders (i.e. league, facility, club) to make a reasonable marketing contribution in terms of resource commitment. (Why spend your money when someone else can spend theirs?) Likewise, it can be a challenge to coordinate the marketing efforts of the various parties, with efforts being duplicated in places and absent in others. These two challenges can easily result in a marketing campaign that does not reach its full potential, namely one that does not produce as many customers as possible and consequently puts fewer dollars in all parties' pockets.

When parties in addition to a league, facility and club as in the professional sport context are factored into facility and event marketing strategy, the coordination challenge noted previously becomes even more complex. For example, major sport events such as the Rugby World Cup require multiple facilities (typically managed by separate entities), and often employ the outsourced marketing services of firms such as Elite Sports Properties (ESP) and the International Management Group (IMG) in addition to their own. Furthermore, and at least in an Australian context, when major facilities are seeking to attract events they are often assisted by the marketing might of government-backed events corporations (e.g. Queensland Events Corporation, Victoria Major Events Corporation) whose purposes are to attract national and international events to their respective states. Finally, we cannot forget the promotional efforts of sponsors and broadcasters, with sponsors assisting promotional efforts by way of logo exposure, and broadcasters delivering the facility's or event's promotional message to a mass audience. It should now be apparent that the question of who is responsible for marketing the facility or event is not necessarily a simple one.

Summary

The emphasis of this chapter has been on the marketing of facilities and their events. Consistent with the definition of marketing presented at the beginning of the chapter, we stress the importance of facility and event marketers identifying, understanding and meeting the needs of a variety of customer markets, including individual consumers as well as businesses. The facility and event product is described in terms of four unique characteristics of services—namely, intangibility, inseparability, heterogeneity, and perishability. These characteristics, as well as their considerable implications, necessitate that facility and event marketers adopt a services marketing approach. A particular focus of this chapter, including the case study, has been on marketing strategy, notably the steps of market segmentation, targeting and positioning. In addition to describing this strategy process, we have introduced several strategy constraints specific to the marketing of facilities and events. We have also emphasised the importance of retaining customers, noting the relationships between service quality, customer satisfaction and customer retention. Consistent with this customer retention focus, we have then looked at relationship marketing, including a conceptual framework to assist facility and event marketers to identify which customers they are best developing and maintaining relationships with. We conclude with a case study exploring the challenges of resource commitment and coordination associated with the multiple marketing stakeholders that typically characterise facilities and events.

Case Study

Multiple marketing stakeholders: facility, league and club

The Melbourne Cricket Ground (MCG) is arguably Australia's premier sporting stadium. The two main spectator sports it hosts are cricket in summer and Australian Rules football (Australia's most popular football code) in winter. The Melbourne Cricket Club (MCC) manages the MCG, on behalf of the state government and the MCG Trust. The Australian Football League (AFL), the governing body of Australian Rules football, is the MCG's most important tenant and therefore the MCC's most important customer. In addition to many finals, including the Grand Final being contracted to be played at the MCG, five of the league's clubs (Collingwood, Essendon, Hawthorn, North Melbourne, Richmond) use the MCG as their home ground. Thus the MCG hosts many games of football throughout the season.

The MCC promotes the various Australian Rules football games it hosts, as does the governing professional league, the AFL. Likewise, the two clubs involved in each game (e.g. the Richmond Tigers and the Melbourne Demons) engage in promotional activities in order to get spectators to attend their games. However, despite the various contractual agreements between these parties, there exists no formal agreement stipulating the extent to which each of these parties take responsibility for, and subsequently expend resources on, an event's marketing. Neither does a plan exist to coordinate and integrate the parties' marketing efforts.

The good news is that recently the MCC and the AFL have commenced talks to better coordinate their marketing activities. In time, perhaps, some of the clubs which have held a reputation for taking advantage of the facility's and league's marketing efforts will see the benefit of working together synergistically. In the meantime, it appears that the MCC and the AFL are moving towards a true relationship—that is, one in which they work together to achieve each other's objectives. In other words, the AFL (event owner) and MCC (facility manager) are moving from being each other's customers to being each other's partners.

Q. Identify some strategies the MCC can introduce to encourage tenant clubs to engage in a marketing partnership.
Q. On what criteria would you recommend that marketing responsibilities and activities be allocated among the three parties central to this case study (i.e. MCC, AFL, clubs)?

Q. Devise a promotional campaign (advertising, public relations, publicity, sales promotion, personal selling, promotional licensing) involving the MCC, AFL and its clubs for a standard mid-season game at the MCG. Consider factors such as the target market(s), likely resources and time frame when you allocate the promotional responsibilities, and be prepared to justify these allocations.

Q. Who should oversee and coordinate the promotional campaign? Why?

Running the sport event: event operations

Chapter focus
Structure, size and trends in the sport facility and sport event sectors
Key success factors of operating sport facilities and running sport events
Developing new sport facilities: feasibility analysis
Developing new sport facilities: design and construction issues
Developing new sport facilities: preparing facility management infrastructure
Operating the new sport facility: attracting events
Operating the new sport facility: preparing event management infrastructure
Attracting customers: marketing the sport facility and the sport events
Running the sport event: event operations
Measuring facility and event performance: a scorecard approach to success
Measuring facility and event performance: impact on and for stakeholders

CHAPTER OBJECTIVES

In this chapter, we will:
- Consider the breadth and depth of management activities involved in the implementation substage of hosting an event.
- Provide an applied overview of a local organising committee operational structure and its unit groupings.
- Identify the key elements of logistics management and outline the practical checklists, on-site logistical tools and coordination methods to effectively stage an event.
- Highlight the needs of different stakeholders through discussion of the practical arrangements required to specifically manage sport event security, incidents and emergencies, spectator special needs, volunteer commitment and on-site media services.

Camera, lights . . . action!

Well, this is it! The moment of truth has at last arrived. All the hours, days, months, and in some cases, years of event preparation are about to be put to the test. Time has run out, the adrenaline and anticipation levels are at an all-time high, and the focus of attention is entirely centred on producing a memorable, quality experience that exceeds stakeholder expectations at the same time as optimising resource utilisation.

To this end we plan to provide here practical insight into the management activities demanded primarily of the implementation substage of the event lifecycle (see Chapter 2, Figure 2.1). Following on from the case study presented in Chapter 2, namely the 2002 Commonwealth Games, you are initially introduced to the event's local organising committee operational management structure, which serves as an illustrative example of the breadth of event operations demanded of the implementation phase. In particular, we draw your attention to the key elements of logistics management, as well as some of the on-site practical tools and coordination methods that help management to create effective and efficient people, information and other resource flows around the actual sport(s) event venue(s).

To provide a greater depth of understanding and analysis of the operational aspects of a major sport event, the remainder of this chapter focuses on some of the practical arrangements in specifically managing event security, incidents and emergencies, special needs, volunteers and the media. These elements have been purposely selected on the basis of their transferability and functional importance to many other sport event scenarios. They also demonstrate the previously established important principles of comprehending different stakeholder needs, and highlight the integrated and complex nature of managing sport events holistically, across the lifecycle of the project.

Operational structures and the XVII Commonwealth Games, Manchester 2002

Due to the sheer complexity of activities that need to be managed at any sport event, the organising committee must initially plan, establish and develop its human resources into a coordinated team driven by a common purpose. As people are in effect the doers of all work, they need to be optimally motivated and appropriately deployed if the quality performance outcomes are to be realised. At the event implementation substage this means that both paid and voluntary staff need to know exactly to whom they are responsible, as well as what they are meant to do, when and how. To this end, managing and coordinating groups of people are considered fundamental requirements to successful sport event management.

Formal or informal hierarchical unit groupings exist in every organisation. However, in the sport event management scenario they must operate particularly effectively and efficiently, as time is usually the limiting factor encountered by the event manager. As Goldblatt (1997, pp. 12–13) elaborates, 'it is the one commodity that once invested is gone forever'; and, in the implementation management phase, quite literally hundreds of decisions need to be taken and speedily acted on in a very short period of time. The event implementation unit groupings (usually referred to as the operational structure) are usually established quite early on in the project (at the detailed planning and preparation substage). Furthermore, they must be coherent, be communicated to all staff, be meticulously coordinated, and above all be appropriate to the demands of the event.

So what actually happened in the Manchester 2002 Commonwealth Games scenario? Table 2.1 (Chapter 2) provided an overview of the many stakeholders and multiorganisational elements of the event, but the actual M2002 management operational structure can be seen in Figure 9.1.

Diagrammatically it appears that there were three discrete unit groupings at this event (Operations, Commercial, and Creative and Communications), which were further subdivided into divisions (each with a respective manager/head) and then functional departments (see Table 9.1). Although these hierarchical units might seem to be working as separate identities, in practice this multi-venue organisational structure was largely based on heavily integrated relationships and project activity, thereby adopting the matrix and network structure principles introduced in Chapter 5.

As illustrated in Table 9.1, it is now considered good practice to formalise the operational structure by defining the event management's units or teams of operation, responsibilities of action, chains of command, as well as determining the respective spans of control. In just reviewing the functional departments column of Table 9.1 it becomes apparent that there is a very broad cross-section of interrelated activities. These need minimally to be project-managed against a common master timeline and overall plan if the event is to run smoothly and successfully.

Figure 9.1 Manchester 2002 Limited (local operating company) operational management structure

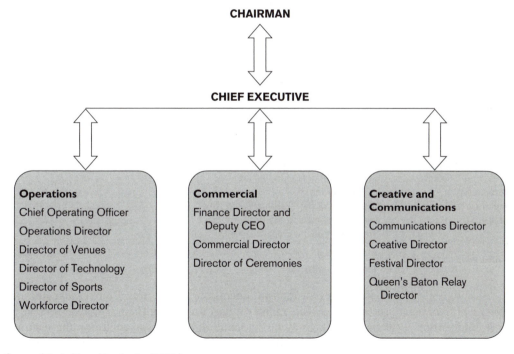

Source: Adapted from Manchester (2002a).

Table 9.1 Divisional responsibilities and departments of the XVII Commonwealth Games, Manchester 2002

	Divisional responsibility	Functional departments
Operations		
Chief Operating Officer	Coordination of all games operational activities	Program management; strategy and integration
Operations Director	Delivery of a range of support services across the whole games organisation	Transport; security; catering; cleaning and waste; accommodation; accreditation; village
Director of Venues	Development of venues to allow the provision of space, services and support to perform their games time tasks	Venue planning; venue fit-out; venue operations
Director of Technology	Provision of all information technology for the games	Telecommunications; results and timing; information technology
Director of Sports	Delivery of all sporting events in accordance with the rules of the International Sports Federation of each sport	Sport operations; medical; anti-doping control
Workforce Director	Detailed planning of all aspects of the Commonwealth Games workforce	Human resources; administration; volunteers; pre-volunteer program; uniforms
Commercial		
Finance Director and Deputy Chief Executive	Provides central support services for the other divisions within M2002	Finance; procurement and logistics; CGA relations; protocol; risk management; broadcasting
Commercial Director	Revenue generation, marketing and festivals	Sponsorship; licensing and marketing; ceremonies; spirit of friendship; ticketing; hospitality; look of the games; corporate relations
Creative and communications		
Communications Director	Marketing the Games and contact with external media agencies and the general public	Marketing; publicity; public relations; public information; media services
Creative Director, Festival Director and Director of Ceremonies	Opening and closing ceremonies; Spirit of Friendship; and all creative media activities	—
Director of Queen's Jubilee Baton Relay	All aspects of the Queen's Baton Relay, which will be raising the profile of the Games across the Commonwealth	—

Source: Adapted from Manchester (2002a).

Although, diagrammatically, event internal operational structures often appear uniquely different, further analysis usually reveals many similarities among them. For example, at the sport competition level there is likely to be someone directly responsible for the technical requirements of the respective governing body needs (competitors, officials, media services, sport facilities and equipment). At the project management level, the generic management disciplines of marketing, finance, law and human resources commonly form many of the units of the management structure. Indeed, Emery (1997) identified that, despite a considerable breadth of terminology used in unit groupings, most major sport events were arranged around the following task groups: administration/protocols, accommodation, finance and legal, transport, technical (rules), venue, staffing, and marketing (publicity).

The chosen event management operational structure should clearly be dependent on the exact nature of the event, its accompanying risks and resource availability, as well as the stakeholder expectations, commitment and expertise. This means that to fulfil the unique requirements of the sport event, numerous tasks will need to be carefully integrated into a coordinated and controlled production schedule in exactly the same way as any other aspect of the entertainment industry. The diversity of the event tasks should not be underestimated. For example, even a relatively small annual 10-kilometre road race is likely to involve many of the tasks identified in the generic listing provided in Table 9.2. (Please note that this list is far from exhaustive.)

In summary, operational structures (staffing responsibilities, roles, functions) and task-oriented checklists are the very first components of preparatory activity for the implementation phase. As early as the planning stage, the systematic process of determining the event's operating structure begins. Logically derived from agreed performance indicators, this operating structure is vital to establish a unity of purpose and event integration from which further coordination activities can be logically planned. As suggested by Watt (1998, pp. 38–9):

Table 9.2 Generic checklist for event implementation

Accommodation	Medals/trophies/prizes
Accreditation	Media
Admission	Medical provision
Advertising—stadium, program	Merchandising
Arrival/departure—of teams/officials/VIPs	Photocopying/printing
Artwork	Photography
Car parking	Police
Catering	Program
Ceremonies	Registration
Communications	Seating
Concessions	Security
Decoration—flags, bunting external/internal	Signage—external/internal
Emergency procedures	Sponsorship
Equipment	Staff
Facilities—competition/training/changing/toilets/	Tickets
storage/reception/secure areas/sales points/	Transport
medical/crèches/disabled/exhibition space/hospitality	
Fundraising	
Insurance	
Invitations	
Licensing	
Lost property	

Source: Adapted from Croner Publications (1988, pp. 208–17).

A structure may be appropriate and people may do work, but little will be achieved unless their efforts are coordinated . . . In general terms, coordination comes from having a shared goal and common objectives, within an appropriate culture and structure.

Torkildsen similarly makes the point (1999, p. 476):

Unfortunately, with many event organisations, the structures are poor and without coordination. The result is that informal dealings flourish without co-ordination; misunderstandings and miscommunications abound, leaving many parts of the planning to fall between two stools.

At the local level, how many of the following sound familiar, or how easy is it to recall embarrassing mistakes at a sports event? Again Torkildsen (1999, p. 476):

. . . there was no staging; the public address did not work, lights did not come on; the changing rooms were in the nearest school a mile away; the VIPs at a national event were standing in the rain trying to convince the doorman that they had been invited; players at an All Stars match could not get into the ground because the entrance was blocked with traffic; and the grand piano for the concert at the sports centre had been delivered to the theatre!

Unity of purpose and coordination through effective and efficient communication channels are so essential to establish early on, to preserve and maintain through all aspects of the event lifecycle, that without them any event is likely to be a disaster!

Logistics management

Effective coordination and communication at the event implementation stage requires a clear understanding of the project goals, the different stakeholder needs, and an ability to manage practical logistics within the physical constraints of the venue(s). Logistics, defined as 'the time-related positioning of resources to meet user requirements' by the Institute for Logistics and Transport (cited in Bowdin, McDonnell, Allen & O'Toole 2001, p. 216), is practically about making sure the right people, equipment and services are available in the right place at the right time.

In the event management scenario this means establishing coordinated systems, which ideally permit effective and efficient flows of people, information and other resources around the event venue(s). As highlighted in Figure 9.2, the essential elements of establishing an overall event logistics system to achieve this coordination are to consider the supply of customers, products and facilities to the event, around the event, and then to determine the event shutdown arrangements.

Event logistics, then, should be part of the overall planning process that includes establishing the event theme, unique atmosphere and staging detail. Timing, secrecy and explicit management of the five senses (tactile, smell, taste, visual, auditory) have now become an art form in attempting to make the event a memorable success. But, as expressed by one event organiser (cited in Bowdin, McDonnell, Allen & O'Toole 2001, pp. 249–50):

Figure 9.2 Elements of the logistics system

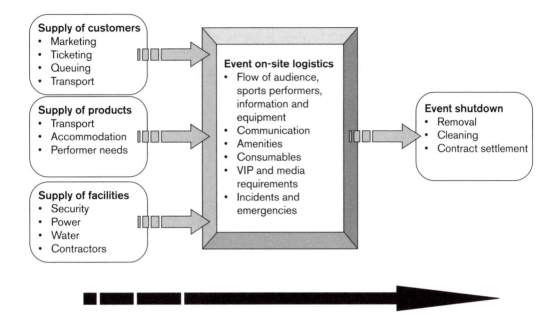

Source: Adapted from Bowdin, McDonnell, Allen and O'Toole (2001, p. 217).

... meticulous planning and staging are crucial when trying to create a spontaneous and vibrant atmosphere. This can be understood in terms of 'staging' because things like lighting, space and noise and furniture are tools of 'mood' to be manipulated ... Stage managing their environment can often ensure that the guests do not have to be 'ferried' around and will 'naturally' go home at the right time! It is interesting that the most tightly staged environment will often inspire guests to feel a natural part of a very exciting party.

Ideally, at any particular moment in time everything will be perfectly controlled, coordinated and in its rightful place if the event quality targets are to be fully realised. The sport and technical facilities and equipment (including power supplies) must be of an appropriate standard and be arranged according to the event owner's as well as national legislative requirements. The officials, athletes and staff must similarly be professionally turned out, and as per the media, support services, spectators and guests; they must all be aware of when, how and where they can gain access to the venue immediately before, during and after the sporting contest.

On-site logistics at the event

Regardless of the event venue(s), the flows of materials, people and information around the site (including sport and non-sporting venues such as hotels and airports) become critical elements in exceeding stakeholder satisfaction levels. The ultimate aim must always be to create a safe secure environment for all, which unfortunately has not historically always been the case. The secondary aim, and probably the *raison d'être* of the organising committee's work, is to create an enjoyable and positively memorable experience for all concerned. Although these may sound like basic ideals, they are not necessarily easy to achieve due to the complex nature of the event management environment (as introduced in Chapter 2). For example, sport events are usually dependent on working with large numbers of volunteers (whose reliability and competence are largely untested) as well as many different organisations, each with their own agenda and assumption of expectations of the local organising committee. Temporary physical structures (e.g. corporate hospitality marquees, media facilities, participant/spectator toilets, performer stages, spectator seating areas) and other service utilities are also often needed, each demanding its own 'bump-in'/'set-up' and 'bump-out'/ 'break-down' arrangements, which again have largely been untested.

Furthermore, and as previously mentioned, time is the limiting factor for all concerned. As the event draws near, the tempo accelerates and everything becomes classified as urgent. Long working hours, confrontations and a distinct lack of sleep are common occurrences at many sport events. On the one hand, the working environment is likely to become a highly energised and rewarding experience; on the other, it has the potential to be very stressful, where the smallest incident can create annoyance, conflict and a crisis. Obviously, the easiest solution is to try to manage these uncertainties by preparing rationally for potential contingencies. In practice, this means involving experienced personnel in the production of integrated operational systems and plans that are logically linked to the achievement of the event goals as well as to the organisational strategic and overall master plans.

The outcomes of these operational plans and systems need to be communicated and where possible tested by the relevant stakeholders prior to the event. According to Bowdin et al. (2001), this normally will include use of the following tools:

- *venue site plan* (often includes details of the entrances/exits, fixtures, access arrangements, car parking, electrics, accreditation zones, and the location of the support services);
- *contact list and communication system details* (e.g. the lines and means of communication, radio channel usage, incident and emergency procedures);
- *production schedule* (chronological master document with activities, timings, locations and responsibilities);
- *run sheets* (for specific jobs, e.g. VIP speeches and other announcements); and
- *cue sheets* (for prompting, if things do not go according to plan).

In briefly elaborating on each tool, the venue site plan usually refers to the sport(s) event venue(s) (although major sport events are also likely to include a venue plan of some of the non-sporting venues, such as the athletes' village). In sport event terms, on-site logistics are usually arranged around the following key areas, which clearly target specific stakeholder requirements:

- *front of house*—general circulation areas, where services are provided for the public (e.g. toilets, catering, merchandising outlets);
- *back of house*—the operational and management areas, which are rarely seen by the public (e.g. storage areas, meeting rooms and the essential event control centre);
- *field of play*—which includes the sport performance and preparation areas.

These are then subdivided into 'facility zones' (see Chapter 4) or in the case of many events form the basis of establishing the all-important 'accreditation zones' (more details on these later on). Typically, venue plans are presented in diagrammatic form and are customised to the needs of each stakeholder. For example, Figure 9.3 summarises the important location details of the key media facilities at the 9th IAAF World Indoor Championships in Athletics (2003).

Such a venue plan, as depicted in Figure 9.3, is normally supported by a written guide, in the language(s) stipulated by the event owner, that details many of the other operational aspects that directly influence the quality of service provision. In this instance the event media guide, for example, included the competition timetable, access, accreditation and transport arrangements, the nature of the electrical and information technology provision, as well as the details of the support services, other social events, and the vitally important contact and communication arrangements should further information be required.

The contact list and communication systems for the whole event clearly need to be thought through in some detail. With the advances in technology, closed-circuit television systems, radio channel usage and mobile telephones have now become the norm to update venue management continuously on what is happening both within and external to the sporting venue(s). Coordinated through an on-site control centre, lines of communication and radio channel usage must be carefully planned, tested and reviewed to avoid congested

Figure 9.3 Media facilities within the National Indoor Arena, 2003 World Indoor Athletics Championships

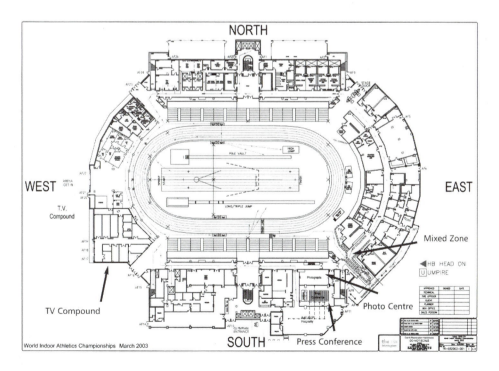

Source: Reproduced with permission from World Indoor Championships in Athletics (2003a, p. 10).

channel traffic and inappropriate behaviour. One example of this is illustrated in Figure 9.4, which highlights the established communication arrangements at a professional football stadium in England.

In essence, it is the on-site logistics plan that tries to identify the likely movement of people and information through the eyes of each group of stakeholders. This in turn determines their specific demands and needs at key moments in time, which in turn establishes the requirements of the integrated communication systems needed to implement a successful event. This stakeholder focus is clearly exemplified by France's 100-metre runner Issa

Figure 9.4 Professional football match communication arrangements

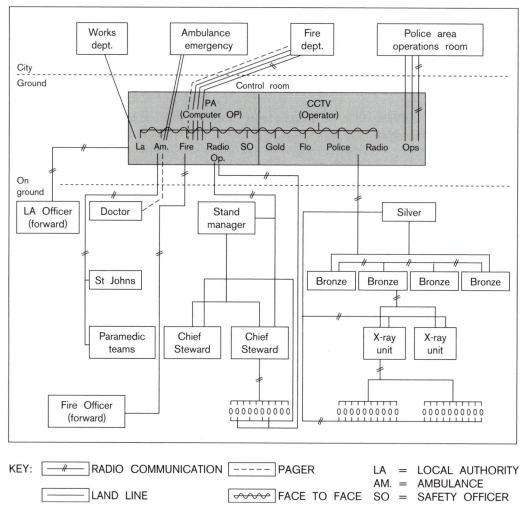

Source: Reproduced with permission from Martin (1996).

N'Thépé (2003) from the 9th IAAF World Championships in Athletics, who provides a unique chronological insight (Table 9.3) into the journey within the Stade de France® immediately before the competition in the field of play venue zone.

The more important the stakeholder to the successful operation of the event at any moment in time, the greater the depth of logistical analysis, planning and stakeholder involvement required. In the Table 9.3 example, where the 100-metre televised live race is one of the highlights of the championships, it is vital that all of the finalists be on the start line together. Although perhaps a little obvious and easy to say, how easy is this to achieve given the traffic and security arrangements experienced at most large sport events today? This is the reason why event organisers now carefully attempt to manage the sports performers' pre-event activities, which normally includes providing a 'meet-and-greet service' at the airport/train station, transport to and from the athletes' village as well as to all of the training, competition and social venues, and chaperoning them around the sport venue(s) at the moment of competition.

Table 9.3 Pre-event chronological athlete perspective

Specific locations	N'Thépé comments
The warm-up stadium	'Located fifty metres from the Stade de France® . . . It is here that the athletes come about one and a half hours before their event. A private tunnel then takes them directly into the stadium proper to complete their final preparations, before going out onto the track.'
The bowels of the Stade de France®	'A corridor that looks more like a street, then pedestrian crossings, then a tunnel . . . we walk along the pavement for about fifty metres before reaching the call room. It's best to keep up with the guides—if I ended up on my own here, I'd get completely lost.'
The call room	'This is the zone of reckoning and focus, the airlock before entry onto the track. It's a large, sparsely furnished room in which around 30 athletes can be gathered to wait together. This is where the officials check our spikes, cover up the logos of sponsors not allowed to appear in the stadium and confiscate electronic equipment such as radios or walkmans. For the athletes, concentration reaches its peak here.'
The entry of the athletes	'This is the most awesome moment of all, for me. After leaving the call room we follow a corridor for a few metres leading as far as the track, which we then walk along to the middle of the back straight. As you go, you can see the stands rise and rise before you . . . it's as if the sky's never going to appear. This is the moment when the athlete becomes fully aware of the immense scale of the Stade de France®.'
The stadium and track	'This stadium can be very intimidating the first time you enter it . . . The only little gripe I have is the distance between the inside lanes and the crowd. But I don't mean to worry the spectators: we can hear them perfectly well.'
The mixed zone	'As soon as the event finishes, the athletes are swamped by journalists in what's known as the "mixed zone", the area just at the exit from the track, where they take part in question and answer sessions . . . We collect our personal belongings. All that remains then is to leave the stadium to take a shower back at the hotel, or go and sit in the stand reserved for the athletes, sometimes after doping control.'

Source: Adapted from N'Thépé (2003).

The complexity of such arrangements (due to the diversity of stakeholders and numbers at major events) means that project management techniques (see Chapter 4) are no longer being used purely for the pre-event stage but also in some cases for the event stage of the life-cycle. Such detailed operational planning is then summarised in the form of a production schedule(s) as well as run and cue sheets.

Whereas production schedules provide a chronological list of management activities against time (see Table 9.4 taken from the French 1998 Football World Cup), run and cue sheets tend to provide more detail, such as the scripted content of key speeches and compère announcements. For example, the following emergency action plan announcement was made after the guests of the 2003 North East Sport Awards Ceremony were seated (Sunderland City Council 2003):

> Ladies and Gentleman, this is an emergency action plan announcement. Should the fire alarm sound during this evening's event please remain in your event area whilst the alarm is being investigated. You will be advised of the necessary action to take, following investigations by the Centre-staff.

Furthermore, scripted announcements were prepared just in case the fire alarm went off, evacuation and re-entry procedures were activated, or (in the ultimate case) if the decision was actually made to cancel the event.

Up to this point, the general breadth of tasks associated with the effective operation of an event, as well as the process and tools of logistics management, have been our centre of discussion. However, successful event management usually demands a greater level of task understanding and application than currently presented. In the remainder of this chapter we will therefore provide a more detailed and specific focus on just a few key activities associated with the management of the event implementation phase.

Key activities in event implementation phase

Specific activities

Every organisation should be committed to establishing high standards of health and safety for the continuing quality reputation and image of the event, the venue(s), as well as all of the people associated with it. But as Limb (2003, p. 20) comments:

> Why do we still not take health and safety seriously? A number of recent litigation cases [in the UK] have revealed significant contraventions in health and safety compliance resulting in civil claims ... and, in one recent case, imprisonment. Why? Is it a lack of understanding of the law or a blatant disregard? Is it looked upon as a bureaucratic paper-producing exercise, merely existing to keep the law enforcers and insurance companies happy? ... We need to have appropriate site design, appropriate safety measures and standards and competent contractors, tailored to suit the event. Under- or over-provision can cost time, money and, of course, lives.

The bottom line clearly is that event organisers *must* ensure the safety of all of the event's stakeholders and comply with appropriate legislation by taking all reasonable and

Table 9.4 Football World Cup, countdown match day for the Argentina and Croatia game

Time	Activity
7:00	Opening of the Key Distribution Centre
	Opening of the Broadcasting Centre
	Opening of the Centre for Volunteers
	Opening of the Operations Centre
9:00	Daily meeting of Organisation Committee/FIFA
	Coordination of organisational activities/taskforces activated
10:00	End preparation of the pitch
	Placing of public signage
	Watering the pitch
	Pre-opening of the official village
13:00	Finish checking out the stadium
	Opening of prestige space 'Gold'
14:00	Count-down—synchronisation of watches FIFA
	Opening of corporate boxes
	Opening of prestige space 'Silver'
	Stadium floodlight to 1300 Lux
15:10	End of 2nd curtain-raising match
15:15	Players begin warm-up on field
15:30	Synchronisation of watches
15:40	Players leave—end of warm-up
	1st test of fanfare announcements
15:42	Welcome announcement over loudspeakers—teams listed
	Final verification of pitch markings (FIFA)
15:44	2nd check of fanfares
	1st broadcast transmission
	Fanfare arrival onto the pitch
15:45	6 youngsters from FIFA Fair Play ready in the tunnel
15:50	Youngsters in national dress march onto the pitch
15:51	Line-up of players leaving the changing room
	The 6 youngsters from FIFA Fair Play come onto the pitch followed by FIFA coordinator, the referees/linesmen/two teams
	Playing of the FIFA anthem
15:52	National anthems: announce anthem A and anthem B
	3 fanfares sounded—bands withdrawn from pitch
15:53	Introductions/handshaking—2 teams
15:57	Official team photographs taken
15:58	Toss of coin for choice of direction
16:00	Kick-off—1st half

Note: Match schedule plan continues until 2 am the next day, with the final activity being the close-down of the IT bureau.

Source: Adapted from France '98 (1998).

practicable steps to prevent, control and guard against risks that directly affect the event. What then are some of the practical considerations that the event manager has to consider within the implementation phase of an event to make this possible?

Event security and accreditation

In light of the terrorist acts of 11 September 2001, high-profile sport events, attended by world-famous celebrities and receiving intense global media coverage, are particularly vulnerable to all types of risks and extreme activities. This means that every event manager must now be prepared to confront a wide variety of risks that need to be professionally managed. (Many of the techniques and processes of identifying and dealing with these risks have already been covered in the planning chapters of this text.)

Risk management (often covered under a variety of event terminology and roles such as health and safety, security, risk assessment, insurance, compliance and emergency management), for example, is considered so fundamental to any type of event success that a senior member of management staff is usually assigned this responsibility. For example in the M2002 scenario, Table 9.1 revealed that event security was largely the responsibility of the Operations Director. However, this in itself is a little simplistic, as everyone involved with an event has a responsibility for the health and safety of others. Illustrating the integrated matrix nature of the 2002 Commonwealth Games operations, external organisations (e.g. the emergency services) as well as all of the senior operational managers were actually involved in the preparation of the safety documentation as well as the practicality of its implementation. Internally, the viability of the Operations Director's security and accreditation plans were clearly dependent on knowledge of the sporting program (Director of Sports), the number and competence of staff available (Workforce Director), the geographically specialist and disparate venue requirements (Director of Venues), the information technology systems available (Director of Technology), as well as an in-depth understanding of how these systems would be integrated into the overall event management program (Chief Operating Officer).

The actual event security systems and risk management plans of M2002, as with most other venue-based major sport events around the world, were largely based on the venue's standard operational procedures (SOPs) (venue-specific daily operational procedures) as well as workable emergency action plans (EAPs). Both of these formalised procedures need to be regularly reviewed to ensure their effectiveness and currency.

As these plans are usually determined in the first instance by the physical entrance (ingress) and exit (egress) parameters of each venue, it probably comes as no surprise to learn that the event's security systems usually involve trained staff being strategically located at these points to check access rights at both the venue perimeter and the internally restricted zones. For spectators, entrance to the 2002 Commonwealth Games front-of-house activities generally meant ticket inspection at the main entrance followed by a progression through airport-style metal detectors and accompanying baggage being checked by X-ray machines. Given the popularity of some events and the likely queues that would result from these and other related security procedures, opening ceremony spectators were advised to arrive at least two hours before the start of the event.

For other stakeholders (e.g. the athletes, officials, media, sponsors, VIPs, and event staff) that need to access the back-of-house and field-of-play activities of different venues, alternative entrances and exits are used. Similar procedures to those for spectators are usually implemented at the main perimeter entrance but, rather than using a ticket, entrance normally takes place through some form of official identification, commonly referred to as accreditation. This typically takes the format of a sealed laminate identity card/pass that includes at least the name, position and photograph of the wearer, as well as details of the particular zones of access. Yet such is the increased concern for people's safety at mega-sport events (Salt Lake Winter Olympic Games spent $US400 million on event security) that advanced computer security packages are now being developed to apply cutting-edge, non-intrusive biometric techniques to the accreditation process, such as iris/fingerprint scanning and voice/face-recognition systems to considerably improve the validity of the identification and verification processes (Ammon 2002).

Accreditation, the purpose of which is to confirm identity and provide appropriate access rights and benefits to a particular venue and designated area within a venue, must clearly be directly related to each stakeholder's needs. As explained regarding the Olympic Games (International Olympic Committee 1998, p. 9):

> Athletes must be able to participate in the sports competitions under optimum conditions in order to give their best performance in accordance with the Olympic motto, 'Citius, Altius, Fortius'.

Accreditation has a significant impact on these objectives, in that:

- it ensures that only the appropriately qualified and eligible people are entitled to participate in or attend the Games;
- it limits participants' access to areas they need to perform their official function and keeps unauthorised people out of secure competition zones;
- it assists in determining the appropriate size and capacity for facilities and services; and
- it ensures that participants reach these areas in a safe and orderly manner.

Whereas accreditation may be less significant in smaller events and involve only face recognition or fluorescent bracelets as the means of access, in the case of major sport events the process of issuing passes to each group of stakeholders needs to be carefully thought through. Key deadlines need to be established and the method(s) of accreditation pass distribution communicated to all relevant parties in a timely manner. This is to ensure that vital police checks and other security approvals can be achieved on time, thus avoiding embarrassing and often heated conflicts at the moment of venue entry.

Normally there is at least one accreditation centre to issue these passes, which is set up close to, yet outside, the main sporting venue. This centre is supported by appropriate IT hardware and software that collects and securely stores the necessary anagraphical data, which are then used for security purposes. At the same time and location, staff are usually allocated their official event uniform. Common sense suggests that this uniform should be ordered to size to optimise resource utilisation, and staff collection times staggered to avoid the inevitable volunteer queues. However, considerable personal event volunteer experience suggests that common sense rarely prevails! Even if coherent systems are established, additional 'what-if scenarios' should always be under consideration. For example, what happens if people lose/forget their accreditation passes or cannot pick them up at the designated time? Or perhaps need to access an area urgently to fulfil a task that they do not have accreditation approval for? Flexibility may be permitted in certain circumstances, but never at the expense of reducing event security.

In many cases, accreditation privileges of major sport events are formally established by the event owners within the event management protocols section of the initial bidding documentation. For example, M2002 had to adhere to six pages of 'venue and zone access, dining and transportation privileges'. These were prioritised and defined according to Federation, Commonwealth Games Association, Organising Committee, Future Organising Committee, International Federation, Broadcaster, Sponsors, as well as Press and Photographer categories. Table 9.5 illustrates just a selection of some of these privileges and access rights.

The above accreditation process and outputs are common to most major sport events. The event owner normally determines its key stakeholders and the local organising committee then designs and manages the specific operational systems, accreditation venues and zones that adhere to the higher-order owner needs. For example, in the 2003 World Indoor Athletic Championships held in Birmingham, England, the accreditation process was designed and developed by the local organising committee, in consultation with the IAAF, an official accreditation company and the venue security staff. This specific event involved just one sport and one competition venue yet established 12 accreditation zones and three accreditation centres (one for the volunteers, staff, media and contractors; one for the athletes and officials; and one for the VIPs and VVIPs). Again, the lead-in time and pre-event checks should not be underestimated. In the case of the written and photographic press accreditation for the Athens 2004 Olympic Games, the process started 16 months before the event, with the passes being collected in person at the earliest just one month before the event from one of four media accreditation sites, one of which was the main airport (Athens 2004 International Media Relations 2003).

Incidents, emergencies and crisis management

The impact of a security breach or an incident occurring at a large sport event should similarly never be underestimated. The 1989 Hillsborough Stadium football disaster (in Sheffield, England) reminds us of how a relatively minor incident, of late fans arriving, quickly escalated into panic and a major crisis, where 95 fans died. As a result of such event tragedies occurring around the globe, it has now become common practice for national legislation to insist that event and venue managers produce a workable incident, emergency and crisis management plan before any major sport activity or event can take place.

It is the local organising committee in consultation with the key multi-agencies of the police and other emergency services that initiate this plan and draw on the management process of scenario development. Being derived primarily from the risk management process, this plan needs to address the many incidents requiring emergency action, such as fire, overcrowding, loss of electrical power, a bomb or bomb-threat as well as other acts of violence or terrorism. On the other hand, event incidents and emergencies by their very nature are often unpredictable, so it is important from the outset to realise that no emergency action plan will ever cover detailed procedures for every potential scenario. Flexible arrangements must always exist, but key principles relating to the formalisation of specific responsibilities, the establishment of synchronous communication mediums (see Figure 9.4), and clear procedures for reporting and monitoring incidents are essential if stakeholder safety is to be paramount in the manager's mind.

Table 9.5: Commonwealth Games 'venue and zone access, dining and transportation privileges'

Category	Population	Venue access	Zone access	Seating	Transport	Dining
HRH	Her Majesty the Queen	Infinity, IBC, MPC, CGV	Blue, 1, 2, 3, R	Officials' Stand	T1	Yes
G	Distinguished guests of Federation category	Access only with ticket	n/a	Stand of Honour	T2	No
CGF	Members of the Medical Commission	Infinity, IBC, MPC, CGV	Blue, 1, 2, 3, R	Stand of Honour	T2	Yes
Ao	Team officials	Own sport venues, CGV	Blue 2, R	Athletes' Stand	T3	Yes
G	Mayor of next host city	Infinity, IBC, MPC, CGV	Red 1, 2, 3	Stand of Honour	T2	No
B	International Federation technical delegates	Infinity	Blue 1, 2	Federation Stand	T2	No
HBb	Host broadcasters' production and technical personnel	Infinity, IBC, MPC	Yellow 2, 3	RT Stand	T4	No
SPV	Chairman and CEO of major sponsors	Infinity, IBC, MPC, CGV	Red 1, 2, 3	Officials' Stand	T2	No
Eps	Sport-specific photographers	Own sport venues, MPC	Yellow 2	Photo positions	T4	No
ENR	Electronic press personnel of non-rights-holding media	Infinity, MPC	Yellow 2	E Stand	T4	No

Key: Venues   Infinity = All competition and training venues
                      IBC = International broadcast centre
                      MPC = Main press centre
                      CGV = Athletes' village

        Zones Yellow = General circulation areas/front of house
        Red = Operational areas/back of house
        Blue = Field of play/athletes' preparation areas
        R = Residential zone of the athlete's village
        1 = Hospitality lounge; 2 = Press areas; 3 = Rights holding areas.

        Transport T1 = Personal car with driver; T2 = On-call fleet; T3 = Team buses; T4 = Shuttle buses.

*The dining privilege refers to access to this service only at the Athletes' Village

Source: Adapted from Commonwealth Games Federation (2001, pp. 44–50).

To illustrate the depth of planning detail required of management, let us draw again on the incident, emergency and crisis management arrangements for the 2003 World Indoor Championships in Athletics (WICA), which are summarised in Figures 9.5 and 9.6.

From Figure 9.5, which largely focuses on the emergency incidents occurring at the sport venue itself (other arrangements are made for alternative venues), it is evident that a clear hierarchical line of communication and control exists. This needs to be communicated and understood by all of the event staff, whether internal or external, whether working in a paid or voluntary capacity. Volunteers are often the very first persons to identify incidents and

Figure 9.5 2003 World Indoor Athletics Championship's incident communications

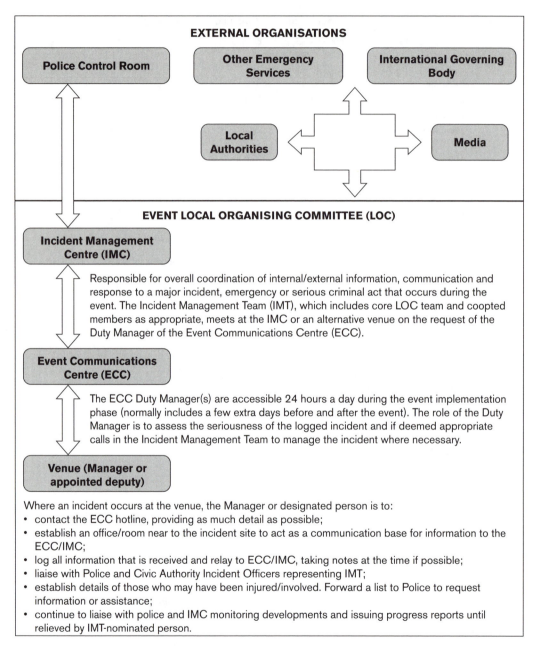

EXTERNAL ORGANISATIONS

Police Control Room

Other Emergency Services

International Governing Body

Local Authorities

Media

EVENT LOCAL ORGANISING COMMITTEE (LOC)

Incident Management Centre (IMC)

Responsible for overall coordination of internal/external information, communication and response to a major incident, emergency or serious criminal act that occurs during the event. The Incident Management Team (IMT), which includes core LOC team and coopted members as appropriate, meets at the IMC or an alternative venue on the request of the Duty Manager of the Event Communications Centre (ECC).

Event Communications Centre (ECC)

The ECC Duty Manager(s) are accessible 24 hours a day during the event implementation phase (normally includes a few extra days before and after the event). The role of the Duty Manager is to assess the seriousness of the logged incident and if deemed appropriate calls in the Incident Management Team to manage the incident where necessary.

Venue (Manager or appointed deputy)

Where an incident occurs at the venue, the Manager or designated person is to:
- contact the ECC hotline, providing as much detail as possible;
- establish an office/room near to the incident site to act as a communication base for information to the ECC/IMC;
- log all information that is received and relay to ECC/IMC, taking notes at the time if possible;
- liaise with Police and Civic Authority Incident Officers representing IMT;
- establish details of those who may have been injured/involved. Forward a list to Police to request information or assistance;
- continue to liaise with police and IMC monitoring developments and issuing progress reports until relieved by IMT-nominated person.

Source: Adapted from World Indoor Championships in Athletics (2003b).

they, like everyone else, need to be made aware of their role and the behaviour expected of them in case an incident does occur. Unfortunately, in the event industry today, management often adopts the 'it'll be alright on the night' and the 'it'll never happen to me' philosophies, which means many volunteers do not even know who their line managers are or the emergency procedures to implement if urgent action becomes necessary.

For example, in the 2003 World Indoor Athletics Championship (WICA) scenario, the operational procedure for informing the key decision makers of an incident was planned to be implemented as follows. If a volunteer identified an incident, they should verbally communicate the nature of it to the line manager, who would inform the venue manager by radio or telephone if it was considered to require their attention. Using closed-circuit television cameras and radio or telephone communications to source and allocate additional resources to the incident location if necessary meant that the incident might be resolved at the local-venue level. However, if this were not possible, the venue manager would contact the event communications centre, which in turn would inform the incident management centre and, in the ultimate case, involve contact with the police control room. Obviously, the nature of the incident would dictate both the urgency and primary means of the communication as well as the direct line of communication. For example, the identification of a serious fire or violent incident between sports fans would probably involve direct communication with the respective emergency services, via a spectator, participant, staff member, or by the representative of the emergency service member(s) actually present at the event. In such a situation, simultaneous communications are likely to exist. This is why the overall control centre usually contains the senior multi-agency staff of the event—so that they can collectively manage the incident through information gained from their own (e.g. police site incident officer) and other staff, as well as through the most advanced information technology on-site. Emergency procedures should have been discussed and rehearsed in advance to determine the most appropriate implementation actions. As briefly highlighted earlier, this normally includes prescripted announcements to the general public as well as pretyped forms that permit transfer of responsibility between stakeholders (e.g. from the event organiser to the police) through just two signatures.

In common with most other major sport events, the WICA incident, emergency and crisis management plan included organisational policy and procedures that related not just to the athletic competition venue but also to the training and social venues, the athlete, media and governing body hotels, as well as the transport service/hub operated by the local organising committee. Furthermore, all recordable incidents, defined as 'any incident that deviates from what is planned' (World Indoor Championships in Athletics 2003b, p. 6), required usage of the incident telephone hotline, which was directly linked to the events communications centre (ECC). As elaborated by the World Indoor Championships in Athletics (2003b, p. 6), this meant reporting:

> ... something that is deemed minor such as a delay to the opening of the training centre by 5 minutes. It is still a deviation from what is planned and has to be recorded. It may be something far more serious and which will require escalation to the core IMT ... Once a recordable incident is logged at the ECC it will be assessed by the Duty Manager ... available at all times ... Where a log has been closed without escalation it will be for the Duty Manager to decide whether anyone needs to be informed urgently. If not it can wait for the next update meeting. If required the IMT will be contacted and will meet at the IMC to manage the major incident.

In other words, the system of incident reporting needs to be coherent, logical and efficient, and decisions and communication flows are thus usually documented in diagrammatic form, as illustrated in Figure 9.6.

Safety, incident and risk management are synonymous with professional management, and should exist at all levels of management and be applied across all stages of the event life-cycle. Goldblatt (1997) adds that, to protect legal interests, financial investments, stakeholder

Figure 9.6 2003 World Indoor Athletics Championship's reporting and escalation process

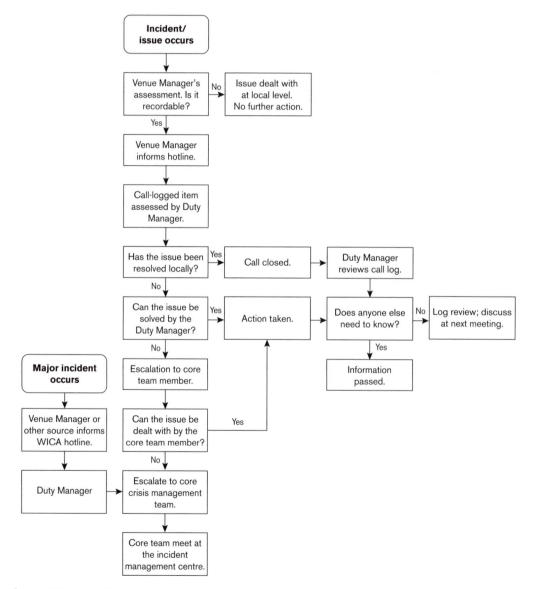

Source: Adapted from World Indoor Championships in Athletics (2003b).

safety and public perceptions, professional management should not only require an understanding of the relevant permits, licences, regulations and laws but also involve ethical and socially inclusive practices that include specific considerations of disabled people.

Special needs

In most developed countries around the world, organisations are rightly being pressured to remove physical and social access barriers that have existed for many years and disadvantaged many groups of the population. In the United Kingdom, for instance, the Disability Discrimination Act directly affects all event and facility providers: for example, venues had to be accessible to those with restricted mobility by October 2004. As suggested by Bunce (2003), to comply with this law many physical changes to sport and leisure facilities in the UK are now evident, and include:

- improved signage for the visually impaired;
- installation of ramps and lifts;
- lowering of reception counter height;
- designated parking spaces; and
- installation of induction loops for those with impaired hearing.

To specifically meet the disability needs of spectators at major sport events, it is not uncommon to involve such groups in the planning process, as was the case in the 2002 'inclusive Commonwealth Games'. As well as establishing important marketing networks, long-term relationships and key employees for the event, such meetings accompanied by site visits provided vital information for the event organisers that enhanced the experience of all spectators. From such knowledge, spectator expectation and the demand for particular services can be more effectively planned and promotional activity more specifically targeted to spectator needs. For example, in the M2002 situation, spectators buying tickets were initially asked whether they would like wheelchair positions, companion seats, easy-access seats, and access to an induction loop or verbal commentary. Additional information explaining 'what you can expect' (e.g. wheelchair-accessible venues with appropriate parking, ramps/lifts, signage and toilets; escort service for spectators with a visual impairment; an induction loop system that could be linked to hearing aids) and similarly 'what you can not expect' (e.g. short-term loan of mobility equipment; assistance with medication, feeding or personal hygiene) proved highly valuable to both service provider and consumer. This inclusive approach was further demonstrated through the practices of some of the individual sponsors and partners of the 2002 event. For example, United Utilities (the official event partner and regional provider of water and electricity services) initiated a 'Uniting Communities Program' and 'Community Champions Award' scheme that gave away approximately 10 000 event tickets to special-needs groups and the people assisting them (Guardian Media Group 2002).

Managing volunteers

As mentioned in Chapter 2, volunteers are one of the key stakeholder groups that determine whether the quality outputs of the event will be met. Globally, they are the backbone of sport, and many suggest that without them the majority of sport events would cease to exist

(Goldblatt 1997; Sport England 2001). As suggested by Angelopoulou-Daskalaki (2003), President of the Athens Olympic Committee, when referring to the Olympic Games:

> The greatest celebration of humanity is only possible through the will, the passion, the dedication and the professionalism of each volunteer.

Given their importance to the successful implementation of an event, volunteers must be carefully selected and be provided with enriching opportunities that attempt to match their aspirations, previous experiences and current competencies to the tasks to be carried out. Effective volunteer management therefore minimally implies excellent people skills and the ability to manage activities across the full breadth of the event lifecycle, and in many cases beyond. For example:

- *Pre-event activities*—Usually include establishing job remits, as well as developing promotional, recruitment and training systems, procedures and actions.
- *Event activities*—Often include the provision of a uniform, accreditation, a shift roster, car parking or public transport passes (where appropriate), an acceptable level of subsistence, as well as motivating volunteers to perform optimally, possibly through the creation of a happy and appreciative working culture, daily newsletters and merit awards.
- *Post-event activities*—Normally involve one or more social events, public and private thanks, a review process, as well as the establishment of a database for future volunteer activities.

It must be remembered that volunteer involvement is not founded on the basis of receipt of an income but on the satisfying of unique and often undeclared motivations. In this sense volunteers are, ironically, a human resource strength as well as a weakness. On the one hand, they have chosen to give of their own free time and are therefore personally committed to the event, possessing expectations to be fulfilled. On the other hand, if their expectations are not managed they can and will walk away at any time, potentially involving a high risk and reactive strategy for achieving your quality targets. To avoid this disastrous and worst-case scenario, volunteers must be listened to and sincerely valued at every opportunity.

From the very first contact made with volunteers, they are expecting to work with an organised, knowledgeable and professional team of staff who are driven by a clear sense of purpose and unity. To establish such unity and purpose it is now considered normal practice at most major sports events to use workforce staff identities, tag lines or key words and values with which volunteers can readily identify. For example, all of the permanent and volunteer staff of the M2002 event worked under the collective name of 'Crew 2002', and their mantra became 'Choose it, share it, show it' ('*choosing* to really enjoy the experience and make the most of every moment; *sharing* their enthusiasm with their teams and making sure everyone's spirits are high; *showing* everyone they come into contact with how much fun they're having and making sure you enjoy it too') (Guardian Media Group 2002, p. 59).

It is also not uncommon for major events to have an official staffing sponsor and management agency of the event volunteer program. In the 2002 Commonwealth Games this was Adecco, which very successfully promoted the volunteer as 'the face of the games' (the first person a visitor or athlete is likely to come in contact with) and reported (Guardian Media Group 2002, pp. 56–60) that:

- We had nearly three times more applicants than volunteer positions.
- Nearly 600 applications came from overseas, and 52 per cent of these were from Australia.
- 237 volunteers were over 70 (the oldest being 87).
- Some people used up their annual holiday entitlement to participate in the Games; for others, volunteering gave them a stepping-stone back into permanent employment. One even gave up her honeymoon to be part of it!

From a management perspective, minimum general and specific requirements need to be established, and in the M2002 case this meant that all volunteers were at least 16 years of age (for legal and insurance purposes), that they would commit to work for at least 10 days across a 24-day period, and furthermore that they would possess the essential aspects designated for the position for which they applied. For example, the position of 'Doping Control Chaperone' meant, among other personal attributes, that they would 'attend at least three sporting events prior to the Games' (Guardian Media Group 2002, p. 97).

To ensure equal access and opportunity for the northwest communities of England, the event organisers additionally created a unique pre-volunteer program (PVP) that included four core modules (first aid, health and safety, customer care, role of the ambassador) and culminated in working at the Games. As explained by the Guardian Media Group (2002, p. 61), this unique project:

> ... targeted many groups and communities which may not have traditionally been involved in an event of this type. Over 6,000 people from regeneration areas, ethnic minority communities, unemployed people and people with disabilities took part in the program which, as well as giving them an increased chance of becoming a volunteer at Games time, also helped them gain new skills and experience.

Although this vocational training program was initially 'introduced to enhance the skill base of young unemployed people across the region' (Commonwealth Games 2002), it further provided a sustainable legacy to accompany the Sport England facility infrastructure training programs. For example, for the program volunteer it did not end with the Games itself—rather, it provided a nationally accredited and valued qualification that could be used in other volunteer or sport development positions both in the region and beyond. Such was the success of the program that it was described by the United Nations (2001) as 'a most creative and dynamic social legacy program' and has subsequently cascaded to other regeneration areas in the country to help 'people gain employment opportunities through the new skills, knowledge and experience gained as volunteers' (Guardian Media Group 2002, p. 61).

On being accepted, all M2002 volunteers were invited to attend a pre-event training program where they were introduced to the event organisation, the venue in which they would be working, while the expectations of their role were clarified both verbally and through the receipt of a pocket-sized handbook. The latter typically included a summary of the volunteer's general duties, communication arrangements (e.g. radio call signs, line manager), alert codes and emergency procedures; lost property/person systems; venue maps; and incident reports. An example of the type of information received and remit of a volunteer's role is illustrated in Table 9.6, which details some of the expectations required of a steward at the Sportcity venue.

Table 9.6 Volunteer expectations: steward at Sportcity

General requirements	As a Steward employed at Sportcity, it is expected that you will have been provided with and undertaken the following: • Training—Minimum one day course in Event Stewarding • Familiarisation training at the City of Manchester stadium • Appropriate job description • Appropriate uniform
General duties of a steward	Effective stewarding should prevent overcrowding in areas of the stadium, reduce the likelihood and incidence of disorder, help disperse spectators in such a manner as to reduce crowd pressure, and provide the means to investigate, report and take any early action in an emergency. It is emphasised that you are employed to assist in the safe operation of the stadium, not to view the event taking place. There are six basic duties that Stewards are required to undertake: • Control or direct spectators who are entering or leaving the stadium to achieve an even flow of people to the viewing areas. • Recognise crowd densities, signs of crowd distress and crowd dynamics so as to help ensure safe dispersal of spectators within the stadium. • Patrol the allotted area to address any emergencies (e.g. raising alarms, tackling early stages of fire or to address potential crowd problems). • Staff entrances, exits and other strategic points to and from the viewing areas, especially exit doors and exit gates from the stadium, which are not continually open while the stadium is in use. • Assist or liaise with the police as appropriate or as requested by security or the Event Control Room. • Undertake specified duties in an emergency.
Examples of typical tasks	Ensure that spectators sit in the seat(s) allocated. Refer any member of the public with a duplicate ticket to the appropriate Quadrant Manager. DO NOT ALLOW THEM TO TAKE ANOTHER SEAT (this escalates the problem). Warn any spectator using foul or abusive language, or making obscene gestures, about their conduct. If they persist, then they should be ejected on advice from the Event Control Room via your Manager. No ejection should take place without prior notice to Event Control who will probably wish to video the ejection. Know the location of the first aid rooms and any first aid equipment kept elsewhere.

Source: Adapted from Manchester (2002b).

More specifically referring to the practical implementation phase of managing volunteers, each volunteer must be fully accounted for and be provided with details of their full shift roster before the event begins. Event organisers normally request that before starting a shift each volunteer must check in (usually via the volunteer rest room), when attendance is recorded, meal vouchers are distributed, and up-to-date information is provided often in the form of a daily event newspaper or central noticeboard. Once checked in, the volunteer needs to report directly to the team leader, who confirms their specific role for the day as well as rest and meal breaks for the shift. In this way, the appropriate team leader or substitute line manager is formally identified and both parties become aware of each other's general location should any unforeseen incident occur.

But effective volunteer management entails considerably more than just a polite introduction of names and faces. As Walker (2001) suggests, research has identified that there are commonly five main incentives for becoming a volunteer—namely, achievement, power, affiliation, recognition, and altruism. All volunteers are likely to have their own expectations, and management needs to recognise and reward these, applying the basic motivating principle of equity within the particular resource constraints. For many volunteers the tangible reward of receiving branded clothing or other memorabilia will be sufficient to satisfy their needs, particularly as these provide external social symbols that last well beyond the duration of the event.

On the other hand, if volunteers are expected to provide the enthusiastic professional customer care service demanded of an event, they need to encounter a similar working environment of friendliness, openness, trust and respect. As many volunteer training programs suggest, 'a friendly smile supported by warm body language are internationally contagious'. Line managers must therefore lead by example and take every opportunity to listen, involve and inspire volunteers both as individuals and collectively as a team. In many cases, volunteers just enjoy the feeling of being of use (purposive objectives)—that their ideas and actions might have helped in some small way to achieve the event/department goals. External and internal praise must be constantly given to reinforce the very important 'valuing of volunteer efforts'. This might be in the form of daily verbal (de)briefing(s), written comments in the event newsletter, or even rewarding excellence through job enrichment or enlargement opportunities, volunteer merit schemes, or by creating spontaneous and unique photographic opportunities and thereby providing even more enduring memories.

To further thank volunteers, it is customary practice to organise a social party directly after the event. This provides another opportunity to sincerely demonstrate appreciation of volunteer effort but also helps to meet affiliation objectives. For many volunteers at the M2002 event, the sole purpose for becoming involved was to meet and make new international friends. Through team building and social activities very strong bonds were developed that provided additional opportunities for friendship and network development, particularly for other volunteering experiences in the future. Indeed, such was the success of the volunteer program of the M2002 event that 'volunteer camaraderie' was the subject of many event and post-event news articles and television documentaries.

Media services

Without doubt, in this global and technological world the media have become an increasingly significant stakeholder to be managed at events. Conveying messages and images to more than 99 per cent of the target audience population of many major sports events, Emery (2001, p. 10) elaborates:

> Possessing considerable power as a significant 'enabler' of mass communication, the media have the potential to make or break an event by creating positive or negative images of the event and the region.

While the 1996 Atlanta Olympic Games perhaps epitomises the negative messages that can be spread around the world—newsprint headlines included 'Atlanta Chaos' (*The Observer*

1996); 'Groans and Gridlock as Atlanta Grinds to a Halt' (*Independent* 1996); and 'Olympians Give Atlanta Full Marks for Chaos' (*The Times* 1996)—the 2002 Commonwealth Games received unprecedented positive media acclaim—'The Real Commonwealthy' (Yates 2002); 'Mancs for the Memory' (West 2002).

Given the media's power and influence, as well as the fact that at mega-sport events there are nearly as many media personnel as competing athletes to service, let us conclude this specialist event activity focus by describing how the media can be managed at the event to maximum effect. Probably this is easiest to achieve by understanding who they are and what they need at the live event. Collectively known as the media, this is a diverse group of organisations and individuals that includes written journalists, accredited photographers, rights-holding television and radio representatives and agents to other media sources. Put simply, they continuously require timely event information via verbal, electronic and paper means so that they can communicate their individual contemporary and creative messages to their paymasters. Print deadlines are usually very tight, and the experience of broadcasting sports activities live means that there is often only one opportunity for them to get it right. A missed photograph opportunity or late report will not please the publisher. So media personnel normally operate in a very hectic and stressful environment and require the very latest technological and human means to support their work. From a management perspective this means establishing clear, effective and efficient internal and external communication systems, fully tested and supported hardware and software, appropriate physical locations, accreditation and subsistence arrangements, as well as highly reliable and helpful staff who can problem-solve under considerable pressure.

The types of media services provided by management are obviously matched to the demands of the sport, the nature of the event as well as the specific requirements of the governing body(s). For example, the nature of an athletic competition is such that the event provides ongoing winners throughout the duration of the event, unlike that of a team sports event, where there is only one winner which usually signifies the end of the spectator venue experience. As the sport of athletics is one that creates perhaps the most complex demands of media services, this will form the main focus of sport event examples utilised below.

Most major athletic championships, such as the 2003 World Indoor Athletics Championships, entail the establishment of temporary physical structures that host the local organising committee media office, and the international governing body (IAAF) press office. Overseen by the head or director of media services, the following interconnected locations are then specifically organised and usually coordinated via a manager, an assistant, and a team of volunteers to carry out their respective servicing functions.

Media centre

This is the main central in-situ working and information area, where all accredited media staff can gain access to competition and general information, as well as be provided with the technical means to communicate globally (e.g. Internet and pay phones). It usually contains a staffed media help desk, which is the coordination point, verbally and physically via runners, between the other media sites. As the main registration point it provides media guides, pigeonholes for up-to-date event information, a message board, locker access, refreshments, and many other support services such as photocopying or useful contacts to arrange transport, accommodation, or tickets.

Photo centre

This is similar in nature to the media centre, but it specifically focuses on the needs of the photographic press. Services again include a help desk; seated desks with Internet connections for digital photography needs; a camera loan and repair service, along with a film processing and dispatch desk; a hospitality area for refreshments; lockers and the inevitable pigeonholes containing the news, start lists, results, and qualification lists.

Media tribune

This is the working area set aside for the media that overlooks the 'field of play'. In the case of athletics, these are the tabled and non-tabled seats located in the stadia at the finish line. As most of the media in the tribune are providing live commentary, Internet connections and power cables need to be carefully taped down and be accessible to every tabled seat. Volunteers, commonly referred to as 'runners', assist the media by quickly distributing start lists, results and athlete quotes by hand and in a non-intrusive manner. In practice, this is one of the most physically demanding volunteer positions, as it requires fit and agile volunteers to negotiate narrow rows and stairways as they constantly run to and from photocopying facilities and the media staff.

Mixed zone

This has already been alluded to in Table 9.3. It is the secured exit immediately after the sporting competition is finished where athletics and journalists meet just off the track. Athletes are obliged to walk through the entire mixed zone, which logistically takes them to the anti-doping testing centre before the medal ceremonies and, where appropriate, to the press conference centre. In other words the mixed zone provides the accredited media with the first opportunity to ask the athletes questions on the competitive outcome. As well as external media there is usually an internal news agency team present in the mixed zone. It is their job to obtain 'info or flash quotes' from the athletes, and to distribute this information along with daily previews, reviews as well as press conference summaries and other miscellaneous news items through the media centre.

Press conference

This is obviously where the official press conferences take place with the event medallists; it also includes special news bulletin items, such as announcements of drug test results. The room is typically laid out in a conference style, and communication with persons on the top table is managed through a chairperson and the use of remote microphones.

It is apparent that media service needs at a sport event can be very specific and quite diverse. It might be more appropriate to classify the management activities of media service requirements into four strands, namely:

• informational
• opportunity

- technological
- support service needs.

While informational and support service needs may be common to all media personnel, specialist provision of opportunity and technology activities/equipment needs to be very carefully planned and tested in consultation with both the event owner and category of stakeholder. For example, photographic media needs and procedures are likely to be very different from radio broadcasting and written journalist needs, and could specifically include:

- the expectation of a raised platform on the outfield for 100-metre head-on shots and medal ceremonies;
- a system to manage the maximum number of photographers permitted on the infield at any one time;
- volunteers on mountain bikes for speedy photo-processing services;
- on-site digital enhancement hardware and software, along with a camera rental and a repair service.

Such attention to detail, including media access to specialist equipment and facilities 24 hours a day and seven days a week (as was the case in Athens 2004), is considered essential if the event is to be regarded a success. The inevitable search for excellence to exceed stakeholder expectations while optimally managing the golden triangle of project quality, cost and time is the ultimate challenge that lies ahead of every sport event manager. But no-one said that the sport event management role was an easy one!

Summary

To provide a memorable and high-quality event experience is clearly not an easy task, particularly within the unique and complex environment encountered at most major sport events. However, successful event management is possible and personally very rewarding, provided it is founded on the basics of competent planning, organisation, implementation and control. Whereas many of the generic management functions and tools of planning and organisation have been introduced in previous chapters, this chapter has extended their application, additionally highlighting the breadth and depth of management activities required for effective event implementation.

Initially, it was suggested that to simplify the event complexity and improve communication in this substage, the workforce must be organised into coordinated unit groupings (the event operational structure), with each unit being assigned responsibility for specifically defined subproject activity. To fulfil the objectives of these subprojects and ultimately those of the event, these unit groupings usually have to work with external stakeholders, creating task-oriented multi-agency management scenarios.

While the process of logistics management can provide a general understanding of the likely multi-agency flows of people, information and other resources typically experienced at the event, the on-site logistical tools of a venue site plan, production schedule, run or cue sheets, contact list and communication systems are all used to implement and coordinate the detailed action plans of the event.

To further highlight the depth of integrated management activity normally experienced at an event, we have discussed the practicalities of managing security, incidents and emergencies, spectator special needs, volunteers and the increasingly important media services. Selected on the basis of their transferability and functional importance to other sports events, these activities demonstrate the importance of really understanding the diverse needs and support services of different stakeholders and place heavy emphasis on the establishment of effective and efficient communication systems in the implementation phase of an event.

We have tried in this chapter, through applied examples, to build on previous event and facility management knowledge and to reinforce the notion of managing organisational synergy across a breadth of interrelated activities, organisations, teams and individuals, as well as across the duration of the event lifecycle. How well you perform, and what evidence you collect to substantiate your claims, is the subject of Chapters 10 and 11.

Case study

Hong Kong International Races Day—accreditation

Hong Kong is where the 'Sport of Kings' (i.e. thoroughbred racing) is definitely the 'King of Sports'! Thoroughbred racing is Hong Kong's number one sport, with more money being bet per race there than anywhere else in the world.

Held annually during the second weekend of December, the Hong Kong International Races Day is the country's premier race day. One of the most exciting and prestigious events on the international racing calendar, the race meet attracts the world's best horses, best jockeys and biggest punters. It comprises four feature races: the Hong Kong Cup; the Hong Kong Mile; the Hong Kong Vase; and the Hong Kong Sprint. These races carry a total prize money of approximately $US7 million.

Sha Tin, one of Hong Kong's two race tracks, was opened in 1978 and, with ongoing redevelopment, is one of the most modern racecourses in the world. Sha Tin has an impressive grandstand that holds up to 85 000 people and on International Races Day it is filled to capacity. The races can also be viewed from other areas of the racecourse, including the public lawn, corporate marquees, bars, lounges, private boxes and dining rooms.

As with most race days, International Races Day spectators fall into several different categories—namely, general admission, members (and guests of members), sponsors, corporate guests and VIPs. International tourists are particularly well looked after at Sha Tin: on showing their passports they have access to the members' stand rather than being restricted to the general public areas. Members, sponsors and corporate guests have the privilege of superior dining options, including the right to purchase fine-dining hospitality packages. These spectator groups also have access to the racecourse's best views and betting facilities.

The Hong Kong Jockey Club (HKJC) manages almost all aspects of Hong Kong's thoroughbred racing industry, including International Races Day. The HKJC's key source of revenue is betting. Essentially, the more people that bet, the more revenue the club makes. It is thus in the club's best interests to ensure that betting facilities, particularly at major race meetings like International Races Day, are of the highest possible standard. Furthermore, it is critical that a sufficient number of betting facilities be available. When on-course, betters can place their bets with the totalisator; electronically through betting machines; or via their phone accounts.

The ability of the HKJC to maximise gambling revenue from International Races Day is not only dependent on the quality and quantity of betting facilities—it also rests on the sport being 'clean'. That is, people won't bet if they believe that a race is rigged (except, of course, those people involved in the rigging). Fortunately, the HKJC is known internationally for its commitment to clean racing. It protects the integrity of racing via several methods, including: (a) employing hundreds of thoroughly trained computer and security staff; (b) conducting extensive security checks on everyone who works in the stable area; (c) installing surveillance cameras in the barns and tote rooms; (d) strictly monitoring jockeys for interference during racing; (e) conducting drug testing on the horses both pre- and post-race; and (f) utilising one of the most modern drug-testing laboratories in the world.

All the horses competing on International Races Day are stabled at Sha Tin in two- and three-level barns, with ramps leading to each level. Prior to racing, just like any athlete, the horses need to be warmed up. Strappers walk the horses around briskly. The horses are then led out to the mounting yard to their jockeys. The horses canter towards the barriers, where stewards (the 'officials' of thoroughbred racing) are located to help the jockeys get their horses into the barriers. When the barrier gates open and racing commences, the race caller 'comes to life' and takes centre stage with the horses and the jockeys. With the crowd's attention focused on the race, hardly anyone notices the ambulance that circles the inside of the track behind the horses and their jockeys.

After racing, the jockeys dismount and stewards accompany them back to the jockeys' room. It is here that the jockeys are weighed in after every race (nobody is even allowed to touch them before this). While the jockeys are being weighed, and again in the presence of stewards, the strappers take the horses on another walk to cool down and then back to their stables. It is in the stables that the horses are tested for illegal substances.

For the people who go to watch the horses (i.e. the spectators) and the athletes themselves (i.e. the horses and their jockeys), a day at the Hong Kong International Races offers much more than just the racing. Akin to other famous race meetings, such as the Melbourne Cup, the Kentucky Derby and the Dubai World Cup, International Races Day at Sha Tin is as much about socialising, fun, fashion, entertainment, hospitality and networking as it is about racing and betting. One particular breed of racegoers (i.e. the 'partygoers') may not even watch a race, let alone bet on one, given that there are so many other things to do.

To support the tens of thousands of people who attend International Races Day, there are hundreds of staff working in the areas of ticketing, gate entry, catering, hospitality, security, cleaning, gardening, maintenance, administration and wagering. Then there are the staff more directly concerned with the actual racing, including the stewards, strappers, stable hands, veterinarians and laboratory attendants. In addition to the staff employed by the racecourse and the HKJC are other people who need access to the racecourse, such as emergency services, various contractors (e.g. electricians and carpenters), and the media, not to mention the horse owners and trainers.

Although spectators access Sha Tin racecourse only during opening hours, most staff have to get there earlier. Likewise, for the stages, marquees and corporate hospitality venues to be set up, contractors need to arrive much earlier to 'bump the event in', as do the people responsible for delivering hundreds of tonnes of food and thousands of litres of beverages.

Q. Develop an accreditation plan for Hong Kong International Races Day. You will need to consider all parties who require access to the racecourse, not only during the actual day but those who need to access it prior to race day in order to bump the event in, as well as those people who need to bump the event out. (Tip: Don't forget the horses!) Your plan should include the following:
- *identification of the various accreditation zones;*
- *identification of those with access to the various accreditation zones;*
- *justification of access to the various accreditation zones;*
- *overview of the accreditation process, including (a) how accreditation passes are applied for or are awarded, (b) when the accreditation process begins, and (c) when and where accreditation passes are received or picked up;*
- *a policy on lost, forgotten or stolen accreditation passes (i.e. the processes you would recommend that the HKJC follow if a spectator, staff member or contractor arrived at the course without accreditation);*
- *a policy on emergency access to an unaccredited area (i.e. the processes you would recommend that the HKJC follow if an emergency necessitated spectators, staff members or contractors accessing an area they were not accredited to enter).*

10

Measuring facility and event performance: a scorecard approach

CHAPTER OBJECTIVES

In this chapter, we will:

- Highlight the need for performance measurement.
- Introduce the balanced scorecard approach to measuring performance.
- Examine methods for generating key performance measures.
- Identify key metrics for facility and event performance.
- Discuss the effective use of performance measures for the strategic management of facilities and events.

Why measure performance?

Sporting competitions measure the performance of teams and athletes. We keep records of sport performances, times, wins and losses, and myriad other measures. Athletes and coaches use these records to measure their own (or their team's) progress. These are considered performance measures and are used as benchmarks to measure changes in performance. Like coaches, trainers and athletes, facility and event managers track performance and benchmark their own performance against competitors' and industry leaders' and even their own organisation's past performance. However, the performance of a facility or event organisation is rarely as straightforward a measure as winning or losing an athletic competition, and appropriate benchmarks are much more difficult to identify. Still, an organisation can make little progress towards its goals if it makes no attempt to track its progress.

Performance measures serve a number of purposes and work at a variety of organisational levels (Behn 2003). Meyer's (2002) model, specifying the purposes of performance measures, was introduced in Chapter 2. In this model, Meyer specifies seven distinctive purposes of performance measures: (1) to look ahead, (2) to look back, (3) to motivate, (4) to compensate, (5) to roll up, (6) to cascade down, and (7) to compare. At the organisational level in particular, it is important to look back at past accomplishments in order to build on the successes (and learn from and redress the failures) of the past. Similarly, it is important to look ahead to understand the context in which the organisation will operate, and to set goals and objectives for the organisation. Performance measures that look ahead can keep employees focused on the activities that will meet the strategic objectives of the organisation. Further, performance measures can be effective tools to motivate and compensate employees at all levels of an organisation. Properly linked, performance measures can focus activities and attention on the strategic objectives of an organisational unit. Benchmarks can motivate individuals and teams to achieve goals, as performance-based compensation requires the use of performance measures to determine rewards. Lastly, performance measures can be used to compare output and outcomes across units and to provide specific, bidirectional feedback throughout the organisation.

The purpose of any particular performance measure foreshadows both the type of measure that is appropriate and the way in which each measure can be used (see Table 10.1). Yet individual measures provide only a partial view of performance. Using a single measure is akin to measuring the performance of a basketball team solely by the number of points it scores. The measure cannot possibly be equated with competitive success (i.e. winning) without also measuring the number of points allowed. A single measure can be a useful benchmark for improvement in one area, but it fails as a measure of overall performance. Worse yet, organisations may then focus their efforts on improving that single dimension at the cost of others. More practice in shooting baskets takes time away from practising defensive techniques. Thus, this effort could result in an even poorer overall performance on the court. This example is a simple one. Measuring the performance of a facility or an event is decidedly more complex. But the same principle applies: What gets measured gets done! This poses a real danger to organisations whose performance measurement systems focus on a narrow range of measures or on measures that are either irrelevant or misleading. The wrong performance measures can lead a company to divert scarce resources or to use them unproductively. The purpose of measuring performance is not necessarily to maximise performance on each measure: it is to determine progress in attaining organisational objectives.

Table 10.1 Potential uses of performance measures

Purpose	Question the measure can help to answer	Need to achieve purpose
Evaluate	How well is the facility/event performing?	Outcomes, combined with inputs and with the effects of external factors
Control	How can I ensure that my employees are doing what they should?	Inputs that can be regulated and controlled
Budget	On what programs, employees, projects or events should my organisation spend its money?	Efficiency measures (specifically, outcomes or outputs divided by inputs)
Motivate	How can I motivate staff, managers, stakeholders and community members to do the things necessary to improve performance?	Almost real-time outputs compared with production targets or output measures
Promote	How can I convince government, ministers, stakeholders, media and the community that my organisation is doing a good job?	Easily understood aspects of performance that people really care about
Celebrate	What accomplishments are worthy of the important organisational ritual of celebrating success?	Periodic and significant performance targets that, when achieved, provide people with a real sense of accomplishment
Learn	Why are things working or not working?	Disaggregated data that can reveal differences from what's expected
Improve	What exactly should we do differently to improve performance?	Inside-the-black-box relationships that connect changes in operations to changes in outputs and outcomes

Source: Adapted from Behn (2003).

Facility and event organisations each operate in a unique environment, structure themselves in a unique way, and set objectives that serve the unique purpose of their organisations. Consequently, every organisation will measure success in its own way. Performance measures must take into account the internal and external environment facing the facility or event, the inputs and processes that produce the products and services, and the outputs and outcomes desired by the organisation and its stakeholders. Each internal and external system influences the other. An effective performance measurement system, therefore, must account for the interrelationship of the systems (Jensen & Sage 1995). As discussed in Chapter 2, this is known as systems theory (see Figure 2.5). It provides the framework for developing an integrated performance measurement system, rather than just a collection of ad-hoc performance measures.

Traditionally, performance measures have been used for evaluation and control (Robbins & DeCenzo 2004). Historically, performance measures emerged from a financial accounting model directed at maintaining financial control. Accounting has often been termed the language of business; hence, it is not surprising that performance measures have overwhelmingly focused on financial performance (Eigenmann 2001; Finnerty 1986). While financial performance is necessary to the success of any business, it is not, by itself, sufficient to predict business success (Eccles 1991). Financial indicators are insufficient for two reasons: namely, timing and breadth.

Timing

Key performance indicators (KPIs) typically measure things like profitability, liquidity, turnover and leverage. Note the focus on short-term financial performance. Long-term performance is much more difficult to measure. Further, standard financial measures indicate past performance (e.g. last quarter's earnings). Information about past performance can certainly provide information relevant to future performance, but there is also a need for forward-looking information (AICPA Special Committee on Financial Reporting, 1994). Leading indicators not only provide up-to-date information about current performance—they can also help managers look forward by measuring the *drivers* of future performance. For example, sport facility managers might measure participants' satisfaction with the local fixtures. Satisfaction is often an indication of potential repurchase or, in this case, repeat participation. Early indication of participant dissatisfaction can provide facility managers with the chance to make changes *before* losing customers.

Lagging indicators (i.e. most financial measures) help managers to understand what has already happened. Leading indicators reduce uncertainty about what will happen. Attention to and balance of these two types of indicators can help a manager to better plan and to successfully implement strategies and tactics. Thus the timing issues associated with financial indicators highlight the need to go beyond the standard lagging indicators of financial performance.

Breadth

Another outcome of the financial roots of performance measurement is the absence of ways to capture the value of intangible and intellectual assets. These assets are particularly important to the success of service entities such as facility and event organisations. For example, customer service is critical to successful service organisations. Caring and knowledgeable employees are often cited as an important component of quality management (Howat, Murray & Crilley 1999; O'Neill, Getz & Carlson 1999), and significantly affect customer satisfaction, loyalty and repurchase intentions (Athanassopoulos 2000). However, intangible assets such as these are difficult to value. Consequently, they are rarely included in standard financial reports. Yet in today's business environment it is the intangibles (e.g. employee skills, customer loyalty, process capabilities) that are critical to success.

Many organisations do in fact measure some intangibles. However, this is often done in isolation. For example, a health and fitness centre may systematically measure the quality of service provided to its members, and may do so by surveying customers to obtain evaluations of the service provided. Service quality measures may be used to evaluate employee performance, to design employee training, or to reward good customer service. They may even be used as proxy indicators of customer satisfaction. Clearly, service quality measures are useful indicators of performance. But how does a measure of service quality link to the overall performance of the business? What effect does customer satisfaction have on the financial performance of the business? Or on the overall strategic thrust of the organisation? Customer evaluations of service quality need to be considered with reference to other information about the business and its performance.

The same organisation might track the number of people attending each of its cardiovascular exercise programs, or the number and type of equipment breakdowns. Each of these measures is important to the overall performance of the company. However, the main consumers of the information provided by each indicator may be isolated from the others. Although staff responsible for facility maintenance might focus on data regarding equipment breakdown, marketing might focus on service quality information, and programs on participant numbers. If these indicators remain compartmentalised, it can become difficult for managers in each area to understand the way the performance of their own department relates to the overall performance of the organisation, and thus to its overall strategy. For example, programs might use participant numbers as the basis for eliminating a program, even though the organisation is seeking to expand its membership in the market segment targeted by that program. Similarly, by compartmentalising information, staff may fail to recognise the interrelationships of departments. For example, participant numbers in a program may depend on perception of service quality, which in turn depends on equipment quality and reliability. Numbers in a potentially popular program could be down because the equipment has been unreliable or maintenance has not been promptly carried out. In such an instance, the correct organisational response might be to upgrade to more reliable equipment or to adjust the maintenance schedule, rather than to cancel the program. However, that would become apparent only if the various indicators were considered jointly.

As these examples illustrate, what is measured matters; how it is measured matters; and how measures are used matters. Indeed, measures can lead to quite erroneous conclusions if not considered with reference to overall operations and objectives. Note, for example, that maintenance might look excellent if there are few equipment breakdowns. However, if the lack of breakdowns is a consequence of low utilisation because the equipment is difficult to use or out of date, then the correct conclusion would not be that maintenance is effective or the equipment is reliable; the correct conclusion would be that the equipment needs to be modified or replaced. The point, then, is that performance measures should be linked to the overall operational structure and the strategic goals of the organisation. Each component of the system can then understand its place in the performance of the business as a whole.

In summary, performance measurement has been hindered by three problems. First, no performance measure can be considered in isolation. Single indicators are not valid indicators of performance: a performance management *system* is required. Second, performance measures are often backward-looking: they report on past performance rather than providing lead indicators of impending performance issues. There needs to be a balance between lead and lag indicators of performance. Third, there is often a bias towards exclusive use of financial performance measures. This prevents a company from focusing on underlying intangible assets and processes. In effect, a purely financial analysis fails to consider changes in human and process capabilities that could lead to improved performance. Nor does it promote ownership and commitment to the strategies and objectives of the organisation.

The balanced scorecard

The balanced scorecard has been advocated as a means by which to overcome the problems described above (Kaplan & Norton 1992, 1996). It provides a conceptual framework for translating the strategic objectives of a facility or event into a set of cohesive performance measures and indicators organised along four dimensions: finance, customer, internal business processes, and learning and growth. But the beauty of the scorecard approach lies in its ability to communicate mission and strategy by measuring and articulating the outcome desired by the organisation and the drivers of those outcomes. Unlike other performance management approaches, the balanced scorecard is not focused on compliance or control. Rather, it provides a framework within which to articulate and communicate strategy and to align organisational, departmental cross-departmental and individual initiatives in order to achieve a common goal. We next examine each perspective in turn, and then discuss the creation of a balanced scorecard to measure facility and event performance.

The four perspectives of the balanced scorecard

Finance perspective: how do we look to shareholders?

Financial performance measures are the indicators that are traditionally used to determine whether the facility's or event's strategy and operations are contributing to the bottom line. Although the balanced scorecard considers financial measures to be insufficient indicators in and of themselves, financial measures are nonetheless vital elements of the overall constellation of measures. Traditionally, financial analysis has focused on such measures as return on investment, debt-to-equity ratio, and related ratios calculated from the organisation's financial statements. Although these may still be important to management when using the balanced scorecard, there are several other financial indicators that contribute significant information when considered in conjunction with other measures used in a balanced scorecard. In keeping with its underlying premise that measures need to be developed specifically for each organisation's strategic goals and context, the balanced scorecard does not prescribe specific indicators. Rather, three types of indicators are recommended.

The first are measures of *revenue growth and mix*. These are measures that indicate the degree to which the organisation is expanding its revenues, reaching new markets, or improving its market share. Which specific measures are chosen will depend on the organisation's strategic objectives. For example, if an event were seeking to increase its revenues from media rights and sales of licensed merchandise, then it would include measures of the degree to which earnings from those two sources had grown. It might also include measures of the percentage of total revenue for which these sources were responsible. Similarly, if a facility's strategy aimed to increase the number of women who became members, then it would include measures of the growth in revenue associated with women's membership. In order to determine whether the growth in women's membership was particularly pronounced, it might also include a measure of the change in percentage of total revenue resulting from women's memberships.

The second type of recommended measures is those that assess *cost reduction/productivity improvement*. Here the objective is to assess improvements in efficiency. These measures look for improved profitability. For example, by improving ticket sales through the Internet, an event might reduce the number of sales staff required, or it might reduce the amount of time that sales staff spend per sale. The result would be that the average cost per sale would drop. Similarly, if a facility were to improve sight lines and placement of security staff, it might be able to reduce total security costs. Again, if these improvements in productivity were part of the organisation's strategic plan, then these outcomes should be measured.

The final measures recommended have to do with *asset utilisation*. These measures are comparable to those used in traditional financial analysis, such as return on investment. The objective of these measures is to determine how efficiently the organisation's assets are being allocated. It is useful to note here that these indicators may need to include measures that are specifically related to the organisation's strategic plan. For example, if databases or personnel are being shared across functional areas of an event, then there should be an indicator demonstrating the costs and returns associated with that sharing. There might also be some comparison with the costs and returns if that sharing was not undertaken.

Each type of financial indicator is linked to the long-term goal of the organisation—to provide optimal returns for the capital invested in the business. By the way, this long-term 'return on capital invested' goal is applicable to a non-profit organisation as much as to a for-profit organisation. Capital invested simply 'returns' different things to non-profit organisations than to for-profit entities. The balanced scorecard takes this approach one step further. Not only does it specify the measures by which the long-term success of the organisation will be evaluated—the balanced scorecard also provides indicators for the variables that create and drive long-term outcomes. Thus, all objectives and measures from the other scorecard perspectives will be linked to at least one objective within the financial perspective. So, for example, an organisation trying to increase its market share (financial perspective) might develop indicators for customer retention (customer perspective), average waiting time for entry (internal-business process perspective), and the percentage of staff trained to handle customer complaints (learning and growth perspective).

Customer perspective: how do customers see us?

The customer perspective begins with the identification and selection of customers and market segments. After all, the targeted consumers will be responsible for delivering the revenues indicated by the financial perspective. Two types of performance indicators for the customer perspective address the organisation's performance in its selected market segments: core customer outcomes and performance drivers. The former are lagging indicators; the latter are leading indicators. Both types of measures are needed.

Core customer outcomes are fairly generic measures of interest to facility managers, event managers, and nearly every other service organisation. The core measures include market share, customer acquisition, customer retention, customer satisfaction and customer profitability. As lagging measures, these help the manager determine how the organisation has been doing.

Market share reflects the proportion of business that an organisation generates within the selected market. For example, the manager of a local tennis event might measure the proportion of registered tennis players that participate in the tournament. Customer acquisition is a measure of the rate at which a business attracts new customers. Facility managers might track the number of new events held in the facility or the percentage growth in new customers contracting to use the facility. Similarly, customer retention measures provide an indication of the organisation's ability to maintain its customer base. Repeat attendance, sponsorships renewed and membership renewals are common examples of customer retention measures.

Both customer acquisition and customer retention are dependent on meeting customers' needs. Customer satisfaction measures provide feedback on how well the organisation is meeting customers' needs. Measures of customer profitability provide balance and prevent an organisation from becoming overly responsive to customers' needs. Not all customer demands can be satisfied in a profitable manner. For example, members of a fitness centre may desire state-of-the-art equipment in all areas of the centre. The costs associated with equipment updates could be higher than the net increase in membership that the purchase of new equipment engenders. Hence, organisations should create measures to provide an indication of the profitability of each customer segment.

By viewing customers in terms of both market segment and profitability, managers obtain valuable feedback on the effectiveness of their segmentation strategies. However, outcome variables such as these provide little insight into what drives customer satisfaction and profitability. These indicators provide insight into what has been happening in the business, but not into why it has been happening. Consequently, the manager also needs to measure those things that are expected to drive customer satisfaction. These are considered 'leading indicators'.

Customer value propositions drive customer outcomes. They represent the attributes of an organisation that create satisfaction and develop loyalty among targeted customer segments. In other words, these are the attributes by which customers determine the value of your product or service. The attributes are categorised along three dimensions: (1) good/service attributes, (2) customer relationships, and (3) image and reputation of the business.

Good and service attributes include the functionality, quality and price of the organisation's products and services. An aquatic facility may focus on two primary customer segments: competitive swimmers (and their coaches), and young families. The competitive swimmers may value the facility for the quality of its equipment, the timing of its availability and the functionality of its layout. Young families, on the other hand, may value the same facility for its low cost and the breadth of its programs. Consequently, measures should be developed to measure the service attributes of importance to each customer segment.

The same is true of the *customer relationship* dimension, which focuses on the delivery of the product or service. Indicators in this category may include focus on operational issues such as responsiveness, as well as on the affective response of the customer (e.g. how they *feel* about buying the company's goods and services). So an event company putting on a triathlon series may identify as a customer relationship objective that it will build and maintain high expectations about the way every athlete is treated. This might require the company to train workers to understand and recognise the needs of each of its triathlete customer segments and to work proactively to satisfy those needs. In other words, the triathlon series will differentiate itself within its target markets by staffing the event with knowledgeable people who are responsive to the needs of the athletes and customers. If these objectives are met, each athlete will come away from the event feeling cared for and well treated. The drivers in this case might include response times, increases or decreases in complaints, or percentage of service recovery successes. Each should be measured for each market segment identified.

The *image and reputation* dimension includes the intangible aspects that attract a customer to the facility or event. These may be communicated to customers through advertising, through promotions, or by word-of-mouth. In effect, this dimension enables an organisation to define itself for its users. For example, a golf club may define itself based on its users. Wealthy, educated club members portray an image of exclusivity and elitism. Successful diffusion of this image might be measured by the premium price earned on club-branded items (e.g. the difference in the prices commanded for a jumper with the golf club's logo embroidered on it and a comparable but unbranded jumper). Similarly, the image and reputation of a 10-kilometre race event might be captured in the difference in entry fees commanded.

In order to formulate performance indicators for the customer perspective, facility and event managers must first identify their targeted customer segments. Once that has been done, a set of core outcome measurements can be generated. However, customer outcome measures share with traditional financial indicators the limitation that they are lagging measures. Leading indicators are identified by determining what target markets value about your products and services. These become the basis for creating measures of product and service attributes, customer relationship, and image and reputation. The attributes dimensions can serve as an early warning system, alerting the organisation to areas of potential customer dissatisfaction.

Internal business process perspective: what internal processes must we excel at?

In the internal business process perspective, managers identify the critical internal processes necessary for the organisation to meet its objectives. This perspective builds on both financial and customer perspectives. Internal business processes are those which deliver the value propositions that attract and retain targeted customers, which in turn affect the organisation's ability to meet its financial objectives. Consequently, internal business process measures focus on the processes that have the greatest impact on customer satisfaction and on achieving an organisation's financial objectives. Kaplan and Norton (1996) recommend examining internal business processes throughout the value chain (see Figure 10.1). Three principal business processes form the value chain linking customer need identification to customer satisfaction: (1) innovation processes, (2) operations processes, and (3) post-sale service processes. Operational excellence is often seen as the dominant factor in the value chain. It makes sense that a facility or event should focus on processes that deliver superior goods and services, so we will examine operational processes first.

Service organisations such as sport facilities and event providers have been particularly sensitive to quality issues in the *operations process* (Chelladurai, Scott & Haywood-Farmer 1987). Service quality is an important means to differentiate one's facility or event from its competitors (Cronin, Brady & Hult 2000; Disney 1999). Measures of service quality focus an organisation on improving the existing service delivery processes that are necessary to satisfy the needs of its customers. Seating comfort, facility cleanliness, knowledgeable and pleasant staff, and crowd handling are some (of many) common components of service quality for both facilities and events. Customer satisfaction with these aspects is an often used indicator of service quality. However, as we have discussed, customer satisfaction is an outcome variable.

By itself, customer satisfaction provides managers with little insight into how to go about *improving* the components of service quality. For that, one needs to examine the internal

Figure 10.1 Sport facility and event management value chain

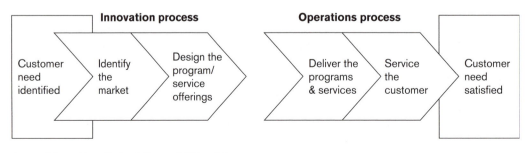

Source: Adapted from Kaplan & Norton (1996, p. 96).

business processes that *produce* the service. What, for example, do we do operationally that can affect customers' perceptions of the cleanliness of our facility? The most obvious answer is that someone cleans the facility. But how does the cleaning process work? Who cleans the facility? Is it done in-house or contracted out? When is the facility cleaned? How often? Is cleaning linked to use patterns? What is the procedure for responding to customer complaints or alerts about cleanliness? Each of these questions corresponds to a business process that can be measured and monitored. Thus, the facility manager might measure the frequency of cleaning, the duration of cleaning, or average response time to customer complaints.

Similarly, perceptions of crowding can negatively affect event patrons' experiences. Event managers might examine the internal processes that can affect perceptions of crowding. What type of queuing system is used? How many ticket booths are available? How much space is allotted to crowd movement? Is there adequate signage to ensure good crowd flow? Performance indicators might include measures of the average wait time to purchase a ticket, food and beverage, or a souvenir; or number of tickets sold per hour. A lead indicator for crowd flow could be a measure of the number of times patrons requested directions per time period.

Both facility and event managers would do well to attend to service recovery processes. By definition, services are produced and consumed simultaneously. Consequently, service providers such as sport facilities and events do not have many post-sales processes distinct from operations. Traditional post-sales processes for product-based companies have focused on warranties and repairs. Facility and event managers must be able to 'repair' service breakdowns as they occur. Service recovery processes, then, become part of the operations process. We discuss methods for developing the scorecard and its measures later, but important to note here is that measures must be linked to the internal processes that produce customer outcomes. This is also true of the first link in the value chain, the *innovation process*.

Operations processes tend to emphasise short-term value creation. That is, the operations provide value for the duration of the customer's visit to the facility or event. Long-term value creation can be enhanced through the first stage of the value chain, the *innovation process*. This is the process of researching the emerging needs of customers and creating products and services that will meet those needs. Whereas the operations process focuses on improving operations and enhancing existing operations to enhance value, the innovation process focuses on creating new value. During the innovation process new customers and new markets are identified and nurtured, then new products and services are designed to reach those customers. Thus, innovation processes are the research and development functions that consist of two types of processes, those which identify the market and those which create new product and service offerings. Two questions, suggested by Hamel and Prahalad (1994), can be used to guide innovation processes. First, what range of benefits will customers value in tomorrow's products and services? Second, how might you, through innovative product and service design, pre-empt competitors in delivering those benefits to the marketplace?

The first of these questions points to processes through which to identify new customers and market segments. Convenience and responsiveness to lifestyle are increasingly valued benefits for participation-based facility users. Sport facility schedules and programs are often not convenient for mothers with young children. On the one hand, these potential customers have primary child-minding responsibilities during the day, and their evenings may be filled with family activities and responsibilities. On the other hand, this potential target market may place a high value on its own sport and leisure activities. The challenge for the facility, then, is to design (or redesign) products or services to help these customers to overcome the barriers to their use of the facility. Similarly, event patrons' expectations of their event experience continue to escalate. Whereas sport events were historically attended by young men, the potential audience for sport events has expanded to include men and women of all ages. Consequently, the challenge for event managers is to identify a latent need or desire in a potential customer group.

Potential performance indicators for market identification processes would quantify market research processes aimed at understanding customer needs, and providing reliable and valid information on such factors as market size, market accessibility, and customer preferences. They might also include such outcome measures as percentage increase in customers from a specified target market.

The *service creation process* is the development aspect of the business. This process translates the information on new markets, customer needs and desires into products and services that can meet those needs. To attract the mothers discussed in the previous example, facility managers might create family sport programs held in the early evenings or introduce child-minding services for daytime programs. Event owners have made events more family-friendly (thus reaching beyond the young male audience) by providing special seating areas, food choices, and pre-game, half-time and post-game entertainment options. Outcome measures (i.e. lagging indicators) are obvious. Increased attendance by selected demographic segments and increased participation in daytime programs are two of many indicators of successful outcomes. However, like all lagging indicators these fail to provide timely feedback on the actual processes used to create the new products and services. Leading indicators of successful product design might consider instead the number of new products or services developed, the value of those products to the targeted customer, the cost of development, and the time to develop a new product or service.

The inclusion of indicators of successful innovation processes allows management to emphasise research and development processes that may yield new products, services and markets. Measures of operations processes provide a means of tracking the success of an organisation's existing operational processes. Together, these processes create the value chain linking customer need identification to customer satisfaction. When combined with the customer perspective, the internal-business-process perspective identifies the factors most critical to current and future success. So to maintain superior performance in the facility and event industries requires that an organisation continually improve its capabilities and the capabilities of its employees.

Learning and growth perspective: how can we continue to improve and create value?

The learning and growth perspective references the infrastructure necessary to create long-term growth and improvement. The objectives in this perspective are the drivers for achieving the objectives from each of the other three perspectives. The objectives and measures in the first three perspectives identify *where* the facility or event organisation must excel. The learning and growth perspective identifies the capabilities necessary to achieve the performance targets identified. In effect, performance in organisational learning and growth builds the capacity of the organisation to develop and implement the necessary business processes to meet customer and shareholder needs and expectations. Organisational learning and growth emerge from three principal sources within the organisation: (1) employee outcomes and capabilities, (2) information systems capabilities, and (3) organisational procedures and alignment. Organisational learning and growth is particularly important in the events industry. Rarely do any two events have the same requirements or target the same audience. Consequently, event staff must constantly build their expertise, information systems must remain flexible, and procedures can never be set in stone. It is through capacity building that facility managers can expand their repertoire of events and event managers can successfully bid on an increasing array of events.

Like the customer perspective, *employee outcomes and capability* measures of organisational learning and growth include a smattering of generic outcome measures, as well as some business-specific drivers which serve to enable the desired outcomes (see Figure 10.2). Standard outcome measures include employee satisfaction, employee retention, and employee productivity. Employee satisfaction is seen to drive retention and productivity (Mondy, Noe & Premeaux 2002; Rosser 2004). Unsatisfied employees are less productive and tend to leave the organisation. Satisfied employees are essential to providing quality service. Employee morale is particularly important for service providers such as sport facilities and events. Often the lowest-paid workers have the most interaction with customers. Consequently, these employees are a significant part of the service experience. Like customer satisfaction, employee satisfaction is usually measured via a survey. Typical components of employee satisfaction would include: involvement with decisions, recognition, access to information, encouragement to use initiative, support, and overall satisfaction with the organisation.

Employee retention is an important component of organisational learning. This is a particularly difficult objective to achieve for many event organisations. Due to the cyclical nature

Figure 10.2 Employee outcomes and measures

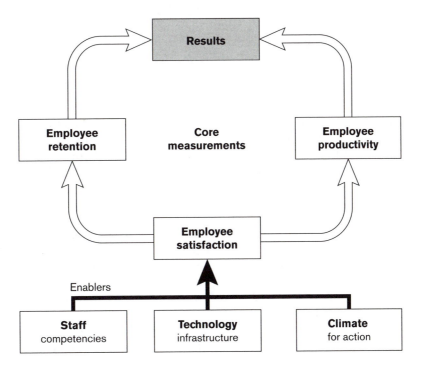

of event employment, a great deal of organisational knowledge is lost with the loss of employees after an event (Hanlon & Jago 2001). This is true for paid staff as well as volunteers. Retaining volunteers from one event to the next can significantly reduce staff time spent training volunteers, and can cut the costs of recruiting new volunteers. The organisational knowledge lost with the departure of full-time staff can be significantly greater. Generally, employee retention is measured by the percentage of staff turnover by program, by event, or by functional area.

Employee productivity is a function of the impact of 'enhancing employee satisfaction, innovation, improving internal processes, and satisfying customers' (Kaplan & Norton 1996, p. 131). Productivity measures, then, should be a function of the number of employees and the amount produced by those employees. In a strict manufacturing context, one could measure the number of units of a product produced per employee. Facilities with multiple programs might use a comparable measure, such as number of members using a particular program by the number of employees producing the program. However, the simplest measure for service providers is a measure of revenue generated per employee. Tickets sold per employee might provide event managers with an early indication of their marketing and sales success. But tickets per employee would fail to recognise the type of ticket sold. If the objective is merely to sell tickets, this is a good measure. If the objective is to maximise ticket revenues, then not all tickets are created equal. Ten $100 tickets sold would be better than twenty $10 tickets sold. In this case, revenue per employee is the better measure.

In addition to the core employee indicators discussed above, each facility and event may have unique, situation-specific drivers of learning and growth. While the actual measures may be unique to the facility or event, they tend to be drawn from three critical enabling factors: (1) staff competencies, (2) technology infrastructure, and (3) a climate for action.

In order to achieve customer and internal-business-process objectives, employees may face new responsibilities. New responsibilities often necessitate changes in the skills required to carry out those responsibilities effectively. *Staff competencies* form part of the infrastructure necessary to meet the organisation's objectives. When responsibilities change, there may be a demand for reskilling employees to meet new objectives. For example, an event company specialising in 10-kilometre running events may have identified a new customer segment—beginning triathletes. The new internal-business processes may have developed a triathlon series to meet the needs of this market. Note that a significant portion of the event staff now requires new competencies in such things as developing a swim course, designing and supervising changeover stations, and developing marketing collateral for a new market. Both the level of reskilling and the percentage of the workforce requiring reskilling will affect the success of this new strategy. These aspects can be measured using the strategic job coverage ratio. The ratio monitors the number of employees qualified for specific jobs relative to the anticipated needs of the organisation. The value chain can be used to identify the critical job skills of the future. The strategic job coverage ratio exposes the gap between future needs and current competencies. Thus, a ratio of 50 per cent would mean that only half of the skills, knowledge and attitudes necessary to implement the triathlon initiative exist in our current workforce.

Systems performance is indicated by the availability of accurate, critical customer and internal process information to employees at the coalface. Measures of one's *technology infrastructure* should provide an indication of the degree to which your internal systems provide decision makers with the information necessary to take action. Employees may have the job skills necessary to achieve organisational objectives, but they need information about their customers, internal processes, and the financial consequences of their decisions. Front-line employees need information about all products and services offered. For example, employees refereeing a facility's netball competition may be asked about other programs offered by the facility. Program instructors may be asked about membership prices or renewal policies. Many organisations measure the availability of strategic information via an information coverage ratio. Much like the job coverage ratio, this measure assesses current availability of information relative to anticipated information needs. Thus, a ratio of 85 per cent would indicate that 85 per cent of the information needed to meet anticipated demand is currently available to employees.

The third enabler for learning and growth objectives is a *climate for action*. Highly skilled employees with access to necessary information still may not lead to organisational success. Employees need to be motivated to contribute to the success of the facility or event. Further, they need to be empowered to make decisions and take action to ensure the success of the organisation. In short, employees need to feel that they have a voice and a stake in the success of the organisation. The ongoing participation of employees might be measured by the number of suggestions for improvement made per employee.

Quality of suggestions can be incorporated by measuring the number of suggestions implemented. The outcome of suggestions might also be measured. For example, on the first day of a multi-day volleyball tournament, an employee noticed that passers-by were slowing down to see what was going on inside the facility but did not enter the building. She suggested that a sign be placed outside the building indicating the event and advertising free admission (the event did not charge admission, but did issue wristbands to track attendance). Her suggestion was implemented the following session. The change in attendance by locals provided a measure of the success of her suggestion. It will also provide an outcome measure of the degree of alignment between individual and organisational objectives. When goal alignment is achieved, employees are actively participating in organisational improvement activities. Alignment of individual and organisational goals ensures that everyone is working to achieve the same objectives. Successful suggestions are a visible and measurable indication of this alignment.

Quality performance requires a significant investment in your workforce, your information systems and your climate. Objectives and measures of those factors that build the capacity for future performance provide a foundation for achieving performance outcomes in each of the other perspectives: internal-business processes, customer indicators, and financial indicators. However, measurement itself is not sufficient to improve performance.

Each scorecard measure must be linked to the organisation's strategy. The strategy of the facility or event is illustrated by linking your outcome and performance driver measures through a series of cause-and-effect relationships. Ultimately, all causal paths from all the measures on the scorecard should be linked in some way to the organisation's financial objectives.

Identifying critical measures

The balanced scorecard provides a means to measure business performance retrospectively and prospectively, and to do so in a manner that is consistent with the organisation's strategic plan. We have seen what the elements of a balanced scorecard are; next we need to consider how to create measures that are specific to your particular organisation. Measures of each type are created by cascading objectives (see Figure 10.3).

Figure 10.3 Cascading objectives for sport facility and event management

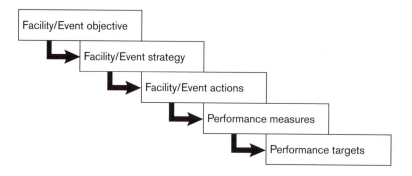

The process begins by identifying an overall *objective*, usually a financial objective. For example, Mega Events, Inc., a major sport event company, might choose revenue growth as its top financial objective. The next step is to consider which *strategies* would help to achieve the objective. Mega Events might consider any of the following strategies: improve ticket sales, obtain more sponsors, or do more advertising. Each is a valid strategy, as are others not mentioned here. To keep the example simple, we will limit the strategy to one—improving ticket sales. The next step is to consider any *actions* that need to occur to ensure that the strategy is carried out. To improve ticket sales, Mega Events might provide sales training to all employees, hire more experienced salespeople, or lower the price of tickets. Typically, each objective will have more than one strategy, each strategy will have multiple actions, each action will have more than one measure etc.

Step four of the process is to create *measures* to check progress in achieving the actions and strategies. Appropriate measures for Mega Events might include percentage of staff with sales training and sales staff turnover. Note that these measures are future predictors (i.e. lead indicators) of sales. The level of sales training today is a good indicator of the growth in sales tomorrow, assuming that Mega Events' strategy is effective. Note also that the measure provides a clear link back through the actions taken to the strategy selected. Further, it is all linked to the overall financial objective of revenue growth. It is easy for staff at all levels (e.g. salespeople, sales trainers, managers) to understand how their own actions affect Mega Events' performance. Employees at all levels now contribute to the same goal. The *targets* provide both strategic feedback (does the strategy work?) and tactical feedback (did we implement the actions properly?). If Mega Events meets its targets of 85 per cent staff with sales training and less than 25 per cent turnover in sales staff, then it will show improved revenue growth.

The balanced scorecard as a strategic management system

The balanced scorecard ensures that performance measures are fully integrated with an organisation's strategy. Yet the balanced scorecard is more than a systematic performance measurement initiative (Kaplan & Norton 1993). It can be used as a strategic management system. A balanced scorecard approach can help a facility or event management company to: '(1) clarify and translate vision and strategy, (2) communicate and link strategic objectives and measures, (3) plan, set targets, and align strategic initiatives, and (4) enhance strategic feedback and learning' (Kaplan & Norton 1996, p. 10).

Clarify and translate vision and strategy

The balanced scorecard is a top-down strategic initiative. The process begins with the senior management team clarifying its vision for the organisation. It is important to reach consensus regarding the strategic vision for the organisation. Often, senior executives come from different functional areas. As a result, they may have different visions and priorities for the organisation. The balanced scorecard process highlights potential differences and forces the group to work together to articulate a shared vision. So the balanced scorecard creates consensus and teamwork among senior staff, and has the added benefit of holding senior management accountable to the agreed-on objectives and strategies.

Communicate and link strategic objectives and measures

The balanced scorecard signals, to all employees, the objectives that are critical to the organisation's performance. Importantly, it also provides actions, measures and targets for all levels of the organisation. In this way, the balanced scorecard can communicate and gain commitment to the organisation's goals and the strategies to achieve those goals. This allows individual employees to formulate local actions and align their own goals to those of the organisation.

Plan, set targets, and align strategic initiatives

The planning and target-setting process assists the organisation in quantifying the long-term outcomes that it wants to achieve while also establishing short-term goals for the financial and non-financial measures on the scorecard. In addition, it can help to identify the strategies and actions for achieving both long- and short-term outcomes and provide a rationale for obtaining the resources necessary to achieve them.

Enhance strategic feedback and learning

The balanced scorecard is unusual in its ability to provide senior management with feedback about its strategy, and to test the hypotheses on which the strategy is based. Further, it provides regular feedback that allows management to learn about and adjust the organisation's strategy or the way in which it is implemented. The balanced scorecard can be used by managers to gain clarification, to reach consensus, to focus on strategy, and to communicate that strategy throughout the organisation. However, its real strength lies in its ability to function as a fully integrated strategic management system.

Summary

Consistent performance measurement allows sport facility and event managers to monitor and control the strategies, processes and outcomes of the organisation and its employees. Further, it is a useful way to benchmark performance against industry standards and one's own competitors. Effective performance measurement requires an organisation to develop an array of measures that provide a reasonably complete picture of the processes and outcomes of the organisation's operations, and should be linked to its strategies and objectives. This chapter contends that the balanced scorecard approach developed by Kaplan and Norton (1992, 1993, 1996) provides facility and event managers with a comprehensive approach by which to develop and implement an effective performance management system that begins with the strategic objectives of the facility or event. It then helps the manager to translate organisational objectives into a set of cohesive performance indicators organised along four dimensions: finance, customer, internal business processes, and learning and growth. Measures within these four dimensions provide a balance between process and outcome, and between leading and lagging indicators. Together, the indicators provide managers with a systematic performance measurement initiative that is fully integrated with the organisation's strategic management system.

Case study

Event performance measurement at the City of Melbourne

From international events such as the Australian Open to cycling with friends along the Yarra River, the City of Melbourne offers something for everyone when it comes to sports and recreation. The City of Melbourne manages and supports a large and diverse range of clubs, facilities and grounds catering to players of football, netball, tennis, hockey, athletics, soccer, cricket and much more. Swimming pools such as the historical City Baths are easily accessible for recreational users. The city also has one of the most beautiful jogging tracks in Australia, the Tan Track, which skirts the boundaries of the Royal Botanic Gardens, Kings Domain and Government House. Each year the City of Melbourne offers the 'Summer Fun in the Parks' program. This program celebrates Melbourne's parks and gardens, by providing a variety of free events throughout summer for residents and visitors.

A fundamental role of the City of Melbourne is to provide high-quality services and activities to members of the public. This philosophy has been integrated into its contractual agreements with all service providers. A variety of performance measurement systems are also used to meet the needs and expectations of all stakeholders.

Recreation facilities—facility performance measurement

The primary performance measurement instrument used by the City of Melbourne to evaluate its wide range of facilities is the CERM performance indicators. The Centre for Environmental and Recreation Management (CERM) at the University of South Australia initially developed facility management performance indicators in collaboration with the managers of local government indoor sports and leisure centres in Australia. This collaboration has been extended to New Zealand and the United Kingdom.

The CERM performance indicators provide protocols for reliable data collection and indicators in the following three areas:

- operational management (resource utilisation);
- effectiveness (customer service quality—CSQ); and
- appropriateness (community service obligations—CSO).

These performance indicators and demographic data are used to improve operational decision making, including regular internal and external benchmarking against similar operations. The City of Melbourne believes the CERM performance indicators are the most appropriate measuring stick available to compare like with like. The council uses CERM to measure its customer service for its main recreation facilities, swimming pools, golf course and the skate park.

In addition to the CERM measures, contracts between service providers and the City of Melbourne specify quality control requirements. The City of Melbourne's Parks and Recreation officers regularly assess each facility against a number of occupational health and safety (OH&S) measures. Each of these measures is used by the City of Melbourne to provide performance bonuses within the contractual arrangements with service providers.

Summer Fun in the Parks—event performance measurement

Summer Fun in the Parks is an annual program of free events in parks and gardens throughout the city. The events have included a series of free lunchtime concerts, classes in Tai Chi, massages and free dance classes. The program is delivered under contract by an external provider.

The City of Melbourne has developed a number of key performance indicators (KPIs) to effectively measure the performance of the wide variety of summer fun in the parks events. These KPIs are integrated into the contracts with service providers and set the levels for minimum threshold performance scores.

Each KPI sets the required level of performance in a specific area. These are:

- a range of free events that are educational with diverse community involvement
- first-class customer service
- care and protection of parklands
- OH&S and risk management
- increased visitation (set percentage)
- timely delivery as advertised
- milestone dates
- documentation and reporting
- cooperation between client and provider
- embracing change in the development of new programs.

Against each of these KPIs, a number of deliverables and instructions detail the required level of performance. For example, event participants are asked to complete a satisfaction survey to measure customer service. The benchmark deliverable for the service providers is to have an increase in the number of favourable surveys, and a decrease in the number of negative surveys, compared with the previous year. The KPIs are also subject to review and improvement. Detailed instructions to service providers are being developed around the expectations of the City of Melbourne to assist providers to understand the needs of the City.

When evaluating the overall performance of the Summer Fun in the Parks program, the City of Melbourne uses these KPIs to:

- Foster an environment of continuous improvement in the event program, by using performance measures and minimum threshold scores as both a mechanism for providing a bonus, or conversely withholding a percentage of the management fee for underperformance
- Provide an additional measure of control over the service provider.

The City of Melbourne's performance management strategies ensure the facility and event services are providing value for money, and also act as a mechanism for accountability to the council and ratepayers. Measuring the performance of the facilities and events within the City of Melbourne assures participants and stakeholders that they are being provided with high-quality sport and recreation services. Performance management is an integral component of effective planning and management.

Q. Select either a major sporting event, or high-profile facility, and devise a set of key performance indicators against which to measure performance.
Q. Based on your recommended KPIs, organise them using the balanced scorecard approach.
Q. Identify strengths and weaknesses associated with using the balanced scorecard to organise your KPIs. List these strengths and weaknesses.
Q. Describe the importance of customers in your recommended KPIs. What measures do you recommend to assess performance associated with customers?

Case prepared by Emma Sherry.

11

Measuring facility and event performance: impact on and for stakeholders

Chapter focus
Structure, size and trends in the sport facility and sport event sectors
Key success factors of operating sport facilities and running sport events
Developing new sport facilities: feasibility analysis
Developing new sport facilities: design and construction issues
Developing new sport facilities: preparing facility management infrastructure
Operating the new sport facility: attracting events
Operating the new sport facility: preparing event management infrastructure
Attracting customers: marketing the sport facility and the sport events
Running the sport event: event operations
Measuring facility and event performance: a scorecard approach to success
Measuring facility and event performance: impact on and for stakeholders

CHAPTER OBJECTIVES

In this chapter, we will:
- Discuss the triple bottom line of facility and event performance.
- Examine the economic, environmental and social impacts of facility and event performance.
- Consider ways to measure and monitor the economic, environmental and social impacts of facilities and events.
- Suggest ways in which managers can minimise the negative and maximise the positive impacts of their facilities and events.
- Describe the importance and purpose of stakeholder analysis in facility and event planning and management.

The construction of sport facilities, the maintenance of sport facilities and the hosting of sport events each represent substantial financial investments. In many instances, the costs are not fully covered by the revenues generated (Crompton 2001; Mules & Faulkner 1996). This fact has led to increasing interest in the impact that facilities and events have on the wider communities that host them. Initially, that interest has been in terms of the economic impact (Dwyer, Mellor, Mistilis & Mules 2001; Swindell & Rosentraub 1998). However, in recent years there has also been some concern about the environmental impact (Cantelon & Letters 2000) and the social impact (Fredline & Faulkner 2000, 2002) of facilities and events.

Social and environmental impacts have been recognised in recent years as necessary complements to economic impact when assessing the effects and value of investments, technology and infrastructure. Taken together, economic impact, environmental impact and social impact are known as 'the triple bottom line'. Tschopp (2003) points out that accountants are increasingly being expected to develop procedures and reports that assess each element of the triple bottom line. Smith (2004) notes that engineers are using the triple bottom line to ascertain the sustainability of their systems and technologies. Molnar and Mulvihill (2003) observe that organisations are having to adapt their cultures and their record keeping in order to incorporate the triple bottom line in their operations.

This chapter introduces the tools and considers the challenges for evaluating facility and event impacts. Economic, environmental and social impact assessment methods are each introduced. The effect of different assessment procedures on stakeholders and the need for stakeholder management are then considered.

Economic impact

The development (and redevelopment) of major sport facilities is often dependent on government funding. Telstra Stadium cost $A690 million to build; the redevelopment of SunCorp Stadium in Brisbane cost $A279.7 million. A substantial portion of those funds was provided by government. Similarly, local sports grounds and indoor facilities are often funded with local council expenditures (Daly 1995). Major events are also heavily reliant on government funds. Government subsidises bids for and production of sport events. In return, facilities and events are expected to provide a significant return on government investment. However, the return is rarely expected to occur solely through operating profits. Instead, facilities and events are expected to provide the community at large with economic benefit. They are expected to induce spending in the local area, thus profiting local businesses. The induced spending spills over into tax collections in the form of sales taxes or goods and services taxes. Ultimately, more money circulating in the area stimulates a growth in earnings and employment (Coates & Humphreys 2003). Consequently, economic impact is an increasingly important measure of facility and event performance.

Assessing economic impact

Economic impact is assessed in terms of two components—namely, direct and indirect impacts. Direct economic impact consists of any new spending that is directly stimulated by a facility or sport event. It is important to note that this spending must be new to the economy. Examples of direct expenditures include the money spent by visitors (local, national and international) on tickets, food, accommodation, entertainment, shopping and transport. Other direct expenditures may be related to participants, organisers and sponsors. The key determinant is that expenditures would not otherwise have occurred; they would have been spent somewhere else or not at all.

Conducting an economic impact study

The first challenge in conducting an economic impact study is to estimate visitor numbers. At first glance, this may seem straightforward. Events typically have readily available data regarding tickets sold. Facilities may also have data on the number of people using their facilities. Attendance and user numbers provide a good initial estimate of visitor numbers. But other visitor groups must also be estimated. For example, facilities and events may have vendors living outside the local area. Vendors are not usually considered attendees, yet they are often deemed to be visitors. Events often focus purely on spectator attendance and fail to consider the spending of players, officials, administrators and/or corporate sponsors. Each of these groups may be accompanied by one or more others who may or may not attend the event. Consequently, when estimating visitor numbers, one should begin by identifying potential spending groups.

Once groups have been identified, the size of each group should be estimated. As economic impact is estimated by extrapolating data collected from a sample of visitors to the total number of visitors, an economic impact study is only as accurate as its estimate of visitor numbers (Crompton, Lee & Shuster 2001). Care should be taken to avoid double-counting visitors. This can be problematic for multi-day events in particular. Estimates can be obtained from the visitor survey itself by asking respondents to indicate which days they attended the event. When extrapolating to the entire visitor population, ratios can be calculated to estimate single-day attendees, two-day attendees, and so on. In the same way, the proportion of local versus out-of-town visitors can be determined.

Economic impact is clearly linked to out-of-town spending. Thus, it is important to determine the boundaries for any economic impact study. Who will be considered local? How will that be determined? The area of impact can vary. Will events supported by a local council be interested only in the impact within the council or city limits? Postcodes are a simple way of defining the geographic limits of any impacts. Respondents listing postcodes within the local shire or county are considered locals. Those with other postcodes are considered non-locals. For state-supported events, locals are often defined as those residents whose primary residence is within the state. An event funded by the Queensland Events Corporation (an organisation specifically set up to attract events to Queensland), for example, would show very little impact on the state of Queensland if the majority of attendees at an event in Townsville (a city in Queensland) came from Brisbane (the capital of Queensland). However, the economic impact of the event for Townsville could be significant. Consequently, it is important to determine the boundaries of expected impacts early in the measurement process.

Once the area of impact has been determined and a procedure has been devised to measure visitor numbers, visitor surveys can be implemented. Remember, direct economic impact is a measure of stimulated spend. Standard economic impact studies use one of several tools to collect spending information. Visitors may be asked to keep a diary of their expenditures while visiting a city to attend an event or visit a facility. Diaries have the advantage that they do not rely on recollections of what was spent. However, the act of recording expenditures has been shown to influence the spending of participants (Faulkner & Raybould 1995). Alternatively, visitors may be asked to complete a brief questionnaire that requires them to estimate their spending while visiting. These are commonly completed as on-site exit interviews. Minimally, these questionnaires gather information about the size of the travelling party, length of stay, spending in a variety of categories, and postcode. Figure 11.1 is an example of a visitor survey on a series of events in the city of Austin, Texas (USA).

All questionnaires should have a way to differentiate locals from out-of-town visitors. Locals do not provide any new spending. Local spending is spending that would have occurred in the local community anyway. A local resident's expenditure at a local restaurant, for example, does not represent a new source of funds for the local economy. Postcodes,

Figure 11.1 Visitor survey

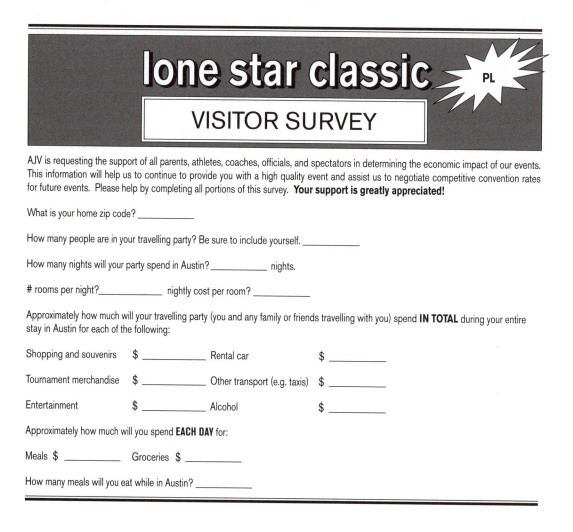

lone star classic PL

VISITOR SURVEY

AJV is requesting the support of all parents, athletes, coaches, officials, and spectators in determining the economic impact of our events. This information will help us to continue to provide you with a high quality event and assist us to negotiate competitive convention rates for future events. Please help by completing all portions of this survey. **Your support is greatly appreciated!**

What is your home zip code? _____

How many people are in your travelling party? Be sure to include yourself. _____

How many nights will your party spend in Austin? _____ nights.

rooms per night?_____ nightly cost per room? _____

Approximately how much will your travelling party (you and any family or friends travelling with you) spend **IN TOTAL** during your entire stay in Austin for each of the following:

Shopping and souvenirs $ _____   Rental car $ _____

Tournament merchandise $ _____   Other transport (e.g. taxis) $ _____

Entertainment $ _____   Alcohol $ _____

Approximately how much will you spend **EACH DAY** for:

Meals $ _____   Groceries $ _____

How many meals will you eat while in Austin? _____

home towns or home states are common items used to differentiate locals from non-locals. Similarly, a question addressing the number of days attended helps to differentiate repeat visitors from new visitors. In this way, no attendee is counted more than once. It also assists agencies in comparing the economic impact of events of various lengths.

Locals are not the only group that should be excluded. Time-switchers and casuals (Crompton 1999) should also be excluded from the analysis. Time-switchers are visitors to the event destination, but they are visitors who were intending to visit anyway. These visitors merely changed the dates of their visit to coincide with the event. Thus, they would have spent money in the local economy anyway, just at a different time. Consequently, their spending was not a result of the event and cannot be included in the economic impact of the event. The same is true of casuals. Casuals are event attendees who were already at the destination and happened to go to the event during their stay. Expenditures by casuals would have occurred even without the event. Like expenditures by time-switchers, expenditures by casuals cannot be attributed to the event and should not be included in measures of the economic impact of the event. There is an exception, however: some time-switchers and casuals may stay longer at the destination because of the event. In this case, the additional spending can be included in the analysis. Screening questions can be embedded in the visitor survey to identify time-switchers and casuals. For example, a visitor survey for the Asia-Pacific Masters Games held on Australia's Gold Coast might include the following questions to identify casuals and time-switchers:

- Would you have come to the Gold Coast *at this time* even if this event had not been held?
- If yes, will you stay longer than you would have if this event had not been held?
- If yes, how much longer?
- Would you have come to the Gold Coast in the next three months if you had not come at this time for this event?

Knowledge of group size is important in that it helps to prevent researchers from over-estimating spending. Visitors often travel with others and often are responsible for paying for others in their travel party. For example, a parent typically pays the bills for all family members on a family holiday. Thus, one person's spending estimates may include spending on others. As most studies report per person expenditure, group size is an important variable in any economic impact analysis.

Respondents are asked to estimate the amount that was (or will be) spent by their travel group in a number of categories. Common categories include: food and beverage; night clubs, lounges and bars; other entertainment (e.g. theatres, museums, amusement parks, other tourist attractions); retail shopping; accommodation; transport *during* the stay; and any other expenses. It is often useful to have respondents estimate their spending within the area of interest (i.e. city, region, state, country) and their spending outside the area of interest (Crompton et al. 2001). This helps respondents to differentiate between spending on their trip (which may include spending on the way to and from the destination) and spending while at the event destination (the expenditure of interest). Total expenditures by non-locals can be calculated as follows:

$$\frac{\text{Total non-local visitors}}{\text{Average group size}} - \text{Average expenditure per group}$$

Spending in each of the specified categories is aggregated to determine direct expenditures. However, spending in each category affects the economy in different ways. The ways in which revenues are spent and respent vary by industry and by locality. The circulation (and recirculation) of revenues within the economy provides additional, indirect benefits to the economy. Indirect benefits are estimated via the use of 'multipliers'. Multipliers are used to account for the ripple effect of money through the economy. Money that is spent and respent within the economy has a cumulative impact greater than the initial visitor expenditure. Multipliers are designed to account for the cumulative impact by estimating the indirect expenditures resulting from initial spending.

However, not all direct expenditures circulate entirely within the local economy. Expenditures leaving the local economy are referred to as 'leakage'.

Figure 11.2 shows the direct, indirect and induced impacts of $100 spent by a non-local event. The $100 spent at a local restaurant is considered a direct expenditure. Now let's consider the indirect effects of the $100 spent in the restaurant. The local restaurant spends this money again. It buys produce from a local grocer and pays its chef, who lives in the local community. Thus, $50 is recirculated in the local economy. The other $50 is leakage. It is used to pay bills outside the local area (e.g. insurance, out-of-town employees). The $50 that stays in the local economy is again respent. The grocer spends $10 on vegetables from a local farm, and sends $35 to its parent company in another state. These are indirect impacts. The

Figure 11.2 The multiplier effect: direct, indirect and induced spending at an event

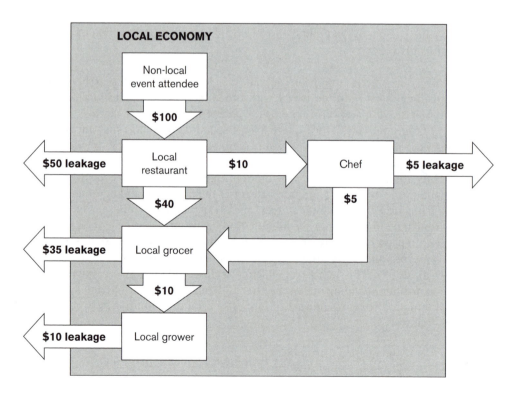

chef spends $5 at the local grocery, and $5 outside the local community. Secondary spendings in the community by employees of affected businesses are called induced impacts. Thus, the chef's purchase at the local grocery store is an example of induced impact. Direct, indirect and induced impacts contribute to the total impact of building a facility or hosting an event. In this example, the recirculation of revenues results in an impact of $100 (direct) + $40 (indirect) + $10 (indirect) + $10 (indirect) + $5 (induced), or $165 total impact.

Rather than try to trace actual expenditures through the economy, multipliers are used to represent the indirect impact of the direct expenditures. Three types of multipliers are commonly reported in economic impact studies: (1) sales, (2) income, and (3) employment multipliers. A sales multiplier measures the direct, indirect and induced effect of an extra unit of visitor spending on economic activity within the local area. If the example shown was indicative of spending patterns in the restaurant industry in a particular region, then a sales multiplier of 1.65 would be appropriate for the food and beverage category. Sales multipliers are substantially higher than income multipliers. But, as Crompton (1999, p. 21) notes, 'in an economic impact analysis sales multipliers are not useful . . . [residents] have no interest in value of sales per se because it has no impact on their standard of living'. Income multipliers, on the other hand, measure the effect of an extra unit of visitor spending on changes in residents' household income. Income multipliers can be expressed as follows:

$$\frac{\text{Direct} + \text{indirect} + \text{induced income}}{\text{Visitor expenditure}}$$

Employment multipliers are often included, and often misrepresented, in economic impact studies. An employment multiplier measures the effect of an extra unit of visitor spending on local employment. The outcome is reported in full-time equivalent (FTE) job opportunities. Employment multipliers are the least reliable of the multipliers (Fletcher & Snee 1989). Consider an event reporting an impact of 62 full-time equivalent jobs. Does this mean that 62 new full-time jobs were created? Probably not. Events, particularly one-off events, rarely warrant the creation of full-time jobs. Rather, the existing workforce usually is asked to work additional days or hours to meet the increased demand for labour. FTEs generated by facilities, on the other hand, may be more reliable indicators of the effect of the facility on the labour market. Facilities, unlike events, are stable, ongoing enterprises. Thus, a new sport facility may result in the creation of new jobs.

No matter which multipliers are reported, they must be calculated for each spending category and for each economy. As discussed earlier, each industry and each geographic location has a unique pattern of revenue circulation. A small town may rely heavily on foods imported from outside its area. In that instance, most of the spending would be in the form of leakage from the local economy. Other categories of spending may differ. For example, the same small town may have few chain hotels, and may rely mainly on independent local accommodation providers. In this case, less revenue would go to corporations based outside the local economy. The choice of multiplier can greatly affect overall estimates of economic impact. The best multipliers are those that have been developed specific to a particular industry within a particular economy. Economics researchers in government and in universities have often calculated the multiplier for spending categories (or in general) for local economies. Thus, in practice, it is normally possible to obtain a good estimate of the appropriate multipliers to use for spending at an event.

Intangible impacts

Economic impact studies can provide reasonable indications of the tangible impacts of sport facilities and sport events. However, these same studies often fail to measure the intangible impacts of a sport facility or event. Admittedly, intangible impacts are more difficult to measure. Yet they are no less important.

Sport facilities are the prime enabler of sport events. With few exceptions (e.g. surf lifesaving, road races, sailing), the success of major sporting events is dependent on the host facility or facilities. In fact, the existence or promise of the requisite facility(s) is a necessary component of a bid to host a sport event. However, this intangible benefit (the very fact of 'enabling' sport to be played) is rarely considered in studies of the economic impact of sport facilities.

Sport and recreation have been found to positively affect quality of life (Brown et al. 2003; Elley, Kerse, Arroll & Robinson 2003). Quality of life is an important element in attracting businesses to a city or region, and can be instrumental in retaining workers (Kotler, Haider & Rein 1993; Ward 2000). Thus, sport facilities, through their impact on the quality of life of workers and community residents, can have a significant economic impact on a city or region. However, it is difficult to measure with precision the impact of a facility on businesses' decisions to locate in a city or on residents' decisions to remain in the local community.

Increasingly, sport facilities are an important component of a destination's tourism mix. It has been argued that appropriate integration of sport facilities in the destination's product mix can generate longer visitor stays and greater visitor spend (Chalip 2001). Further, some sport facilities have become tourist attractions in themselves. FC Barcelona's Nou Camp football stadium in Spain and the Melbourne Cricket Ground (MCG) in Australia are prime examples of the attraction of sport facilities to tourists. In fact, for highly involved Australian Rules football fans, a visit to the MCG could be considered a form of pilgrimage (Graburn 1983). Significantly, these venues attract tourists at times when no events are scheduled. Rarely have these benefits been quantified in economic impact studies.

Economic impact studies of sport events are so focused on the visitor spend stimulated by the event that most of them fail to consider secondary benefits. Events play an increasingly important role in destination branding (Brown, Chalip, Jago & Mules 2002; Jago, Chalip, Brown, Mules & Ali 2003). For example, the publicity and advertising surrounding an event can add saliency and dimension to the host destination's profile among tourists and businesses. Similarly, event visitors may 'talk up' the host city to their friends, thus increasing a city's attractiveness as a place for tourism or business.

When economic impact assessments seek to incorporate estimates of the impact of event publicity, comparable worth estimates are typically used (Dwyer et al. 2001; Higham 1999). Accordingly, the cost of purchasing advertising time or space equivalent to that obtained by event publicity is used as a proxy for the value of event advertising. As publicity is thought to have greater credibility than advertising, the comparable worth of the publicity is typically multiplied by a factor between two and three to obtain an estimate of the value of the publicity.

There are two fundamental misleading notions in this method. First, destination advertising will be built around a message about the destination and the benefits it offers. There is no guarantee that the same is true of event publicity. Second, astute advertisers will place ads where they are most likely to be seen by the desired target market(s). That is not necessarily the case with event publicity. Recent empirical work demonstrates that the comparable worth method is, indeed, flawed. Chalip, Green and Hill (2003) found that event publicity can actually worsen viewers' image of key dimensions of the host destination. Green, Costa and Fitzgerald (2003) showed that the destination images that appear in an event telecast may not be salient and may not be readily identified with the host destination. Given the logical fallacies and the demonstrated flaws in the comparable worth method, it is not an appropriate proxy for the economic value of event media. Nevertheless, it is clear that when event media are appropriately built into the overall destination marketing mix, they can provide value (Brown et al. 2002). In order for the value to be estimated, what needs to be ascertained is what is being communicated and to which markets it is being communicated.

A further benefit of events can be the social capital that they engender (Jago et al. 2003). Event employees and volunteers can build new skills and enhance their social networks. A successful event may enhance residents' pride in their community. Each of these benefits can have economic value, although that value is difficult to quantify and is not normally included in estimates of event value. Nonetheless, the value of events for social capital may represent a significant benefit to the host community. As we will see, benefits like these can be measured using the techniques of social impact assessment.

Environmental impact

Sport facilities and the events they host often cram large numbers of people into a relatively concentrated space. The effect on the environment can be devastating, as the environmental damage caused by the construction of sport facilities and the running of the 1992 Winter Olympic Games in Albertville clearly demonstrated (Christie 1992). The effect was sufficiently intense to evoke widespread criticism from environmental groups, thereby bringing sport facilities and events under heightened environmental scrutiny. The International Olympic Committee (IOC) responded in 1994 by adopting the environment as the third pillar of the Olympic Movement (along with sport and culture), and followed with the creation of a Sport and the Environment Commission. The World Conference on Sport and the Environment in 2001, sponsored by the IOC in cooperation with the United Nations, called on all participants and enterprises associated with sport to continue and intensify their efforts in implementing environmental, economic and social sustainability in all of their policies and activities. In fact, the resolution reflected pressure on sport organisations at all levels that was already causing them to consider environmental issues in all that they did. Indeed, organisers of the Sydney Olympics formed a partnership with the environmental organisation Greenpeace in order to implement as environmentally friendly an event as possible (Greenpeace 2000).

In the years following the 1992 Winter Olympics in Albertville, a number of reports and guidelines were developed for sport facilities and sport events. The United Nations Environmental Programme later sponsored a handbook for the environmental management of sport facilities and events (Chernushenko, van der Kamp & Stubbs 2001). Each kind of facility—gymnasia, ice arenas, swimming pools, ski fields—raises its own set of environmental problems. Similarly, the specific environmental issues raised by different kinds of sport vary as a function of the environment and the sports' characteristics. For example, swimming events and golf events both make extensive use of chemicals. However, the chemicals are different—water treatment chemicals in the case of swimming, and herbicides and fertilisers in the case of golf. Thus, the specific management problems are different. Similarly, a mountain biking event raises fewer problems having to do with chemical management but serious issues having to do with management of erosion and protection of the natural watershed. Nevertheless, there are some general principles that can guide facility and event managers when planning, maintaining and operating their facilities and events.

Environmentally friendly facility management

Sport facilities can use a great deal of energy to operate. Air needs to be heated or cooled; water needs to be heated; ice needs to be kept frozen; lighting needs to be bright enough for competition and safety. Energy production places a demand on the environment, so the more energy a facility uses, the greater its impact on the environment (and the greater the costs of operation). The facility manager can audit the facility to reduce its level of demand for energy. For example, insulation in walls and ceilings can reduce energy loss; low-energy-demand lighting can be installed to reduce the power consumed to illuminate playing areas, spectator seating and parking areas; double-glazed windows can reduce the energy loss due to conduction; efficient water heating systems can be selected.

It is also possible to make effective use of heat pumps to minimise energy lost. For example, swimming pool water needs to be heated, but the ice in an ice arena needs to be cooled. Normally, ice is chilled using an electric heat pump with the heat that is taken from the water (to cool it to ice) then vented into the environment and thus lost. However, if a swimming pool is constructed nearby, the heat that results from cooling the ice can be pumped to heat the swimming pool. Little or no added energy is then needed to heat the pool, and the heat generated by ice making is not vented into the environment. A storage system can be used to retain the heat for later use at a time when the pool (or shower or air-heating system) does not require it.

Many sport facilities make extensive use of chemicals. These can include cleaning solvents, coolants, chemicals to treat water (especially for swimming pools), insecticides, and chemicals used on plants (e.g. herbicides and pesticides). Cooling systems should be tested regularly to prevent leaks, and coolants that do not threaten the ozone layer should be preferred. Biodegradable and environmentally friendly cleaning and sterilising agents should be chosen over those that are not readily biodegradable or that are biodegradable but damaging to the environment. Pools can make use of ozone rather than chlorine or bromine to sterilise water. Insect traps and natural predators (e.g. birds and bats) can be used to minimise use of insecticides. Grass and other plants that are well suited to the environment in which the facility resides can be chosen to minimise the need for herbicides and fertilisers.

Sport facilities can also damage the native habitats of local flora and fauna. The mere presence of a facility often introduces a built environment into what was once a natural habitat. Activities at a facility can increase noise, automobile traffic, pedestrian use, and play in and around the facility. The construction of a facility can be particularly destructive to the local environment, as construction equipment and activities often extend damage beyond the footprint of the facility itself. Care needs to be taken to ensure that local watersheds are not disrupted or overstretched by the location and access pathways of the facility. The placement of the facility, as well as activity areas and access pathways, should be designed to minimally disrupt breeding grounds and nesting areas. Wherever possible, plants and landscaping should be chosen to enhance rather then disrupt pollination within the local ecosystem and feeding opportunities for local wildlife.

Environmentally friendly events

Effective environmental management for an event requires that the culture of the event management organisation explicitly encourage and support positive environmental management throughout the event organisation's work. This includes training and education for staff and volunteers, creation of an environmental policy statement, monitoring of environmental impacts, reporting of environmental risks and impacts, and allocation of resources and rewards for environmentally friendly operations. Of course, the matters noted above regarding facilities apply. Indeed, if an event can use existing facilities or retrofit existing facilities, the environmental impact will be less than if new facilities are constructed. Nevertheless, there are a number of additional realms to consider when seeking to make event operations environmentally friendly, as shown in Table 11.1.

Environmental impact assessment

The effect a facility or an event is likely to have can be forecast using the techniques of environmental impact assessment (Environment Agency 2002). The content and focus of environmental impact assessments can vary as a function of the particular context and concerns being addressed, but the common objective is to ascertain how the environment will be changed by the proposed facility or event. An environmental impact assessment will forecast or measure the effect on such variables as terrestrial flora and fauna, marine biota, local geology and soils, and surface and subsurface waters. In practice, governments often require that an environmental impact assessment be completed before an event takes place or a facility is constructed. An assessment of environmental impacts may also be required periodically while the facility is in operation or after the event has ended.

The environmental impact assessment (EIA) is most commonly undertaken prior to facility construction or event implementation. It is reported in an environmental impact statement (EIS). The EIS considers the justification for the facility or event, and includes a detailed specification of the potential environmental effects. It may also consider alternatives to the project. When completed, it is usually a public document subject to scrutiny and comment by interested persons or groups. Although the most common purpose is to determine the appropriateness of undertaking a particular project, the EIA can also be used to plan the management of a facility or event (Goodenough 1992). By identifying areas of the environment that are most at risk as a result of a facility being built or event being hosted, as well as the particular operations that are most likely to cause environmental disruptions, it is possible to plan or redesign a facility or event in a manner that minimises environmental risks. This should include means to restore environmental damage.

In practice, it has often been left to facility developers or event organisers to undertake the EIA. As the developer or organiser has a vested financial stake in the project, it is in their interests to produce a report that plays down the environmental risks and emphasises the benefits a project might provide. As a result, the validity of EIAs has been strongly criticised (e.g. Schindler 1976; Treweek 1996). In a systematic evaluation of EIAs conducted for 170 Australian projects, Warnken and Buckley (1998) found that significant environmental parameters were ignored, predictions were either untestable or simply inaccurate, and monitoring programs were inadequate to detect likely impacts. Criticisms like these have caused governments to revisit their requirements for EIAs before, during and after

Table 11.1 Making event operations environmentally friendly

Procurement

Reuse products (rather than purchasing new products) wherever possible.

Develop and enforce policies preferring environmentally friendly products.

Prefer products that can be recycled:

- Choose or prefer packaging that minimises waste and that is recyclable.
- Prefer energy-efficient products.
- Prefer products for which disposal will be unnecessary or safe.

Office management

Minimise paper use.

Use recycled paper products.

Use energy-efficient machinery and lighting.

Prefer recyclable, reusable or durable products over disposable products.

Have printers and photocopiers with double-sided capability.

Transport

- Minimise the number of fleet vehicles and maintain them to retain efficiency.
- Prefer energy-efficient vehicles.
- Use public transport wherever possible.
- Minimise the number of trips by teleconferencing where appropriate.
- Encourage car pooling, walking and biking to work by staff.
- Have covered bicycle parking for staff.
- Have showers and change rooms available for staff.

Waste management

Develop systems to minimise waste:

- Audit waste to identify means to reduce waste and to handle it more efficiently.
- Recycle wherever possible.
- Serve food and drink in reusable containers wherever possible.

Publications

Use electronic forms of publishing where appropriate:

- Use both sides of the paper.
- Avoid colours or coatings that make recycling difficult.

Marketing

Publicise and advertise your environmentally friendly policies.

Encourage sponsors to be environmentally friendly in their event-related activities and publicity.

Avoid 'blanketing' an area with the same signs by placing signs strategically.

Make signage reusable wherever possible.

projects. Consequently, the requirements for environmental impact assessments are likely to become more stringent in years to come.

Social impact

Sport facilities can affect the behaviours of people within their critical trading radius. It is easier for people who live or work near a sport facility to attend events at the facility or to participate in activities at the facility than it is for those who live or work further away. Thus, sport facilities can have a noticeable impact on the social lives of those who live or work nearby.

Similarly, sport events can have a substantial impact on the lives of people in the host community. Crowding, traffic, pollution and noise may all become more intense. On the other hand, there may be a party-like atmosphere or heightened community pride during the event. Consequently, events can also have a significant effect on the lives of people who reside in the host community (Fredline & Faulkner 2000, 2002).

The intended and unintended consequences of facilities and events are measured and managed through social impact assessment. Social impact assessment can be used to evaluate the impact of facilities or events on the behaviour, attitudes, interests, health or economic wellbeing of residents, organisations, social movements and political systems. Social impact assessment examines the effects that facilities and events have on the objective and subjective quality of life for people and organisations in the community.

Although social impact assessment has not yet had the political impact enjoyed by economic impact analysis or the kinds of legislative mandate common to environmental impact assessment, the emergence of triple-bottom-line frameworks has heightened the appeal of social impact assessment to governments and community groups. Consequently, it is reasonable to expect that social impact assessments will be undertaken with increasing frequency and increasing rigour. The specific methods used in any particular social impact assessment (e.g. surveys, interviews, media analysis, behavioural observation) will vary as a function of the expected impacts and the context. However, the fundamental process will generally follow the nine steps outlined in Table 11.2.

Stakeholders

We have already mentioned stakeholders. A stakeholder is any person or group that will be interested in, affected by, or is a necessary participant in the project. Identification and management of stakeholder interests has been shown to be a necessary element of effective business administration and policy making (Walker & Marr 2001; Wheeler & Sillanpaa 1997).

As our previous discussion shows, stakeholders are not merely those who are responsible for building or running the facility or its events. Government, local retailers, tourism

Table 11.2 Steps in social impact assessment

1. Establish the terms of reference for the study.
2. Identify alternative pathways that project development might take.
3. Determine the current social condition, identify stakeholders, and ascertain what and who are likely to be affected.
4. Project what is likely to happen and who might be affected under the alternative pathway scenarios identified in step 2.
5. On the basis of steps 3 and 4, identify indicators to be examined and measures to be used; then determine the nature and magnitude of likely impacts under alternative scenarios.
6. Evaluate net benefits for stakeholder groups, and determine who benefits, who loses, and whether the aggregate impact is acceptable.
7. Identify means to counteract unacceptable impacts.
8. Monitor ongoing impacts, and compare with predicted impacts.
9. Feed findings from step 8 into ongoing planning and implementation.

businesses, environmental groups, local residents and sport organisations are all stakeholders likely to be affected. Each of these groups is likely to have a stake in the economic, environmental and social impacts of a facility or an event. If they perceive the effects to be sufficiently negative, they may challenge the facility or event, thus making it politically impractical (e.g. Barnes 2000; Lenskyj 1997). On the other hand, strong stakeholder support can enable a facility or an event to proceed despite significant opposition (e.g. Burbank, Andranovich & Heying 2001; Covell 2001).

One reason why it can be particularly valuable to map stakeholder interests is that the benefits to accrue from a facility or an event may depend on stakeholder cooperation (Chalip & Leyns 2002; Webb 2001). Local businesses may need to cooperate in order to attract visitor spending or provide necessary services. Government may need to work closely with facility managers and event organisers in order to manage traffic congestion or deliver security services. Sport and tourism organisations may need to cooperate in order to optimise economic and social outcomes. Yet recent work demonstrates that the requisite cooperation is often lacking (Chalip & Leyns 2002).

The technique for managing stakeholders is called stakeholder analysis (Brugha & Varvasovsky 2000; Varvasovsky & Brugha 2000). Fundamentally, stakeholder analysis requires that the groups and individuals that are likely to have a stake in the proposed project be identified and their particular stakes be explored. This typically requires a substantial amount of research—first to identify stakeholders, and then to obtain details about the contingencies driving their particular interests, concerns, needs and objectives. A core objective of stakeholder analysis is to determine whether each stakeholder is likely to be in favour of or opposed to the proposed project, whether their support will be active or latent, and why. Once stakeholders have been identified and their stakes have been mapped, strategies to optimise active support and minimise opposition can then be formulated. Given the public visibility and level of expenditure often associated with sport facilities and events, stakeholder analysis is a vital tool for their planning and management (Thoma & Chalip 1996).

Summary

This chapter has introduced the concept of triple-bottom-line measurement and reporting. The triple bottom line includes economic, environmental and social accounts. It was shown that each type of account is relevant for sport facilities and events.

The economic impact of sport facilities and events has been commonly assessed by estimating the spending stimulated (direct impact) and the flow-on effects of that spending (indirect and induced impact). Facilities and events can also render intangible benefits that are not typically accounted for in economic impact assessments. These include effects on the host destination's brand as well as effects on social capital. It was noted that comparable worth estimates do not adequately capture the effects of event publicity on destination brand.

Sport facilities and events can have a substantial impact on the environment. Facility managers can reduce their facility's detrimental impact on the environment by promoting efficient use of energy, using chemicals for cleaning and operations that are not environmentally toxic, using plants that are well adapted to the local ecology, being careful not to overload or erode local watershed, and minimising the impact of facility siting and activities on local breeding, nesting and feeding habitats. Event managers can foster environmentally friendly operations by promoting, auditing and rewarding staff and attendee behaviours that min-imise stress on the environment. Environmental impact assessments are used to forecast, monitor and manage environmental impacts.

The social impacts of sport facilities and events can affect the quality of life in the host community. Social impact assessment can identify the social effects of facilities and events, including which stakeholders benefit and which may be negatively affected. Social impact assessments can be used to identify policies and procedures to optimise positive social effects and to eliminate or minimise negative effects.

Stakeholder analysis provides a means to identify individuals and groups likely to have a stake in the facility or event. It is an essential tool for sport facilities and events, because a substantial array of stakeholders must cooperate if the benefits of the facility or event are to be optimised and negative outcomes minimised. Stakeholder analysis provides the informa-tion required to optimise support for a facility and its events and to minimise opposition.

Case study

The Greek economy going for gold

In the face of spiralling costs and a frenzy of last-minute preparations, the organisers of the Athens 2004 Olympics declared themselves ready for the official opening of the Games on 13 August 2004. The venues were completed on time, transport systems were open and ran smoothly, and more than 10 000 athletes from 199 countries competed in the 301 scheduled events. However, before the party even began, the government worried about how to deal with the hangover that will follow. Soaring spending on the Games is expected to push Greece's budget deficit far above the 3 per cent of GDP ceiling permissible under the EU's Stability and Growth Pact, and could, perversely, have a dampening effect on GDP growth.

A ballooning deficit

Following a Herculean effort during the last few months before the Games, all 38 Olympic venues were finally completed in early August, with just days to spare. Partly as a result of this last-minute scramble to ensure that Athens was ready in time, the costs of staging the Games have increased dramatically. The price tag was originally estimated at around €5.9 billion (€1.8 bn from the organising committee, Athens 2004, and €4.1 bn from the government). These costs are now approaching €10 billion (€2 bn from the organisers, €5.5 bn from the government, and a further €2.5 bn from state coffers for ancillary projects). And they could go higher still.

The impact on the 2004 budget is already being felt. Public investment spending on the Games from national sources was put at around €1.8 billion in 2003 (1.2 per cent of GDP) and €1.4 billion in 2004 (0.9 per cent of GDP). Last-minute spending will ensure that the 2004 figure climbs sharply, although by just how much is not yet clear. According to preliminary data released by the State Accounting Office in early August, general budget outlays increased by 12.7 per cent during the first half of the year, compared with a target of 4.9 per cent. This has pushed the deficit for the first half of the year to €8.7 billion, a rise of 26 per cent over the same period one year earlier.

Unless there is a dramatic turnaround in the second half of the year, this could push up the state budget deficit for 2004 as a whole to approximately 4 per cent of GDP. The New Democracy government that took office in March has already been forced to revise the 2003 deficit from 1.7 per cent of GDP, as calculated by the previous Panhellenic Socialist Movement (Pasok) government, to 3.2 per cent of GDP. As a result, EU finance ministers set a deadline of November for the Greek government to announce corrective measures worth some 1 per cent of GDP over the course of this year and next. With the deficit now expected to climb even higher, further austerity measures may become necessary.

A post-Olympic slowdown

Preparations for the Olympics have helped spur economic growth in recent years, but it seems unlikely that high GDP growth rates will outlive the Games. In 2003 the Greek economy grew by 4.3 per cent, driven largely by sharply increased construction activity. The government now expects GDP growth to decelerate to 3.7 per cent in 2004. Private consumption, which accounts for around two-thirds of GDP, continues to grow strongly, increasing by 3.4 per cent year on year during the first half of the year. But the rate of growth in fixed investment (public and private), which accounts for around 28 per cent of GDP, is expected to slow markedly from 15.5 per cent in 2003 to just 3.4 per cent in 2004 (it was up by just 4.5 per cent during the first half).

Greece won't be the first country to experience a post-Olympics slowdown: a similar trend emerged following the Sydney 2000 Olympics and the Barcelona Olympics in 1992. But the need to channel funds into Olympics-related projects has meant that Greece has been forced to accept lower transfers from the EU under the third Community Support Framework (CSF III). The EU has co-financed some projects, including the new tram system, a suburban light railway, an extension of the Metro to Athens airport, and upgrades to health facilities. However, most public spending on the Olympics—including spending on venues, associated infrastructure and a massive €1.2 billion bill for security—was not eligible for co-financing and had to come from the national public investment budget. The result has been a reduction in the amount of EU transfers, which ordinarily buoy budget revenue, so that total public investment has been curbed. The effects should be reversed in 2005, when the funds now being spent on the Olympics are diverted back to CSF projects, but in the short term the Games are taking their toll on the public finances, as well delaying investment in the wider economy.

Short-term pain, long-term gain

Set against the costs are the huge potential benefits of staging the Olympics. A study carried out for the Pasok government in 2001 by the Centre of Planning and

Economic Research (KEPE) suggested that overall the Games should pay for themselves by the end of this decade. The research concluded that the total volume of investments to be made would generate some €8.4 billion in economic activity between 1998 and 2010, adding 6 percentage points to total GDP growth, with the maximum contribution of 1.2 percentage points in 2004.

The value of this assessment, however, is highly questionable, because it was based on assumptions that have since changed. For example, the study posited that the Games would attract an extra 2 million tourists to Athens this summer (2004), while preliminary estimates suggest that fewer than half that number arrived. Moreover, the tourism sector in Greece—the country's largest single sector—is already on course for a disappointing season, a result of competition from cheaper locations, including neighbouring Turkey, and concern over terrorism following the bombings in Bali, Istanbul and Madrid. The number of tourists visiting Greece fell in the first half of the year in comparison with previous years, and there are already suggestions that tourist arrivals could fall by 10 per cent over the year as a whole.

With spending on the Games topping €10 billion and tourism receipts down, it may be well into the next decade before Greece can claim to have reached the breakeven point for the Games; one government official recently predicted that Greece won't recoup its investments until the end of the decade at least. But besides the boost to tourism for the duration of the Games, there are many other factors that must be considered in a long-term cost–benefit analysis of staging the Olympics:

Games-related spending

Of the €2 billion being spent by the organisers, Athens 2004, around 60 per cent is coming through the International Olympic Committee in the form of broadcasting rights, sponsorship and merchandising deals. This is new money entering the Greek economy. The remaining 40 per cent will be financed from local sponsorship, ticket sales and licensing deals. As of 10 August, Athens 2004 had sold only around half of the total number of tickets available. However, with the most expensive tickets being snapped up first, ticket sales have already generated more than 80 per cent of anticipated revenue. Given that ticket sales were budgeted to provide just 9 per cent of total revenue, the shortfall should not cause significant problems for the organisers (or for the state, which would ultimately be required to foot the bill for any losses).

Tax revenue is likely to be higher

The Australian government calculated that it got back about one-third of its total investment in the Sydney Olympics from additional flows of corporate and sales taxes from companies connected with the Games. Even considering that tax evasion is a Greek national sport, the Greek authorities should, in theory, be able to claw back around one-fifth to one-quarter of their expenditure in new tax revenue. (The government has done the calculations, but has not released the estimates.)

New facilities

Now that the Games are over, the venues are supposed to pass to a new state-owned company, Olympic Properties, which has a brief to develop them as convention centres, concert halls, and sites for international athletics events. This could boost tourism over the medium term, and also help to spread the number of arrivals throughout the year.

A better business environment

Public spending to upgrade the transport, communications, security and health systems might have happened eventually, but without the spur of the Games this is far from certain. Perhaps the most important legacy from the Olympics will therefore be the improvements to Athens' infrastructure, which is now on a par with the most advanced European capitals and should help make the country a more attractive base for foreign direct investment.

Finally, the Games were viewed by a worldwide television audience of between 4 and 5 billion people. This is 'free advertising' for Greece that the country could never have hoped for without the Games. This could have a major impact on future tourism, boosting receipts in the long term, and perhaps helping to raise investment.

Q. Identify the advantages and disadvantages to Greece of hosting the 2004 Olympic Games.

Q. List the economic benefits and non-economic benefits to Greece of hosting the 2004 Olympic Games.

Q. Identify other social and environmental benefits to Greece of hosting the Olympic Games not cited in the case.

Q. Identify other social and environmental disadvantages not cited in the case.

Q. Given the ballooning deficit cited in the case, in your view was the overall triple bottom line associated with hosting the Olympic Games worthwhile? Why?

Economist Intelligence Unit—Views Wire, Number 301. Reproduced with permission.

Epilogue

In Chapter 1 we explained why in the book's title we combined the management of facilities and events. Sport events—or, from a wider perspective, entertainment events—are inextricably linked to the place and location in which the events are organised and hosted. High-profile events require high-profile facilities; high-quality events require high-quality facilities; big events require big facilities; community events require facilities that cater to the needs of community groups, and so on. The type of event brings with it an endless list of requirements regarding the eventual success or failure of the event. We argued that 'matching the facility (location) with the event' is the key to achieving success for both 'the facility' and 'the event'. Throughout this book we have attempted to inform you from both perspectives, in order to ensure that facility managers can think in 'event mode' and that event managers can consider issues from a facility management point of view. We thus considered it important to take you through the processes of developing and building the facility, prior to using the facility by organising events in it. Ultimately, this should lead to all managers being in a position to monitor both facility and event performance and to determine the levels of success that have been achieved.

The development of new sport and entertainment facilities is becoming a truly global industry. Teams of specialists working on new facility projects come from all over the world. Add to this the often sizable, multidisciplinary and international project teams that come into the facility on a temporary basis to organise large-scale events, and you are faced with the challenge of managing a professionally and culturally diverse workforce. This of course has as many advantages as it has pitfalls, as professional and cultural enrichment goes hand in hand with overcoming professional and cultural clashes. However, in the context of successfully managing facilities and events, the manager of the future needs to be able to communicate across professional and cultural boundaries. For example, an issue of increasing international importance is safety at events, and in order to successfully manage safety, knowledge of facility layout and event logistics needs to be combined with the ability to bring international stakeholders (e.g. event owners, federations, spectators, athletes) together.

At the conclusion of this book we hope we have succeeded in providing an overall framework that will assist current and future facility and event managers to better understand the context in which they work in order to achieve operational excellence. As we noted in the final chapter of the book, in a world with ever-rising community scrutiny and the resulting need for greater accountability it remains important not only to achieve financial operational excellence but also to contribute to a sustainable natural environment and to enrich people's lives as much as possible.

References

Chapter 1

Anderson, P. (2000). *Sports Facilities Reports*. Volume 1, Number 1. National Sports Law Institute of Marquette University Law School, Milwaukee. (at http://www.mu.edu/law/sports/sfr/sfr11.html).

AT Kearny (2002). *The Main Event: Best Practices for Managing Mega-Sports Events*. AT Kearny, Chicago.

Berg, L. van den, Braun, E. & Otgaar, A. (2000). *Sport and City Marketing in European Cities*. EURICUR, Erasmus University, Rotterdam.

Boon, G. (1999). *Deloitte & Touche Annual Review of Football Finance (1997–1998 Season)*. Deloitte & Touche, Manchester, p. 62.

Britcher, C. (2000). 'The new breed of indoor arenas'. *Sport Business*, January, pp. 26–7.

Goldblatt, J. (2000). 'A future for event management: the analysis of major trends impacting the emerging profession'. Events Beyond 2000: Setting the Agenda, Proceedings of conference on event evaluation, research and education. Sydney, July 2000. Australian Centre for Event Management, School of Leisure, Sport and Tourism, University of Technology, Sydney, pp. 1–8.

Jensen, R. (1999). *The Dream Society*. McGraw-Hill, New York.

Melbourne Cricket Club (2002). Press release: 'MCC commits $580 million to MCG redevelopment'. Wednesday 26 June, 2002 (at http://www.mcg.org.au/news/redev_mcc_release_260602.htm).

Roberts, K. (1999). 'Building finance options: how project financing is helping fund the US stadium boom'. *Sport Business*, September, p. 18.

Sports Facility Reports (2002). Appendices to Volume 3, Number 1. National Sports Law Institute of Marquette University Law School, Milwaukee (at http://www.mu.edu/law/sports/sfr/sfr31.html).

Westerbeek, H. & Smith, A. (2003). *Sport Business in the Global Marketplace*. Palgrave Macmillan, London.

Zoltak, J. (2002). 'U.S. festivals & events market estimated at $15 billion'. *Amusement Business*, 21 January, 114(3), p. 11.

Melbourne Sports and Aquatic Centre Website http://www.msac.com.au

Chapter 2

Bowdin, G., McDonnell, I., Allen, J. & O'Toole, W. (2001). *Events Management*. Oxford, Butterworth-Heinemann.

Briner, W., Geddes, M. & Hasting, C. (1996). *Project Leadership*, 2nd edn. Gower, Aldershot.

Chelladurai, P. (1985). *Sport Management: Macro Perspectives*. Sport Dynamics, Bisley, Surrey.

Cole, G.A. (1999). *Management Theory and Practice*, 5th edn. DP Publications, London.

Commonwealth Games Federation (2001). *Commonwealth Games Federation Constitution, Games Management Protocols, Regulations & Codes of Contact* (at http://www .thecgf.com).

Commonwealth Games (2002). Home page of the XVII Commonwealth Games of Manchester (at http://www.commonwealthgames.com). Accessed 4 April 2004.

Done, F. (2002). Cited in Homer (2002): 'Our Sporting Life'. *The Times*. 24 July, p. 1.

Emery, P.R. (1997). *The Management of Major Sport Events*. Unpublished Master of Business Administration Dissertation, Durham University.

Emery, P.R. (2002). 'Bidding to host a major sports event: the local organising committee perspective'. *International Journal of Public Sector Management*, 15(4), pp. 316–35.

Emery, P.R. (2003). 'Sports event management'. In Trenberth, L. (Ed.), *Managing the Business of Sport*. Dunmore Press, Palmerston North, NZ.

Guardian Media Group (2002). *2002 Manchester: Official Souvenir Brochure of the Commonwealth Games*. Guardian Media Group, Manchester.

ILAM (2002). 'Stadium legacy includes indoor move for track'. *Leisure News* 8–14 August, p. 1. Institute of Leisure and Amenity Management.

Ives, J. (2002). 'Long-term key to "true value"'. *Leisure News* 8–14 August, p. 1. Institute of Leisure and Amenity Management.

Kerzner, H. (2001). *Project Management: A Systems Approach to Planning, Scheduling, and Controlling*, 7th edn. John Wiley & Sons, New York.

Leese, R. (2002). *What the Games Mean to Manchester*. In Guardian Media Group, *2002 Manchester: Official Souvenir Brochure of the Commonwealth Games*. Guardian Media Group, Manchester.

Manchester (2002). *Manchester 2002 Commonwealth Games Corporate Plan*. Manchester 2002 Ltd, Manchester.

McKinnon, G. (2002). In Ives, J., 'Long-term key to "true value"'. *Leisure News* 8–14 August, p. 1. Institute of Leisure and Amenity Management.

Meyer, M.W. (2002). *Rethinking Performance Measurement: Beyond the Balanced Scorecard*. Cambridge University Press, Cambridge.

Moss, V. (2003). 'Empty dome is still costing taxpayers £15m a year'. *Sunday Mirror*. 13 April, p. 21.

Phillips, B. (2002). 'The Evolving Games'. In Guardian Media Group, *2002 Manchester: Official Souvenir Brochure of the Commonwealth Games*. Guardian Media Group, Manchester.

Soucie, D. & Doherty, A. (1994). *An overview of past, present and future sport management research in North America*. Paper presented at the Second European Congress on Sport Management. Florence, Italy.

Sport England (2002). *Manchester 2002 Commonwealth Games Factsheet*. Sport England.

Sports Council (1994). *Written Evaluation of National 2002 Commonwealth Games Bid*. Sports Council.

Torkildsen, G. (1999). *Leisure & Recreation Management*, 4th edn. E. & F. Spon, London.

Watt, D.C. (1992). *Leisure & Tourism Events Management & Organisation Manual*, Longman, Harlow.

Wearne, S. (1989). *Engineering Management—Control of Engineering Projects*, 2nd edn. Thomas Telford, London.

West, L. (2002). 'The action from the final day'. *Daily Mirror*. 5 August, p. 51.
Yates, C. (2002). 'The Real Commonwealthy'. *The Sun*. 16 July, pp. 12–13.

Chapter 3

Bond, C.J. (1991). *Hands-on Financial Controls for Your Small Business*. Liberty Hall Press, Blue Ridge Summit, PA.

Culture, Media and Sport Parliamentary Committee (2001). *Third Report: Staging International Sporting Events, House of Commons*, London (at http://www.volvooceanrace.org).

Government of Western Australia (1995). *How to Undertake a Feasibility Study for a Proposed Sport or Recreation Facility*, Perth July.

Hillary Commission (1999). *Getting What You Need: A Practical Guide to Developing Project Briefs for Sport Facilities in New Zealand*, Auckland February.

Mullin, B., Hardy, S. & Sutton, W. (2000). *Sport Marketing*, 2nd edn. Human Kinetics, Champaign, IL.

Overton, R. (2000). *Feasibility Studies Made Simple*. Martin Management: Australian Business Publications, Sydney.

Porter, M. (1985). *Competitive Advantage: Creating and Sustaining Superior Performance*. The Free Press, New York.

Shilbury, D., Quick, S. & Westerbeek, H. (2003). *Strategic Sport Marketing*, 2nd edn. Allen & Unwin, Sydney.

Chapter 4

Aveni, M. (2001). 'Site constraints, design features result in unusual stadium layout'. *Civil Engineering*, 71(7), pp. 12–15.

Brake, A.G. (2002). 'Onion skins for the old pigskin'. *Architecture*, 91(4), pp. 115–17.

Canter, D., Comber, M. & Uzzell, D. (1989). *Football in its Place: An Environmental Psychology of Football Grounds*. Routledge, London.

Commission for Architecture and the Built Environment (2002). *Supplement to the Client Guide for ACP projects: The Design Brief*. CABE.

Commission for Architecture and the Built Environment (2003). *Supplement to the Client Guide for ACP projects: Selecting The Design Team*. CABE.

Frosdick, S. (1997). 'Designing for safety'. In S. Frosdick & L. Walley (Eds), *Sport and Safety Management*. Butterworth-Heinemann, Oxford.

Gonchar, J. (2001). 'Denver dares to give its new stadium a distinct local personality'. *Engineering News-Record*, 246(13), pp. 20–1.

de Groot, E.H., Mallory-Hill, S.M., van Zutphen, S.M. & de Vries, B. (1999). 'An experimental design system for the very early design stage'. In: Proceedings of the 8th International Conference on Durability of Building Materials and Components, 30 May–3 June 1999, Vancouver, Canada.

Highmore, M. (1997). 'Safety risks in stadia and sports grounds'. In S. Frosdick & L. Walley (Eds), *Sport and Safety Management*. Butterworth-Heinemann, Oxford.

Hope, K. (2003). 'Capitals: an overview of current events and trends in Europe's capitals'. *Europe*, 422, pp. 34–5.

Kennedy, M. (2000). 'Making sports facilities brighter and more energy-efficient'. *American School & University*, 72(11), p. 34.

Kubany, E.H. (2002). 'The only game in town'. *Architecture*, 190(5), p. 245.

Lewandowski, J. (2002). 'Olympic spirit for years to come'. *Parks & Recreation*, 37(3), pp. 86–93.

Locke, M. & Randall, E. (1994). *Management of Value in the British Construction Industry*. SAVE Annual Proceeding: The 1994 International Conference of the Society of American Value Engineers, New Orleans.

McGuigan, C. (2000). 'The good, the bad and the boring'. *Newsweek,* 135(23), pp. 58–60.

Nessen, J. & Blank, E. (2001). 'Want a great skatepark? Put the experts to work!' *Parks & Recreation*, 36(8), pp. 88–93.

Scott, R. (2000). 'The good, the bad and the ugly in natatorium design'. *Parks and Recreation,* 35(11), pp. 46–51.

Sport England (1999). *Design Guidance Note: Floors for Indoor Sports*. Sport England Publications/English Sports Council, Wetherby.

Sport England (2000). *Design Guidance Note: Natural Turf for Sport*. Sport England Publications/English Sports Council, Wetherby.

Sport England (2001). *Design Guidance Note: Village and Community Halls*. Sport England Publications/English Sports Council, Wetherby.

Sport England & CABE (2003). *Better Places for Sports: A Client Guide to Achieving Design Quality*. Sport England/Commission for Architecture and the Built Environment, Wetherby.

Stonor, W. (2001). 'The design of Manchester Aquatics Centre', *Journal of Leisure Property*, 1(2), pp. 162–9.

Weber, B. (2002). 'The new sports architecture, design, and technology'. *Scholastic Coach & Athletic Director*, 71(7), pp. 100–5.

Chapter 5

Anderson, G. (1996). 'Performance appraisal'. In B. Towers (Ed.), *The Handbook of Human Resource Management*, 2nd edn. Blackwood Publishers, London.

Cleanevent (2003). www.cleanevent.com.au/index2.html. Accessed on 31 October 2003.

Cohen-Rosenthal, E. (1995). *Unions Management and Quality: Opportunities for Innovation and Excellence*. Irwin Professional Publishers, Burr Ridge, IL.

Daniel, Z. (2002). 'Cleaning up the world'. Transcript from ABC Radio program Inside Business 29/9/2002. Australian Broadcasting Corporation. Available on: http://www.abc.net.au/insidebusiness/content/2002/s688444.htm. Accessed 31 October 2003.

Ghoshal, S. & Bartlett, C. (1995). 'Changing the role of top management: beyond structure to processes'. *Harvard Business Review*, January–February, pp. 86–96.

Graetz, F. (2002). 'New forms of organising'. In F. Graetz, M. Rimmer, A. Lawrence & A. Smith (Eds), *Managing Organisational Change*. John Wiley & Sons, Melbourne.

Graetz, F., Rimmer, M., Lawrence, A. & Smith, A. (2002). *Managing Organisational Change*. John Wiley & Sons, Melbourne.

Guthrie, J.P. (2001). 'High involvement work practices, turnover and productivity: evidence from New Zealand'. *Academy of Management Journal*, 44(1), pp. 180–91.

Huselid, M. (1995). 'The impact of human resource management practices on turnover, productivity and corporate financial performance'. In C. Mabey, Industry Search (2001–03).

Industry Search Company Profile: Cleanevent Australia Pty Ltd. Available on www.industry-search.com.au/isearch/viewrecord.asp?ID=1558&SearchField=. Accessed 31 October 2003.

Kanter, R.M. (1996). 'Beyond the cowboy and the corpocrat'. In K. Starkey (Ed.), *How Organisations Learn*. International Business Press, London, pp. 13–31.

Kelly, P. (2002). 'Cleanevent to sponsor race at Nashville'. *Infinite Pro Series*. http://www.indyracing.com/pro/press/story.php?story_id=1613. Accessed 31 October 2003.

Limerick, D. & Cunnington, B. (1993). *Managing the New Organisation*. Business & Professional Publishing, Sydney.

Locke, E., Shaw, R., Saari, L. & Latham, G. (1981). 'Goal setting and task performance: 1969–1980'. *Psychological Bulletin*, 97, pp. 125–52.

Masters, R. (2003). 'Punter's trash is gold for cleanevent'. *Sydney Morning Herald*, 8 September 2003. Available on http://www.smh.com.au/articles/2003/09/07/1062901938994.html?from=storyrhs. Accessed 31 October 2003.

Maund, L. (2001). *An Introduction to Human Resource Management: Theory and Practice*. Palgrave, Hampshire.

Nankervis, A.R., Compton, R.L. & McCarthy, T.E. (1993). *Strategic Human Resource Management*. Nelson, Melbourne.

Newton, T. & Findlay, P. (1998). 'Playing god: the performance appraisal'. In C. Mabey, G. Salaman & J. Storey (Eds), *Strategic Human Resource Management: A Reader*, Blackwell, Oxford, pp. 128–43.

Salaman, G. & Storey, J. (Eds) (1998). *Strategic Human Resource Management: A Reader*. Blackwell, Oxford, pp. 128–43.

Savage, A. (2000). 'Small business success stories: Cleanevent'. *NineMSN*. 7 December 2000. Available on http://smallbusiness.ninemsn.com.au/smallbusiness/success_stories/story_539.asp. Accessed on 31 October 2003.

Smith, A. & Stewart, B. (1999). *Sports Management: A Guide to Professional Practice*. Allen & Unwin, Sydney.

Stone, R. (2002). *Human Resource Management*, 4th edn. John Wiley & Sons, Brisbane.

Whittington, R., Pettigrew, A., Peck, S., Fenton, E. & Conyon, M. (1999). 'Change and complementarities in the new competitive landscape: a European panel study, 1992–1996'. *Organisational Science*, 10(5), p. 588.

Chapter 6

Board of Ethics, SLOC (1999, February 8). 'Report to the Board of Trustees'. *Board of Ethics of the Salt Lake Organizing Committee for the Olympic Winter Games of 2002*, Salt Lake City.

Booth, D. & Tatz, C. (1994a). 'Swimming with the big boys? The politics of Sydney's 2000 Olympic bid'. *Sporting Traditions, Journal of the Australian Society for Sports History*, 11(1), pp. 3–29.

Booth, D. & Tatz, C. (1994b, December 93/January 94). 'The games people play'. *Current Affairs Bulletin*, pp. 4–11.

Bose, M. (2003, 14 July). 'Basics first, London told'. *Telegraph Sport*. www.telegraph.co.uk/sport/main.jhtml. Accessed 7 August 2003.

Bowdin, G.A.J., McDonnell, I., Allen, J. & O'Toole, W. (2001). *Events Management*. Butterworth-Heinemann, Oxford.

Crockett, S. (1994). 'Tourism and sport: bidding for international events'. *Journal of Tourism Sport*, 1(4), pp. 11–21.

Emery, P.R. (2002). 'Bidding to host a major sports event: the local organising committee perspective'. *International Journal of Public Sector Management*, 15(4), pp. 316–35.

Erickson, G.S. & Kushner, R.J. (1999). 'Public event networks: an application of marketing theory to sporting events'. *European Journal of Marketing*, 33(3/4), pp. 348–64.

Getz, D. (1997). *Event Management and Event Tourism*. Cognizant Communication Corporation, New York.

Hall, C.M. (1989). 'Hallmark tourist events: analysis, definition, methodology and review'. In G.J. Syme, B.J. Shaw, D.M. Fenton & W.S. Mueller (Eds), *The Planning and Evaluation of Hallmark Events*. Avebury, USA, pp. 3–19.

Ingerson, L. & Westerbeek, H. (2000). 'Determining key success criteria for attracting hallmark sporting events'. *Pacific Tourism Review*, 3(4), pp. 239–53.

IOC *ad hoc* Commission (1999, 24 January). 'Report of the IOC ad hoc Commission to investigate the conduct of certain IOC members and to consider possible changes in the procedures for the allocation of the Games of the Olympiad and Olympic Winter Games'. *Report Presented to the IOC Executive Board*, Lausanne.

IOC Candidate Acceptance Procedure (1999). 'Games of the XXIX Olympiad in 2008 Host City'. *Candidate Acceptance Procedure*. IOC, Lausanne.

McFarlane, D. (1992, December). 'Adelaide 1988—what happened?' *Sportsnetwork*, Australian Society of Sports Administrators, pp. 4–5.

McGeoch, R. & Korporaal, G. (1994). *The Bid: How Australia Won the 2000 Games*. William Heinemann, Melbourne.

Special Bid Oversight Commission (1999, 1 March). *Report of the special bid oversight commission*. United States Olympic Committee (USOC).

Westerbeek, H.M., Turner, P. & Ingerson, L. (2002). 'Key success factors in bidding for hallmark sporting events'. *International Marketing Review*, 19(3), pp. 303–22.

Wilkinson, D. (1988). *The Event Management and Marketing Institute*. Wilkinson Information Group, Canada.

Chapter 7

Farmer, P.J., Mulrooney, A.L. & Ammon, R.A. (1996). *Sport Facility Planning and Management*. Fitness Information Technology, Morgantown, USA.

Graham, S., Goldblatt, J.J. & Delpy, L. (1995). *The Ultimate Guide to Sport Event Management & Marketing*, Irwin, Burr Ridge, IL.

Hughes, R. (1998). 'Risk management for sport'. *21st Century Sport Management Series*, unpublished manuscript, IEA in association with Vicsport and ASSA.

John, G. & Sheard, R. (2000). *Stadia: A Design and Development Guide*, 3rd edn. Architectural Press, Oxford.

Watts, E.W. (1999). 'The elimination of waste through effective capacity management: identifying techniques to improve venue management'. Proceedings of the 7th Congress of the European Association for Sport Management, Thessaloniki, pp. 339–40.

Chapter 8

Bateson, J.E.G. & Hoffman, K.D. (1999). *Managing Services Marketing: Text and Readings*, 4th edn. Dryden Press, Sydney.

Hoffman, K.D. & Bateson, J.E.G. (2002). *Essentials of Services Marketing: Concepts, Strategies, and Cases*, 2nd edn. Harcourt College, Fort Worth, TX.

Kotler, P., Brown, L., Adam, S. & Armstrong, G. (2004). *Marketing*, 5th edn. Prentice Hall, Sydney.

Langeard, E., Bateson, J., Lovelock, C. & Eiglier, P. (1981). *Marketing of Services: New Insights from Consumers and Managers*, report no. 81–104, Marketing Sciences Institute, 1981, Cambridge, MA.

Levitt, T. (1960). 'Marketing myopia'. *Harvard Business Review*, July–August, pp. 45–66.

Lovelock, C.H., Patterson, P.G. & Walker, R.H. (2004). *Services Marketing: An Asia-Pacific Perspective*, 3rd edn. Prentice Hall, Sydney.

McDonald, M.A. & Milne, G.R. (1997). 'Conceptual framework for evaluating marketing relationships in professional sport franchises'. *Sport Marketing Quarterly*, 6(2), pp. 27–32.

Mullin, B.J., Hardy, S. & Sutton, W.A. (2000). *Sport Marketing*, 2nd edn. Human Kinetics, Champaign, IL.

Murray, D. & Howat, G. (2002). 'The relationships among service quality, value, satisfaction, and future intentions of customers at an Australian sports and leisure centre'. *Sport Management Review*, 5(1), pp. 25–43.

Shani, D. (1997). 'Framework for implementing relationship marketing in the sport industry'. *Sport Marketing Quarterly*, 6(2), pp. 9–15.

Shilbury, D., Quick, S. & Westerbeek, H. (2003). *Strategic Sport Marketing*, 2nd edn. Allen & Unwin, Sydney.

Wakefield, K.L. & Blodgett, J.G. (1996). 'The effect of the servicescape on customers' behavioural intentions in leisure service settings'. *Journal of Services Marketing*, 10(6), pp. 45–61.

Chapter 9

Ammon, R. (2002). *Security Issues for the Event Manager Since 9/11: Has Anything Changed?* Paper presented at 10th EASM Conference, Finland.

Angelopoulou-Daskalaki, G. (2003). Cited on www.athens.olympics.org. Accessed on 13/1/2003.

Athens 2004 International Media Relations (2003). *Athletics*, 2nd edn. Athens 2004.

Bowdin, G., McDonnell, I., Allen, J. & O'Toole, W. (2001). *Events Management*. Butterworth-Heinemann, Oxford.

Bunce, D. (2003). *Sport facility management*. Unpublished Distance Learning Materials on the MSc Sport Management Programme, Northumbria University.

Commonwealth Games Federation (2001). *Commonwealth Games Federation Constitution, Games Management Protocols, Regulations & Codes of Contact*. Located at http://www thecgf.com.

Commonwealth Games (2002). Home page of the XVII Commonwealth Games of Manchester. Located at http://www.commonwealthgames.com. Accessed 3 April 2004.

Croner Publications (1988). *A Practical Approach to the Administration of Leisure and Recreation Services*. Croner Publications.

Emery, P.R. (1997). *The management of major sport events.* Unpublished Master of Business Administration Dissertation, Durham University.

Emery, P.R. (2001). *The Great North Run—Everyone's a Winner.* North East Sports Board, Institute of Sport, Newcastle.

France '98 (1998). *Operational plan.* France '98 Coupe du Monde.

Goldblatt, J.J. (1997). *Special Events: Best Practices in Modern Event Management.* Van Nostrand Reinhold, New York.

Guardian Media Group (2002). *2002 Manchester: Official Souvenir Brochure of the Commonwealth Games.* Guardian Media Group, Manchester.

Independent (1996). *Groans and gridlock as Atlanta grinds to a halt.* 23 July.

International Olympic Committee (1998). *Accreditation and Entries at the Olympic Games: Users' Guide.* International Olympic Committee, Lausanne.

Limb, R. (2003). 'New perspective; events: health and safety'. *Leisure Manager,* December 2003/January 2004, p. 20. Institute of Leisure and Amenity Management.

Manchester (2002a). *Staff Induction Handbook.* Manchester 2002 Ltd, Manchester.

Manchester (2002b). *Stewards' Handbook.* Manchester 2002 Ltd, Manchester.

Martin, O. (1996). *The policing of football matches—the implications of Hillsborough on planning, procedure and cost.* Unpublished BSc (Hons) Sport Management Dissertation. Northumbria University.

N'Thépé, I. (2003). *Behind the scenes.* Article in the Official Program of the 9th IAAF World Championships in Athletics, Paris Organising Committee.

The Observer (1996). *Atlanta Chaos.* 21 July.

Rees, J. (20 April 2003). 'Hong Kong: where the sport of kings is the king of sports'. Accessed at http://www.courier-journal.com/cjsports/news2003/04/20/sp042003s398685.htm.

Sport England (2001). *Volunteer Investment Programme: Volunteering Matters.* Sport England.

Sport England (2002). *Manchester 2002 Commonwealth Games Factsheet.* Sport England.

Sunderland City Council (2003). *North East Sports Awards Ceremony.* Operational Emergency Action Plan, Sunderland City Council.

The Times (1996). *Olympians give Atlanta full marks for chaos.* 23 July.

Torkildsen, G. (1999). *Leisure & Recreation Management,* 4th edn. E. & F. Spon, London

United Nations (2001). Cited in Guardian Media Group (2002). *2002 Manchester: Official Souvenir Brochure of the Commonwealth Games.* Guardian Media Group, Manchester.

Walker, D. (2001). *Motivating Yourself and Your Volunteers.* Leadership and Development.

Watt, D.C. (1998). *Event Management in Leisure and Tourism.* Addison Wesley Longman, New York.

West, L. (2002). 'Mancs for the memory'. *Daily Mirror.* 5 August, p. 51.

World Indoor Championships in Athletics (2003a). *Media Guide: 9th IAAF World Indoor Championships in Athletics.* Birmingham.

World Indoor Championships in Athletics (2003b). *Operational Manual.* Birmingham.

Yates, C. (2002). 'The real commonwealthy'. *The Sun.* 16 July, pp. 12–13.

Chapter 10

AICPA Special Committee on Financial Reporting (1994). *Improving Business Reporting—A Customer Focus: Meeting the Information Needs of Investors and Creditors.* American Institute of Certified Public Accountants, New York.

Athanassopoulos, A.D. (2000). 'Customer satisfaction cues to support market segmentation and explain switching behavior'. *Journal of Business Research*, 47, 191–207.

Behn, R.D. (2003). 'Why measure performance? Different purposes require different measures'. *Public Administration Review*, 63, 586–606.

Chelladurai, P., Scott, F.L. & Haywood-Farmer, J. (1987). 'Dimensions of fitness services: development of a model'. *Journal of Sport Management*, 1, 159–72.

Cronin, J.J. Jr., Brady, M.K. & Hult, G.T.M. (2000). 'Assessing the effects of quality, value, and customer satisfaction on consumer behavioural intentions in service environments'. *Journal of Retailing*, 76, 193–216.

Disney, J. (1999). 'Customer satisfaction and loyalty: the critical elements of service quality'. *Total Quality Management*, 10, 491–7.

Eccles, R.G. (1991). 'The performance measurement manifesto'. *Harvard Business Review*, Jan–Feb, 1–8.

Eigenmann, R. (Ed.) (2001). *Performance Evaluation and Benchmarking with Realistic Applications*. MIT Press, Cambridge, MA.

Finnerty, J.D. (1986). *Corporate Financial Analysis*. McGraw-Hill, New York.

Hamel, G. & Prahalad, C.K. (1994). *Competing for the Future: Breakthrough Strategies for Seizing Control of Your Industry and Creating the Markets of Tomorrow*. Harvard Business School Press, Boston, MA.

Hanlon, C. & Jago, J. (2001). 'Pulsating sporting events: an organisational structure to optimize performance'. In *Events Beyond 2000*. University of Technology, Sydney.

Howat, G., Murray, D. & Crilley, G. (1999). 'The relationship between service problems and perceptions of service quality, satisfaction, and behavioral intentions of Australian public sports and leisure center customers'. *Journal of Park and Recreation Administration*, 17(2), 42–64.

Jensen, A.J. & Sage, A.P. (1995). 'The role of information in organisational performance improvement strategies'. *Information and Systems Engineering*, 1(3/4), 193–206.

Kaplan, R.S. & Norton, D.P. (1992). 'The balanced scorecard—measures that drive performance'. *Harvard Business Review*, Jan–Feb, 70–9.

Kaplan, R.S. & Norton, D.P. (1993). 'Putting the balanced scorecard to work'. *Harvard Business Review*, Sept–Oct.

Kaplan, R.S. & Norton, D.P. (1996). *The Balanced Scorecard*. Harvard Business School Press, Boston, MA.

Meyer, M.W. (2002). *Rethinking Performance Measurement: Beyond the Balanced Scorecard*. Cambridge University Press, Cambridge.

Mondy, R.W., Noe, R.M. & Premeaux, S.R. (2002). *Human Resource Management*, 8th edn). Prentice Hall, Upper Saddle River, NJ.

O'Neill, M., Getz, D. & Carlson, J. (1999). 'Evaluation of service quality at events: the 1998 Coca-Cola Masters Surfing event at Margaret River, Western Australia'. *Managing Service Quality*, 9, 158–66.

Robbins, S.P. & DeCenzo, D. (2004). *Fundamentals of Management*, 4th edn. Prentice Hall, Upper Saddle River, NJ.

Rosser, V. (2004). 'Faculty members' intentions to leave: a national study on their worklife and satisfaction'. *Research in Higher Education*, 45, 285–310.

Chapter 11

Barnes, J.E. (2000, 19 January). 'City drops plan to build stadium in parade grounds'. *New York Times*, 149(51272), B3.

Brown, D.W., Balluz, L.S., Heath, G.W., Moriarty, D.G., Ford, E.S., Giles, W.H. & Mokdad, A.H. (2003). 'Associations between recommended levels of *physical activity* and health-related *quality* of *life*: findings from the 2001 Behavioral Risk Factor Surveillance System (BRFSS) survey'. *Preventive Medicine*, 37, 520–9.

Brown, G., Chalip, L., Jago, L. & Mules, T. (2002). 'The Sydney Olympics and Brand Australia'. In N. Morgan, A. Pritchard & R. Pride (Eds). *Destination Branding: Creating the Unique Destination Proposition*. Butterworth-Heinemann, Oxford, pp. 163–185.

Brugha, R. & Varvasovsky, Z. (2000). 'Stakeholder analysis: a review'. *Health Policy and Planning*, 15, 239–46.

Burbank, M.J., Andranovich, G.D. & Heying, C.H. (2001). *Olympic Dreams: The Impact of Mega-Events on Local Politics*. Lynne Rienner Publishers, Boulder, CO.

Cantelon, H. & Letters, M. (2000). 'The making of the IOC environmental policy as the third dimension of the Olympic Movement'. *International Review for the Sociology of Sport*, 35, 294–308.

Chalip, L. (2001). 'Sport and tourism: capitalising on the linkage'. In D. Kluka & G. Schilling (Eds), *The Business of Sport*. Meyer & Meyer, Oxford, pp. 71–90.

Chalip, L. & Leyns, A. (2002). 'Local business leveraging of a sport event: managing an event for economic benefit'. *Journal of Sport Management*, 16, 132–58.

Chalip, L., Green, B.C. & Hill, B. (2003). 'Effects of event media on destination image and intention to visit'. *Journal of Sport Management*, 17, 214–34.

Chernushenko, D., van der Kamp, A. & Stubbs, D. (2001). *Sustainable Sport Management: Running an Environmentally, Socially, and Economically Responsible Organisation*. Unipub, New York.

Christie, J. (1992, 12 February). 'Employment and environment create a delicate balance'. *Globe and Mail*, E6.

Coates, D. & Humphreys, B.R. (2003). 'The effect of professional sports on earnings and employment in the services and retail sectors in US cities'. *Regional Science and Urban Economics*, 33, 175–98.

Covell, D. (2001). 'The political arena: the construction of the William D. Mullins Memorial Center at the University of Massachusetts'. *International Sports Journal*, 5(2), 50–69.

Crompton, J.L. (1999). 'Economic impact analysis of sports facilities and events: eleven sources of misapplication'. *Journal of Sport Management*, 9, 14–35.

Crompton, J.L. (2001). 'Public subsidies to professional team sport facilities in the USA'. In C. Gratton & I. Henry (Eds), *Sport in the City*. Routledge, London, pp. 15–34.

Crompton, J.L., Lee, S. & Shuster, T.J. (2001). 'A guide for undertaking economic impact studies: the Springfest example'. *Journal of Travel Research*, 40, 79–87.

Daly, J. (1995). *Recreation and Sport Planning and Design*. Office for Recreation and Sport South Australia, Adelaide.

Dwyer, L., Mellor, R, Mistilis, N. & Mules, T. (2001). 'A framework for assessing "tangible" and "intangible" impacts of events and conventions'. *Event Management*, 6, 175–89.

Elley, C.R., Kerse, N., Arroll, B. & Robinson, E. (2003). 'Effectiveness of counselling patients on physical activity in general practice: cluster randomised controlled trial'. *British Medical Journal*, 326, 793–7.

Environment Agency (2002). *A Handbook for Scoping Projects: Environmental Impact Assessment (EIA)*. Environment Agency, Bristol, UK.

Faulkner, B. & Raybould, M. (1995). 'Monitoring event expenditure associated with attendance at sporting events: an experimental assessment of the diary and recall methods'. *Festival Management and Event Tourism*, 3, 73–81.

Fletcher, J. & Snee, H. (1989). 'Tourism multiplier effects'. In S.F. Wit & L. Moutinho (Eds), *Tourism Marketing and Management Handbook*. Prentice Hall, Hemel Hempstead, UK, pp. 529–531.

Fredline, E. & Faulkner, B. (2000). 'Host community reactions: a cluster analysis'. *Annals of Tourism Research*, 27, 764–85.

Fredline, E. & Faulkner, B. (2002). 'Variations in residents' reactions to major motorsport events: why residents perceive the impacts of events differently'. *Event Management*, 7, 115–25.

Getz, D. (1997). *Event Management and Event Tourism*. Cognizant Communication, New York.

Goodenough, R. (1992). 'The use of environmental impact assessment in the management of open space and recreational land in California'. *International Journal of Environmental Studies*, 40, 171–84.

Graburn, N. (1983). 'The anthropology of tourism'. *Annals of Tourism Research*, 10, 9–33.

Green, B.C., Costa, C. & Fitzgerald, M. (2003). 'Marketing the host city: analyzing exposure generated by a sport event'. *International Journal of Sports Marketing and Sponsorship*, 4, 335–52.

Greenpeace (2000). *How Green the Games? Greenpeace's Environmental Assessment of the Sydney 2000 Olympics*. Sydney.

Higham, J. (1999). 'Commentary—sport as an avenue of tourism development: an analysis of the positive and negative impacts of sport tourism'. *Current Issues in Tourism*, 2, 82–90.

Jago, L., Chalip, L., Brown, G., Mules, T. & Ali, S. (2003). 'Building events into destination branding: insights from experts'. *Event Management*, 8, 3–14.

Kotler, P., Haider, D.H. & Rein, I. (1993). *Marketing Places: Attracting Investment, Industry, and Tourism to Cities, States, and Nations*. Free Press, New York.

Lenskyj, H.J. (1997). 'The case against Toronto's bid for the 2008 Olympics'. *Policy Options/Options Politiques*, 18(3), 16–18.

Molnar, E. & Mulvihill, P.R. (2003). 'Sustainability-focused organisational learning: recent experiences and new challenges'. *Journal of Environmental Planning and Management*, 46, 167–76.

Mules, T. & Faulkner, B. (1996). 'An economic perspective on special events'. *Tourism Economics*, 2(2), 107–18.

Schindler, D.W. (1976). 'The impact statement boondoggle'. *Science*, 192, 509.

Smith, L.R. (2004). 'The triple bottom line'. *Quality Progress*, 37(2), 23–9.

Swindell, D. & Rosentraub, M.S. (1998). 'Who benefits from the presence of professional sports teams? The implications for public funding of stadiums and arenas'. *Public Administration Review*, 58, 11–20.

Thoma, J. & Chalip, L. (1996). *Sport Governance in the Global Community*. F.I.T., Morgantown, WV.

Treweek, J. (1996). 'Ecology and environmental impact assessment'. *Journal of Applied Ecology*, 33, 191–9.

Tschopp, D. (2003). 'It's time for triple bottom line reporting'. *CPA Journal*, 73(12), 11.

Varvasovsky, Z. & Brugha, R. (2000). 'How to do (or not to do) a stakeholder analysis'. *Health Policy and Planning*, 15, 338–45.

Walker, S.F. & Marr, J.W. (2001). *Stakeholder Power: A Winning Strategy for Building Stakeholder Commitment and Driving Corporate Growth*. Perseus, Cambridge, MA.

Ward, J. (2000). 'Come one! Come all!' *American City and County*, 115(6), 35–40.

Warnken, J. & Buckley, R. (1998). 'Scientific quality of tourism environmental impact assessment'. *Journal of Applied Ecology*, 35, 1–8.

Webb, T. (2001). *The Collaborative Games: The Story Behind the Spectacle*. Pluto Press, Sydney.

Wheeler, D. & Sillanpaa, M. (1997). *The Stakeholder Corporation: A Blueprint for Maximizing Stakeholder Value*. Pitman, London.

Index